# ADVANCES IN CHARACTER RECOGNITION

Edited by **Xiaoqing Ding**

**Advances in Character Recognition**
http://dx.doi.org/10.5772/2575
Edited by Xiaoqing Ding

**Contributors**

W. David Pan, Antonio Carlos Gay Thomé, Bilan Zhu and Masaki Nakagawa, W.T. Chan, T.Y. Lo, C.P. Tso and K.S. Sim, Chih-Chang Yu, Ming-Gang Wen, Kuo-Chin Fan and Hsin-Te Lue, Stephen Karungaru, Kenji Terada and Minoru Fukumi, Nadia Ben Amor and Najoua Essoukri Ben Amara, Fu Chang and Chan-Cheng Liu, Gabriel Pereira e Silva and Rafael Dueire Lins, K.C. Santosh and Eizaburo Iwata, Yasuhiro Matsuda and Tsuneshi Isomura, Shinji Tsuruoka, Masahiro Hattori, Yasuji Miyake, Haruhiko Takase and Hiroharu Kawanaka

**Published by InTech**

Janeza Trdine 9, 51000 Rijeka, Croatia



**Publishing Process Manager** Marija Radja
**Technical Editor** InTech DTP team
**Cover** InTech Design team

Additional hard copies can be obtained from orders@intechopen.com

Advances in Character Recognition, Edited by Xiaoqing Ding
p. cm.
ISBN 978-953-51-0823-8

For EU product safety concerns:
IN TECH d.o.o., Prolaz Marije Krucifikse Kozulić 3, 51000 Rijeka, Croatia,
info@intechopen.com or visit our website at intechopen.com.

# Meet the editor

Ding Xiaoping, graduated from Tsinghua University, China, in 1962 with the graduate Golden Medal. Now she is a professor and PhD supervisor in Department of Electronic Engineering, Tsinghua University. She is an IEEE fellow and IAPR Fellow. Her research interests include pattern recognition, image processing, characters recognition, biometric identification, computer vision etc. She has a grearesearch achievements on character & document recognition in Chines & multi-languages (Japanese, Korean, Arabic, Tibetan, Uygur, Mongolia& English etc.) and also on face recognition etc... She has won four most prestigious National Scientific and Technical Progress Awards in China in 1992, 1998, 2003 and 2008. She has published more than 550 papers, coauthored 7 books and holds 24 Invention Patents.

# Contents

Chapter 1

# Efficient Transformation Estimation Using Lie Operators: Theory, Algorithms, and Computational Efficiencies

W. David Pan

Additional information is available at the end of the chapter

http://dx.doi.org/10.5772/53271

## 1. Introduction

In many pattern recognition problems such as handwritten character recognition, it would be a challenge to design a good classification function, which can eliminate irrelevant variabilities among objects of the same class, while at the same time, being able to identify meaningful differences between objects of different classes. For example, in order for an automatic technique to "recognize" a handwritten digit, the incoming digit pattern needs to be accurately classified into one out of ten possible categories (from "0" to "9"). One straightforward yet inefficient way of implementation would be to match the pattern with a set of prototypes, where almost all possible instances (e.g., different sizes, angles, skews, etc.) of the digit in each category must be stored, according to a certain distance measure. Consequently, the pattern will be classified into the category where the closest match with one of its prototype instances was found. This approach would lead to impractically large prototype sets in order to achieve high recognition accuracy. An alternative method is to use only one prototype for each category, where different "deformed" instances of the same prototype can be generated by geometric transformations (e.g., thickened or rotated) during the matching process so as to best fit the incoming digit pattern. To this end, the concept of *Lie operators* for the transformations would be applicable.

More precisely, the pixel values of an incoming pattern (an digital image with $N \times N$ pixels) can be viewed as the components of a $N^2$-dimensional ($N^2$-D) vector. One pattern, or one prototype, is a point in this $N^2$-D space. If we assume that the set of allowable transformations is continuous, then the set of all the patterns that can be obtained by transforming one prototype using one or a combination of allowable transformations is a surface in the $N^2$-D pixel space. For instance, when a pattern $I$ is transformed (e.g., rotated by an angle $\theta$) according to a transformation $s(I, \theta)$, where $\theta$ is the only parameter, then the set of all the transformed patterns

$$T_I = \{x | \exists \theta, \text{for which } x = s(I, \theta)\} \tag{1}$$

is a one-dimensional curve in the $N^2$-D space. Here we assume that $s$ is differentiable with respect to both $I$ and $\theta$, and $s(I,0) = I$. When the set of transformations is parameterized by $m$ parameters $\theta_i$, where $i = 1,2,...,m$, $T_I$ becomes a manifold (topological surface) with an intrinsic dimension being $m$. For instance, if the allowable transformations of character images are rotations and scaling, the surface will be a 2-D manifold.

In practice, the search for the best matching deformation of a prototype for an incoming pattern would be expensive computationally, if the set of all the patterns that can be obtained by transforming one prototype using one or a combination of allowable transformations is large. Therefore, computationally efficient transformation estimation methods for pattern matching will be highly desired. It turns out that the surface of possible transforms of a pattern can be approximated by its *tangent plane* at the pattern [18]. More specifically, a linear approximation to the transform $s(I,\theta)$ of the pattern $I$ can be obtained by the Taylor expansion of $s$ around $\theta = 0$:

$$s(I,\theta) = s(I,0) + \theta\frac{\partial s(I,\theta)}{\partial \theta} + O(\theta^2) \approx I + \theta L, \tag{2}$$

where $L = \frac{\partial s(I,\theta)}{\partial \theta}$ is called the Lie Derivative of the transform $s$, which is also known as the tangent vector.

To facilitate a better understanding of the key concepts of Lie derivatives, which establish a connection between groups of transformations of the input space and their effect on a functional of that space, as well as Lie operators, which can be used to approximate the transformed pattern in a computationally efficient way, we first provide an explanation of the theory in Section 2, by working through some concrete examples of Lie groups and algebras. We then address in Section 3 the key problem of transformation estimation where both fast and accurate estimation methods are desired. The computational efficiency of transformation estimation algorithms based on Lie operator based approach is then investigated in Section 4, where several fast search algorithms for transformation estimation in video coding are presented. Further investigation is conducted in Section 5, by comparing the Lie operator based approach against transformation estimation based on a full affine transform model, in terms of the tradeoffs between accuracies and computational efficiencies.

## 2. Theory

### 2.1. Lie groups

Being an algebraic structure, a group is a set with an operation that combines any two of its elements to form a third element. To qualify as a group, the set and the operation must satisfy four conditions, namely, closure, associativity, identity, and invertibility (see definition below). For instance, the integers endowed with the addition operation form a group.

**Definition**: A set with elements $g_i, g_j, g_k, \ldots$, together with a combinatorial operation $\circ$ form a group $G$ if the following axioms are satisfied [5]:

(i) **Closure**: If $g_i \in G$ and $g_j \in G$, then $g_i \circ g_j \in G$.

(ii) **Associativity**: If $g_i \in G, g_j \in G$, and $g_k \in G$, then $(g_i \circ g_j) \circ g_k = g_i \circ (g_j \circ g_k)$.

(iii) **Identity**: There exists an element $e$ such that for every element $g_i \in G$, we have

$$g_i \circ e = g_i = e \circ g_i.$$

(iv) **Inverse**: Every group element $g_i$ has an inverse (called $g_i^{-1}$), with the property

$$g_i \circ g_i^{-1} = e = g_i^{-1} \circ g_i.$$

Some groups carry additional geometric structures. For example, Lie groups are groups that also have a smooth (differentiable) manifold structure. The circle and the sphere are examples of smooth manifolds. Named after Sophus Lie, a nineteenth century Norwegian mathematician who laid the foundations of the theory of continuous transformation groups, Lie groups lie at the intersection of two fundamental fields of mathematics: algebra and geometry. A Lie group has the property that the group operations are compatible with its smooth structure. That is, the group operations are differentiable. More precisely, we have

**Definition**: A Lie group consists of a manifold $\mathcal{M}^n$ that parameterizes the group elements $g(x), x \in \mathcal{M}^n$ and a combinatorial operation defined by $g(x) \circ g(y) = g(z)$, where the coordinate $z \in \mathcal{M}^n$ depends on the coordinates $x \in \mathcal{M}^n$, and $y \in \mathcal{M}^n$ through a function $z = \Phi(x, y)$. There are two topological axioms for a Lie group [5].

(i) **Smoothness of the group composition map**: The group composition map $z = \Phi(x, y)$ is differentiable.

(ii) **Smoothness of the group inversion map**: The group inversion map $y = \psi(x)$, defined by $g(x)^{-1} = g(y)$, is differentiable.

Almost every Lie group is either a matrix group or equivalent to a matrix group, which greatly simplifies the description of the algebraic, topological, and continuity properties of the Lie groups. Let us consider the following example encountered in pattern recognition, where a prototype pattern can be represented as a computer image $P[i, j]$, which can be interpreted as the discrete version of the continuous function $f(X) = f(x, y)$. Assume that $f$ is a differential function that maps points $X = (x, y)$ in the plane $\Re^2$ to $\Re$, which is the intensity (or pixel value) of the point $X$.

$$f : X \in \Re^2 \mapsto f(X) \in \Re. \tag{3}$$

Next, the image is deformed (e.g., rotate by an angle $\theta$)) via a transformation $T_\theta$ (parameterized by $\theta$), which maps bijectively a point of $\Re^2$ back to a point of $\Re^2$:

$$T_\theta : X \in \Re^2 \mapsto T_\theta(X) \in \Re^2. \tag{4}$$

For example, $T_\theta$ could represent rotating the pattern by an angle $\theta$:

$$T_\theta : (u, v) \mapsto (u \cos\theta - v \sin\theta, u \sin\theta + v \cos\theta). \tag{5}$$

These transformations form a group $G$, which can be represented by a matrix group, with the combinatorial operation $\circ$ being the matrix multiplication. In particular, each element $g(\theta)$ of $G$ is parameterized by one parameter $\theta$:

$$g(\theta) = \begin{pmatrix} \cos\theta & \sin\theta \\ -\sin\theta & \cos\theta \end{pmatrix}. \tag{6}$$

We show that $G$ is indeed a group:

(i) **Closure**: If $g(\theta_1) \in G$ and $g(\theta_2) \in G$, then

$$g(\theta_1) \circ g(\theta_2) = \begin{pmatrix} \cos\theta_2 & \sin\theta_2 \\ -\sin\theta_2 & \cos\theta_2 \end{pmatrix} \begin{pmatrix} \cos\theta_1 & \sin\theta_1 \\ -\sin\theta_1 & \cos\theta_1 \end{pmatrix} = \begin{pmatrix} \cos(\theta_1+\theta_2) & \sin(\theta_1+\theta_2) \\ -\sin(\theta_1+\theta_2) & \cos(\theta_1+\theta_2) \end{pmatrix}$$
$$= g(\theta_1+\theta_2) \in G. \tag{7}$$

(ii) **Associativity**: If $g(\theta_1) \in G, g(\theta_2) \in G$, and $g(\theta_3) \in G$, then

$$(g(\theta_1) \circ g(\theta_2)) \circ g(\theta_3) = g(\theta_1+\theta_2) \circ g(\theta_3) = g(\theta_1+\theta_2+\theta_3), \tag{8}$$

and

$$g(\theta_1) \circ (g(\theta_2) \circ g(\theta_3)) = g(\theta_1) \circ g(\theta_2+\theta_3) = g(\theta_1+\theta_2+\theta_3). \tag{9}$$

Thus

$$(g(\theta_1) \circ g(\theta_2)) \circ g(\theta_3) = g(\theta_1) \circ (g(\theta_2) \circ g(\theta_3)). \tag{10}$$

(iii) **Identity**: There exists an element $e = g(0) = I_2 = \begin{pmatrix} 1 & 0 \\ 0 & 1 \end{pmatrix}$ such that for every element $g(\theta) \in G$, we have

$$g(\theta) \circ e = g(\theta) = e \circ g_i.$$

(iv) **Inverse**: Every group element $g(\theta)$ has an inverse $g(\theta)^{-1} = g(-\theta)$, such that

$$g(\theta) \circ g(\theta)^{-1} = I_2 = e = g(\theta)^{-1} \circ g(\theta).$$

We further show that $G$ is also a Lie group with one parameter. To verify the two topological axioms for a Lie group, consider the group elements $g(\theta_1)$, $g(\theta_2)$, and $g(\theta_3)$, which are parameterized by $\theta_i \in M$, where $M$ is one-dimensional curve (a smooth manifold). Given the combinatorial operation $g(\theta_1) \circ g(\theta_2) = g(\theta_3)$, it follows that the group composition map

$$\theta_3(\theta_1, \theta_2) = \theta_1 + \theta_2 \tag{11}$$

is differentiable. Furthermore, given the inverse $g(\theta_1)^{-1} = g(\theta_2)$ the group inversion map

$$\theta_2(\theta_1) = -\theta_1 \tag{12}$$

is also differentiable.

The study of Lie groups can be greatly simplified by linearizing the group in the neighborhood of its identity. This results in a linear vector space called a *Lie algebra* [4]. The Lie algebra retains most of the properties of the original Lie group. Next, we use again the rotation of an image as an example of transformation to illustrate how to linearize the Lie transformation group.

## 2.2. Lie operators and Lie algebras

Assume that the intensity of the original 2D image at location $(u, v)$ is given by $f(u, v)$, where $f$ is a differentiable function. In order to determine the intensity of the rotated image at a point $(x, y)$, we need to calculate the location from which the rotation operation originated. This can be accomplished by taking the inverse transformation as

$$T_\theta^{-1} : (x, y) \mapsto (x\cos\theta + y\sin\theta, -x\sin\theta + y\cos\theta). \tag{13}$$

Let $s(f,\theta)(x,y)$ denote the intensity of the rotated image at point $(x,y)$, then

$$s(f,\theta)(x,y) = f(x\cos\theta + y\sin\theta, -x\sin\theta + y\cos\theta). \tag{14}$$

That is, the intensity of the rotated pattern at point $(x,y)$ equals to the intensity of the original pattern at the coordinate found by applying $T_\theta^{-1}$ on $(x,y)$. Differentiating $s$ with respect to $\theta$ around $\theta = 0$ gives

$$\begin{aligned}
&\frac{\partial s(f,\theta)}{\partial\theta}(x,y)\bigg|_{\theta=0} \\
&= \frac{\partial f}{\partial x}(x,y)\cdot\frac{\partial}{\partial\theta}(x\cos\theta + y\sin\theta)\bigg|_{\theta=0} + \frac{\partial f}{\partial y}(x,y)\cdot\frac{\partial}{\partial\theta}(-x\sin\theta + y\cos\theta)\bigg|_{\theta=0} \\
&= y\frac{\partial f}{\partial x}(x,y) - x\frac{\partial f}{\partial y}(x,y)
\end{aligned} \tag{15}$$

Using Taylor series expansion, we have

$$s(f,\theta)(x,y) = f(x,y) + \theta\left[y\frac{\partial f}{\partial x}(x,y) - x\frac{\partial f}{\partial y}(x,y)\right] + o(\|\theta\|^2)f(x,y). \tag{16}$$

Thus the intensity of the rotated pattern image can be approximated by

$$s(f,\theta)(x,y) \approx f(x,y) + \theta\cdot L_\theta(f(x,y)), \tag{17}$$

where $L_\theta$ is the so-called *Lie operator*, given by

$$L_\theta = y\frac{\partial}{\partial x} - x\frac{\partial}{\partial y} \tag{18}$$

Each rotated image with a certain angle $\theta$ corresponds to a point from a Lie group with one parameter.

More generally, if the transformation group is a Lie group with $m$ parameters $\Theta = (\theta_1, \theta_2, \ldots, \theta_m)$, then after transformation, the intensity of the deformed image, $s(f,\Theta)$ is related to the original image $f$ by the following approximation:

$$s(f,\Theta) = f + \theta_1\cdot L_{\theta_1}(f) + \theta_2\cdot L_{\theta_2}(f) + \cdots + \theta_m\cdot L_{\theta_m}(f) + o(\|\Theta\|^2)(f), \tag{19}$$

where the operators $L_{\theta_1}, L_{\theta_2}, \cdots, L_{\theta_m}$ are said to generate a Lie algebra, which is a linear vector space. A vector space is a mathematical structure formed by a collection of vectors, which may be added together and multiplied by numbers (scalars). More precisely,

**Definition**: A **Lie algebra** is a vector space $V$ over a field $\mathbb{F}$, with an product operation $V \times V \to V$ denoted by $[X,Y]$, which is called the Lie bracket of $X \in V$ and $Y \in V$, with the following axioms [16]:

(i) The bracket operation is bilinear.

(ii) $[X,X] = 0, \forall X \in V$.

(iii) **Jacobi identity**: $[X,[Y,Z]] + [Y,[Z,X]] + [Z,[X,Y]] = 0$. $(X,Y,Z \in V)$.

In axiom (i), the bilinear operation refers to a function that combining two elements of the vector space to yield a third element in the vector space, which is linear in each of its arguments. As an example, matrix multiplication is bilinear: $M_1(n,n)M_2(n,n) = M_3(n,n)$.

To illustrate the concept of Lie brackets, let us consider another transformation with three parameters $(a,b,c)$

$$T^{-1}_{(a,b,c)} : (x,y) \mapsto (ax + c, by), \tag{20}$$

which corresponds to the matrix group

$$g(a,b,c) = \begin{pmatrix} a & 0 & 0 \\ 0 & b & 0 \\ c & 0 & 1 \end{pmatrix}. \tag{21}$$

Similar to the group $g(\theta)$ in (6), it can be shown that $g(a,b,c)$ is also a Lie group. However, the intensity of the pattern image after this new transformation is given by

$$s(f,a,b,c)(x,y) = f(ax + c, by). \tag{22}$$

By following the procedure outlined in (15) through (18), we can obtain the three Lie operators as follows:

$$L_a = x\frac{\partial}{\partial x}, \ L_b = y\frac{\partial}{\partial y}, \text{ and } L_c = \frac{\partial}{\partial x}. \tag{23}$$

These three Lie operators generate a Lie algebra, with the Lie bracket between any two operators $X$ and $Y$ defined as

$$[X,Y] = X \circ Y - Y \circ X, \tag{24}$$

where $X \circ Y$ denotes the operation of applying the operator $Y$, followed by applying the operator $X$.

It can be easily checked that the Lie bracket $[X,Y]$ is bilinear (axiom (i) of Lie algebra). Next, for any operator $X \in L_a, L_b, L_c$, we have $[X,X] = X \circ X - X \circ X = 0$, thereby satisfying axiom (ii). Verifying the Jacob identify requires additional efforts. First, we have

$$L_a \circ L_b = x\frac{\partial}{\partial x}\left(y\frac{\partial}{\partial y}\right) = xy\frac{\partial^2}{\partial x \partial y} = y\frac{\partial}{\partial y}\left(x\frac{\partial}{\partial x}\right) = L_b \circ L_a, \tag{25}$$

Hence

$$[L_a, L_b] = L_a \circ L_b - L_b \circ L_a = 0. \tag{26}$$

Similarly,

$$\begin{aligned} [L_a, L_c] &= L_a \circ L_c - L_c \circ L_a = x\frac{\partial}{\partial x}\left(\frac{\partial}{\partial x}\right) - \frac{\partial}{\partial x}\left(x\frac{\partial}{\partial x}\right) = x\frac{\partial^2}{\partial x^2} - \left(\frac{\partial}{\partial x} + x\frac{\partial^2}{\partial x^2}\right) \\ &= -\frac{\partial}{\partial x} = -L_c, \end{aligned} \tag{27}$$

and

$$[L_b, L_c] = L_b \circ L_c - L_c \circ L_b = y\frac{\partial}{\partial y}\left(\frac{\partial}{\partial x}\right) - \frac{\partial}{\partial x}\left(y\frac{\partial}{\partial y}\right) = y\frac{\partial^2}{\partial y \partial x} - y\frac{\partial^2}{\partial x \partial y} = 0. \tag{28}$$

Therefore,

$$[L_a,[L_b,L_c]] = [L_a,0] = 0,\ [L_b,[L_c,L_a]] = [L_b,L_c] = 0,\ \text{and}\ [L_c,[L_a,L_b]] = [L_c,0] = 0. \quad (29)$$

It follows that the Jacob identity holds.

The result of applying the three Lie operators to a function $f$, which is a 2D image in our example, is the set of vectors known as *tangent vectors* (also called the *Lie derivatives* of the transformation). These tangent vectors generate the so-called *tangent space*. Each point in the tangent space corresponds to a transformation, and any transformation of the Lie group $g(a,b,c)$ corresponds to a point in the tangent space.

## 2.3. Lie operators on discrete images

As shown in (17), given a continuous image $f$, by applying the Lie operator ($L_\theta$) for rotation, we can approximate the rotated image as $s(f,\theta) = f + \theta \cdot L_\theta(f)$. However, in many practical applications, we need to deal with computer images. Given a discrete image $I$, in order to apply a Lie operator, which involves derivatives, we first convert $I$ into a continuous one ($f$) by means of convolution: $f = I * g_\sigma$, where $g_\sigma$ is a 2D Gaussian function defined in [18] as:

$$g_\sigma = \exp\left(-\frac{x^2+y^2}{2\sigma^2}\right). \quad (30)$$

In our study, besides rotation ($R$), we will consider several other types of transformations, such as scaling ($S$), parallel deformation ($P$), and diagonal deformation ($D$), as defined in Table 1. To distinguish the Lie operators for different types of transformations, we use $L_R$ to denote the Lie operator for rotation. After applying $L_R = y\frac{\partial}{\partial x} - x\frac{\partial}{\partial y}$, we have

$$L_R(f) = \left(y\frac{\partial}{\partial x} - x\frac{\partial}{\partial y}\right)(I * g_\sigma) = y\left(I * \frac{\partial g_\sigma}{\partial x}\right) - x\left(I * \frac{\partial g_\sigma}{\partial y}\right). \quad (31)$$

To avoid high computational complexity associated with the convolution operation and the calculation of the partial derivatives of the Gaussian function in (30), we can apply the Lie operator on the discrete image directly, by using the following approximations [14].

$$L_R(f) \approx L_R(I) = \left(y\frac{\partial}{\partial x} - x\frac{\partial}{\partial y}\right) I = y\left(\frac{\partial I}{\partial x}\right) - x\left(\frac{\partial I}{\partial y}\right), \quad (32)$$

where

$$\frac{\partial I}{\partial x} \approx \frac{1}{2}\left[I(x+1,y) - I(x-1,y)\right],\ \text{and}\ \frac{\partial I}{\partial y} \approx \frac{1}{2}\left[I(x,y+1) - I(x,y-1)\right]. \quad (33)$$

After the Lie operator is applied, the rotated version of the image $I$ can then be easily obtained as

$$I_R = I + \theta \times L_R(I). \quad (34)$$

For small angles ($\theta$), the approximation tends to be reasonably good.

Similarly, we can obtain the transformed images for other types of transformations, based on their associated Lie operators (summarized in the third column of Table 1), which can be derived in a similar fashion to $L_R$.

| Transformation | Transformation matrix $T_\theta$ (adapted from [18]) | Lie operator and the transformed image |
|---|---|---|
| Rotation ($R$) | $\begin{pmatrix} \cos\theta, & -\sin\theta \\ \sin\theta, & \cos\theta \end{pmatrix}$ | $L_R = y\frac{\partial}{\partial x} - x\frac{\partial}{\partial y}$ <br> $I_R = I + \theta \times L_R(I)$ |
| Scaling ($S$) | $\begin{pmatrix} 1+\theta, & 0 \\ 0, & 1+\theta \end{pmatrix}$ | $L_S = x\frac{\partial}{\partial x} + y\frac{\partial}{\partial y}$ <br> $I_S = I + \theta \times L_S(I)$ |
| Scaling ($S_x$) | $\begin{pmatrix} 1+\theta, & 0 \\ 0, & 1 \end{pmatrix}$ | $L_{S_x} = x\frac{\partial}{\partial x}$ <br> $I_{S_x} = I + \theta \times L_{S_x}(I)$ |
| Scaling ($S_y$) | $\begin{pmatrix} 1, & 0 \\ 0, & 1+\theta \end{pmatrix}$ | $L_{S_y} = y\frac{\partial}{\partial y}$ <br> $I_{S_y} = I + \theta \times L_{S_y}(I)$ |
| Parallel Deformation ($P$) | $\begin{pmatrix} 1+\theta, & 0 \\ 0, & 1-\theta \end{pmatrix}$ | $L_P = x\frac{\partial}{\partial x} - y\frac{\partial}{\partial y}$ <br> $I_P = I + \theta \times L_P(I)$ |
| Diagonal Deformation ($D$) | $\begin{pmatrix} 1, & \theta \\ \theta, & 1 \end{pmatrix}$ | $L_D = y\frac{\partial}{\partial x} + x\frac{\partial}{\partial y}$ <br> $I_D = I + \theta \times L_D(I)$ |

**Table 1.** Six types of transformation and their associated Lie operators ($\theta$ is the degree of the transformations).

We can see from (32) that only simple subtractions and multiplications are involved in applying the Lie operator to obtain $L_R(I)$, which needs to be calculated just once, since a different transformed version $I_R$ corresponding to a different degree of transformation ($\theta$) can be obtained by using the same $L_R(I)$. Therefore, the implementation of Lie operators has fairly low computational complexity.

## 2.4. Lie operators for transformation estimation

Lie operators were proposed in [18] as an effective method for handling transformation invariance in handwritten digit pattern recognition [19]. In order for an automatic method to "recognize" a handwritten digit, the incoming digit pattern needs to be accurately classified into one out of ten possible categories. one method is to use an only one prototype image ($I$) for each category, with different "deformed" instances, $s(I, \Theta)$, of the same prototype image being generated by geometric transformations during the matching process so as to best fit the incoming digit pattern. As mentioned in the section 1, when the set of transformations is parameterized by $m$ parameters $\theta_i \in \Theta$ (rotation, scaling, etc.), the transformed image $s(I, \Theta)$ is a surface (manifold) with intrinsic dimension of at most $m$. In general, such a manifold is not linear. Matching a deformable prototype to an incoming pattern now amounts to finding the point on the manifold that is at a minimum distance from the point in the pixel space corresponding to the incoming pattern. Because the manifold has no analytical expression, the matching process can be very difficult. However, if the set of transformations happens to be linear in the pixel space, then the manifold is a linear subspace (a plane). The matching procedure is then reduced to finding the shortest distance between a point (vector) and a plane, or between two tangent planes corresponding to their original manifolds, which is the idea of *tangent distance* in [18]. While the tangent distance is able to capture the transformation invariance, it involves solving of a complicated least-square problem, which is not only computationally expensive, but also prone to numerical instability issues associated with solving linear systems. Therefore, conventional Euclidean distance between patterns, due to its fast and easy calculation, was also used in conjunction with the tangent distance in actual implementation.

On the other hand, for many pattern recognition tasks, e.g., character recognition, a set of allowable deformations of the prototype might have been known *a priori*. Therefore, one can generate on-the-fly a set of varying transformed versions of the same prototype $I$, by using the Lie operators associated with the transforms, in a computationally efficient way. For example, a set of rotated images $I_R(\theta_i)$, where $i = 1, 2, \ldots, n$, can be readily obtained by

$$I_R(\theta_i) = I + \theta_i \times L_R(I), \tag{35}$$

where $L_R(I)$ can be pre-computed and shared by calculations of different $I_R(\theta_i)$.

Thus, *transformation estimation* refers to matching an incoming pattern image $P$ to the "closest" $I_R(\theta_i)$, which has the shortest distance with $P$. For simplicity, the Euclidean distance could be used.

In transformation estimation, we search for a value for $\theta$ that best matches the degree of transformation the prototype has undergone in relation to the incoming pattern. If the best $\theta$ value is found to be zero in the case of rotation, then the resultant rotated version will be the same as the original prototype. If $\theta$ has a larger search range, then the probability of finding a better match may be increased; however, the complexity of searching will be increased as we have to examine more candidates. On the other hand, the step size of $\theta$ is also an important parameter that controls the "granularity" of the searching. By decreasing the step size, we may be able to enlarge the searching range of $\theta$ without increasing the search complexity. We can further lower the searching complexity by using variable step sizes. For example, we can employ finer-granular searching by taking smaller step sizes for small $\theta$ values, whereas the step size increases as the search drifts away from the centers of the range of allowable $\theta$ values [11].

Transformation estimation can be viewed as a generalized operation of the translation motion estimation. In the following, we present a case study to illustrate the design of computationally efficient transformation estimation algorithms based on Lie operators, by selecting the subject of local motion estimation in video coding, where both accurate and fast motion estimation is critical [12]. We then discuss several methods in which multiple Lie operators can be combined to detect smaller degrees of object motions in video frames such as scaling, rotations and deformations, with varying computational complexities. We then provide both analytical and empirically obtained results regarding the tradeoffs between estimation accuracies and computational complexities for these methods [13].

## 3. Transformation estimation in video coding

Motion estimation is a critical component of almost every video coding system [10][17][23]. Most compression techniques exploit the temporal redundancy that exists between the succeeding frames. In motion estimation, we search for any object in the previous frame that provides a good match of an object in the current frame within a sequence of images (frames). Motion compensation refers to representing objects in the current frame by their match objects in the previous frame. Conventional motion estimation algorithms in video coding consider only translations as an approximation to a combination of potential motions of objects in a video scene, including scaling, rotation, deformations and so on.

### 3.1. Block-based translation motion estimation

Block-based motion estimation [10][23] has been adopted in international standards for video coding such as MPEGs and H.264, where each frame is partitioned evenly into square blocks. Motion estimation is applied on a block-by-block basis so that each block is associated with a motion vector. Motion vectors are used to produce a motion-compensated prediction of a frame to be transmitted from a previously transmitted reference frame [1][7]. Motion estimation enables us to transmit the frame difference as an update between the current frame and the motion-compensated prediction of the current frame from the previous frame, rather than the entire current frame, thereby achieving compression by user fewer bits to code the current frame.

In block-based motion estimation, each frame is divided into evenly partitioned square blocks ($4 \times 4$, $8 \times 8$, ..., etc.). We attempt to predict the current frame ($F_2$) from the previous frame ($F_1$). The prediction is obtained by taking the best match of each block of $F_2$ within the searching window of $F_1$. The match criterion is typically based on mean square error (MSE). The block with the minimum MSE is considered to be the best match, and its associated motion vector $(dx, dy)$ is given by

$$(dx, dy) = \arg \min_{(du,dv)\in[-R,R]} \{\mathrm{MSE}_{m,n} = \sum_{i,j=0}^{B-1} [(F_2(x,y) - F_1(x+du, y+dv)]^2\}, \tag{36}$$

where B is the block size, $[-R, R]$ is the searching window, and $x = m \times B + i$, and $y = n \times B + j$ for the block $(m, n)$. Note that the motion vector for a still block is $(0, 0)$.

After finding in $F_1$ the best match block of each block in $F_2$, the prediction frame ($P_1$) of $F_2$ can then be constructed. To determine the accuracy of the prediction, the PSNR between $F_2$ and $P1$ is calculated as

$$\mathrm{PSNR} = 10 \log_{10} \frac{255^2}{\mathrm{MSE}_{avg}}, \tag{37}$$

where $MSE_{avg}$ is the average mean square error between $F_2$ and $P_1$ as given by

$$\mathrm{MSE}_{avg} = \sum_{m=0}^{M} \sum_{n=0}^{N} \frac{\mathrm{MSE}_{m,n}}{M \times N}. \tag{38}$$

Note that $\mathrm{MSE}_{m,n}$ is defined in (36), and $M \times N$ is the total number of blocks in a frame.

Conventional motion estimation algorithms in video coding consider only translations as an approximation to a variety of object motions; therefore, they have limitations in capturing potential motions such as scaling, rotations and deformations in a video scene other than the translation. The reason for the widespread use of the translation model lies partly in its simplicity - translation model can be readily characterized by displacement motion vectors and can thus be implemented with much lower complexity than other non-linear motion models used to describe non-translation motions. Nonetheless, the accuracy of the motion estimation would be sacrificed by considering the translation model alone.

### 3.2. Block-based transformation estimation

Non-translational transformation estimation can be introduced into video coding to further increase the overall motion estimation accuracy. More specifically, the conventional (translation) motion estimation is applied on the previous frame ($F_1$) based on the current frame ($F_2$). We can construct a predicted frame $P$ (of the current frame) from the previous frame by using the resulting motion vectors associated with each block in the current frame (see Fig. 4). The accuracy of the predicted frame $P$ (relative to the current frame $F_2$) can be represented by $\text{PSNR}_1$. Next, transformation estimation based on the Lie operators is applied on the match blocks ($B_P$) in the predicted frame $P$ to further improve the motion estimation accuracy. For each block $B_P$ in $P$, we search for the best parameter $\theta$ from the set of candidate parameters that yields the smallest mean square error between the transformed version $B_T$ and the corresponding block ($B_C$) in the current frame $F_2$. Consequently, a new predicted frame $P_T$ can be formed by the resulting blocks of $B_T$. The accuracy of the newly predicted frame $P_T$ can be represented as $\text{PSNR}_2$. As expected, $P_T$ will become a better prediction of the current frame than $P$, thereby achieving an increased accuracy in motion estimation and prediction. The accuracy of the motion estimation can be measured by the PSNR between the current frame and the predicted frame. The improved accuracy due to the motion models is calculated as ($\text{PSNR}_2 - \text{PSNR}_1$). The accuracy of the motion estimation can be improved by considering other types of transformations as well.

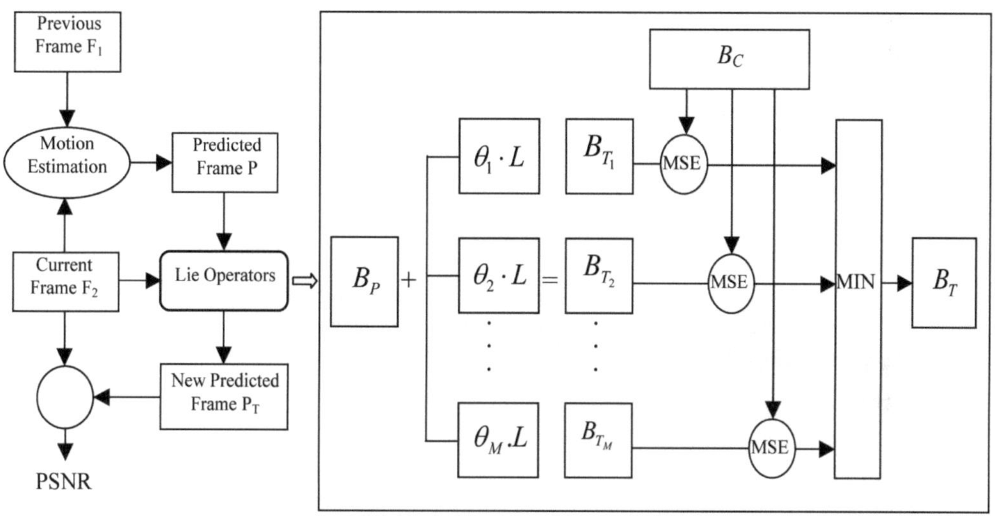


**Figure 1.** The transformation estimation system using a Lie operator: We search for the best $\theta$ in the set of candidates $[\theta_1, \theta_2, \ldots, \theta_M]$ such that the transformed block $B_T$ of the block $B_P$ in the prediction frame $P$ will have the smallest MSE compared to the corresponding block $B_C$ in $F_2$.

## 4. Computational efficiencies of transformation estimation using multiple Lie operators

We first examine the full search method that exhaustively searches for the best combination of four types of Lie operators ($R$, $S$, $P$ and $D$). In order to reduce the high computational complexity associated with the full search method, we then consider the following three parameter-search methods: *dynamic programming* (DP)-like search, *iterative* search, and *serial* search. They combine the Lie operators in different ways, with varying accuracy-complexity tradeoffs [13].

### 4.1. Full search

Fig. 2 illustrates all possible combinations of the Lie operators for rotation, scaling, parallel deformation, and diagonal deformation. The highlighted path shows one combination ($D \to P \to S \to R$), which means that block $B_P$ will be first diagonally deformed, and then the deformed block will go through the parallel deformation. The resultant block will be scaled and then rotated to obtain $B_T$. The degree of motions ($\theta$) associated with each participating operator is optimized by the searching procedure illustrated in Fig. 1. The full search is the

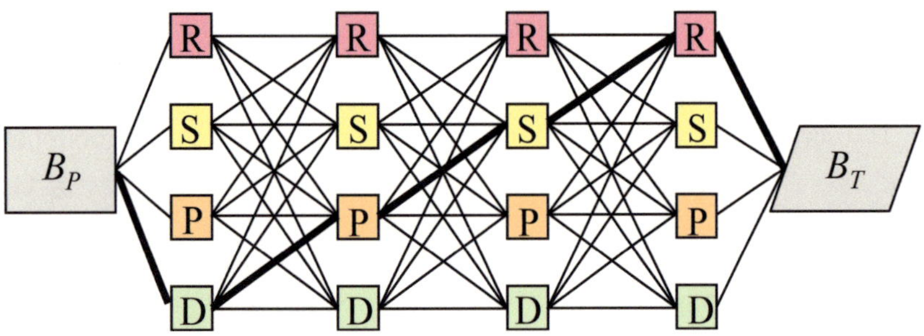


**Figure 2.** The trellis structure of the combined Lie operators. The output block $B_T$ is expected to provide more accurate prediction than the input block $B_P$.

most straightforward and yet the most computationally expensive method. In this method, we search through all possible ($4^4 = 256$) paths that start from block $B_P$ (of the predicted frame $P$) and end on the transformed block $B_T$ (of a more accurately predicted frame than $P$), and select the path (i.e., the combination of the four Lie operators) whose output block $B_T$ is the most accurately predicted version of block $B_C$ in the current frame.

Assume that $x$ is the computational complexity of motion estimation for a single Lie operator. Thus the complexity associated with any path of four operators from $B_P$ to $B_T$ in Fig. 2 is $4x$. Since we need to search all 256 possible paths, the overall complexity of the full search method will be $1024x$.

We can reduce the complexity of this brute-force search approach by dividing the estimation process into four stages, with each stage corresponding to one column of operators in Fig. 2. In the first stage, there will be four estimation operations for $R$, $S$, $P$, and $D$, respectively, with complexity being $4x$. In the second stage, we will apply the same four operators on one of the four candidate transformed blocks generated by one of the four operators in stage one. For example, starting with $R$ in the first stage, we will examine $R \to R$ ($R$ in the first stage, followed by $R$ in the second stage), $R \to S$, $R \to P$, and $R \to D$. Note that applying the $R$ operator again on a block already rotated by the best $\theta$ value as found in the first stage of estimation would not be beneficial in general. However, further gains in the estimation accuracy might be achievable by considering other combinations such as $R \to S$, $R \to P$, and $R \to D$. Therefore, the total complexity of the second stage will be $4 \times 4x = 16x$. Likewise, the complexity of the third stage will be $4 \times 16x = 64x$. In the last stage, the complexity will amount to $4 \times 64x = 256x$. Therefore, the overall complexity of the reduced-complexity full search method is $340x$ ( $= 4x + 16x + 64x + 256x$), merely $1/3$ of that of the brute-force full search method. Even so, the complexity of the full search is still unacceptably high in practical applications. In order to further reduce the complexity, let us consider the following search methods.

## 4.2. Dynamic-programming-like search

Compared to the full search, the DP search method is a sub-optimal search method, which has a flavor of the dynamic-programming (DP) solution in finding the shortest path through a weighted graph [2]. Similar to the Viterbi algorithm used in the decoding of convolutional codes [9], the DP search method keeps only those "survivors" (i.e., the best result obtained by each operator) in each stage (of the four stages in Fig. 2) for further searching operations. In the first stage, there are four transformed blocks ("survivors"), corresponding to the four Lie operators considered, as a result of the estimation operations (with complexity being 4x). In the second stage, four operators will be again applied to the survivors of stage 1. Take operator R as an example. Out of the four possible partial paths ($R \to R$, $S \to R$, $P \to R$, and $D \to R$) entering into $R$ in the second stage, we choose the one that gives a transformed version with the smallest MSE value (as compared against the block in the current frame to be predicted). The transformed block so obtained will be stored as the survivor for operator $R$ in the second stage, so will its originating operator in the first stage. Information about all other inferior partial paths will be discarded. In order to obtain other survivor blocks for stage two, the same procedure will be repeated for the other three operators. Therefore, the total complexity for stage two will be $4 \times 4x = 16x$. The four surviving blocks obtained in stage two will then be used for obtaining another four survivors in stage three in the same fashion, with the partial paths leading to the survivors getting longer. The same procedure will be repeated for stage four in order to obtain yet another four survivors, one of which with the least MSE will be the final winner. Hence the overall complexity for the DP-like method is $52x$ ( $= 4x + 3 \times 16x$), which is less than $1/6$ of that of the reduced-complexity full search method. Although there is no guarantee of optimality in theory for this DP-like method, we expect its search results to be reasonably close to those yielded by the full search method.

## 4.3. Iterative search

To further reduce computational complexity, we introduce the iterative search method that performs the motion-parameter estimation through multiple iterations. In each iteration, we choose the best Lie operator (Fig. 3). For example, in the first iteration, the $S$ operator may turn out to be the best operator. The scaled block will go through the same estimation process in the next iteration, which will output a transformed block with lower MSE values. Here we consider only four iterations to ensure fair comparison between this method and the other two methods previously discussed. Therefore, the overall complexity of this method will be $4 \times 4x = 16x$, which is slightly less than $1/3$ of the complexity of the DP-like method.

## 4.4. Serial search

In the foregoing two search methods, the best quadruplet of Lie operators will not be known until the search is completed. Their complexities are higher than a simplified search method, where Lie operators are applied sequentially in a pre-determined order (e.g., the order of $R \to S \to P \to D$ in Fig. 4). Although this serial search method has the lowest complexity ($4x$), it

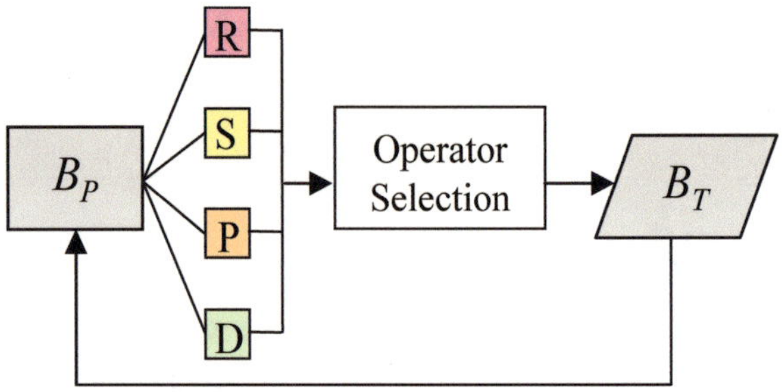


**Figure 3.** Iterative search. In each iteration, the best operator is selected as the one with the largest MSE reduction on the input block $B_P$. The transformed block $B_T$ generated by the best operator found will be further transformed optimally in the next iteration.

is unlikely to provide very accurate transformation estimation due to the non-communicative nature of the transformations.

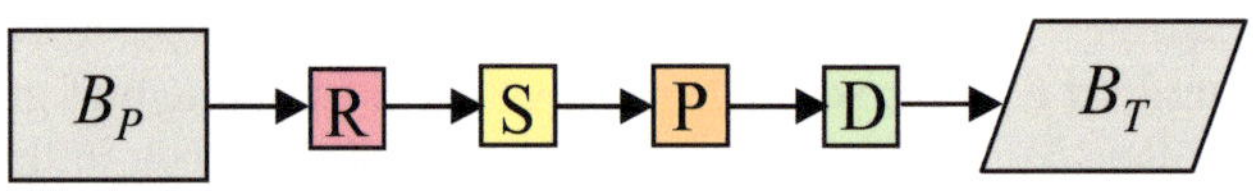


**Figure 4.** Serial search: we apply $R$, $S$, $P$ and $D$ operators sequentially to obtain the transformed block $B_T$.

## 4.5. Comparison of computational complexity

As summarized in Table 2, the complexity of the DP-like search is 13 times that of the serial search and the complexity of the iterative search is 4 times that of the serial search.

| Search Method | Complexity |
|---|---|
| DP-like | $52x$ |
| Iterative | $16x$ |
| Serial | $4x$ |

**Table 2.** Complexities required by the three search methods ($x$ is the complexity associated with estimation using an individual operator). $\theta$ was chosen from $[-0.14, 0.14]$, with a step size of 0.02.

## 4.6. Simulation results

We tested the above mentioned methods on three standard video sequences "Table Tennis", "Mobile Calendar", and "Tempete", all in the CIF format (288 $\times$ 352). Some samples frames of these sequences are shown in Figure 6.

In the simulations, a block size of (4 $\times$ 4) was used. The size of the search window is chosen to be $\pm$15 pixels in translation motion estimation that precedes the transformation estimation using Lie operators. The search range of $\pm$0.14 (with step size being 0.02) is chosen for $\theta_R$, $\theta_S$, $\theta_P$, and $\theta_D$ for the DP-like, iterative, and serial search methods.

Simulation results are illustrated in Fig. 6, Fig. 7, and Fig. 8 for the three test sequences. Some statistics (maximum, minimum and the average values) of the PSNR improvements effected by the three search methods are listed in Table 3. We can see in Table 3 that the DP-like method significantly increases the accuracy of the predicted frames of all three sequences by as high

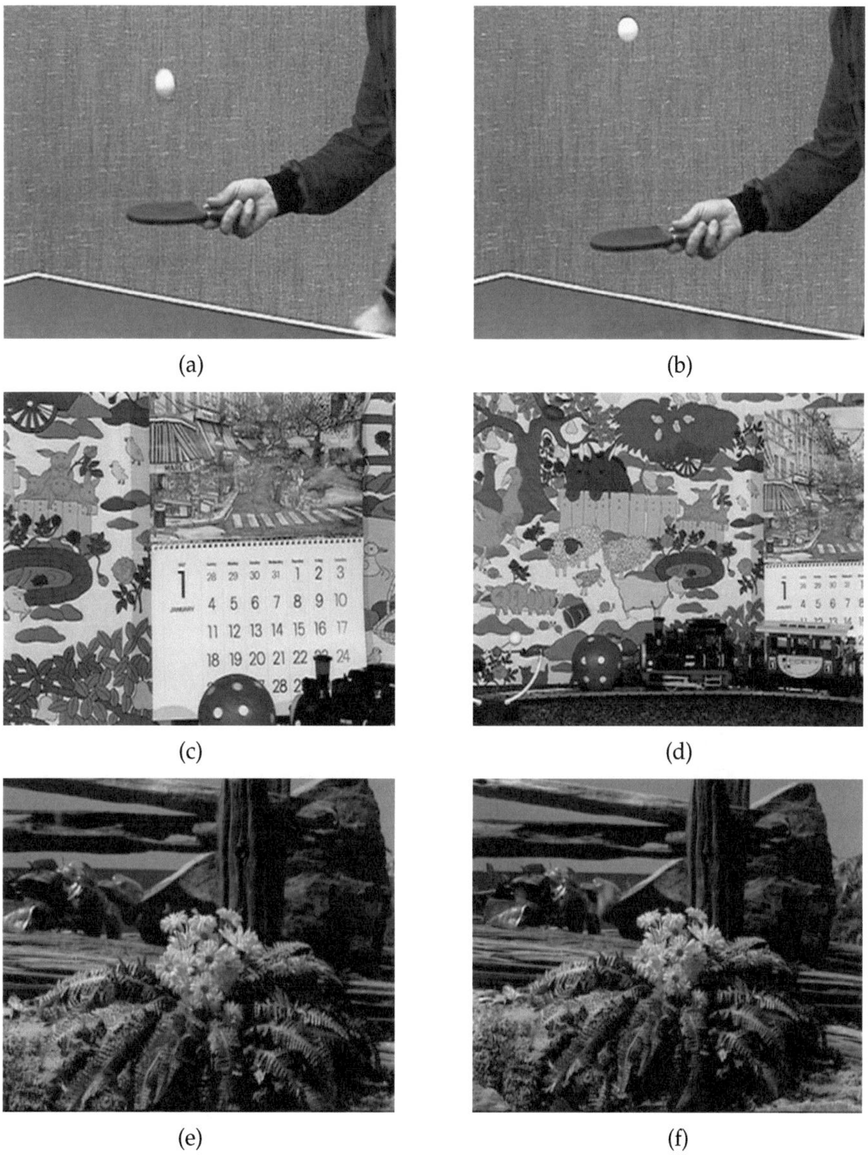


**Figure 5.** Sample frames of the video sequences. (a) The 1st frame of the "Table Tennis" sequence. (b) The 20th frame of the "Table Tennis" sequence. (c) The 1st frame of the "Mobile Calendar" sequence. (d) The 200th frame of the "Mobile Calendar" sequence. (e) The 1st frame of the "Tempete" sequence. (f) The 50th frame of the "Tempete" sequence.

as 2.6 dB and above 2.1 dB on average. The largest improvement (2.47 dB on average) is observed in "Mobile Calendar". This may be attributed to the existence of a great deal of non-translational motions in "Mobile Calendar" (e.g., the ball keeps rotating, and the camera is zooming out). On the other two sequences, about 2.1 dB increase can be achieved by the DP-like method.

| Search Method | Table Tennis | | | Mobile Calendar | | | Tempete | | |
|---|---|---|---|---|---|---|---|---|---|
| | Max | Min | Avg | Max | Min | Avg | Max | Min | Avg |
| DP-like | 2.67 | 0.68 | 2.19 | 2.65 | 2.15 | 2.47 | 2.30 | 1.46 | 2.12 |
| Iterative | 2.12 | 0.45 | 1.75 | 2.31 | 1.73 | 2.04 | 1.81 | 1.19 | 1.66 |
| Serial | 1.70 | 0.30 | 1.35 | 1.84 | 1.36 | 1.60 | 1.39 | 0.91 | 1.27 |

**Table 3.** Increased estimation accuracy (in dB) for the three video sequences.

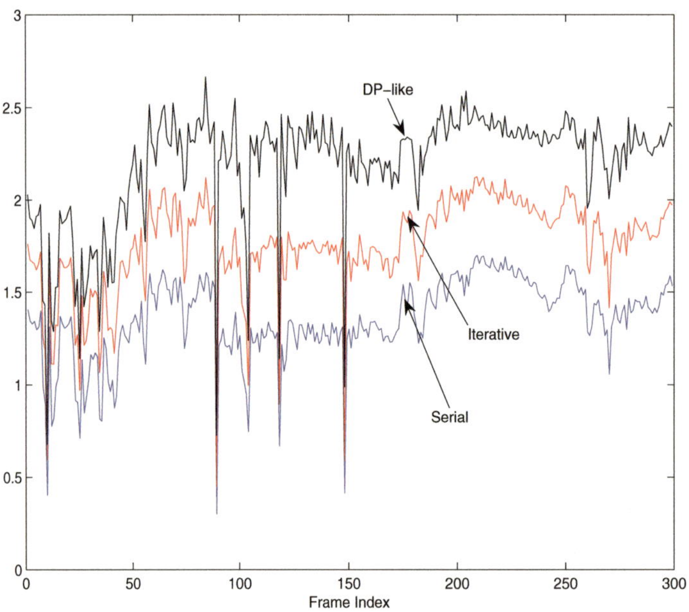


**Figure 6.** PSNR improvements (in dB) for "Tennis".

With less than 1/3 of the complexity required by the DP-like method, the iterative search can deliver an impressive estimation accuracy, especially on the "Mobile Calendar" (up to 2.31 dB and about 2dB on average). Similar to the case with the DP-like method, slightly lower PSNR improvements are observed on the other two sequences: on average, 1.75 dB and 1.66 dB for the sequences "Table Tennis" and "Tempete", respectively. As can be observed in Fig. 6, numerous deep plunges of the PSNR improvement (occurring in a range of frames around, e.g., 90 and 149) affect adversely the average PSNR improvement for "Table Tennis". These plunges occur whenever there is a scene change. For "Tempete", although there is no major scene change, a continuous influx of large number of new objects (e.g., small leaves blown by wind) tends to make transformation estimation less effective.

With only one quarter of the complexity required by the iterative search, the serial search achieves average PSNR improvements of 1.60dB, 1.35dB and 1.27 dB on "Mobile Calendar", "Table Tennis", and "Tempete", respectively. The accuracy of this method is the lowest, which

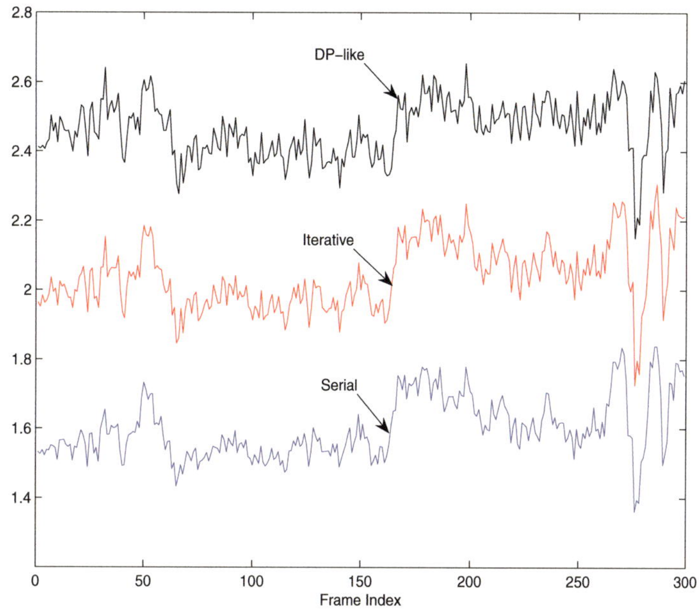


**Figure 7.** PSNR improvements (in dB) for "Mobile Calendar".

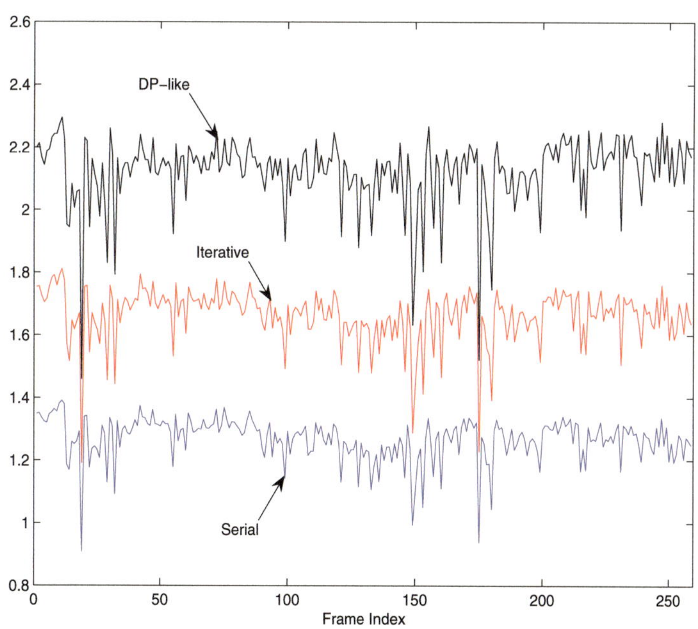


**Figure 8.** PSNR improvements (in dB) for "Tempete".

indicates that changing the order of the Lie operators in a sequence does affects the motion estimation accuracy.

We also measured the actual computation times of the three search methods on a PC running Windows XP (with 3.40 GHz Pentium 4 CPU and 2GB RAM). The total running time of the subroutine for each method was first measured over all the frames in a test sequence. Then the average running time per block for each search method was calculated and listed in Table 4. On average, Time (DP like search) / Time (Serial Search) = 13.12, and Time (Iterative) / Time (Serial Search) = 4.03, which is in agreement with the analytical results listed in Table 2. As a reference, the average time was also measured for executing the subroutine for the conventional translation-only motion estimation that precedes the transformation estimation. As shown in Table 4, the complexity of the DP-like search, iterative search and the serial search methods is 69%, 21% and 5%, respectively, relative to that of the translation-only motion estimation method.

| Search Method | Table Tennis | Mobile Calendar | Tempete | Average | Normalized Complexity |
|---|---|---|---|---|---|
| DP-like | 2.469 | 2.500 | 2.470 | 2.480 | 0.69 |
| Iterative | 0.763 | 0.766 | 0.756 | 0.762 | 0.21 |
| Serial | 0.181 | 0.195 | 0.192 | 0.189 | 0.05 |

**Table 4.** Computation times (in ms / block) of the three methods for three video sequences. The normalized complexity is calculated as the ratio between the average computation time for each search method and the reference time (3.60 ms/block) for translation-only motion estimation method.

Fig. 9 shows the empirical tradeoffs between the accuracies of these three search methods and their complexities. The best performance achievable is again observed in "Mobile Calendar" - an increase of 2.47 dB, 2.04 dB and 1.60 dB can be achieved with additional computational complexity of approximately 69%, 21% and 5% of that of the translation-only motion estimation.

## 5. Comparison with full affine transformation model

We want to compare the computational complexity of transformation estimation using Lie-operators to the complexity of transformation estimation using a full transformation model. We consider the affine model [8, 20, 21, 24], which was widely used in the literature to detect non-translation motions due to its ability to offer good compromise between complexity and performance. In its generic form, the 6-parameter affine model can be expressed as

$$\begin{pmatrix} x \\ y \end{pmatrix} \mapsto \begin{pmatrix} u \\ v \end{pmatrix} = \begin{pmatrix} a_1x + a_2y + a_3 \\ b_1x + b_2y + b_3 \end{pmatrix} \tag{39}$$

Since $a_3$ and $b_3$ in (39) are translational displacements, the 6-parameter affine model can be simplified to a 4-parameter model by estimating the translation motions using the conventional block matching method. In fact, even if the more complex gradient descent method is used for motion parameter estimation, to assure convergence, translation motion estimation is often employed as an initial stage that computes a coarse estimate of the translation component of the set of the motion parameters, so that the starting point of the gradient descent should be within the "basin" of the global minimum [3, 8].

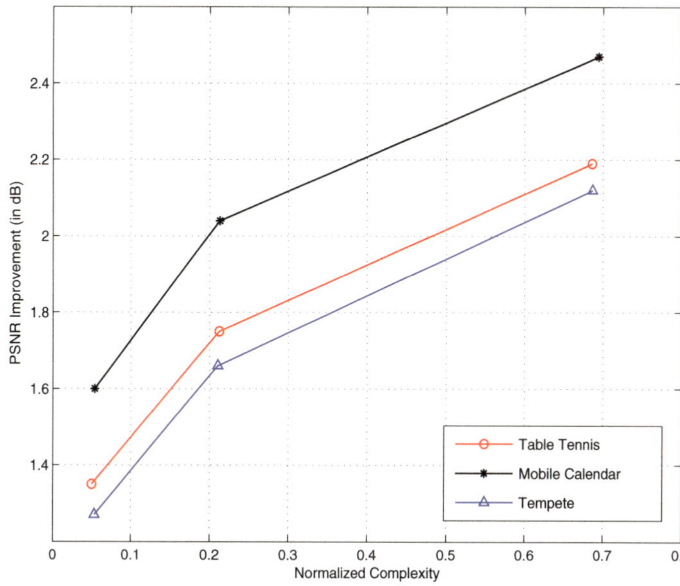


**Figure 9.** Increased accuracy vs. complexity. For each of the three sequences, from the right to the left, the three operating points correspond to the DP-like search, iterative search and the serial search methods, respectively. The normalized complexity is calculated as the ratio between the computation time for each search method and that for the translation-only motion estimation method as shown in Table 4.

## 5.1. A five-parameter affine transform model

Based on the above discussions, we choose the following affine motion model, which was used in [6] to improve the local translation motion compensation by taking into account rotation and scaling of small objects.

$$\begin{pmatrix} u \\ v \end{pmatrix} = \begin{pmatrix} \cos\theta & \sin\theta \\ -\sin\theta & \cos\theta \end{pmatrix} \begin{pmatrix} K_x & 0 \\ 0 & K_y \end{pmatrix} \begin{pmatrix} x \\ y \end{pmatrix} + \begin{pmatrix} t_x \\ t_y \end{pmatrix} \tag{40}$$

The five parameters in (40) are estimated by using a two-step search method [6, 22]. First, parameters $(t_x, t_y)$ corresponding to the translational motion between blocks in the current frame and the reference frame are searched for. This is a common step also shared by the Lie-operator approach (see Fig. 1), which operates on top of the match block yielded by the conventional translation block matching process. In the second step, the remaining three parameters for rotation and scaling $(\theta, K_x, K_y)$ are searched for. For ease of coding, $\theta$, $K_x$ and $K_y$ are chosen from small sets of discrete values. For example, $\theta \in [-0.02\pi, 0, 0.02\pi]$, and $K_x, K_y \in [0.9, 1.0, 1.1]$ were chosen in [6]. On the other hand, the Lie-operator method is also suitable for the estimation of these small degrees of transformation. For example, the iterative approach discussed in Section 4.3 with three operators ($R$, $S_x$ and $S_y$ in Table 1) can be employed. Since $(u,v)$ calculated by (40) can be real numbers, the pixel values at $(u,v)$ have to be interpolated from the pixel values of the surrounding pixels. Bilinear interpolations are often employed [6][24, pp. 59]. More specifically, we assume that the four surrounding pixels in the reference frame have values $I_{\lfloor u \rfloor, \lfloor v \rfloor}$, $I_{\lfloor u+1 \rfloor, \lfloor v \rfloor}$, $I_{\lfloor u \rfloor, \lfloor v+1 \rfloor}$, and $I_{\lfloor u+1 \rfloor, \lfloor v+1 \rfloor}$, where $\lfloor s \rfloor$ is the *floor* function, which returns the nearest integer less than or equal to $s$. Thus the signal value at $(u,v)$ can be interpolated as

$$I_{u,v} = I_1 + r_1 \cdot (I_2 - I_1), \tag{41}$$

where

$$I_1 = I_{\lfloor u \rfloor, \lfloor v \rfloor} + r_2 \cdot \left( I_{\lfloor u+1 \rfloor, \lfloor v \rfloor} - I_{\lfloor u \rfloor, \lfloor v \rfloor} \right), \tag{42}$$

$$I_2 = I_{\lfloor u \rfloor, \lfloor v+1 \rfloor} + r_2 \cdot \left( I_{\lfloor u+1 \rfloor, \lfloor v+1 \rfloor} - I_{\lfloor u \rfloor, \lfloor v+1 \rfloor} \right), \tag{43}$$

and

$$r_1 = v - \lfloor v \rfloor, \qquad r_2 = u - \lfloor u \rfloor. \tag{44}$$

Clearly, there will be extra computation cost incurred by these interpolation operations, which is not required by the Lie-operator approach.

## 5.2. Comparison of computational complexity

We now analyze the complexity required by motion estimation using the affine model described in Section 5.1, and the iterative Lie-operator approach described in Section 4.3, which can offer variable tradeoffs between the increased estimation accuracy and computational complexity by varying the number of iterations. The computational complexity is estimated by counting the number of additions/subtractions ($C_{add}$), and the number of multiplications ($C_{mult}$).

As shown in Table 5, the complexity of applying the affine model is

$$C_{Affine} = (C_{add}, C_{mult}) = (12MW^3, 12MW^3), \tag{45}$$

since one has to search for the best combination of the three types of motion parameters from $W^3$ possible choices, where $W$ is the dimensionality of the candidate set for each motion parameter, which is assumed to be the same for each type of parameter, for ease of analysis and without much loss of generality. In the case of the above affine model given in Section 5.1, $W = 3$ was chosen [6].

| Operation | $C_{add}$ | $C_{mult}$ |
|---|---|---|
| $u = xK_x \cos\theta + yK_y \sin\theta$, $v = -xK_x \sin\theta + yK_y \cos\theta$ (by Eq.(40)) | $2M$ | $8M$ |
| Bilinear interpolation for $I(u,v)$ (by Eqs. (41)-(44)) | $8M$ | $3M$ |
| MSE calculation (by Eq.(36)) | $2M$ | $M$ |
| Total complexity / one combination of ($\theta$,$K_x$, $K_y$) | $12M$ | $12M$ |

**Table 5.** Number of arithmetic operations (per block) required by the transformation estimation using the affine model in (40), based on a displaced block with motion vector ($t_x$,$t_y$). Assume that values of $\sin\theta$ and $\cos\theta$ can be obtained by looking up from a pre-calculated table, and that $M$ is the number of pixels in a block.

On the other hand, the complexity of the iterative Lie-operator approach is given in Table 6 for each iteration involving three operators ($R$, $S_x$ and $S_y$). Therefore, if $Q$ iterations are used, the total complexity is

$$C_{Lie} = (C_{add}, C_{mult}) = (M(5+9W)Q, M(8+6W)Q). \tag{46}$$

| Type | Operation | $C_{add}$ | $C_{mult}$ |
|---|---|---|---|
| $R$ | $\frac{\partial B}{\partial x}$ and $\frac{\partial B}{\partial y}$ (by Eq.(33)) | $2M$ | $2M$ |
| | $L_R(B) = y\left(\frac{\partial B}{\partial x}\right) - x\left(\frac{\partial B}{\partial y}\right)$ (by Eq.(32)) calculated once for $W$ distinct $\theta_R$ values | $M$ | $2M$ |
| | $B_R^{\theta_R} = B + \theta_R \times L_R(B)$ (by Eq.(34)) repeated for $W$ distinct $\theta_R$ values | $MW$ | $MW$ |
| | MSE calculation (by Eq.(36)) repeated for $W$ distinct $\theta_R$ values | $2MW$ | $MW$ |
| | Sub-total for $R$ | $3M(1+W)$ | $2M(2+W)$ |
| $S_x$ | $\frac{\partial B}{\partial x}$ (by Eq.(33)) | $M$ | $M$ |
| | $L_{S_x}(B) = x\left(\frac{\partial B}{\partial x}\right)$ (see Table 1) calculated once for $W$ distinct $\theta_{S_x}$ values | 0 | $M$ |
| | $B_{S_x}^{\theta_{S_x}} = B + \theta_{S_x} \times L_{S_x}(B)$ (see Table 1) repeated for $W$ distinct $\theta_{S_x}$ values | $MW$ | $MW$ |
| | MSE calculation (by Eq.(36)) repeated for $W$ distinct $\theta_{S_x}$ values | $2MW$ | $MW$ |
| | Sub-total for $S_x$ | $M(1+3W)$ | $2M(1+W)$ |
| $S_y$ | Sub-total for $S_y$ (same as that for $S_x$) | $M(1+3W)$ | $2M(1+W)$ |
| Total complexity of ($R$, $S_x$ and $S_y$) / iteration | | $M(5+9W)$ | $M(8+6W)$ |

**Table 6.** Number of arithmetic operations required for finding the best transformed block (per iteration) using the iterative Lie-operator approach, based on a displaced block with motion vector ($t_x$,$t_y$). In each iteration, three types of operators ($R$, $S_x$, and $S_y$) are considered. Assume that $M$ is the number of pixels in a block, and that the dimensionality of the set of candidate $\theta_R$ values for operator $R$ is $W$, which is the same for the parameters $\theta_{S_x}$ and $\theta_{S_y}$ (for operators $S_x$ and $S_y$, respectively).

From (45) and (46), it can be shown that as long as the number of candidate parameters for each type of motion $W \geq 3$, we have $C_{Lie} < 0.3\ C_{Affine}$ if the number of iterations $Q = 3$; and $C_{Lie} < 0.4\ C_{Affine}$ if $Q = 4$. The larger the $W$ value is, the smaller the complexity of the iterative Lie operator becomes, relative to that of the estimation using the affine model.

Table 7 summarizes the increased accuracies obtained empirically for the iterative Lie-operator approach (using operators $R$, $S_x$ and $S_y$ in each iteration) and the affine model approach discussed in Section 5.1, which searches for the best combination of the parameters for rotation and scaling ($\theta$, $K_x$, $K_y$), where $\theta \in [-0.02\pi, 0, 0.02\pi]$, and $K_x, K_y \in [0.9, 1.0, 1.1]$. The corresponding set of parameters for the Lie operators are thus chosen to be $\theta_R \in [-0.02\pi, 0, 0.02\pi]$, and $\theta_{S_x}, \theta_{S_y} \in [-0.1, 0, 0.1]$.

| Search Method | Table Tennis | | | Mobile Calendar | | | Tempete | | |
|---|---|---|---|---|---|---|---|---|---|
| | Max | Min | Avg | Max | Min | Avg | Max | Min | Avg |
| Affine Model | 1.58 | 0.24 | 1.14 | 1.63 | 0.99 | 1.41 | 1.29 | 0.85 | 1.14 |
| $RS_xS_y$ ($Q = 4$) | 1.36 | 0.28 | 1.08 | 1.49 | 1.06 | 1.27 | 1.08 | 0.69 | 0.98 |
| $RS_xS_y$ ($Q = 3$) | 1.23 | 0.22 | 0.95 | 1.35 | 0.94 | 1.11 | 0.93 | 0.60 | 0.84 |

**Table 7.** Increased estimation accuracy (in dB) of the iterative Lie-operator method versus that of the affine model approach. $Q$ denotes the number of iterations.

It can be seen from Table 7 that with only 3 iterations, the Lie operator method performs closely to the affine model approach in terms of PSNR improvement; with one additional round of iteration, the Lie operator approach comes very close (within less than 0.1 dB) to the affine model approach. On a PC running Windows XP (with 3.40 GHz Pentium 4 CPU and 2GB RAM), the average running times of these two approaches were measured to be 0.46 ms/block (Lie operator, 4 iterations) and 1.46 ms/block (affine model). That is, Time (Lie operator, $Q = 4$) $\approx 1/3$ Time (affine model), which agrees with our analysis in Section 5.2. On the other hand, by comparing the data for iterative Lie operator approach in Table 3 and Table 7, it is obvious that the accuracy of the motion estimation can be increased significantly by using larger sets of candidate parameters (i.e., by increasing $W$ in (46)) and considering more operators. Nevertheless, for the affine model, using a large $W$ can lead to unacceptably large complexity, which increases linearly with $W^3$ in (45), as opposed to the almost linearly increased complexity of the Lie operator approach with $W$ in (46). Therefore, the Lie operators have a clear advantage in terms of computational complexity, as long as they can provide good approximations to small degrees of transformation. Nevertheless, in the case of large degrees of transformations, the search method based on the full affine transformation model would be more accurate than the fast method based on Lie operator.

## 6. Conclusion

Lie operators are useful for efficient handwritten character recognition. Multiple operators can be combined to approximate small degrees of object transformations, such as scaling, rotations and deformations. In this chapter, we first explained in a tutorial fashion the underlying theory of Lie groups and Lie algebras. We then addressed the key problem of transformation estimation based on Lie operators, where exhaustive full search method is often impractical due to its prohibitively huge computational complexity. To illustrate the design of computationally efficient transformation estimation algorithms based on Lie operators, we selected the subject of motion and transformation estimation in video coding as an example. We presented several fast search algorithms (including the dynamic programming like, serial, and iterative search methods), which integrated multiple Lie operators to detect smaller degrees of transformation in video scenes. We provided a detailed analysis of the varying tradeoffs between estimation accuracies and computational complexities for these transformation estimation algorithms. We demonstrated that non-translational transformation estimation based on Lie operators could be used to improve the overall accuracy of motion estimation in video coding, with only a modest increase of its overall computational complexity. In particular, we showed that the iterative search method based on Lie operators has much lower complexity than the transformation estimation method based on the full affine transformation model, with only negligibly small degradation in the estimation accuracy.

## Author details

W. David Pan
*Department of Electrical and Computer Engineering, University of Alabama in Huntsville, Huntsville, Alabama 35899, USA.*

## 7. References

[1] B. Carpentieri, Block matching displacement estimation: a sliding window approach, Information Sciences 135 (1-2), (2001) 71–86.
[2] T. H. Cormen, C. E. Leiserson, R. L. Rivest, C. Stein, Introduction to Algorithms, Second Edition, MIT Press, 2001.
[3] F. Dufaux, J. Konrad, Efficient, robust, and fast global motion estimation for videocoding, IEEE Trans. Image Processing 9 (3) (2000) 497–501.
[4] R. Gilmore, Lie Groups, Lie Algebras and Some of Their Applications, John Wiley & Sons, 1974.
[5] R. Gilmore, Lie Groups, Physics, and Geometry: An Introduction for Physicists, Engineers and Chemists, Cambridge University Press, 2008.
[6] H. Jozawa, K. Kamikura, A. Sagata, H. Kotera, H. Watanabe, Two-stage motion compensation using adaptive global MC and local affine MC, IEEE Trans. Circuits and Systems for Video Technology 7 (1) (1997) 75–85.
[7] T. C. T. Kuo, A. L. P. Chen, A mask matching approach for video segmentation on compressed data, Information Sciences 141 (1-2) (2002) 169–191.
[8] W. Li, J.-R. Ohm, M. van der Schaar, H. Jiang, S. Li, MPEG-4 video verification model version 18.0, in: ISO/IEC JTC1/SC29/WG11 N3908, Pisa, Italy, 2001.
[9] S. Lin, D. J. Costello, Error Control Coding, Second Edition, Pearson Prentice Hall, 2004.
[10] J. L. Mitchell, W. B. Pennebaker, C. E. Fogg, D. J. LeGall, MPEG Video Compression Standard, Chapman & Hall, 1996.
[11] M. Nalasani, W. D. Pan, On the complexity and accuracy of the lie operator based motion estimation, in: Proc. IEEE Southeastern Symposium on System Theory (SSST), Atlanta, Georgia, 2004, pp. 16–20.
[12] W. D. Pan, S.-M. Yoo, M. Nalasani, P. G. Cox, Efficient local transformation estimation using Lie operators, Information Sciences, 177 (2007) 815-831.
[13] W. D. Pan, S.-M. Yoo, C.-H. Park, Complexity accuracy tradeoffs of Lie operators in motion estimation, Pattern Recognition Letters 28 (2007) 778–787.
[14] C. A. Papadopoulos, T. G. Clarkson, Motion estimation using second-order geometric transformations, IEEE Trans. Circuits and Systems on Video Technology 5 (4) (1995) 319–331.
[15] H. Richter, A. Smolic, B. Stabernack, E. Muller, Real time global motion estimation for an MPEG-4 video encoder, in: Proc. Picture Coding Symposium (PCS), Seoul, Korea, 2001.
[16] H. Samelson, Notes on Lie Algebras, Springer, 1990.
[17] K. Sayood, Introduction to Data Compression, Morgan Kaufmann, 2000.
[18] P. Y. Simard, Y. A. LeCun, J. S. Denker, B. Victorri, Transformation invariance in pattern recognition - tangent distance and tangent propagation, International Journal of Imaging Systems & Technology 11 (3) (1998) 239–274.
[19] K. Sookhanaphibarn, C. Lursinsap, A new feature extractor invariant to intensity, rotation, and scaling of color images, Information Sciences 176 (14) (2006) 2097–2119.
[20] C. Stiller, J. Konrad, Estimating motion in image sequences, IEEE Signal Processing Magazine (1999) 70–91.
[21] Y. Su, M.-T. Sun, V. Hsu, Global motion estimation from coarsely sampled motion vector field and the applications, IEEE Trans. Circuits and Systems on Video Technology 15 (2) (2005) 232–242.

[22] Y. T. Tse, R. L. Baker, Global zoom/pan estimation and compensation for video compression, in: Proc. International Conference on Acoustics, Speech, and Signal Processing (ICASSP), Toronto, Canada, 1991, pp. 2725–2728.
[23] Y. Wang, J. Ostermann, Y.-Q. Zhang, Video Processing and Communications, Prentice Hall, 2002.
[24] G. Wolberg, Digital Image Warping, IEEE Computer Society Press, 1990.

Chapter 2

# SVM Classifiers – Concepts and Applications to Character Recognition

Antonio Carlos Gay Thomé

Additional information is available at the end of the chapter

http://dx.doi.org/10.5772/52009

## 1. Introduction

Support Vector Machines – SVMs, represent the cutting edge of ranking algorithms and have been receiving special attention from the international scientific community. Many successful applications, based on SVMs, can be found in different domains of knowledge, such as in text categorization, digital image analysis, character recognition and bioinformatics.

SVMs are relatively new approach compared to other supervised classification techniques, they are based on statistical learning theory developed by the Russian scientist Vladimir Naumovich Vapnik back in 1962 and since then, his original ideas have been perfected by a series of new techniques and algorithms.

Since the introduction of the concepts by Vladimir, a large and increasing number of researchers have worked on the algorithmic and the theoretical analysis of SVM, merging concepts from disciplines as distant as statistics, functional analysis, optimization, and machine learning. The soft margin classifier was introduced few years later by Cortes and Vapnik [1], and in 1995 the algorithm was extended to the regression case.

There are several published studies that compare the paradigm of neural networks against to the support vector machines. The main difference between the two paradigms lies in how the decision boundaries between classes are defined. While the neural network algorithms seek to minimize the error between the desired output and the generated by the network, the training of an SVM seeks to maximize the margins between the borders of both classes.

SVM approach has some advantages compared to others classifiers. They are robust, accurate and very effective even in cases where the number of training samples is small. SVM technique also shows greater ability to generalize and greater likelihood of generating good classifiers.

By nature SVMs are essentially binary classifiers, however, based on several researchers' contributions they were adapted to handle multiple classes cases. The two most common approaches used are the One-Against-All and One-Against-One techniques, but this scenario is still an ongoing research topic.

In this chapter we briefly discuss some basic concepts on SVM, describe novel approaches proposed in the literature and discuss some experimental tests applied to character recognition. The chapter is divided into 4 sections. Section 2 presents the theoretical aspects of the Support Vector Machines. Section 3 reviews some strategies to deal with multiple classes. Section 4 details some experiments on the usage of One-Against-All and One-Against-One approach applied to character recognition.

## 2. Theoretical foundations of the SVM

Support vector machines are computational algorithms that construct a hyperplane or a set of hyperplanes in a high or infinite dimensional space. SVMs can be used for classification, regression, or other tasks. Intuitively, a separation between two linearly separable classes is achieved by any hyperplane that provides no misclassification on all data points of any of the considered classes, that is, all points belonging to class A are labeled as +1, for example, and all points belonging to class B are labeled as -1.

This approach is called linear classification however there are many hyperplanes that might classify the same set of data as can be seen in the figure 1 below. SVM is an approach where the objective is to find the best separation hyperplane, that is, the hyperplane that provides the highest margin distance between the nearest points of the two classes (called functional margin). This approach, in general, guarantees that the larger the margin is the lower is the generalization error of the classifier.

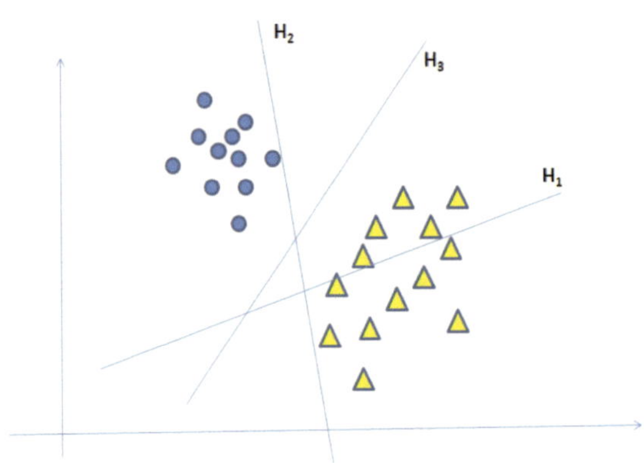


**Figure 1.** Separation hyperplanes. $H_1$ does not separate the two classes; $H_2$ separates but with a very tinny margin between the classes and $H_3$ separates the two classes with much better margin than $H_2$

If such hyperplane exists, it is clear that it provides the best separation border between the two classes and it is known as the maximum-margin hyperplane and such a linear classifier is known as the maximum margin classifier.

## 2.1. Brief history

Research on pattern recognition started in 1936 through the work done by R. A. Fisher who suggested the first algorithm for pattern recognition [2]. After him we have the work done by Frank Rosemblat in 1957 that invented the nowadays well known linear classifier named PERCEPTRON that is the simplest kind of feed forward neural network [3]. In 1963 Vapnik and Lerner introduced the Generalized Portrait algorithm (the algorithm implemented by support vector machines is a nonlinear generalization of the Generalized Portrait algorithm) [4]. Aizerman, Braverman and Rozonoer in 1964, introduced the geometrical interpretation of the kernels as inner products in a feature space [5] and Cover in 1965 discussed large margin hyperplanes in the input space and also sparseness [6].

The field of statistical learning theory was first developed and proposed by Vapnik and Chervonenkis in 1974 [7] and, based on this theory, appears in the year of 1979, the first concepts about SVMs [8]. SVMs close to their current form were first introduced by Boser at al. with a paper presented at the COLT 1992 conference in 1992 [9].

## 2.2. Formal definition of the SVM classifier – The linear model

The surface model used by SVM to perform the separation is the hyperplane. Let then **W** and **b** be, respectively, the vector normal to the hyperplane and its displacement relative to the origin [10]. Thus, we have that the decision function for an input **x** is given by equation (1).

$$D(x) = W \bullet x - b \tag{1}$$

where,

$$x \in \begin{cases} A & if\ D(x) > 0 \\ B & if\ D(x) < 0 \end{cases} \tag{2}$$

As can be seen in figure 2 below, the distance from **x** (with signal) to the hyperplane is given by 3.

$$\frac{D(x)}{\|W\|} \tag{3}$$

Thus, D(**x1**) and D(**x2**) will have opposite signs (belong to different sets) if and only if **x1** and **x2** are on opposite sides of the separation hyperplane.

Figure 2 shoes that the Vector **W** is perpendicular to the hyperplane and the parameter $\frac{|b|}{\|W\|}$ determines the offset of the hyperplane from the origin along the normal vector. It is desired to choose **W** and **b** to maximize the margin M that represents the distance between the parallel hyperplanes that are as far apart as possible while still separating the both set of data. These two hyperplanes can be described respectively by the following equations (4).

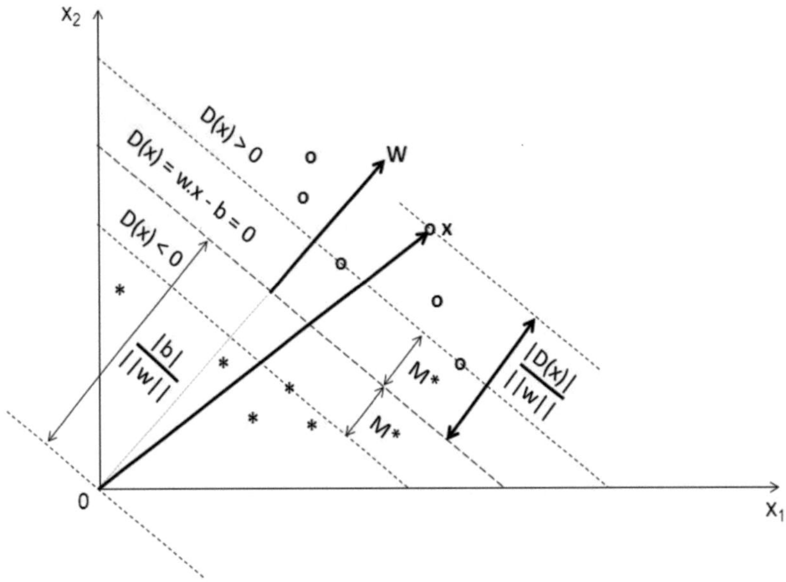


**Figure 2.** Example of the separating hyperplane (in two dimensions), distances and margins (from Boser et al, 1992 [9]).

$$\begin{gathered} W \bullet x - b = +1 \\ and \\ W \bullet x - b = -1 \end{gathered} \tag{4}$$

Let the set of sample points be represented by $\mathbf{x}_1, \ldots, \mathbf{x}_p$ and their respective group classification be represented by $y_1, \ldots, y_p$ where

$$y_i = \begin{cases} +1 & if\ x_i \in A \\ -1 & if\ x_i \in B \end{cases} \tag{5}$$

If the two groups of samples in the training data are linearly separable it is then possible to select the two hyperplanes in a way that there are no points between them and then try to maximize the distance between the two hyperplanes [11].

The distance between these two hyperplanes is given by $\frac{2}{\|W\|}$ and to maximize it implies to minimize **W** and, in order to prevent data points falling into the margin M, we add the following constraint to each equation (6):

$$\begin{gathered} W \bullet x_i - b \geq +1 \quad \forall i, y_i = +1 \\ and \\ W \bullet x_i - b \leq -1 \quad \forall i, y_i = -1 \end{gathered} \tag{6}$$

Multiplying each equation by its corresponding $y_i$ they are transformed into just one equation as following (7):

$$y_i \bullet (W \bullet x_i - b) \geq 1 \quad \forall i, i = 1 \ldots p \tag{7}$$

Dividing now both sides of the equation by $\|w\|$ it turns into (8)

$$\frac{y_i \bullet (W \bullet x_i - b)}{\|w\|} \geq \frac{1}{\|w\|} = M \quad \forall i, i = 1 \ldots p \tag{8}$$

To maximize M we need to minimize $\|w\|$ subject to the following constraint (9).

$$\begin{aligned} &\min\,(in\ w,b) \\ &\quad \|w\| \\ &subject\ to\ \forall i, i = 1 \ldots p \\ &\quad y_i \bullet (w \bullet x_i - b) - 1 \geq 0 \end{aligned} \tag{9}$$

The optimization problem above is difficult to solve because it depends on $\|w\|$, the norm of **w**, which involves a square root. Fortunately it is possible to alter the equation substituting $\|w\|$ by $\frac{1}{2}\|w\|^2$ without changing the solution (the minimum of the original and the modified equations have the same **w*** and **b***). The problem now belongs to the quadratic programming (QP) optimization that is easier to be computed and is stated as in (10).

$$\begin{aligned} &\min\,(in\ w,b) \\ &\quad \frac{1}{2}\|w\|^2 \\ &subject\ to\ \forall i, i = 1 \ldots p \\ &\quad y_i \bullet (w \bullet x_i - b) - 1 \geq 0 \end{aligned} \tag{10}$$

The factor of 1/2 is used for mathematical convenience and the problem can now be solved by standard quadratic programming techniques. Applying non negative Lagrange multipliers $\alpha_i$ ($i = 1 \ldots p$) to the objective function turns the problem into its dual form as in (11).

$$\begin{aligned} &L(w,b,\alpha) = \frac{1}{2}\|w\|^2 - \sum_{i=1}^{p} \alpha_i \left( y_i \left( w \bullet x_i - b \right) - 1 \right) \\ &subject\ to \\ &\quad \alpha_i \geq 0 \quad \forall i, i = 1 \ldots p \end{aligned} \tag{11}$$

Considering now that in the solution point the gradient of **L()** is null, the equation can be handled in order to obtain a new quadratic programming problem as in (12):

$$\begin{aligned} &\frac{\partial L}{\partial w}\Big|_{w=w^*} = w^* - \sum_{i=1}^{p} \alpha_i y_i x_i = 0 \quad \therefore w^* = \sum_{i=1}^{p} \alpha_i y_i x_i \\ &\frac{\partial L}{\partial w}\Big|_{b=b^*} = -\sum_{i=1}^{p} \alpha_i y_i = 0 \quad \therefore \sum_{i=1}^{p} \alpha_i y_i = 0 \end{aligned} \tag{12}$$

In this case, the minimum point with respect to **w** and **b** is the same to the maximum with respect to **α**, and the problem can be stated as in (13).

$$\begin{aligned} & \max\,(in\ \alpha_i) \\ & \quad \alpha^T \bullet 1 - \frac{1}{2}\alpha^T \bullet H \bullet \alpha \\ & subject\ to\ \forall i, i = 1...p \\ & \quad \alpha_i \geq 0, \\ & \quad \alpha^T \bullet y = 0 \end{aligned} \tag{13}$$

Where $\boldsymbol{\alpha} = (\alpha_1, \ldots, \alpha_p)^T$, $\mathbf{y} = (y_1, \ldots, y_p)^T$, **0** and **1** have size p, and $H_{p \times p}$ is such that

$$H_{i,j} = y_i y_j x_i^T \bullet x_j \tag{14}$$

A condition imposed by the Kühn-Tucker Theorem is that

$$\alpha_i^* \left( y_i \left( w^* \bullet x_i - b^* \right) - 1 \right) = 0 \quad \forall i, i = 1...p \tag{15}$$

so that, if $\alpha_i^* \neq 0$ then

$$y_i \left( w^* \bullet x_i - b^* \right) - 1 = 0 \quad \forall i, i = 1...p \tag{16}$$

that is,

$$y_i \left( w^* \bullet x_i - b^* \right) = 1 \tag{17}$$

Any $\mathbf{x}_i$ that satisfies equation (17) is called **support vector** and the SVM trainings are reduced to the set of such vectors.

In the cases where the samples are not linearly separable the approach described above would diverge and grow arbitrarily. In order to deal with the problem it is then introduced a set of slack variables (δ) in equation (6) as showed in (18).

$$\begin{aligned} & D(x_i) = W \bullet x_i - b \geq +1 - \delta_i \quad \forall i, y_i = +1 \\ & and \\ & D(x_i) = W \bullet x_i - b \leq -1 + \delta_i \quad \forall i, y_i = -1 \\ & where \\ & \delta_i \geq 0, \quad \forall i, i = 1...p \end{aligned} \tag{18}$$

These equations can be rewritten as

$$y_i D(x_i) \geq +1 - \delta_i \quad \forall i, i = 1...p \tag{19}$$

The slack variables provide some freedom to the system allowing some samples do not respect the original equations. It is necessary however to minimize the number of such samples and also the absolute value of the slack variables. The way to do this is introducing a penalization term into the objective function as follows (19):

$$\begin{aligned}
&\max\,(in\ w, b) \\
&\quad \frac{1}{2}\|w\|^2 + C\sum_{i=1}^{p}\delta_i \\
&subject\ to\ \forall i, i = 1 \ldots p \\
&\quad y_i\left(w \bullet x_i - b\right) - 1 + \delta_i \geq 0, \\
&\quad \delta_i \geq 0
\end{aligned} \tag{20}$$

Variable C indicates the strength of the penalization to be applied. Introducing Lagrange multipliers on the penalization variables the dual form of the problem becomes as in (21).

$$\begin{aligned}
&L(w,b,\alpha,\delta,\lambda) = \frac{1}{2}\|w\|^2 + C\sum_{i=1}^{p}\delta_i - \sum_{i=1}^{p}\alpha_i\left(y_i\left(w \bullet x_i - b\right) - 1\right) - \sum_{i=1}^{p}\lambda_i\delta_i \\
&subject\ to\ \forall i, i = 1 \ldots p \\
&\quad \alpha_i \geq 0 \\
&\quad \lambda_i \geq 0
\end{aligned} \tag{21}$$

Where $\delta = \left(\delta_i \ldots \delta_p\right)^T$ $and$ $\lambda = \left(\lambda_i \ldots \lambda_p\right)^T$

From here, as before, the problem can be represented into its quadratic form in terms of $\alpha$(22).

$$\begin{aligned}
&\max\,(in\ \alpha_i) \\
&\quad \alpha^T \bullet 1 - \frac{1}{2}\alpha^T \bullet H \bullet \alpha \\
&subject\ to\ \forall i, i = 1 \ldots p \\
&\quad \alpha^T \bullet y = 0, \\
&\quad 0 \leq \alpha \leq c
\end{aligned} \tag{22}$$

Where c = (C … C) is a p dimension vector with all values equal C.

### 2.3. The non-linear model

Whereas the original problem as proposed by Vladimir Vapnik in 1979 [8], was stated for a finite dimensional space, it often happens that the sets to be discriminated are not linearly separable in their original space. For this reason, it was proposed by Isabelle Guyon, Bernhard Boser and Vapnik in 1992 [9], that the original finite-dimensional space was mapped into a higher-dimensional space, presumably making the separation easier in the new space.

In order to achieve non-linear separation, instead of generating a new quadratic programming problem as in previous section, it is possible to modify the vectors of the input space into vectors of a feature space through a chosen transform function ϕ◎ with N ≥ n and then compute the separation hyperplane on the feature space. Figure 3 shows an example of such scheme.

$$\Phi : \Re^n \rightarrow \Re^N$$

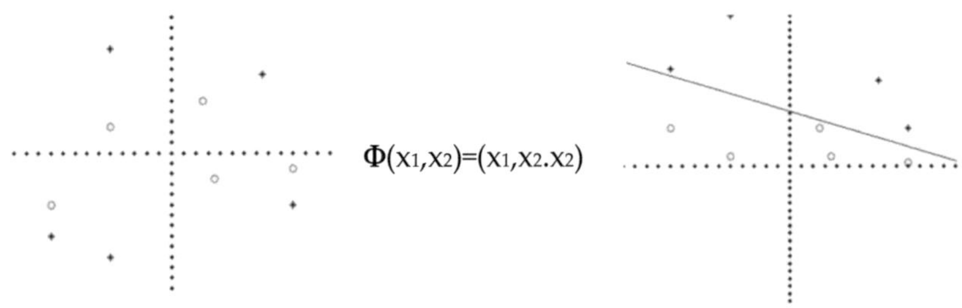


**Figure 3.** The transform function maintains the same dimension of the input space but makes the representation in feature space be linearly separable

The computation of the separation hyperplane is not done explicit on the feature space but using a scheme where every occurrence of **ϕ(u).ϕ(v)** is replaced by a function **K(u,v)** called kernel function and the H() function as seen before becomes (23):

$$H_{i,j} = y_i y_j K(x_i , x_j) \tag{23}$$

The optimum **W** vector is given by

$$w^* = \sum_{i=1}^{p} \alpha_i y_i \Phi(x_i) \tag{24}$$

And the support vector machine decision function becomes

$$D(x) = \sum_{i=1}^{p} \alpha_i y_i K(x_i , x) - b \tag{25}$$

To keep the computational load reasonable, the mapping used by SVM schemes are designed to ensure that dot products may be computed easily in terms of the variables in the original space, by defining them in terms of a kernel function K(x,y) selected to suit the problem. The hyperplanes in the higher dimensional space are defined as the set of points whose inner product with a vector in that space is constant. The vectors defining the hyperplanes can be chosen to be linear combinations of feature vectors that occur in the data base. With this choice of a hyperplane, the points **x** in the feature space that are mapped into the hyperplane are defined by the relation:

$$\sum_{i} \alpha_i K(x_i , x) = constant \tag{26}$$

This approach allows the algorithm to find the maximum-margin hyperplane into the transformed feature space. The transformation may be non-linear and / or the transformed space may be of high dimension. The classifier, in the feature space, draws a hyperplane that represents a non-linear separation curve in the original input space.

If the kernel used is a Gaussian radial basis function, the corresponding feature space is a Hilbert space of infinite dimension. Maximum margin classifiers are well regularized, so the infinite dimension does not spoil the results. Some common kernels include:

Polynomial (homogeneous): $K(x_i, x) = (x_i \bullet x)^d$

Radial Basis Function: $K(x_i, x) = \exp(-\lambda \|x_i - x\|^2); \lambda > 0$

Gaussian Radial basis function: $K(x_i, x) = \exp(-\frac{\|x_i - x\|^2}{2\sigma^2})$

Sigmoid: $K(x_i, x) = \tanh(kx_i \bullet x + c);\ for\ some\ (but\ not\ every)\ k > 0\ and\ c < 0$

## 3. The multiclass classification strategies

Multiclass SVM approach aims to assign labels to a finite set of several elements based on a set of linear or non-linear basic SVMs. The dominant approach for doing so in the literature is to reduce the single multiclass problem into multiple binary problems [12 – 15].

Doing so, each of the problems can be seen then as a binary classification, which is assumed to produce an output function that gives relatively large values for those examples that belong to the positive class and relatively small values for the examples that belong to the negative class.

Two common methods to build such binary classifiers are those where each classifier is trained to distinguish: (i) one of the labels against to all the rest of labels (known as one-versus-all) [16] or (ii) every pair of classes (known as one-versus-one). Classification of new instances for one-versus-all case is done by a winner-takes-all strategy, in which the classifier with the highest output function assigns the class. The classification of one-versus-one case is done by a max-wins voting strategy, in which every classifier assigns the instance to one of the two classes, then the vote for the assigned class is increased by one vote, and finally, the class with more votes determines the instance classification.

### 3.1. The one-versus-all strategy

One-Against-All multiclassifier is compound by a number of binary classifiers, one for each class. Using a Winner-Takes-All strategy, each binary classifier is trained taking the examples from one of the classes as positive and the examples from all other classes as negative. The multiclassifier output is activated for the class whose binary classifier gives the greatest output amongst all. Formally, given a vector **y** with the outputs of the binary classifiers, the multiclassifier generates a vector $\mathbf{L} = (l_1, \ldots, l_s)$, in the following way (27):

$$i^* = \arg\max_{i=1\ldots s}\{y_i\},$$
$$L_i = \begin{cases} +1 & if\, i = i^*, i = 1\ldots s \\ -1 & otherwise \end{cases} \quad (27)$$

Where 's' represents the total number of classes.

As seen, a one-against-all multiclassifier for 's' different classes requires the construction of 's' distinct binary classifiers, each one responsible for distinguishing one class from all the others. However, doing so does not guarantee that the resulting multi-class classifier is good. The problem is that all binary classifiers are assumed to show equal competence distinguishing their respective class, in other words, there is an underlying assumption that all binary classifiers are totally trustable and equally reliable, which does not always hold in multi-class cases as Yi Liu [17] shows through a simple example as in figure 4.

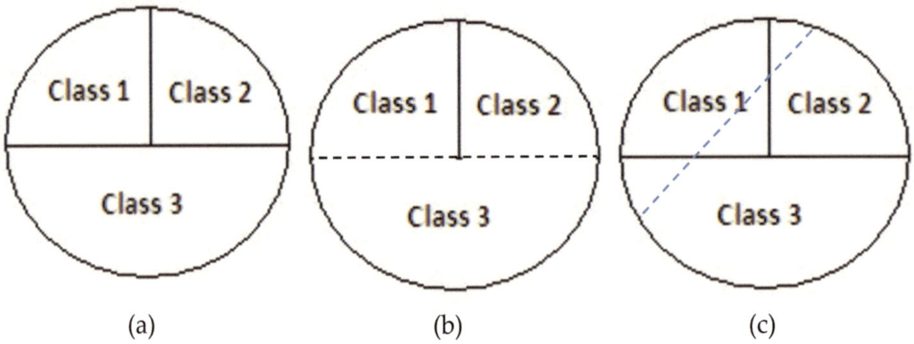


**Figure 4.** (a) Three classes problem and respective boundaries; (b) binary classifier that distinguishes well class 3 from all others (dashed line); (c) binary classifier that does not distinguish well class 1 from all others (dashed line). The example was taken from [15].

The same error occurs with the binary classifier for class 2 and so, the multi-class classifier based on these three binary classifiers would not provide good accuracy. In order to mitigate such problem, Liu [15] suggests two reliability measures: SRM – static reliability measure and DRM – dynamic reliability measure.

### *3.1.1. Static reliability measure*

As pointed out by Vapnik [17] and Cortes [1], a small training set error does not guarantee a small generalization error when the number of training samples is relative small with respect to the feature vector **x** dimension. SVM training is done minimizing the objective function and as the objective function becomes smaller, smaller also becomes the generalization error. Based on this fact, Liu rewrites the objective function as seen in (28) and proposes the SRM as in (29).

$$Obj = \frac{1}{2}\|w\|^2 + C\sum_{i=1}^{N}(1 - y_i D(x_i))_+ \tag{28}$$

Where $(u)_+ = u$ if $u > 0$ and 0 if $u \leq 0$.

$$\lambda_{SRM} = \exp\left( -\frac{1/2\|w\|^2 + C\sum_{i=1}^{N}(1 - y_i D(x_i))_+}{\sigma} \right) \tag{29}$$

Where $D(x_i) = w^T x_i + b$, and the parameter $\sigma = CN$ is a normalization factor to offset the effect of the different regularization parameter C and training size N. This $\lambda_{SRM}$ metric is reduced to (30) for those linearly separable cases where $(1 - y_i D(x_i))_+ = 0$ for all training samples.

$$\lambda_{SRM} = \exp\left( -\frac{\|w\|^2}{2CN} \right) \tag{30}$$

From (28) we notice that $2/\|w\|^2$ is the classification margin. Small $\|w\|$ corresponds to large margin and more accurate classifier. Small $\|w\|$ also corresponds to larger reliability measure $\lambda_{SRM}$.

### 3.1.2. *Dynamic reliability measure*

The basic idea, differently of the static measure that is global over the whole training samples, is to estimate the classifier's reliability in a local region of feature space surrounding the test sample **x**. The 'k' surrounding samples of **x** are denoted by $N_k(x)$.

Suppose A(**x**) ∊ {1, -1} is the class label assigned to **x** by a SVM classifier and let $N_k^{A(x)}(x)$ denote the set of the training samples that belong to the set of 'k' nearest neighbors of **x** and are classified to the same class of **x**. Now, rewriting equation (28) as in (31)

$$Obj = \sum_{i=1}^{N}\frac{1}{2N}\|w\|^2 + C\sum_{i=1}^{N}(1 - y_i D(x_i))_+ = \sum_{i=1}^{N} Obj(x_i) \tag{31}$$

Liu formulate the local version of OBJ as in (32)

$$Obj_{local} = \sum Obj(\hat{x}_i) = \sum_{i=1}^{k_x}\left( \frac{1}{2N}\|w\|^2 + C\sum_{i=1}^{N}(1 - y_i D(x_i))_+ \right) \tag{32}$$

Where $\hat{x}_i \in N_k^{A(x)}(x), (\hat{x}_i, \hat{y}_i)$ is the training pair, and $k_x$ is the number of training samples in the set $N_k^{A(x)}(x)$. And the dynamic reliability measure becomes as in (33).

$$\lambda_{DRM}(x) = \exp\left( -\frac{Obj_{local}}{C \cdot k_x} \right) \tag{33}$$

### 3.1.3. SRM and DRM decision rule

For a test sample **x**, assuming 'M' trained support vector machines each with its decision function, we evaluate D(x) for each classifier and after, generate the corresponding soft decision output $y_i \in [-1,+1]$ assuming that all classifiers are completely trustable (34)

$$y_i = sign\left(D_i(x)\right)\left(1 - \exp\left(\left|D_i\left(x\right)\right|\right)\right) \tag{34}$$

Now, assuming that $\lambda_i$ denotes either the SRM or DRM reliability measure we have (35)

$$\begin{aligned} &\tilde{y}_i = y_i \cdot \lambda_i \\ &and \\ &i^* = \underset{i=1\ldots M}{\arg\max}\, \tilde{y}_i \end{aligned} \tag{35}$$

Mota in [18] sees the same problem from a different point of view. According to them in the One-Against-All method, SVM binary classifiers are obtained by solving different optimization problems and the outputs from these binary classifiers may have different distributions, even when they are trained with the same set of parameters and so, comparing these outputs using equation (27) may not work very well.

The output mapping, as suggested in [18], tries to mitigate such problem normalizing the outputs of the binary classifiers in such way to make them comparable by the equation (27). Four strategies are suggested: MND, BND, DNCD and MLP, based, respectively, on distance normalization (the first three) and base on a neural network model (the last one).

### 3.1.4. MND output mapping strategy

Analyzing the histogram of the raw outputs (original outputs) from a typical SVM binary classifier (figure 5) we observe a bimodal distribution consisting of two normal functions each with different mean and standard deviation. Different binary classifiers show different values of mean and standard deviation which makes unfair to compare their outputs. Then, before applying equation (10), the outputs from each binary classifier are normalized in a way that they all provide a normal distribution with mean at −1 or +1 and a standard deviation equal to 1.

Using a validation data set the samples are grouped into two groups $A_1$ (the current class) and $A_2$ (all the other classes) and the respective output distribution mean and standard deviation are computed and then the normalized output is obtained by equation (36).

$$u_i = \frac{d'_{(y_i,-1)} + d'_{(y_i,+1)}}{2} \tag{36}$$

Where

$$d'_{(y_i,k)} = \frac{y_i - \mu_k}{\sigma_k}, k = \{-1,+1\} \quad (37)$$

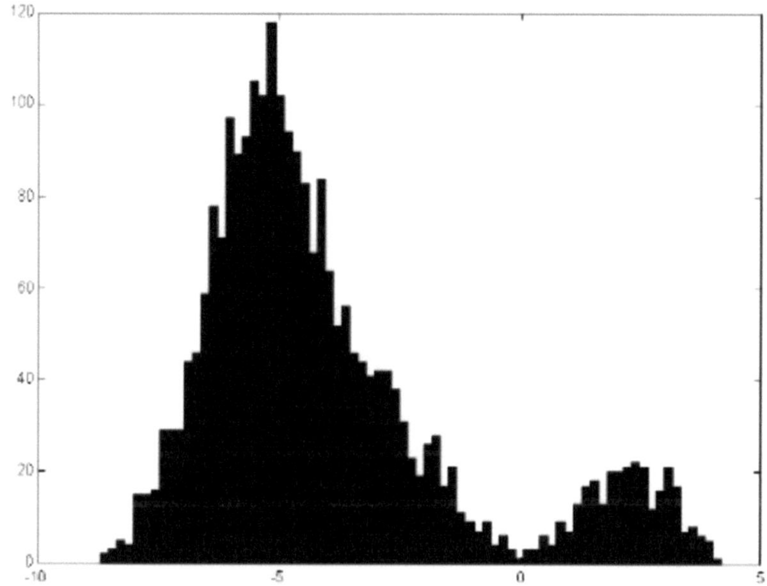


**Figure 5.** Output histogram of a binary one-against-all classifier

### *3.1.5. BND output mapping strategy*

BND Strategy takes into account both normalized distances using the equation (38). When both distances $d'_{(y_i,k)}, k = \{-1,+1\}$ are positive (i.e., $y_i$ is on the right side of the centers of both normal functions) then $u_i$ is +1. When both distances are negative $y_i$ is on the left side of both centers and $u_i$ is −1, but when the distance signals are different, $u_i$ is between −1 and +1, closer to +1 if $d'_{(y_i,+1)}$ is greater than $d'_{(y_i,-1)}$, 0 when the distances are equal and closer to −1 otherwise.

$$u_i = \frac{d'_{(y_i,-1)} + d'_{(y_i,+1)}}{\left|d'_{(y_i,-1)}\right| + \left|d'_{(y_i,+1)}\right|} \quad (38)$$

### *3.1.6. DNCD output mapping strategy*

Instead of using normalized distances (like in MND Strategy), DNCD Strategy builds a normalized output by joining the non-normalized distances and normalizing it by the distance between the centers of the normal functions as in equation (39).

$$u_i = \frac{d'_{(y_i,-1)} + d'_{(y_i,+1)}}{\left|\mu_{-1} - \mu_{+1}\right|} \quad (39)$$

### *3.1.7. MLP output mapping strategy*

In this case, instead of having a function which maps each raw output $y_i$ to a normalized output $u_i$, we have a function which maps the entire vector **y** into the vector **u**. The idea of this strategy is to implement the mapping function by using an MLP neural network, trained using a validation data set. The training samples are the outputs given by the multiclassifier for the validation data set. The expected outputs for those samples are the multiclassifier expected outputs, that is, a vector for which all positions have value −1, except for the one which corresponds to the class of that sample, whose value is +1.

Homogeneous M class multiclassifier is the one where its M binary classifiers are all trained with the same set of parameters. This approach, however, may not be the best option once the training of each classifier is independent and so, the chance is high to find a better set of classifiers if the search for different parameters is allowed in each case. But, in these cases, if a number 'g' of such parameters is used then the number of possible combinations of them is $g^s$ and, obviously, even for reasonable values of 'g' the test for all possible combinations is impracticable.

One approach is to choose a subset of alternative parameters composition and train a set of L distinct homogeneous multiclass SVMs. The output mapping is then applied to each of the 'L*s' binary classifiers and the heterogeneous multiclassifier is formed by selecting the best binary classifier from the 'L' homogeneous multiclassifiers. The selection is done through the classification quality metric 'q' as in (40) computed from the confusion matrix of each binary classifier.

$$q_i = \frac{2M_{ii}}{\sum_{j=1}^{s} M_{ij} + \sum_{j=1}^{i} M_{ji}} \tag{40}$$

Where $M_{ij}$ is the value of the i-th row and j-th column of the confusion matrix, which corresponds to the number of samples of class $A_i$ that were missclassified as being of class $A_j$ by the homogeneous multiclassifier. The more $q_i$ approaches to 1 the better is the interaction of the i-th binary SVM among the other ones of the same homogeneous multiclassifier. Thus, not only we take into account the number of hits of an SVM, but also we penalize it for possible confusions in that multiclassifier. Finally, the heterogeneous multiclassifier is produced by the binary SVMs of greatest quality for each class.

## 3.2. The one-versus-one strategy

This method constructs one binary classifier for every pair of distinct classes and so, for M classes, a number of M*(M-1)/2 binary classifiers are constructed. The binary classifier $A_{ij}$ is trained taking the examples from class 'i' as positive and the examples from class 'j' as negative. For a new example **x**, if classifier $A_{ij}$ classifies it as class 'i', then the vote for class 'i' is added by one. Otherwise, the vote for class 'j' is increased by one. After each of the M*(M-

1)/2 binary classifiers makes its vote, the strategy assigns the current example to the class with the largest number of votes.

Two interesting variations for the One-Against-One strategy, not using maximum vote, were proposed, one by Hastie and Tibshirani [19] known as pairwise coupling and other by Platt [20] that is a sigmoid version of the same pairwise coupling approach suggested by Hastie. Another interesting variation of this pairwise is proposed by Moreira and Mayoraz [21].

### *3.2.1. Pairwise coupling*

Considering that each binary classifier $C_{ij}$ on a One-Against-One strategy provides a probabilistic output as $r_{ij} = prob(A_i / A_i \cup A_j), i \neq j$, Hastie and Tibshirani propose to combine them in order to obtain an estimation of the posterior probabilities for all classifiers together $p_i = prob(A_i / x), i = 1...M$. To estimate the $p_i$'s, M*(M-1)/2 auxiliary variables $\mu_{ij}$'s related to the $p_i$'s are introduced such as: $\mu_{ij} = p_i/(p_i + p_j)$ and then, $p_i$'s are determined so that $\mu_{ij}$'s are close to $r_{ij}$'s. Kullback-Leibler distance [22, 23] between $r_{ij}$ and $u_{ij}$ was chosen as the measure of closeness (41).

$$l_p = \sum_{i<j} n_{ij} \left( r_{ij} \log \frac{r_{ij}}{\mu_{ij}} + (1 - r_{ij}) \log \frac{1 - r_{ij}}{1 - \mu_{ij}} \right) \tag{41}$$

where $n_{ij}$ is the number of examples that belongs to the union of both classes ($A_i$ U $A_j$) in the training set. The associated score equations are (42).

$$\sum_{i \neq j} n_{ij} \mu_{ij} = \sum_{i \neq j} n_{ij} r_{ij}, \; i = 1...M, \; subject \; to \sum_{k=1}^{M} p_k = 1 \tag{42}$$

The $p_i$'s are computed using the following iterative procedure:

1. Start from an initial guess of $p_i$'s
2. Compute the corresponding $\mu_{ij}$'s: $\mu_{ij} = \dfrac{p_i}{p_i + p_j}$
3. Repeat (i = 1 … M and so on) until the convergence is reached:

a. $p_i = p_i \dfrac{\sum_{i \neq j} n_{ij} r_{ij}}{\sum_{i \neq j} n_{ij} \mu_{ij}}$

b. Renormalize $p_i$'s: $p_i = \dfrac{p_i}{\sum_{i=1}^{M} p_i}$

c. Recomputed $\mu_{ij}$'s

### *3.2.2. Sigmoid pairwise coupling*

Platt criticized Hastie and Tibshirani's method of generating posterior class probabilities for each binary SVM, and suggested the use of a properly designed sigmoid applied to the SVM output to form these probabilities such as in (43).

$$\Pr(w_1 \mid x) = \frac{1}{1 + e^{Af + B}} \tag{43}$$

Where 'f' is the output of the SVM associated with the example **x** and the parameters 'A' and 'B' are determined by the minimization of the negative log-likelihood function over the validation data. In [20] Platt suggests a pseudo-code for the determination of the parameters 'A' and 'B'.

## 4. Character recognition experiments

The ability to identify machine printed characters in an automated manner has obvious applications in numerous fields (figure 6). *Optical character recognition (OCR), as this field is commonly known,* has been a topic of interest for a long time since the late 1940's, when Jacob Rabinow started his work. Jacob was an engineer and inventor, he lived from 1910 to 1999 and during his life he earned 230 U.S. patents on a variety of mechanical, optical and electrical devices.

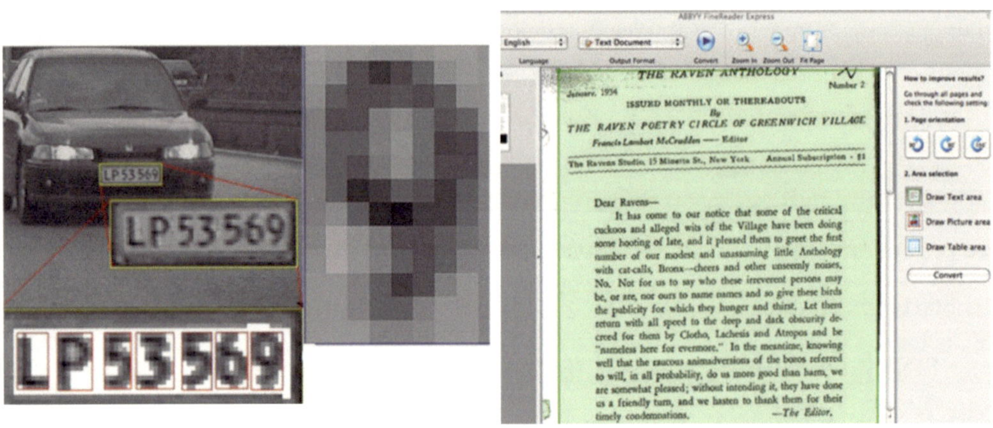


(a) (b)

**Figure 6.** a) Example of a LPR – License Plate Recognition application; b) Example of a text reading from scanned paper

The earliest OCR machines were primitive mechanical devices with fairly high failure rates. As the amount of new written material increased, so did the need to process it all in a fast and reliable manner, and these machines were clearly not up to the task. They quickly gave way to computer-based OCR devices that could outperform them both in terms of speed and reliability.

Today there are many OCR devices in use based on a variety of algorithms. Despite the fact that these OCR devices can offer good accuracy and high speed, they are still far away compared to the performance reached by the human being. Many challenges are still opened not only with respect to the variety of scenarios, as well as, types of printed characters and handwritings, but also with respect to the accuracy by itself. There is no device able to recognize 100%, they always make mistake and, sometimes, bad mistakes like find a character that does not exist or recognize a complete different character than it really is (example: recognize as an 'M' what in fact is an 'S').

## 4.1. Remarks

The research field on automatic algorithms for character recognition is very large including different forms of characters like Chinese, Arabic and others; different origin like printed and handwritten and different approaches to obtain the character image like on line and off line.

The experiments on character recognition reported in the literature vary in many factors such as the sample data, pre-processing techniques, feature representation, classifier structure and learning algorithm. Only a reduced number of these works have compared their proposed methods based on the same set of characters. Obviously that this fact makes tough to get a fair comparison among the reported results.

Some databases were created and divulgated to the researcher's community with the objective to offer a generic and common set of characters to be used as patterns for the researches. Some of the most popular databases are CENPARMI, NIST, MNIST and DEVNAGARI.

License Plate and handwritten numeral recognition are on the most addressed research topics in nowadays and the experiments on handwritten numeral have been done basically using CENPARMI and NIST Special Database 19.

CENPARMI database, for example, contains 4,000 training samples and 2,000 test samples segmented from USPS envelope images. This set is considered difficult but it is easy to achieve in the literature recognition rates reported over 98%. Suen et al. reported accuracy of 98.85% by training neural networks on 450,000 samples [24] training it with 4,000 samples. Liu et al. report rates over 99% using polynomial classifier (PC) and SVMs [25], [26]. They report an accuracy of 99.58% using RBF SVM and 99.45% using Polynomial SVM. In [27] Ahmad et al. report the usage of a hybrid RBF kernel SVM and a HMM – Hidden Markov Model system over an online handwriting problem taken from the IRONOFF-UNIPEN database. The same authors in [28] report a work done on the recognition of words. Pal et al. also report in [29] the usage of a hybrid system based on SVM and MQDF – Modified Quadratic Discriminant Function for the problem of Devnagari Character Recognition. Arora et al., all from India, report in [30] a performance comparison between SVM and ANN – Artificial Neural Network on the problem of Devnagari Character Recognition.

License Plate recognition as well as off line handwritten recognition represents a very tough challenge for the researchers. There are a number of possible difficulties that the recognition algorithm must be able to cope with, which includes, for example: a) poor image resolution, usually because the camera is too far away from the plate; b) poor lighting and low contrast due to overexposure, reflection or shadows; c) object obscuring (part of) the plate, quite often a tow bar, or dirt on the plate; d) bad conservation state of the plate; e) Blurry images, particularly motion blur; and f) lack of global pattern, sometimes even inside a same country or state (figure 7).

**Figure 7.** Example of License plate samples from 50 states of USA [31]

There is plenty of research work on this subject reported in the literature but the accuracy comparison among them is even more complex and difficult than the work done on handwritten. The accuracy not only depends on the type of the plates itself but also on the conditions on which the images were taken and on the level of the problems cited on previous paragraph. Waghmare et al. [32] report the use of 36 One-Against-All multiclass SVM classifier trained to recognize the 10 numeral and 26 letters from Indian plates (figure 8a). Parasuraman and Subin in [33] also report the usage of a Multiclass SVM classifier to recognize plates from Indian motorcycles (figure 8b). Other works on LPR can be found in [34 – 37].

In summary, character recognition is intrinsically a non linear and high dimensional problem. Among to the variety of OCR algorithms found in the literature, the SVM classifier is one of the most popular based on its good accuracy, high response speed and robustness. In the following subsections we describe some experiments in character recognition using both One-Against-All and One-Against-One multiclass SVMs.

(a) (b)

**Figure 8.** Indian plates for car (a) and motorcycle (b)

## 4.2. Using one-against-all strategy

The strategies proposed in [18] are here evaluated when applied to a problem of classifying characters extracted from vehicle plates. Two multiclass SVMs are trained: one to recognize the 10 digits (10 classes) and other to distinguish the 26 letters (26 classes).

For each group of characters, three data sets were formed based on the feature extraction used. In data set 1 (DS1) the feature vector has dimensionality of 288 formed by the $16 \times 16$ character bit matrix and 32 additional values from the character horizontal and vertical projections. Principal Component Analysis [38] reduced the original dimension to 124 (for digits) and 103 (for letters). Data sets 2 (DS2) and 3 (DS3) were generated respectively by 56 and 42 statistical moments extracted from the 16 x 16 character bit matrix.

Each data set was divided in three subsets: one for training, one for validation, and one for test. Table 1 shows how the samples were divided in these three subsets.

| Subset | Digits | Letters |
|---|---|---|
| Training | 2794 | 2088 |
| Validation | 2500 | 1875 |
| Test | 7500 | 5625 |
| Total | 12,794 | 9,588 |

**Table 1.** Number of samples for each data subset

### *4.2.1. Digit recognition*

Based on two kernel functions and a set of different values for two variables as shown in table 2 (standard deviation for the Gaussian kernel and exponent order for the polynomial kernel), a set of 55 Homogeneous multiclassifiers were trained.

| Kernel Function | Kernel Parameter | C value |
|---|---|---|
| Polynomial | [1, 4] | [0.1, 10] |
| Gaussian | [1.0, 3.0] | [5, 80] |

**Table 2.** Number of samples for each data subset

The heterogeneous multiclassifier was formed with 10 binary classifiers selected each one of the 55 homogeneous multiclassifiers using the output mapping and confusion matrices as explained in previous section. The best results achieved for the test subsets of each data set are seen in Table 3. WTA-SVM is the common Winner-Takes-All strategy for One-Against-All approach.

| Strategy | DS1 | DS2 | DS3 |
|---|---|---|---|
| WTA-SVM | 4.16% | 2.95% | 2.77% |
| MND | 4.07% | **2.84%** | 2.73% |
| BND | 4.23% | 2.91% | 2.83% |
| DNCD | 4.33% | 3.05% | 2.87% |
| MLP | **3.48%** | 2.85% | **2.57%** |

**Table 3.** Error results on the test sets

### 4.2.2. *Letter recognition*

The multiclassifier construction was also based on the same two kernel functions and the same two variables as shown in table 4 (standard deviation for the Gaussian kernel and exponent order for the polynomial kernel), a set of 30 Homogeneous multiclassifiers were trained.

| Kernel Function | Kernel Parameter | C value |
|---|---|---|
| Polynomial | [2, 4] | [0.05, 5] |
| Gaussian | [1.0, 3.5] | [1, 20] |

**Table 4.** Number of samples for each data subset

The heterogeneous multiclassifier was formed with 26 binary classifiers selected each one of the 30 homogeneous multiclassifiers using the output mapping and confusion matrices as explained in previous section. The best results achieved for the test subsets of each data set are seen in Table 5. WTA-SVM is the common Winner-Takes-All strategy for One-Against-All approach.

| Strategy | DS1 | DS2 | DS3 |
|---|---|---|---|
| WTA-SVM | 5.24% | 4.36% | 3.29% |
| MND | 5.74% | 4.37% | 3.57% |
| BND | 6.24% | 4.52% | 3.72% |
| DNCD | 5.64% | 4.46% | 3.45% |
| MLP | **4.46%** | **4.12%** | **2.88%** |

**Table 5.** Error results on the test sets

### 4.3. Using one-against-one strategy

Experiments using One-Against-One RBF Kernel SVM are described in [39] for Brazilian plates, a total of 22464 numerals and 16848 letters were used for training and testing the system (Table 6). Brazilian plates show two different patterns (figure 9 – black characters over gray background and white characters over red background).

| Subset | Digits | Letters |
|---|---|---|
| Training | 3942 | 3024 |
| Test | 18522 | 13824 |
| Total | 22,464 | 16,848 |

**Table 6.** Number of samples for each data subset

**Figure 9.** Brazilian patterns of plate

#### 4.3.1. Digit recognition

As reported, an average accuracy of 99.61% was achieved (Table 7) and the worst performance occurred on the recognition of the number 8, which was misclassified 17 times from a total of 1725 samples (Table 8 – 7 times misclassified as 6 and 7 as 9).

| | Correct Classification | | Error | |
|---|---|---|---|---|
| **Label** | **Number** | **%** | **Number** | **%** |
| 0 | 2222 | 99.64% | 8 | 0.36% |
| 1 | 2095 | 99.90% | 2 | 0.10% |
| 2 | 1840 | 99.67% | 6 | 0.33% |
| 3 | 1799 | 99.89% | 2 | 0.11% |
| 4 | 1716 | 99.42% | 10 | 0.58% |
| 5 | 1700 | 99.77% | 4 | 0.23% |
| 6 | 1751 | 99.38% | 11 | 0.62% |
| 7 | 1825 | 99.67% | 6 | 0.33% |
| 8 | 1708 | 99.01% | 17 | 0.99% |
| 9 | 1793 | 99.61% | 7 | 0.39% |
| Total | 18449 | | 73 | |
| Average | | **99.61%** | | **0.39%** |

**Table 7.** Percentage of classification for Digits

| SVM \ Target | 0 | 1 | 2 | 3 | 4 | 5 | 6 | 7 | 8 | 9 |
|---|---|---|---|---|---|---|---|---|---|---|
| 0 | 2222 | 0 | 0 | 0 | 2 | 0 | 0 | 0 | 0 | 0 |
| 1 | 0 | 2095 | 0 | 0 | 0 | 0 | 0 | 0 | 0 | 0 |
| 2 | 1 | 0 | 1840 | 0 | 1 | 2 | 0 | 0 | 0 | 2 |
| 3 | 0 | 0 | 0 | 1799 | 0 | 1 | 0 | 0 | 1 | 0 |
| 4 | 1 | 0 | 0 | 0 | 1716 | 1 | 6 | 1 | 0 | 1 |
| 5 | 0 | 1 | 0 | 0 | 0 | 1700 | 2 | 0 | 0 | 1 |
| 6 | 1 | 0 | 0 | 0 | 1 | 2 | 1751 | 0 | 4 | 3 |
| 7 | 0 | 0 | 2 | 1 | 0 | 0 | 0 | 1825 | 0 | 3 |
| 8 | 2 | 0 | 0 | 0 | 0 | 1 | 7 | 0 | 1708 | 7 |
| 9 | 1 | 0 | 0 | 2 | 0 | 3 | 0 | 0 | 1 | 1793 |

**Table 8.** Digits confusion matrix

### *4.3.2. Letter recognition*

As reported, an average accuracy of 98.60% was achieved (Table 9) and the worst performances showed by letters D (89.76%), O (93.31%) and Q (94.51%).

| | Correct Classification | | Error | | | Correct Classification | | Error | |
|---|---|---|---|---|---|---|---|---|---|
| Label | Number | % | Number | % | Label | Number | % | Number | % |
| A | 408 | 100.00% | 0 | 0.00% | N | 719 | 98.76% | 9 | 1.24% |
| B | 450 | 98.90% | 5 | 1.10% | O | 669 | 93.31% | 48 | 6.69% |
| C | 576 | 99.31% | 4 | 0.69% | P | 440 | 99.32% | 3 | 0.68% |
| D | 298 | 89.76% | 34 | 10.24% | Q | 379 | 94.51% | 22 | 5.49% |
| E | 221 | 98.66% | 3 | 1.34% | R | 401 | 99.01% | 4 | 0.99% |
| F | 177 | 98.88% | 2 | 1.12% | S | 327 | 99.09% | 3 | 0.91% |
| G | 250 | 98.43% | 4 | 1.57% | T | 340 | 99.71% | 1 | 0.29% |
| H | 309 | 98.10% | 6 | 1.90% | U | 531 | 98.88% | 6 | 1.12% |
| I | 168 | 97.67% | 4 | 2.33% | V | 374 | 99.73% | 1 | 0.27% |
| J | 337 | 99.70% | 1 | 0.30% | W | 284 | 98.95% | 3 | 1.05% |
| K | 1590 | 99.69% | 5 | 0.31% | X | 287 | 98.97% | 3 | 1.03% |
| L | 2925 | 99.59% | 12 | 0.41% | Y | 283 | 99.30% | 2 | 0.70% |
| M | 349 | 97.76% | 8 | 2.24% | Z | 538 | 99.81% | 1 | 0.19% |
| Total | 13630 | | 194 | | | | | | |
| Average | | 98.60% | | 1.40% | | | | | |

**Table 9.** Percentage of classification for Digits

Table 10 shows and explains the reasons for such reduced performance in comparison to the other 23 letters. The fact is that these three letters show very similar visual aspect and the SVM misclassified 23 letters 'O' as 'D', 26 'D' as 'O', 17 'Q' as 'O' and 18 'O' as 'Q'.

**Figure 10.** Similarity among letters D, O and Q

| | B | C | D | E | F | G | H | I | J | K | L | M | N | O | P | Q | R | S | T | U | V | W | Z |
|---|---|---|---|---|---|---|---|---|---|---|---|---|---|---|---|---|---|---|---|---|---|---|---|
| B | | | 2 | | | | | | | | | 1 | | | | | 1 | 1 | | | | | |
| C | | | | | 1 | 1 | | | | | 1 | | | | | 1 | | | | | | | |
| D | 3 | 3 | | | | | | | | | | | | **23** | | 3 | | | | | | | |
| E | | | | | 2 | | | | | | | | | | | | | 1 | | | | | |
| F | | | | 2 | | | | | | | | | | | | | | | | | | | |
| G | | 3 | | | | | | | | | | | | | | | 1 | | | | | | |
| H | | | | | | | | | | | | 1 | 1 | | 1 | | 1 | | | | | 2 | |
| I | | | | | | | | | | | 3 | | | | | | | | | | | 1 | |
| J | | | | | | | | 1 | | | | | | | | | | | | | | | |
| K | 1 | | | | | | | | | | | | | | | | | | 1 | | 1 | 2 | |
| L | | 1 | | | | | 2 | 6 | | | | | | | 1 | | | | | 2 | | | |
| M | 1 | | | | | | | 1 | | 3 | | | 2 | | | | | | | | | 1 | |
| N | | | | | | | 1 | | | 1 | | 3 | | | | | | | | | 1 | 3 | |
| O | 1 | 3 | **26** | | | | | | | | | | | | 1 | **17** | | | | | | | |
| P | 1 | | | | 2 | | | | | | | | | | | | | | | | | | |
| Q | | 1 | 1 | | | 2 | | | | | | | | **18** | | | | | | | | | |
| R | | | | | | | | | | | | | | | 2 | | | | | | | 2 | |
| S | 1 | | | | | | | | | 1 | | | | | | | 1 | | | | | | |
| T | | | | | | | | | | | | | | | | | | | | | | | 1 |
| U | | | | | | | 1 | | | | 1 | | | 2 | | 2 | | | | | | | |
| V | | | | | | | | | | 1 | | | | | | | | | | | | | |
| W | | | | | | 2 | | 1 | | | | | | | | | | | | | | | |
| X | | | | | | 3 | | | | | | | | | | | | | | | | | |
| Y | | | | | | | | | | | 1 | | | | | | | | 1 | | | | |
| Z | | | | | | | | | 1 | | | | | | | | | | | | | | |

**Table 10.** Letters confusion matrix

## Author details

Antonio Carlos Gay Thomé
*Federal University of Rio de Janeiro, Brasil*

## 5. References


[1] C. Cortes and V. N. Vapnik, Support vector networks. Machine Learning, vol. 20, no. 3, pp. 273-297, 1995.

[2] Fisher, R. A.. *The use of multiple measurements in taxonomic problems*. Annals of Eugenics, 7, 111–132, 1936.

[3] Rosenblatt, Frank. *Principles of Neurodynamics: Perceptrons and the Theory of Brain Mechanisms*. Washington DC: Spartan Books, 1962.

[4] Vapnik, V., and A. Lerner. *Pattern recognition using generalized portrait method*. Automation and Remote Control, 24, 774–780, 1963.

[5] Aizerman, M. A., E. M. Braverman, and L. I. Rozonoer. *Theoretical foundations of the potential function method in pattern recognition learning*. Automation and Remote Control, 25, 821–837, 1964.

[6] Cover, Thomas M.. *Geometrical and statistical properties of systems of linear inequalities with applications in pattern recognition*. IEEE Transactions on Electronic Computers, 14, 326–334, 1965.

[7] Vapnik, V. N., and A. Ya. Chervonenkis. *Teoriya raspoznavaniya obrazov: Statisticheskie problemy obucheniya*. (in Russian) [Theory of pattern recognition: Statistical problems of learning]. Moscow: Nauka, 1974.

[8] Vapnik, V.. *Estimation of Dependences Based on Empirical Data* [in Russian]. Moscow: Nauka, 1979.

[9] Boser, Bernhard E., Isabelle M. GUYON, and Vladimir N. VAPNIK. *A training algorithm for optimal margin classifiers*. In: COLT '92: Proceedings of the Fifth Annual Workshop on Computational Learning Theory. New York, NY, USA: ACM Press, pp. 144–152, 1992.

[10] Theodoridis, S. and Koutroumbas, K., Pattern Recognition, 4th edition, Elsevier, 2009.

[11] Bishop, C. M., Pattern Recognition and Machine Learning, Springer, ISBN-13: 978-0-387-31073-2, 2006.

[12] C.-W. Hsu and C.-J. Lin, "A comparison of methods for multiclass support vector machines," IEEE Transactions on Neural Networks, vol. 13, no. 2, pp. 415–425, 2002.

[13] J. C. Platt, N. Cristianini, and J. Shawe-taylor, "Large margin dags for multiclass classification," in Advances in Neural Information Processing Systems. MIT Press, pp. 547–553, 2000.

[14] E. L. Allwein, R. E. Schapire, and Y. Singer, "Reducing multiclass to binary: A unifying approach for margin classifiers," The Journal of Machine Learning Research, vol. 1, pp. 113–141, 2001.

[15] Yi Liu, One-against-all multi-class SVM Classification using reliability measures, Neural Networks, IJCNN '05, 2005.

[16] R. M. Rifkin and A. B. R. Klautau, "In defense of one-vs-all classification," The Journal of Machine Learning Research, vol. 5, pp. 101–141, 2004.

[17] V. N. Vapnik, An Overview of Statistical Learning Theory, IEEE Transactions on Neural Networks, vol. 10, no. 5, pp.. 988-999, 1999.

[18] Thiago C. Mota and Antonio C. G. Thomé, One-Against-All-Based Multiclass SVM Strategies Applied to Vehicle Plate Character Recognition, IJCNN, 2009.

[19] Hastie, T., Tibshirani, R., Classification by pairwise coupling. The Annals of Statistics, vol 26, nr. 2, 451-471, 1998.

[20] Platt, J., Probabilistic outputs for support vector machines and comparison to regularized likelihood methods. Advances in Large Margin Classifiers, 61-74, MIT Press, 1999.

[21] Moreira, M., Mayoraz, E., Improved Pairwise Coupling Classification with Correcting Classifiers, Tenth European Conference on Machine Learning, Chemnist - Germany, 1998.

[22] Kullback, S.; Leibler. "On Information and Sufficiency". *Annals of Mathematical Statistics* 22 (1): 79–86, 1951.

[23] Kullback, S.; Burnham, K. P.; Laubscher, N. F.; Dallal, G. E.; Wilkinson, L.; Morrison, D. F.; Loyer, M. W.; Eisenberg, B. et al. "Letter to the Editor: The Kullback–Leibler distance". *The American Statistician* 41 (4): 340–341, 1987.

[24] Suen, C.Y., K. Kiu, N.W. Strathy, Sorting and recognizing cheques and financial documents, Document Analysis Systems: Theory and Practice, S.-W. Lee and Y. Nakano (eds.), LNCS 1655, Springer, pp. 173-187, 1999.

[25] C.-L. Liu, K. Nakashima, H. Sako, H. Fujisawa, Handwritten digit recognition: benchmarking of state-of-the-art techniques, Pattern Recognition, 36(10): 2271-2285, 2003.

[26] C.-L. Liu, K. Nakashima, H. Sako, H. Fujisawa, Handwritten digit recognition: investigation of normalization and feature extraction techniques, Pattern Recognition, 37(2): 265-279, 2004.

[27] Ahmad, A. R., Viard-Gaudin, C., Khalid, M. and Yusof, R., Online Handwriting Recognition using Support Vector Machine, Proceedings of the Second International Conference on Artificial Intelligence in Engineering & Technology, Kota Kinabalu, Sabah, Malaysia, August 3-5 2004.

[28] Ahmad, A. R., Viard-Gaudin, C., Khalid, M., Lexicon-based Word Recognition Using Support Vector Machine and Hidden Markov Model, 10th International Conference on Document Analysis and Recognition, 2009.

[29] Pal, U., Chanda, S., Wakabayashi, T. and Kimura, F., Accuracy Improvement of Devnagari Character Recognition Combining SVM and MQDF.

[30] Arora, S., Bhattacharjee, D., Nasipuri, M., Malik, L., Kundu, M. and Basu, D. K., Performance Comparison of SVM and ANN for Handwritten Devnagari Character Recognition, IJCSI International Journal of Computer Science Issues, Vol. 7, Issue 3, No 6, May 2010.

[31] Li, X., Vehicle License Plate Detection and Recognition, Master Science Thesis presented to the Faculty of the Graduate School at the University of Missouri, 2010.

[32] Waghmare, S. K. and Gulve, V. N. N., Automatic Number Plate Recognition (ANPR) System for Indian Conditions using Support Vector Machine (SVM), International Journal of Computer Science and its Applications, 2010.

[33] Parasuraman, Kumar and Subin, P. S. SVM Based License Plate Recognition System, IEEE International Conference on Computational Intelligence and Computing Research, 2010.

[34] Abdullah, S. N. H. S., PirahanSiah, F., Abidin, N. H. H. Z., and Sahran, S., Multi-threshold approach for license plate recognition system, World Academy of Science, Engineering and Technology 72, 2010.

[35] Tsai, I., Wu, J., Hsieh, J. and Chen, Y., Recognition of Vehicle License Plates from a Video Sequence, IAENG International Journal of Computer Science, 36:1, IJCS_36_1_04, 2004.

[36] Abdullah, S. N. H. S., Intelligent License Plate Recognition System Based on Multi Feature Extractor and Support Vector Machine, Master Science Thesis at Faculty of Electrical Engineering – University of Technology of Malaysia, 2009.

[37] K P Tee, Etienne Burdet, C M Chew, Theodore E Milner, One-Against-All-Based Multiclass SVM Strategies Applied to Vehicle Plate Character Recognition, 2009 International Joint Conference on Neural Networks (2009), Volume: 90, Issue: 4, Publisher: Ieee, Pages: 2153-2159, ISBN: 9781424435531.

[38] I. T. Jolliffe, Principal Component Analysis. New York, NY, USA: Springer-Verlag, 1986.

[39] Medeiros, S., SVM Applied to License Plate Recognition, Technical Report, Federal University of Rio de Janeiro, Computer Science Department, Brazil, 2011.

Chapter 3

# Online Handwritten Chinese/Japanese Character Recognition

Bilan Zhu and Masaki Nakagawa

Additional information is available at the end of the chapter

http://dx.doi.org/10.5772/51474

## 1. Introduction

Handwritten character pattern recognition methods are generally divided into two types: online recognition and offline recognition [1]. Online recognition recognizes character patterns captured from a pen-based or touch-based input device where trajectories of pen-tip or finger-tip movements are recorded, while offline recognition recognizes character patterns captured from a scanner or a camera device as two dimensional images.

Both online and offline recognition methods can be roughly divided into two categories: structural and un-structural. Un-structural methods are also called statistical methods [2] or feature matching methods [3]. Structural methods are based on stroke analysis and use structural features such as sampling points, line segments and/or strokes for offline recognition [3-5] and for online recognition [6-21]. Un-structural methods use un-structural features such as directional features, gradient histogram features and projection features such as those for offline [22-24] and online recognition [25, 26], which eventually achieves stroke-order independence.

Structural methods are weak at collecting global character pattern information, while they are robust against character shape variations. In contrast, un-structural methods are robust against noises but very weak against character shape variations. By combining a structural method (structural recognizer) with an un-structural method (un-structural recognizer), the recognition accuracy improves since they compensate for their respective disadvantages [27, 28].

For online recognition, structural features are often employed with hidden Markov models (HMMs) [12-21] or Markov random field (MRF) [29, 30]. However, since the un-structural features are easily extracted from an online handwritten pattern by discarding temporal and structural information, we can apply the un-structural method as well. Therefore, we can combine the structural and un-structural methods.

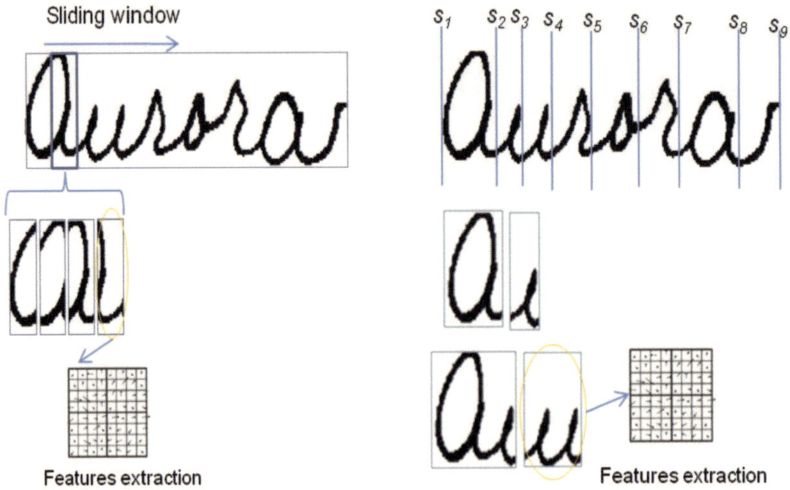


(a) Segmentation-free method (b) Over-segmentation-based method

**Figure 1.** Freely written string recognition

In freely written string recognition, we need to consider whether we should select segmentation-free or over-segmentation-based methods. Character segmentation of cursive handwriting is difficult due to the fact that spaces between characters are not obvious. Without character recognition cues and linguistic context, characters cannot be segmented unambiguously. A feasible way to overcome the ambiguity of segmentation is called integrated segmentation and recognition, which is classified into segmentation-free and over-segmentation-based methods [31, 32] as shown in Figure 1. Segmentation-free methods, mostly combined with hidden Markov model (HMM)-based recognition [20, 21, 33-38], simply slice the word pattern into frames (primitive segments) and label the sliced frames, which are concatenated into characters during recognition. Such methods do not sufficiently incorporate character shape information. On the other hand, over-segmentation-based methods attempt to split character patterns at their true boundaries and label the split character patterns [39-46]. Character patterns may also be split within them, but they are merged later. This is called over-segmentation. It is usually accomplished in two steps: over-segmentation and path search. The string pattern is over-segmented into primitive segments such that each segment composes a single character or part of a character. The segments are combined to generate candidate character patterns (forming a segmentation candidate lattice), which are evaluated using character recognitions incorporating geometric and linguistic contexts. However, character segmentation is a hard problem to solve. When handwritten words are not easily segmented, such as with cursive writing, over-segmentation may result in misrecognition. In this case, a segmentation-free method is appropriate. For Chinese/Japanese recognition, however, segmentation is easier than in English or other western languages.

Segmentation-free offline word recognition methods using un-structural features in sliding windows combined with hidden Markov models (HMMs) [32-38] and those using over-segmentation-based methods [39-43] can also be considered as un-structural methods since they use un-structural features.

Since over-segmentation-based methods can better utilize character shapes, they are considered to outperform segmentation-free methods [2]. Moreover, over-segmentation-based methods produce less primitive segments since they attempt to find the true boundaries of character patterns as segmentation point candidates; therefore, we consider that over-segmentation-based methods are effective and more efficient compared with segmentation-free methods for Chinese/Japanese string recognition. We show our online handwritten Chinese/Japanese string recognition system in Figure 2, where an over-segmentation-based method is used.

In this chapter, we describe the recent technology trends, problems and methods to solve them for the online handwritten Chinese/Japanese character recognition. The rest of this chapter is organized as follows. Section 2 presents an overview of our online handwritten string recognition system. Section 3 presents structural and un-structural recognitions. Section 4 describes coarse classification. Section 5 describes combination of structural and un-structural recognitions. Section 6 presents string recognition, and Section 7 draws conclusions.

## 2. Recognition system overview

We process each online handwritten string pattern as follows:

### 2.1. Segmentation candidate lattice construction

Strokes in a string are grouped into blocks (primitive segments) in accordance with the features such as off-stroke (pen lift between two adjacent strokes) distance and overlap of bounding boxes of adjacent strokes. Each primitive segment is assumed to be a character or a part of a character. An off-stroke between adjacent blocks is called a candidate segmentation point, which can be a true segmentation point (SP) or a non-segmentation point (NSP). One or more consecutive primitive segments form a candidate character pattern. The combination of all candidate patterns is represented by a segmentation candidate lattice.

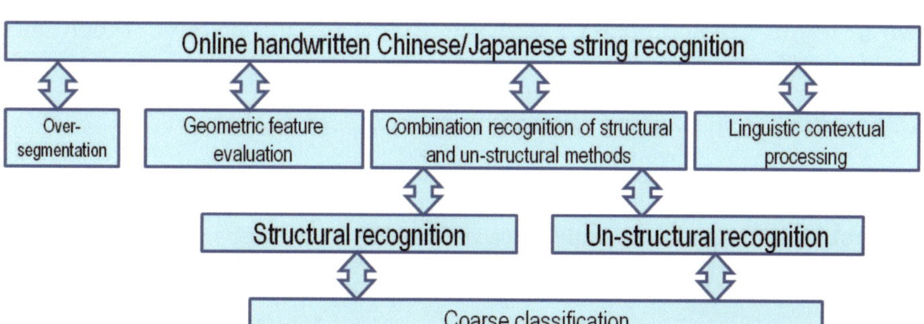


**Figure 2.** Online handwritten Chinese/Japanese string recognition

### 2.2. Character pattern recognition

There are thousands of categories for the Chinese/Japanese language. First, to improve the recognition speed, we reduce recognition candidates by using a coarse classifier for each online candidate character pattern. After coarse classification, we apply a structural recognizer and an un-structural recognizer to recognize the input pattern, and obtain two sets of character candidate classes from the two recognizers. Each candidate class of each set has a corresponding structural or un-structural recognition score. We combine the two sets of candidate classes considering their recognition scores to output a set of candidate classes to nominate them into the candidate lattice.

### 2.3. Search and recognition

We apply the beam search strategy to search for the candidate lattice. During the search, the paths are evaluated in accordance with the path evaluation criterion proposed Zhu et al. [47], which combines the scores of character recognition, linguistic context, and geometric features (character pattern sizes, inner gaps, single-character positions, pair-character positions, candidate segmentation points) with the weighting parameters estimated by a genetic algorithm (GA). This method selects an optimal path as the recognition result.

## 3. Structural and un-structural recognitions

### 3.1. Structural recognition

First, we include a brief description here on our structural character pattern recognition system [48, 49]. Our system first normalizes an input online character pattern by a linear or nonlinear normalization method. An online character pattern is a sequence of strokes and a stroke is a time sequence of coordinates of pen-tip or finger-tip movements. Then, it extracts feature points by such a method as Ramner [50]. First, the start and end points of every stroke are picked up as feature points. Then, the most distant point from the straight line between adjacent feature points is selected as a feature point if the distance to the straight line is greater than a threshold value. This selection is done recursively until no more feature points are selected. The feature point extracting process is shown in Figure 3(a).

Then it uses a MRF model to match the feature points with the states of each character class as shown in Figure 3(b) and obtain a similarity for each character class. It then selects the character class with the largest similarity as the recognition result.

**Site**: Feature points from an input pattern $S=\{s_1, s_2, s_3,\ldots,s_{12}\}$

**Label**: States of a character class $L=\{l_1, l_2, l_3,\ldots, l_{12}\}$

**Labeling problem**: Assign labels to the sites such as $\{s_1= l_1, s_2 = l_1, s_3 = l_3,\ldots,s_{11} = l_9, s_{12} = l_{11}\}$

The system recognizes the input pattern by assigning labels to the sites to make the matching between the input pattern and each character class. MRF model is used to solve the labeling problem.

Structural methods can be further divided into template-based structural methods [3, 6-11] and statistical structural methods [4, 5, 12-21, 39, 40]. Template-based structural methods work well with handwriting recognition for user dependent systems. However, these methods do not take into account the distributions of training patterns, resulting in limited recognition accuracy. Statistical structural methods measure probabilistic primitives and/or relationships so as to better model the shape variations of input patterns [29, 30].

HMMs have been often used with online statistical structural recognition methods and offline English word recognition methods. HMMs were first described in a series of statistical papers [51] and applied to speech recognition [52-53] in the middle of the 1970s. Then, they were applied widely to online handwriting [12-21] and offline word recognition [32-38].

HMMs probabilistically treat a sequence of feature vectors in writing or position order, so that they can only use the neighborhood relationships between the successively adjacent feature vectors in writing or position order (the so-called one-dimensional neighborhood relationships) and the two-dimensional neighborhood relationships, such as those among the neighboring feature vectors, on distances are not explicitly expressed. For one-dimensional neighborhood relationships, HMMs only use the state transition probabilities and unary features, but binary features are not used well. Moreover, the neighborhood relationships among more than two neighboring feature vectors, such as ternary features, cannot be used. Although some HMMs apply binary features, they only merge the binary features into the unary features and use a vector of larger dimension because HMMs do not take a new view of the binary features, which limits recognition accuracy [31].

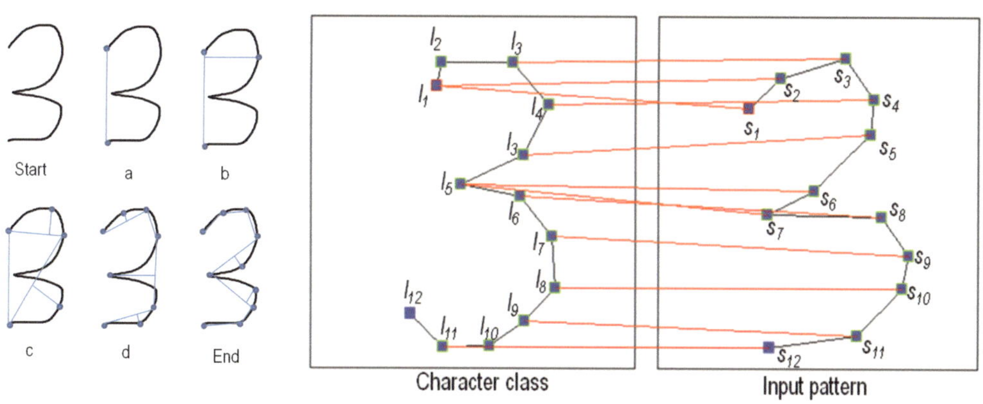


(a) (b)

**Figure 3.** Feature points extraction and labeling

The MRF model is described using an undirected graph in which a set of random variables have a Markov property, and MRFs can be used to effectively integrate information among neighboring feature vectors, such as binary and ternary features, and two-dimensional neighborhood relationships [54]. Therefore, MRFs have been effectively applied to stroke-analysis-based structural offline character recognition [4, 5]. They have also been widely and successfully applied to image processing [55, 56] and online stroke classification [57]. However, MRFs had not been applied to online character recognition until our reports [48, 49]. Current online handwritten character recognition tends to use HMMs (note that HMMs can be viewed as specific cases of MRFs). MRFs have more degrees of freedom than HMMs for explicitly expressing relations among multiple feature vectors.

Saon et al. [33] proposed an HMM-based offline English word recognition method that uses neighboring pixels to estimate the pixel observation probabilities and discussed its performance. However, it is still an HMM-based method, although it uses the neighborhood relationships of the recognition. Based on the advantages of MRFs, we can assume that applying MRFs instead of HMMs to integrate the information among the neighboring feature vectors can improve performance of offline English or other western word recognition using segmentation-free methods [32-38].

Since online character patterns contain temporal information on pen movements, structural methods that discard temporal information and only apply structural information can result in stroke-order independence. However, it is computationally expensive since the neighborhood relationships must be examined in two dimensions. Although the method introducing temporal information is very sensitive to stroke order variations, it is efficient in recognition speed, and combining it with an un-structural method can deal with the stroke-order variations [27, 28]. Even for the one-dimensional neighborhood relationships applying MRFs instead of HMMs to integrate the information of binary features between the successively adjacent feature vectors in writing or position order can improve performance.

Cho et al. [58] proposed a Bayesian network (BN)-based framework for online handwriting recognition. BNs share similarities with MRFs. They are directional acyclic graphs and model the relationships among the neighboring feature vectors as conditional probability distributions, while MRFs are undirected graphs and model the relationships among the neighboring feature vectors as probability distributions of binary or ternary features.

Introducing weighting parameters to MRFs and optimizing them based on conditional random fields (CRFs) [59] or the minimum classification error (MCE) [60] may result in even higher recognition accuracy; CRFs have been successfully applied to online string and offline word recognition [42, 61].

We have proposed an MRF model with weighting parameters optimized by CRFs for online recognition of handwritten Japanese characters [48, 49]. We focused on an online structural method introducing temporal information into one-dimensional neighborhood relationships and compared their effects on HMMs and MRFs. The model effectively integrates unary and binary features and introduces adjustable weighting parameters to the MRFs, which are optimized according to CRF. The proposed method extracts feature points along the pen-tip trace from pen-down to pen-up and matches those feature points with states for character classes probabilistically based on this model. Experimental results demonstrated the superiority of the method and that MRFs exhibited higher recognition accuracy than HMMs.

### 3.2. Un-structural recognition

For the un-structural recognizer, we do not need to transform each online character pattern to an offline character pattern (two dimensional images), and extract directional features directly from the online character pattern. From an online character pattern, we extract directional features: histograms of normalized stroke direction [26]. For coordinate normalization, we apply pseudo 2D bi-moment normalization (P2DBMN) [22]. The local stroke direction is decomposed into eight directions, and from the feature map of each direction, 8x8 values are extracted by Gaussian blurring so that the dimensionality of feature vectors is 512. To improve the Gaussianity of feature distribution, each value of the 512 features is transformed by the Box-Cox transformation (also called variable transformation). The input feature vector is reduced from 512D to *n*D by the Fisher linear discriminant analysis (FLDA) [31]. Then we use the *n*D feature vectors to create a modified quadratic discriminant function (MQDF) recognizer [24] as follows:

$$g_2(\mathbf{x},\omega_i)=\sum_{j=1}^{k}\frac{1}{\lambda_{ij}}[\varphi_{ij}^T(\mathbf{x}-\mu_i)]^2+\frac{1}{\delta}\{\|\mathbf{x}-\mu_i\|^2-\sum_{j=1}^{k}[\varphi_{ij}^T(\mathbf{x}-\mu_i)]^2\}+\sum_{j=1}^{k}\log\lambda_{ij}+(n-k)\log\delta \quad (1)$$

where $\mu_i$ is the mean vector of class $\omega_i$, $\lambda_{ij}$ ($j$ = 1, ..., $k$) are the largest eigenvalues of the covariance matrix and $\phi_{ij}$ are the corresponding eigenvectors, $k$ denotes the number of principal axes, and $\delta$ is a modified eigenvector that is set as a constant. The value of $\delta$ can be optimized on the training data set. However, for a convenience, we simply set it as $\gamma\lambda_{average}$ where $\lambda_{average}$ is the average of $\lambda_{ij}$ ($i,j$ = 1, ..., $n$) for all features of all classes and $\gamma$ is a constant that is larger than 0 and smaller than 1.

According to previous works [23, 26], the best un-structural recognition performance is obtained when $n$ is about 160 and $k$ is about 50 for the MQDF recognizer. When combining structural and un-structural recognizers and then combining them with linguistic context and geometric features for the string recognition, we have found the best combination performance is obtained when $n$ is about 90 and $k$ is about 10 for the MQDF recognizer. Therefore, we take $n$ as 90 and $k$ as 10, respectively.

## 4. Coarse classification

Although character classifiers with high recognition accuracy have been reported [26, 47-49], the demand for speeding up recognition is very high for portable devices as well as for desktop applications for which handwriting recognition is incorporated as one of the modules. The performance of these relatively small devices requires having a fast as possible recognition speed while maintaining high accuracy. Even for a desktop PC with relatively high performance, a recognition speed of within 0.5 seconds per page is required in actual applications. Therefore, we need to refine the recognition scheme to improve the processing speed.

Chinese, Japanese, or Korean have thousands of different categories, and their large character set is problematic not only for the recognition rate but also for the recognition speed. A general approach to improving the recognition speed is to perform coarse classification, pre-classification, or candidate selection before the fine classification [62, 63].

The coarse classification typically uses simpler classification algorithms or fewer features in order to achieve a better speed than does the fine classification. It is used to select a relatively small subset of candidates out of a very large set quickly. The fine classification would then be used on these candidates to match an input pattern so that the whole recognition time is reduced. Current approaches for coarse classification typically use distance measures that are simpler than those for fine classification [64, 65]. The confidence evaluation provides even more precise candidate selection [66]. Others use simple features different from those for fine classification [67]. Sequential (multi-stage) classifications using a partial set of features at each stage have also been used [68].

On the other hands, prototypes may be organized prior to the search itself so that the search is performed on a subset of prototypes. We could mention a number of methodologies that vary slightly in how the data is organized. The simplest ones are proposals for ordered spaces and tree structures. The search on pre-structured spaces aims particularly at alleviating problems with search costs. As a result, recognition is accelerated.

## 5. Combined recognition

How to combine different classifiers is an important problem in multiple classifier approaches. In Japanese character recognition, Oda et al. improved recognition performance by combining a recognizer by a structural method and that by an un-structural method using probabilistic tables to normalize the combination scores [69]. The combination method by probabilistic tables is a generative method, and applying a discriminative method such as the MCE criterion and neural network to estimate and to optimize the combination may bring about higher performance.

Liu investigated the effects of confidence transformation in combining multiple classifiers using various combination rules [70]. Kermorvant et al. constructed a neural network to combine the top rank candidates of three word recognizers [37]. The two works used the discriminative methods to estimate the combination parameters. However, when optimizing the parameters the previous works always only considered the character/word recognition performance, not the string recognition performance. In fact, real applications usually use the string recognition rather than the character recognition. The character recognition is a part of the string recognition. Therefore, when we create a character recognizer, we have to consider the string recognition performance, as done by Tonouchi [71] and Cheriet et al. [71]. The methods that only guarantee the character recognition accuracy do not necessarily provide high string recognition performance. They cannot even be applied for string recognition.

On the other hand, we have to point out that introducing more parameters for a discriminative method dose not bring about higher performance, since we have only a limited amount of samples for training. However, previous works tended to introduce too many parameters for a discriminative method.

We have applied a discriminative method for MCE to optimize the parameters for combinations of structural and un-structural recognizers with a linear or nonlinear function for online handwritten Japanese string recognition [28]. To introduce an effective set of parameters, we applied a *k*-means method to cluster the parameters of all character categories into groups, and for categories belonging to the same group, we introduced the same weight parameters. We investigated how to construct the function and how to introduce effective parameters for discriminative methods under the condition of a limited amount of samples for classifier training. We designed the objective functions of parameter optimization so as to optimize the string performance. Moreover, we used GA to estimate super parameters such as the number of clusters, initial learning rate, and maximum learning times as well as the sigmoid function parameter for the MCE optimization. Experimental results demonstrated the superiority of our method.

## 6. String recognition

### 6.1. Linguistic contextual processing

String recognition applies not only character recognition, but also linguistic contextual processing. As shown in Figure 4 (a), by character recognition, each candidate character pattern is associated with a number of candidate classes with confidence scores. The combination of all character classes is represented by a character recognition candidate lattice. The linguistic contextual processing evaluates the combinations from character classes to character classes. By searching the candidate lattice by the Viterbi algorithm, the optimal path with maximum score gives the final result of string recognition.

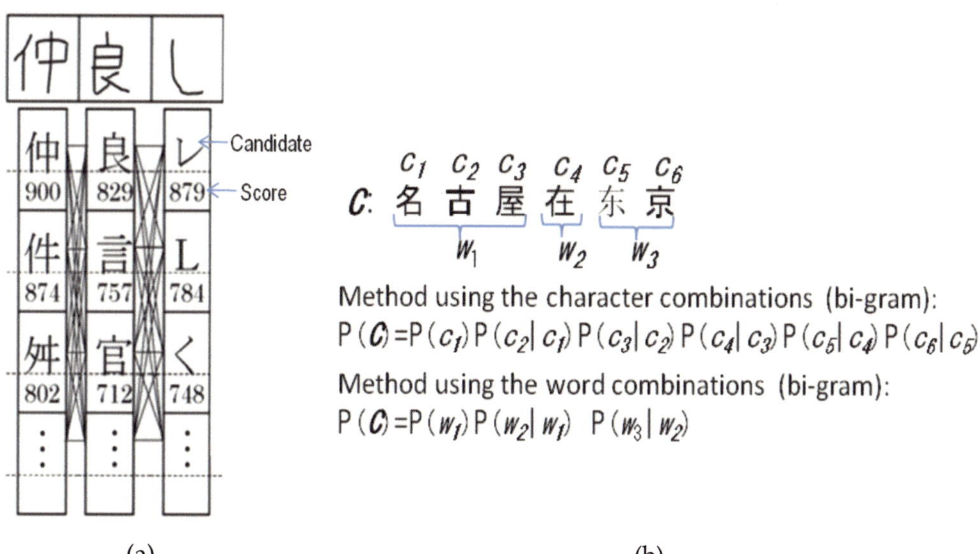


**Figure 4.** Character recogniton candidate lattice and linguistic contextual processing methods

Linguistic contextual processing methods can be roughly divided into two classes: methods using the character combinations and methods using the word combinations. As shown in Figure 4 (b), the linguistic contextual processing evaluates the probability P(C) of the string C that comprises a sequence of characters $\{c_1, c_2, \ldots\}$ or a sequence of words $\{w_1, w_2, \ldots\}$.

The methods using the character combinations evaluate the probability of the character combinations for each string candidate. We can use the appearance probability of only one character (unigram), bi-gram of two characters, tri-gram of three characters and generally called *n*-gram of *n* characters. The tri-gram is smoothed to overcome the imprecision of training with insufficient text by combining unigram, bi-gram and tri-gram using a linear function with weighting parameters.

In our experiment, under the condition with character writing boxes, using bi-gram improved the character recognition rate by 5 points from 92.9%, and using tri-gram improved the character recognition rate by one point. Moreover, under the condition without character writing boxes, using bi-gram improved the character recognition rate by 10 points from 81.3%, and using tri-gram improved the character recognition rate by 3 points.

The methods using the word combinations first divide string into words by morphological analysis, and then evaluate the probability of the word combinations for each string candidate. We can also use the appearance probability of only one word (unigram), bi-gram of two words, tri-gram of three words and generally called *n*-gram of *n* words. Although the methods have some problems such as unknown words and word dictionary memory, Nagata et al. have presented it could save more than 2/3 misrecognitions in a handwriting OCR simulation by dealing with unknown words [73].

Recognition of a limited vocabulary such as addresses, person names, dates and departments is important issues in string recognition. Applying a general-purpose contextual processing method such as tri-gram to recognize specific words would cause misrecognitions. Applying domain specific methods to recognize specific words into the vocabulary set can improve recognition rate significantly [45, 74].

## 6.2. Freely written string recognition

With pen-based or touch-based input devices of large writing areas such as tablet PCs, Pad PCs, electronic whiteboards and digital pens, people tend to write text continuously with little constraints. This urges the need of handwritten string recognition. Compared to isolated character recognition, handwritten string recognition faces the difficulty of character segmentation because characters cannot be reliably segmented before they are recognized. Moreover, in continuous handwriting, characters tend to be written more cursively.

The integrated segmentation and recognition to overcome the ambiguity of segmentation, is dichotomized into segmentation-free method and over-segmentation-based method as shown in Fig. 1 [31]. Based on the advantages of over-segmentation-based method, we apply it for our recognition system.

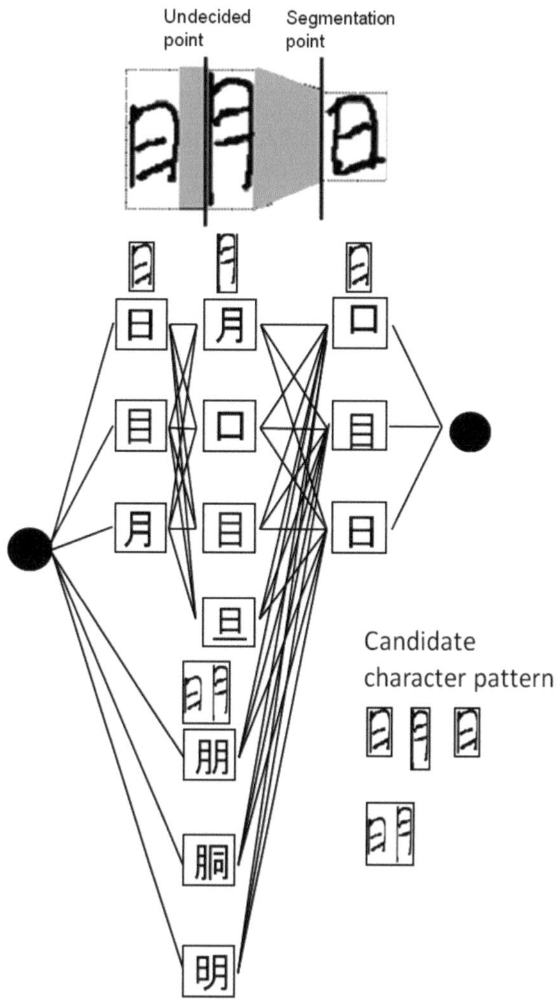


**Figure 5.** Character segmentation-recognition candidate lattice

By character recognition, each candidate character pattern is associated with a number of candidate classes with confidence scores. The combination of all candidate patterns and character classes is represented by a character segmentation-recognition candidate lattice, where each arc denotes a segmentation point and each node denotes a character class assigned to a candidate pattern as shown in Figure 5. The segmentation paths and corresponding string classes in the candidate lattice are evaluated by combining the scores of candidate characters and between-character compatibilities (geometric and linguistic contexts).

In over-segmentation based string recognition, how to evaluate the candidate characters (lying on paths in the candidate lattice) is a key issue. A desirable criterion should make the path of correct segmentation have the largest score. Unlike HMM-based recognition that classifies a unique sequence of feature vectors (each for a frame) on a string, the candidate lattice of over-segmentation has paths of different lengths, each corresponding to a different sequence of feature vectors, thus the comparison of different paths cannot be based on the Bayesian decision theory as for HMM-based recognition. Instead, candidate character recognition and context scores are heuristically combined to evaluate the paths. Such heuristic evaluation criteria can be divided into summation-based ones [75] and normalization-based ones [71]. A summation criterion is the summation of character-wise log-likelihood or the product of probabilistic likelihood. Since the likelihood measure is usually smaller than one, the summation (product) criterion is often biased to paths with fewer characters, and so, tends to over-merge characters. On the other hand, the normalized criterion, obtained by dividing the summation criterion by the number of segmented characters (segmentation length), tends to over-split characters.

To solve the problems, we have proposed a robust context integration model for online handwritten Japanese string recognition [47]. By labeling primitive segments, the proposed method can not only integrate the character shape information into recognition by introducing some adjustable parameters, but also is insensitive to the number of segmented character patterns because the summation is over the primitive segments. Experimental results demonstrated the superiority of our proposed string recognition model.

We include a brief description here on our recognition model [47]. Denote $\mathbf{X} = x_1 \dots x_m$ as successive candidate character patterns of one path, and every candidate character pattern $x_i$ is assigned a candidate class $C_i$. Then $f(\mathbf{X},\mathbf{C})$ is the score of the path $(\mathbf{X},\mathbf{C})$ where $\mathbf{C} = C_1 \dots C_m$. The path evaluation criterion is expressed as follows:

$$f(\mathbf{X},\mathbf{C}) = \sum_{i=1}^{m}\left\{\sum_{h=1}^{6}\left[\lambda_{h1} + \lambda_{h2}\left(k_i - 1\right)\right]\log P_h + \lambda_{71}\log P(g_{j_i} \mid SP) + \lambda_{72}\sum_{j=j_i+1}^{j_i+k_i-1}\log P(g_j \mid NSP)\right\} + m\lambda \quad (2)$$

where $P_h$, $h$=1,…,6, stand for the probabilities of $P(C_i|C_{i-2}C_{i-1})$, $P(b_i|C_i)$, $P(q_i|C_i)$, $P(p^u{}_i|C_i)$, $P(x_i|C_i)$, and $P(p^b{}_i|C_{i-1}C_i)$, respectively. $b_i$, $q_i$, $p^u{}_i$, and $p^b{}_i$ are the feature vectors for character pattern sizes, inner gaps, single-character positions, and pair-character positions, respectively. $g_i$ is the between-segment gap feature vector. $P(C_i|C_{i-2},C_{i-1})$ is the tri-gram probability. $k_i$ is the number of primitive segments contained in the candidate character pattern $x_i$. $\lambda_{h1}$, $\lambda_{h2}$ ($h$=1~7) and $\lambda$ are the weighting parameters estimated by GA. $P(x_i|C_i)$ is estimated by the combination score of the structural and un-structural recognizers. We can also divide it into two parts $P(x^{str}{}_i|C_i)$, $P(x^{un\text{-}str}{}_i|C_i)$ where $x^{str}{}_i$ denotes the structural features of $x_i$, $x^{un\text{-}str}{}_i$ denotes the un-structural features of $x_i$, $P(x^{str}{}_i|C_i)$ is estimated by the score of the structural recognizer and $P(x^{un\text{-}str}{}_i|C_i)$ is estimated by the score of the un-structural recognizer. The path evaluation criterion is changed as follows:

$$f^1(\mathbf{X},\mathbf{C}) = \sum_{i=1}^{m}\left\{\sum_{h=1}^{7}\left[\lambda_{h1} + \lambda_{h2}\left(k_i - 1\right)\right]\log P_h + \lambda_{81}\log P(g_{j_i} \mid SP) + \lambda_{82}\sum_{j=j_i+1}^{j_i+k_i-1}\log P(g_j \mid NSP)\right\} + \\ + m\lambda \quad (3)$$

where $P_h$, $h$=1,...,7, stand for the probabilities of $P(C_i|C_{i-2}C_{i-1})$, $P(b_i|C_i)$, $P(q_i|C_i)$, $P(p^u{}_i|C_i)$, $P(x^{str}{}_i|C_i)$, $P(x^{un\text{-}str}{}_i|C_i)$, and $P(p^b{}_i|C_{i-1}C_i)$, respectively. $\lambda_{h1}$, $\lambda_{h2}$ ($h$=1~8), and $\lambda$ are the weighting parameters estimated by GA. By the path evaluation criterion, we re-estimate the combination of the structural and un-structural recognizers.

# 7. Conclusion

This chapter described the recent trends in online handwritten Chinese/Japanese character recognition and our recognition system. We apply an over-segmentation-based method for our recognition system where the paths are evaluated in accordance with our path evaluation criterion, which combines the scores of character recognition, linguistic context, and geometric features (character pattern sizes, inner gaps, single-character positions, pair-character positions, candidate segmentation points) with the weighting parameters estimated by GA. We combine structural and un-structural methods to recognize each character pattern so that the recognition accuracy improves.

Improving recognition performance is the aim of our future work. This can be achieved by incorporating more effective geometric features, exploiting better geometric context likelihood functions and weighting parameter learning methods, and improving the accuracy of character recognizer. To speed up recognition and reduce memory size is another dimension of our future work. We should consider effective methods to remove invalid patterns from the lattice.

# Author details

Bilan Zhu and Masaki Nakagawa
*Department of Computer and Information Sciences, Tokyo University of Agriculture and Technology, Tokyo, Japan*

# 8. References

[1] R. Plamondon and S.N. Srihari (2000) On-line and off-line handwriting recognition: a comprehensive survey. IEEE Trans. PAMI. 22(1): 63-82.

[2] C.-L. Liu, S. Jaeger and M. Nakagawa (2004) On-line recognition of Chinese characters: the state of the art. IEEE Trans. PAMI. 26(2): 198-213.

[3] C.-L. Liu, I.-J. Kim and J. H. Kim (2001) Model-based stroke extraction and matching for handwritten Chinese character recognition. Pattern Recognition. 34(12): 2339-2352.

[4] J. Zeng and Z.-Q. Liu (2005) Markov random fields for handwritten Chinese character recognition. Proc. 8th ICDAR: 101-105.

[5] J. Zeng and Z.-Q. Liu (2008) Markov random field-based statistical character structure modeling for handwritten Chinese character recognition. IEEE Trans. PAMI. 30(5): 767-780.

[6] Y.-T. Tsay and W.-H. Tsai (1993) Attributed string matching by splitand-merge for on-line Chinese character recognition. IEEE Trans. PAMI. 15(2): 180-185.

[7] M. Nakagawa and K. Akiyama (1994) A linear-time elastic matching for stroke number free recognition of on-line handwritten characters. Proc. 4th IWFHR: 48-56.

[8] J. Liu, W.-K. Cham and M. M. Y. Chang (1996) Stroke order and stroke number free on-line Chinese character recognition using attributed relational graph matching. Proc. 13th ICPR. 3: 259-263.

[9] T. Wakahara and K. Okada (1997) On-line cursive kanji character recognition using stroke-based affine transformation. IEEE Trans. PAMI. 19(12): 1381-1385.

[10] J.-P. Shin and H. Sakoe (1999) Stroke correspondence search method for stroke-order and stroke-number free on-line character recognition—multilayer cube search. Trans. IEICE Japan. J82-D-II (2): 230-239.

[11] A. Kitadai and M. Nakagawa (2002) A learning algorithm for structured character pattern representation used in on-line recognition of handwritten Japanese characters. Proc. 8th IWFHR: 163-168.

[12] M. Nakai, N. Akira, H. Shimodaira and S. Sagayama (2001) Substroke approach to HMM-based on-line kanji handwriting recognition. Prof. 6th ICDAR: 491-495.

[13] M. Nakai, T. Sudo, H. Shimodaira and S. Sagayama (2002) Pen pressure features for writer-independent on-line handwriting recognition based on substroke HMM. Proc. 16th ICPR. 3: 220-223.

[14] M. Nakai, H. Shimodaira and S. Sagayama (2003) Generation of hierarchical dictionary for stroke-order free kanji handwriting recognition based on substroke HMM. Proc. 7th ICDAR: 514-518.

[15] J. Tokuno, N. Inami, S. Matsuda, M. Nakai, H. Shimodaira and S. Sagayama (2002) Context-dependent substroke model for HMM based on-line handwriting recognition. Proc. 8th IWFHR: 78-83.

[16] K. Takahashi, H. Yasuda and T. Matsumoto (1997) A fast HMM algorithm for on-line handwritten character recognition. Proc. 4th ICDAR: 369-375.

[17] H. Yasuda, K. Takahashi and T. Matsumoto (1999) On-line handwriting recognition by discrete HMM with fast learning. Advances in Handwriting Recognition. S.-W. Lee: World Scientific. pp. 19-28.

[18] Y. Katayama, S. Uchida and H. Sakoe (2008) HMM for on-line handwriting recognition by selective use of pen-coordinate feature and pen-direction feature. Trans. IEICE Japan. J91-D (8): 2112-2120.

[19] H. J. Kim, K. H. Kim, S. K. Kim and F. T.-P. Lee (1997) on-line recognition of handwritten Chinese characters based on hidden Markov models. Pattern Recognition. 30(9): 1489-1499.

[20] S. Jaeger, S. Manke, J. Reichert and A. Waibel (2001) Online handwriting recognition: the Npen++ recognizer. IJDAR. 3(1): pp.69-180.

[21] M. Liwicki and H. Bunke (2006) HMM-based on-line recognition of handwritten whiteboard notes. Proc. 10th IWFHR: 595-599.

[22] C.-L. Liu and K. Marukawa (2005) Pseudo two-dimensional shape normalization methods for handwritten Chinese character recognition. Pattern Recognition. 38(12): 2242-2255.

[23] C.-L. Liu (2006) High accuracy handwritten Chinese character recognition using quadratic classifiers with discriminative feature extraction. Proc. 18th ICPR. 2: 942-945.

[24] F. Kimura (1987) Modified quadratic discriminant function and the application to Chinese characters. IEEE Trans. PAMI. 9 (1): 149-153.

[25] A. Kawamura, K. Yura, T. Hayama, Y. Hidai, T. Minamikawa, A. Tanaka and S. Masuda (1992) On-line recognition of freely handwritten Japanese characters using directional feature densities. Proc. 11th ICPR. 2: 183-186.

[26] C.-L. Liu and X.-D. Zhou (2006) Online Japanese character recognition using trajectory-based normalization and direction feature extraction. Proc. 10th IWFHR: 217-222.

[27] H. Tanaka, K. Nakajima, K. Ishigaki, K. Akiyama and M. Nakagawa (1999) Hybrid pen-input character recognition system based on integration of on-line and off-line recognition. Proc. 5th ICDAR: 209-212.

[28] B. Zhu, J. Gao and M. Nakagawa (2011) Objective function design for MCE-based combination of on-line and off-line character recognizers for on-line handwritten Japanese text recognition. Proc. 11th ICDAR: 594-599.

[29] T.-R. Chou and W. T. Chen (1997) A stochastic representation of cursive Chinese characters for on-line recognition. Pattern Recognition. 30(6): 903-920.

[30] J. Zheng, X. Ding, Y. Wu and Z. Lu (1999) Spatio-temporal unified model for on-line handwritten Chinese character recognition. Proc. 5th ICDAR: 649-652.

[31] M. Cheriet, N. Kharma, C.-L Liu and C. Y. Suen (2007) Character recognition systems - A guide for students and practioners. Hoboken. New Jersey: John Wiley & Sons, Inc.

[32] M. Mohamed and P.Gader (1996) Handwritten word recognition using segmentation-free Hidden Markov Model and segmentation-based dynamic programming techniques. IEEE Trans. PAMI, 18(5): 548-544.

[33] G. Saon and A. Belaid (1997) Off-line handwritten word recognition using a mixed HMM-MRF approach. Proc. 4th ICPR. 1: 118-122.

[34] D. Guillevic and C. Y. Suen (1997) HMM word recognition engine. Proc. 4th ICPR. 2: 544-547.

[35] S. Gunter and H. Bunke (2004) HMM-based handwritten word recognition: on the optimization of the number of states, training iterations and gaussian components. Pattern Recognition, 37: 2069-2079.

[36] J.A. Rodriguez and F. Perronnin (2008) Local gradient histogram features for word spotting in unconstrained handwritten documents. Proc. 1stICFHR: 7-12.

[37] C. Kermorvant, F. Menasri, A-L. Bianne, R. AI-Hajj, C. Mokbel and L. Likforman-Sulem (2010) The A2iA-Telecom ParisTech-UOB system for the ICDAR 2009 handwriting recognition competition. Proc. 12th ICFHR: 247-252.

[38] T. Hamamura, B. Irie, T. Nishimoto, N. Ono and S. Sagayama (2011) Concurrent optimization of context clustering and GMM for offline handwritten word recognition using HMM. Proc. 11th ICDAR: 523-527.

[39] F. Kimura, M. Sridhar and Z. Chen (1993) Improvements of lexicon-directed algorithm for recognition of unconstrained hand-written words. Proc. 2nd ICDAR: 18-22.

[40] G. Kim and V. Govindaraju (1997) A lexicon driven approach to handwritten word recognition for real-time applications. IEEE Trans. PAMI, 19(4): 366-379.

[41] J.T. Favata (2001) Offline general word handwritten word recognition using an approximate BEAM matching algorithm. IEEE Trans. PAMI, 23(9): 1009-1021.

[42] S. Shetty, H. Srinivasan and S. Srihari (2007) Handwritten word recognition using conditional random fields. Proc. 9th ICDAR: 1098-1102.

[43] U. Pal, R.K. Roy and F. Kimura (2011) Handwritten street name recognition for Indian postal automation. Proc. 11th ICDAR: 483-487.

[44] M. Koga, R. Mine, H. Sako and H. Fujisawa (1999) Lexical search approach for character-string recognition. In: S.-W. Lee and Y. Nakano editors. Document Analysis Systems: Theory and Practice. Springer . pp. 115-129.

[45] C.-L. Liu, M. Koga and H. Fujisawa (2002) Lexicon-driven segmentation and recognition of handwritten character strings for Japanese address reading. IEEE Trans. PAMI, 24(11): 1425-1437.

[46] M. Koga, R. Mine, H. Sako and H. Fujisawa (2003) A lexicon driven approach for printed address phrase recognition using a trie dictionary. Trans. IEICE Japan. J86-D (2): 1297-1307.

[47] B. Zhu, X.-D. Zhou, C.-L. Liu, M. Nakagawa (2010) A robust model for on-line handwritten Japanese text recognition. IJDAR. 13(2): 121-131.

[48] B. Zhu and M. Nakagawa (2011) A MRF model with parameters optimization by CRF for on-line recognition of handwritten Japanese characters. Proc. Document Recognition and Retrieval XVIII (DRR) that is part of IS&T/SPIE Electronic Imaging. San Jose. CD-ROM.

[49] B. Zhu and M. Nakagawa (2011) On-line handwritten Japanese characters recognition using a MRF model with parameter optimization by CRF. Proc. 11th ICADR: 603-607.

[50] U. Ramer (1972) An iterative procedure for the polygonal approximation of plan closed curves. Computer Graphics and Image Processing. 1: 244-256.

[51] L. E. Baum, T. Petrie, G. Soules and N. Weiss (1970) A maximization technique in the statistical analysis of probabilistic functions of Markov chains. Annals of Mathematical Statistics. 41(1): 164-171.

[52] J. K. Baker (1975) The dragon system – an overview. IEEE Trans. Acoustic, Speech and Signal Processing. ASSP-23. 1: 24-29.

[53] Lawrence R. Rabiner (1989) A tutorial on hidden Markov models and selected applications in speech recognition. Proc. IEEE, 77(2): 257-286.

[54] S. Z. Li (2001) Markov random field modeling in image analysis. Tokyo: Springer.

[55] C. Wolf, D. Doerman (2002) Binarization of low quality text using a Markov random field model. Proc. 16th ICPR. 3: 160 -163.

[56] T. Obafemi-Ajayi, G. Agam and O. Frieder (2008) Efficient MRF approach to document image enhancement. 19th ICPR: 1-4.

[57] X.-D. Zhou and C.-L. Liu (2007) Text/non-text ink stroke classification in Japanese handwriting based on Markov random fields. Proc. 9th ICDAR: 377-381.

[58] S.-J. Cho and J. H. Kim (2004) Bayesian network modeling of strokes and their relationships for on-line handwriting recognition. Pattern Recognition, 37(2): 253-264.

[59] J. Lafferty, A. McCallum, and F. Pereira (2001) Conditional random fields: probabilistic models for segmenting and labeling sequence data. Proc 18th ICML: 282-289.

[60] B.-H. Juang and S. Katagiri (1992) Discriminative learning for minimum error classification. IEEE Trans. Signal Processing, 40(12): 3043-3054.

[61] X.-D. Zhou, C.-L. Liu and M. Nakagawa (2009) Online handwritten Japanese character string recognition using conditional random fields. Proc. 10th ICDAR: 521-525.

[62] S. Mori, K. Yamamoto and M. Yasuda (1984) Research on machine recognition of handprinted characters, IEEE Trans. PAMI. 6: 386-405.

[63] T. H. Hildebrandt, W. T. Liu (1993) Optical recognition of handwritten Chinese characters: Advances since 1980. Pattern Recognition. 26 (2): 05–225.

[64] T. Wakabayashi, Y. Deng, S. Tsuruoka, F. Kimura, Y. Miyake (1995) Accuracy improvement by nonlinear normalization and feature compression in handwritten Chinese character recognition. Technical Report of IEICE Japan. PRU. 95(43): 1-8.

[65] N. Sun, M. Abe, Y. Nemoto (1995) A handwritten character recognition system by using improved directional element feature and subspace method. Trans. IEICE Japan. J78-D-2 (6): 922-930.

[66] C.-L. Liu and M. Nakagawa (2000) Precise candidate selection for large character set recognition by confidence evaluation, IEEE Trans. PAMI, 22 (6): 636-642.

[67] T. Kumamoto, K. Toraichi, T. Horiuchi, K. Yamamoto, H. Yamada (1991) On speeding candidate selection in handprinted chinese character recognition. Pattern Recognition. 24 (8): 793-799.

[68] C.-H. Tung, H.-J. Lee, J.-Y. Tsai (1994) Multi-stage pre-candidate selection in handwritten Chinese character recognition systems. Pattern Recognition. 27 (8): 1093-1102.

[69] H. Oda, B. Zhu, J. Tokuno, M. Onuma, A. Kitadai, M. Nakagawa (2006) A compact on-line and off-line combined recognizer. Proc 10th IWFHR: 133-138.

[70] C.-L. Liu (2005) Classifier combination based on confidence transformation. Pattern Recognition: 38(1):11–28.

[71] C.-L. Liu, H. Sako, H. Fujisawa (2004) Effects of classifier structures and training regimes on integrated segmentation and recognition of handwritten numeral strings. IEEE Trans. PAMI. 26(11): 1395-1407.

[72] Y. Tonouchi (2010) Path evaluation and character classifier training on integrated segmentation and recognition of online handwritten Japanese character string. Proc. 12th ICFHR: 513-517.

[73] M. Nagata (1998) A Japanese OCR error correction method using character shape similarity and statistical language Model. Trans. IEICE Japan. J81-D-2 (11): 2624-2634.

[74] B. Zhu and M. Nakagawa (2011) Trie-lexicon-driven recognition for on-line handwritten Japanese disease names using a time-synchronous method. Proc. 11th ICDAR: 1130-1134.

[75] M. Nakagawa, B. Zhu and M. Onuma (2005) A model of on-line handwritten Japanese text recognition free from line direction and writing format constraints. Trans. IEICE Japan. E88-D (8): 1815-1822.

Chapter 4

# Applying OCR in the Processing of Thermal Images with Temperature Scales

W.T. Chan, T.Y. Lo, C.P. Tso and K.S. Sim

Additional information is available at the end of the chapter

http://dx.doi.org/10.5772/51475

## 1. Introduction

Present-day thermal image processing is dependent on the use of metadata. This metadata, such as colour-to-temperatures indices that help the conversion of the colour value of every pixel in the image into a temperature reading, may be stored within the image files as supplementary information that is not immediately apparent from a glance of the image. Instead, they are kept within the image bytes, to be fetched by metadata-dependent programs that had been designed to examine to work with said metadata.

However, reasons such as company policies on the protection of information or circumstances such as data corruption may cause the loss of metadata. The user may also derive thermal images from sources that do not have metadata, such scans from thermal imaging magazines. In the absence of metadata, the aforementioned programs do not work. Therefore, other methods have to be used to derive the needed information. One of these is the use of optical character recognition.

Optical character recognition (OCR) is the machine equivalent of human reading [1]. Research and development of OCR-based applications has mainly focused on having programs read text that have been written in languages that do not use the Latin alphabet, such as Japanese and Arabic [2]. However, there have been endeavours in more industrious applications, such as having cameras read license plates [3]. This book chapter is dedicated to an application of the latter sort.

The use of OCR scripts is meant to complement the usual method of processing thermal images, which is using metadata, instead of substituting it. This is because fetching and reading metadata for processing parameters is still significantly faster than having the program read temperature scales and derive processing parameters from them. In other words, it is more efficient to use metadata when it is available, and resort to OCR when there is not any. However, OCR has the benefit of being usable on any thermal image as long as it has a temperature scale, and generally, thermal images do have this.

Implementing OCR has challenges, most of which stem from weaknesses of the methods used to have the program capture shapes from the thermal image and recognize these as characters. The quality of the thermal image itself also presents challenges of its own.

This book chapter will elaborate on a method, which has its inspirations from a MatLab project [4]. This method uses a library of pre-existing alphabetical and numerical characters as references to be compared with the shapes of objects, including those of text, captured from a thermal image. The disadvantages of this method and the solutions to overcome it will be mentioned later, along with the results of the comparisons between programs that use this method, manual input and the checking of metadata.

## 2. Body

### 2.1. Problem statement

The first hurdle in implementing OCR is determining the kinds of information that could be derived from the thermal image, if it lacks the metadata that conveniently provides the parameters needed to process the image with. The solution is to have the program examine the temperature scale that is included with the image and derive the temperature range from it. This temperature range is needed for association with the colour range, so that conversion from colour values to temperature readings can be made.

The next problem is to have the program search for the temperature scale without resorting to hard-coding that points that program at a specific region of the image. Hard-coding may be desirable if efficiency is valued over versatility, but the program can only process thermal images of specific formats as a result. The idea of the solution for this can be obtained from examining the layout of the thermal image first. If the temperature scale is placed separately from the image subject, i.e. not imposed onto the image subject itself so as to obscure it, then a separation of the two suffices. Such a layout is usually the case for the majority of thermal images; an example is shown in **Figure 1**.

The next complication is figuring out what aspects of the scale would give the necessary information for the processing. The temperature labels on the scale would give this, but there may be several numbers on it depicting both the intervals in the scale and its limits. Picking the highest and lowest numbers would give the maximum and minimum temperatures in the scale, respectively. The physical distances between the interval labels on the scale can also denote whether the scale is linear or logarithmic.

Figuring out which shapes belong to the characters that make up the numbers in the temperature labels is also a challenge. When designing the program to recognize characters as part of a number, the developer should keep in mind how a human recognizes numbers. The key characteristic of coherently displayed numbers is that the characters in numbers are adjacent to each other and are usually aligned in the same orientation. Therefore, he/she can include these considerations in the program as logical processes.

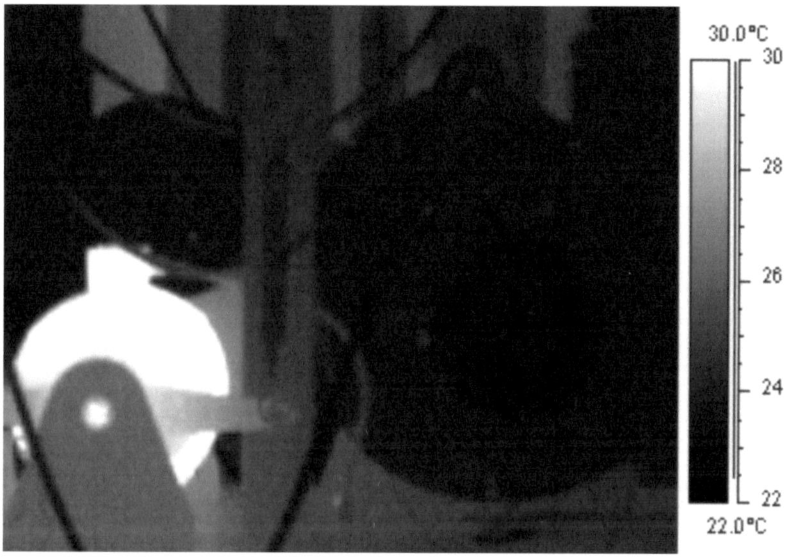


**Figure 1.** Thermal image of a TE84 Centrifugal Fan Test Set

Recognizing which shapes are characters and which are not is important because the processing parameters have to be either coherent numbers or words. Having strings of characters infiltrated by shapes that are mistakenly recognized as characters can result in errors. The use of a correlation coefficient offers a solution for this through the implementation of a threshold value that the shape must surpass if it is to be considered a character.

In summary, most of the problems that would be faced in the development program concerns the processes used to implement OCR. Most of them can be overcome as long as the definition of OCR as the machine equivalent of human reading is kept in mind, i.e. the processes in the OCR scripts are digital versions of the logic processes that humans use to recognize and identify characters in written languages.

## 2.2. Application area

The area that the output of this research is immediately useful in is research in thermal image processing itself. Such research requires the analysis of many thermal images, and samples of these may not be sourced from original thermal images but rather from other media such as science magazines. Such other media obviously do not support the inclusion of metadata in these thermal images, so using an OCR-assisted program on scans or crop-outs of thermal images from these media can be useful.

Preventive maintenance in the industrial sectors may use thermal imaging as one of the tools for examining systems and machines, but company policies on information may prevent the inclusion of metadata in thermal images that are to be used in day-to-day operations or for archiving. Therefore, an OCR-assisted program can provide a solution if already generated thermal images that have to be analyzed again happen not to have metadata.

### 2.3. Research course

The course of this research is to develop a program that can utilize OCR to automatically process batches of thermal images and obtain the information that is usually wanted from a thermal image, such as a chart of temperature readings, one for each pixel on the image. The program must produce the same results as a program that uses manual user input, for the program to be considered a viable upgrade over the latter at processing batches of thermal images without metadata.

The techniques used in implementing OCR can be swapped out for others to achieve better processing times. This is so that the gap in processing time between programs that use OCR and those that rely on metadata can be reduced, such that the former can be more competitive and thus reduce the reliance on metadata.

### 2.4. Methodology

The work-flow of the program is shown in **Figure 2**, **Figure 3** and **Figure 4**. Firstly, the program looks into a directory where thermal images are stored, fetches and makes copies of these. The copies are analyzed and manipulated on throughout the flow of the program, in order to preserve the originals.

Next, the program determines the range of colours that represent the range of temperatures in the image. This is best done by examining the temperature scale that came with the image, so the scale has to be isolated from the image subject. This also helps the capture of characters that make up the temperature labels, if the image subject happens to have paint or labelling that emit infrared radiation on its surface; see **Figure 5** for illustration. Preventing the image subject from being subjected to OCR scripts prevents confusion.

To separate the image subject from the temperature scale, converting the entire image to a binary image changes the objects into discrete blobs that can be identified using connected-component labelling. The image subject should be reduced to a mass of pixels that is the largest object in the entire image, so scripts that check the sizes of objects can identify and isolate it. Scripts can also be introduced to differentiate the colour strip of the scale from its temperature labels, such as through the fact that the strip is generally the larger object.

Any remaining shapes in the region of the image that the temperature scale is located in should belong to characters that compose the temperature labels for the scale, but there may also shapes for blemishes that may have been captured as well, especially if the thermal image came from a scan of a printed image. Therefore, the OCR scripts are performed on these to identify whether they resemble a character or not. Those that are not are discarded.

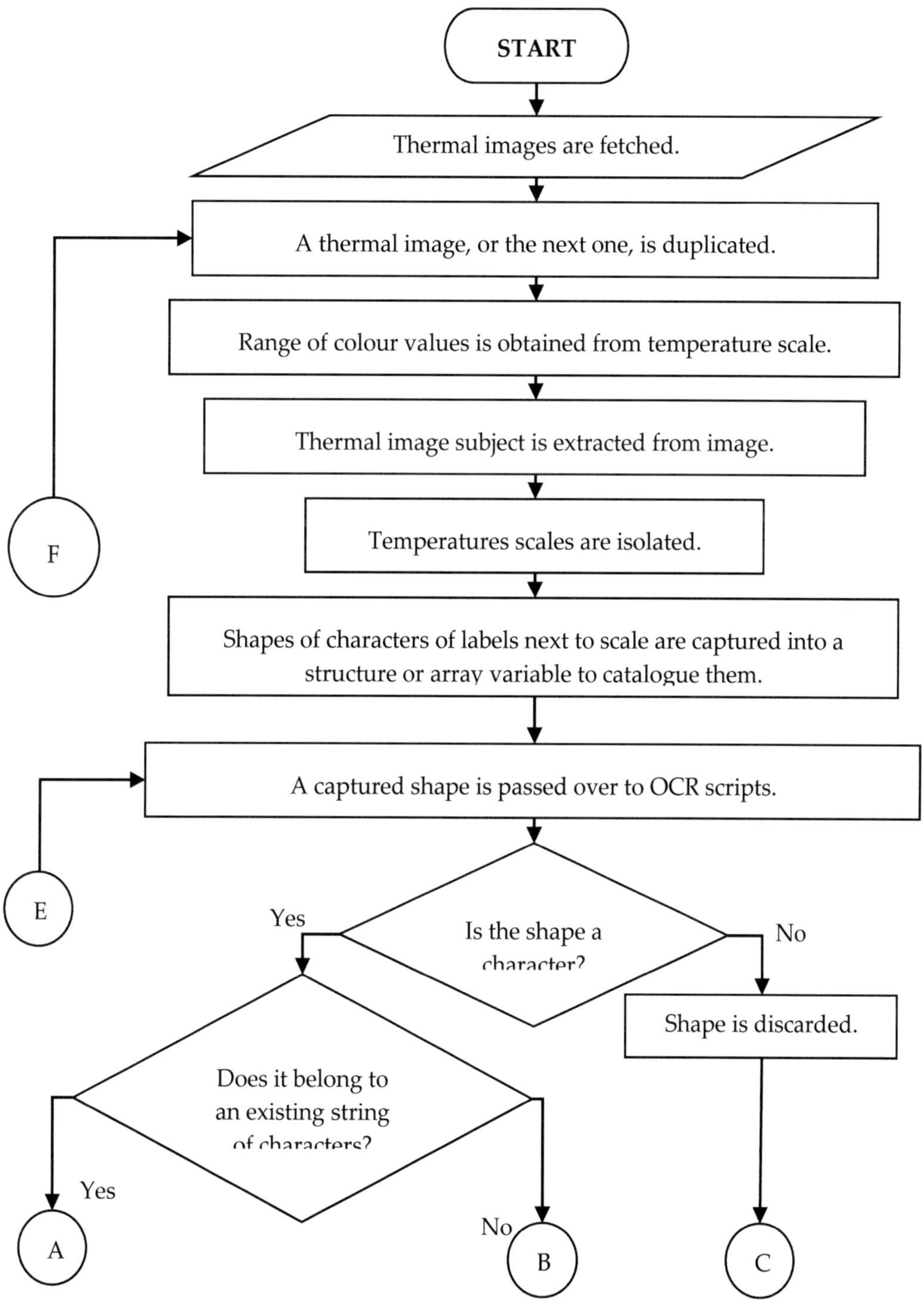


**Figure 2.** Workflow of program (Part 1)

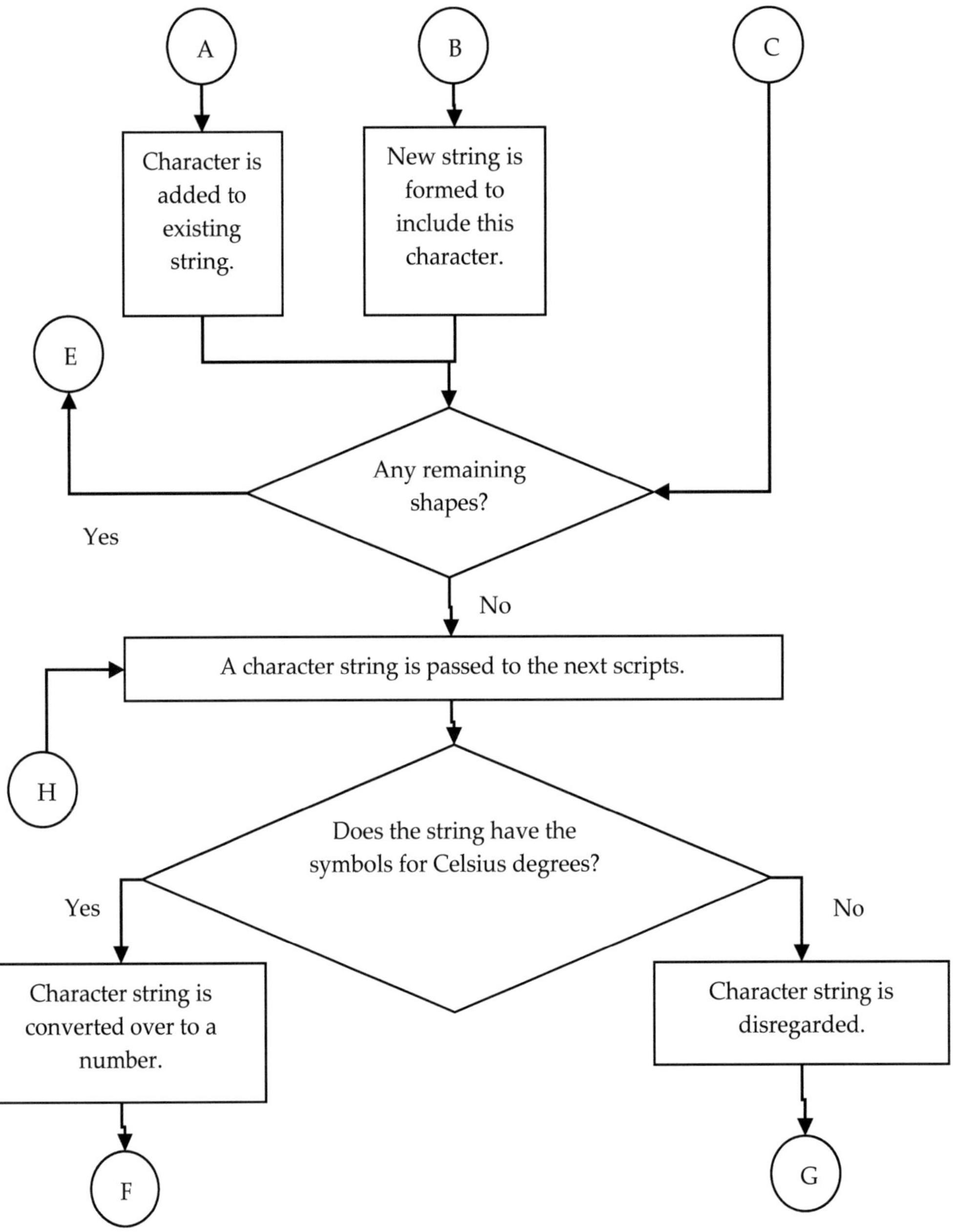


**Figure 3.** Workflow of program (Part 2)

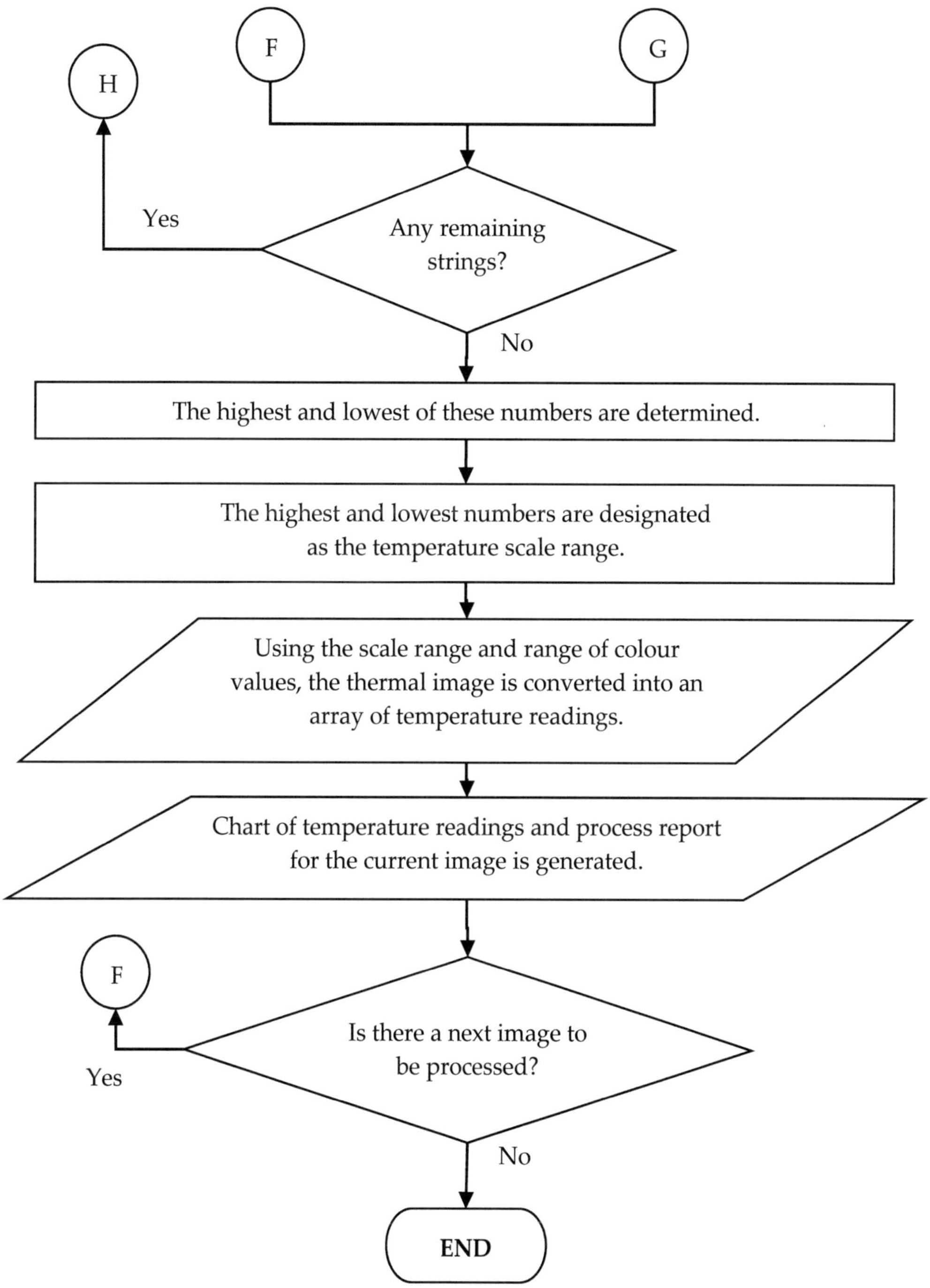


**Figure 4.** Workflow of program (Part 3)

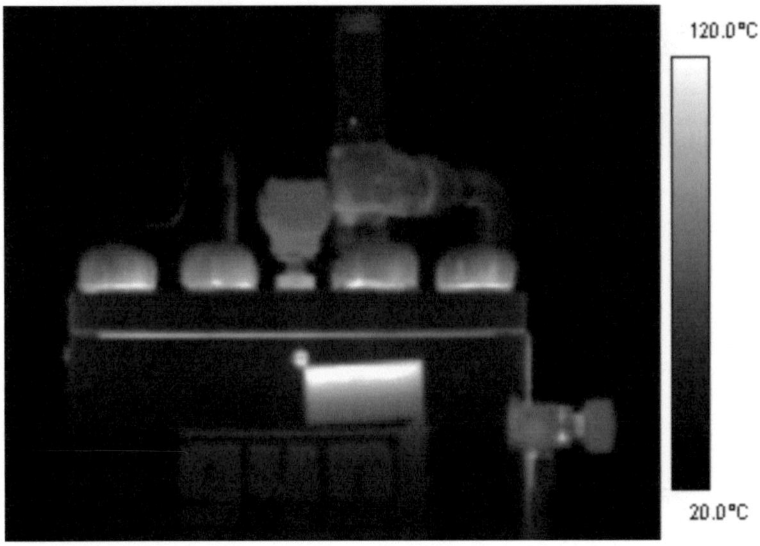


**Figure 5.** Marcet Boiler with logo that emits infrared radiation.

The OCR scripts use the algorithm for correlation coefficient to determine the character that the captured shapes are most similar to. The program compares a captured shape to each entry of an archive of pre-existing images of characters, generating a correlation coefficient from each comparison. If one of the correlation coefficients surpasses a threshold value (which is implemented to prevent illegible shapes from being identified as text characters) and is the highest, the captured shape is identified as this character.

$$r = \frac{\sum_m \sum_n \left(A_{mn} - \bar{A}\right)\left(B_{mn} - \bar{B}\right)}{\sqrt{\left(\sum_m \sum_n \left(A_{mn} - \bar{A}\right)^2\right)\left(\sum_m \sum_n \left(B_{mn} - \bar{B}\right)^2\right)}} \tag{1}$$

The correlation coefficient algorithm cannot be used on simply-shaped characters, such as the period symbol, as this may lead to division-by-zero errors. For these characters, special scripts can be devised to identify captured shapes as such by examining their dimensions.

After the filtering of captured shapes with the OCR scripts, the remaining ones should be those for characters that make up the temperature labels. However, before they can be examined further, they need to be grouped into strings of characters, i.e. words and numbers, as noted in the workflow diagrams above.

The following steps are used to group characters together into strings:

1. A character is picked from the structure or array variable.
2. It is checked for adjacency to any other character. The character and the other one are grouped together into a string.
3. The string is entered into a list of strings, with tags to associate the string with these characters.

4. The current character is marked as having been examined, and the next one is fetched.
5. The next character is checked for any existing tags; these tags will be passed to any character found to be adjacent to this one.
6. Afterwards, steps 2 to 5 are repeated until all characters are accounted for.

To decide whether the strings formed are temperature values or not, they can be first examined to see if they contain digits; if they do not, they are most certainly not temperature labels. To confirm whether they are temperature values or not, they are either examined for any adjacency to symbols for Celsius degrees; these are definite indications that they are temperature labels.

If they are not adjacent to the symbols, the thermal image is checked for the presence of these anyway; a thermal image should have text that denotes the unit of measurement used. If the temperature-to-colour index is presented in a manner similar to how axes are presented on charts, then the strings are examined to determine if they are wholly composed of digits and/or period symbols, if any.

Once all characters have been accounted for, there should be a list of character strings that are all temperature labels. The limits for the temperature scale can be obtained from these by searching for the highest and lowest values. These are then associated with the highest and lowest colour values, respectively.

The program should then examine the thermal image for any indication that the temperature scale is logarithmic or linear. Most thermal images use linear temperature scales, so simple interpolation can be used to convert the colour value of every pixel over to a temperature reading. Otherwise, the program may have to examine the distances of every temperature label to the others; if the distance of separation between them changes exponentially, this is an indication that the scale is logarithmic, and thus the conversion has to be designed accordingly.

The temperature readings can be grouped into a chart of the same dimensions as the image subject. It is preferable to use universal file formats for these charts, such as Comma-Separated Value, to avoid compatibility issues or the technical limitations of more specific file formats. Any other output, such as a report on the peak and lowest temperature readings can be derived from the chart.

To measure the expected benefit of using OCR to automate the analysis of the temperature scale over human reading, another version of the program has been created. It is similar to the one that uses OCR scripts, with the exception that the OCR scripts have been replaced with a user interface that requests for manual input of the temperature scale limits; to aid this, the thermal image being processed is displayed for the user to examine. The processing times for the two versions of the program are compared over a range of numbers of thermal images to be processed.

The processing time is defined as the time from the launch of a program to the generation of the results. Therefore, the time taken for the user to examine the thermal image is considered too for the manual-input version. To reduce the uncertainties in the measurements for the manual-input version, the user practices to achieve the shortest possible times.

Another version of the program that checks for metadata instead of using OCR has also been created and subjected to the tests above as a control test. To this end, the header bytes of the thermal image files are embedded with metadata, which this version of the program checks for.

### 2.5. Status

The program is complete and working in two formats, MatLAB m-file and Visual C#. Currently, the program is made for thermal images in grayscale, though it can also be used for broader colour palettes by simply converting them over to grayscale first. This is justified if the colour scale organizes colour values in the same arrangement as the temperature scale. The program also works for thermal images of any size.

The methods used in this program do not work for thermal images with text that is so small as to be illegible for human reading. As OCR is the machine equivalent of human reading, a program that uses OCR is incapable of reading what a human cannot possibly read. Even if they are legible, small, low-resolution text may give rise to problems such as mistaking one character for another, as a human would if he/she did not further scrutinize said character. **Figure 6** shows an example of such an occurrence.

**Figure 6.** Mistaking a low-resolution zero digit as the letter 'D'.

Currently, the problem overcomes such a problem by examining any character that is next to the dubious character. If the other character is a digit, then the logic that since the characters are expected to compose the numbers that make up temperature labels, the dubious character is likely a digit as well.

As the average resolution of thermal images increases as the resolution of thermal imagers improves due to technological advances, more legible text can be used for the labelling of temperature scales. It is expected that this thermal image processing program and others would not have to encounter such problems in the future.

Any flaws incurred during the generation of the thermal image in the first place may be carried over to the processing of the thermal image. For example, failure to present the digits in the temperature labels as distinctly separate characters may cause problems for certain pattern-recognition techniques like connected-component labelling. **Figure 7** shows such a case for the digits "40", as capture by a FLIR A20M, which would be identified by connected-component labelling techniques as a single object.

**Figure 7.** The digits for number "40" conjoined.

The solution for this example of a flaw is to examine the dimensions of the conjoined characters. If the composite object is too big to be a single character, it is likely a pair or more of conjoined characters, and can be split according to its dimensions into its constituents, which can then be analyzed separately.

## 2.6. Results

The measurements of processing times for the OCR-implemented and manual-input versions of the program are as shown in **Table 1**. A graphical presentation of the measurements is shown in **Figure 7**. The measurements were obtained with the MatLab version of the program, ran with MatLAB R2008b IDE, Windows XP Service Pack 2 and Intel Core2Duo E4700 CPU.

The implementation of the OCR scripts is found to have decreased the time taken for the program to process the same thermal images from that it would have if manual-input was used instead. Therefore, the automation of the examination and processing of thermal images without metadata is feasible with the utilization of OCR.

However, for thermal images with metadata, the version of the program with OCR scripts is not as competitive as the program that checks the metadata immediately. The differences should be apparent in **Table 2** and **Figure 8**.

| No.of Images | OCR-Implemented Program | | | | Manual User Input Program | | | |
|---|---|---|---|---|---|---|---|---|
| | Time Measured for Run no. (s) | | | | Time Measured for Run no. (s) | | | |
| | 1 | 2 | 3 | Average | 1 | 2 | 3 | Average |
| 1 | 0.2779 | 0.2764 | 0.2743 | **0.2762** | 3.9782 | 2.6486 | 3.0375 | **3.2214** |
| 2 | 0.5558 | 0.557 | 0.5574 | **0.5567** | 8.5646 | 9.2787 | 9.1721 | **9.0051** |
| 3 | 0.8411 | 0.8325 | 0.8428 | **0.8388** | 11.7308 | 11.2316 | 11.7690 | **11.5771** |
| 4 | 1.1037 | 1.1135 | 1.1138 | **1.1103** | 12.7000 | 12.8020 | 11.5818 | **12.3613** |
| 5 | 1.3929 | 1.371 | 1.3781 | **1.3807** | 14.3850 | 14.8614 | 14.5479 | **14.5981** |
| 10 | 2.6240 | 2.6541 | 2.6741 | **2.6507** | 29.0014 | 29.0213 | 30.0042 | **29.3423** |
| 15 | 4.1154 | 4.0098 | 4.016 | **4.0471** | 45.9954 | 46.0872 | 46.1534 | **46.0787** |
| 20 | 5.5412 | 5.4001 | 5.4003 | **5.4472** | 62.9987 | 63.5599 | 63.5401. | **63.2793** |
| 25 | 7.0141 | 7.0098 | 6.9421 | **6.9887** | 77.1524 | 77.0016 | 78.0003 | **77.3848** |
| 30 | 8.4386 | 8.445 | 8.4825 | **8.4554** | 97.0983 | 97.3609 | 95.5554 | **96.6715** |

**Table 1.** Processing Times of OCR-Implemented versus Manual-Input

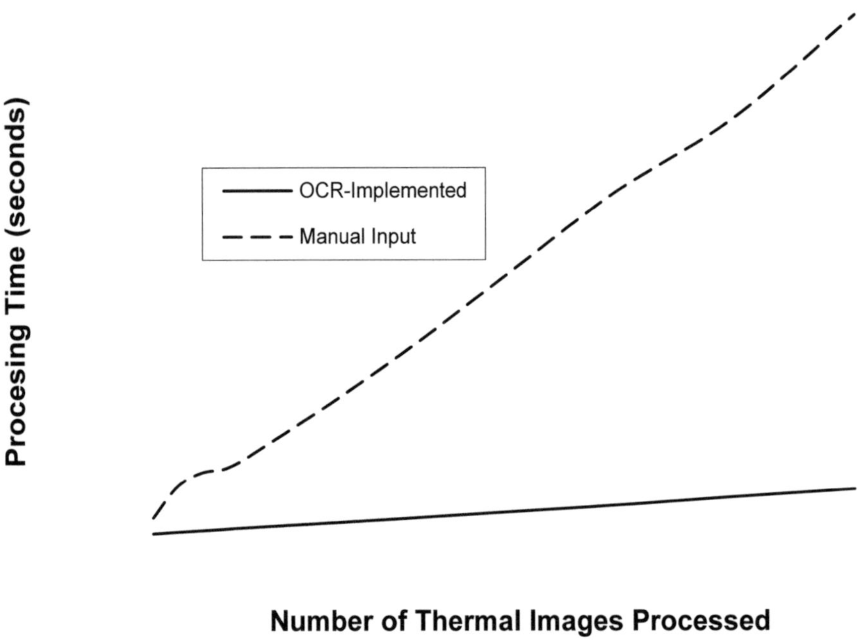


**Figure 8.** Processing Times of OCR-Implemented versus Manual-Input

| No. of Images | OCR-Implemented Program | | | | Metadata-Checking Program | | | |
|---|---|---|---|---|---|---|---|---|
| | Time Measured for Run no. (s) | | | | Time Measured for Run no. (s) | | | |
| | 1 | 2 | 3 | Average | 1 | 2 | 3 | Average |
| 1 | 0.2779 | 0.2764 | 0.2743 | **0.2762** | 0.0554 | 0.0560 | 0.0562 | **0.0559** |
| 2 | 0.5558 | 0.557 | 0.5574 | **0.5567** | 0.1543 | 0.1464 | 0.1472 | **0.1493** |
| 3 | 0.8411 | 0.8325 | 0.8428 | **0.8388** | 0.2541 | 0.2498 | 0.2513 | **0.2517** |
| 4 | 1.1037 | 1.1135 | 1.1138 | **1.1103** | 0.3498 | 0.3501 | 0.3478 | **0.3492** |
| 5 | 1.3929 | 1.371 | 1.3781 | **1.3807** | 0.4453 | 0.4532 | 0.4501 | **0.4495** |
| 10 | 2.6240 | 2.6541 | 2.6741 | **2.6507** | 0.5399 | 0.5468 | 0.5513 | **0.5460** |
| 15 | 4.1154 | 4.0098 | 4.016 | **4.0471** | 0.6534 | 0.6501 | 0.6521 | **0.6519** |
| 20 | 5.5412 | 5.4001 | 5.4003 | **5.4472** | 0.7521 | 0.7498 | 0.7501 | **0.7507** |
| 25 | 7.0141 | 7.0098 | 6.9421 | **6.9887** | 0.8600 | 0.8512 | 0.8532 | **0.8548** |
| 30 | 8.4386 | 8.445 | 8.4825 | **8.4554** | 0.9564 | 0.9513 | 0.9498 | **0.9525** |

**Table 2.** Processing Times of OCR-Implemented versus Metadata-Checking

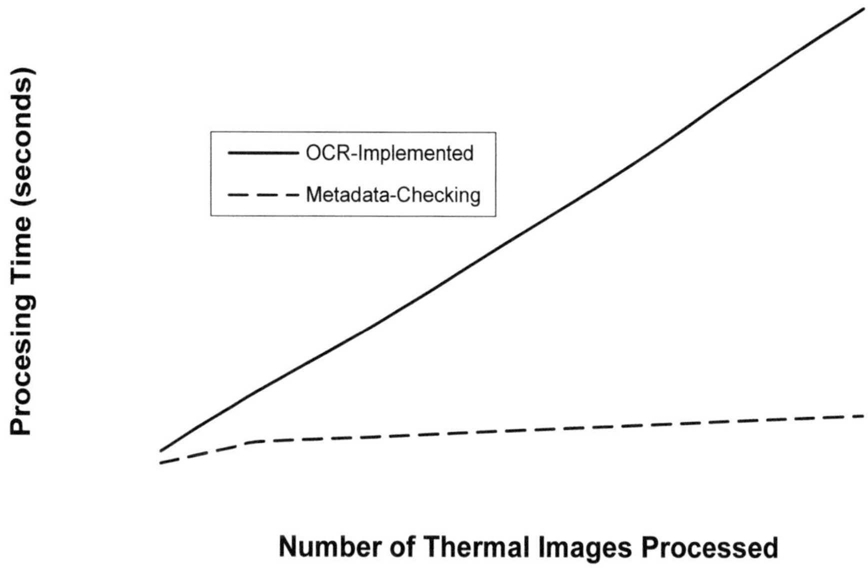


**Figure 9.** Processing Times of OCR-Implemented versus Metadata-Checking

Much of the time taken by the version that uses OCR is spent on running the OCR scripts. The more labels there are on the temperature scale, the longer it takes. Some reduction could be achieved by hard-coding into the program some short-cuts, such as where it looks in the thermal image for the temperature scale limits, but this reduces the versatility of the program. However, such a finding also shows where there is room for improvement.

### 2.7. Future research

Currently, the program is most suitable for the processing of thermal images without metadata. It can process thermal images with metadata as well, as long as it has a temperature scale. However, as shown earlier, it takes a longer time to produce results than checking for metadata does.

While hard-coding is not a desired solution to increase their competitiveness, the OCR scripts can be improved with more efficient techniques. Of particular interest are the ways used in the program to recognize and capture shapes from the image, and the ways to filter and identify shapes as characters. It is the hope of this future research that the OCR-utilizing method can become as competitive as the methods that relies on metadata.

## 3. Conclusion

Optical character recognition is feasible for use as a method in the processing of thermal images for information. It forgoes the need for metadata and can be used on any thermal image as long as it has a legible temperature scale, but the OCR scripts used may consume time that can be otherwise saved if metadata had been available instead.

Therefore, it is currently practical only for thermal images that happen to have no metadata or has damaged metadata. However, it has been shown to be useful in automating the processing of large numbers of thermal images without metadata, which would otherwise be a daunting task if the user has to manually input the processing parameters used.

Considering that there are more methods of optical character recognition than the one shown in this book chapter that utilizes correlation coefficients, processing thermal images with OCR can be developed to be as close to competitive as the use of metadata.

## Author details

W. T. Chan, T. Y. Lo and K. S. Sim
*Faculty of Engineering and Technology, Multimedia University, Melaka, Malaysia*

C. P. Tso
*School of Mechanical and Aerospace Engineering, Nanyang Technological University, Singapore*

## 4. Acknowledgement

The authors would like to thank W.K. Wong of Multimedia University for allowing the use of the FLIR A20M thermal imager under his purview, and D.O.B. Guerrero for having published his MatLab work on OCR.

## 5. References

[1] V.K Govindan , A.P Shivaprasad (1990), Abstract: Character recognition — A review, Pattern Recognition, Volume 23, Issue 7, 671-683.

[2] Hiromichi Fujisawa (2008), Forty years of research in character and document recognition—an industrial perspective, Pattern Recognition, Volume 41, Issue 8, 2435-2446.

[3] Amir Sedighi, Mansur Vafadust (2011), A new and robust method for character segmentation and recognition in license plate images, Expert Systems with Applications, Volume 38, Issue 11, 13497–13504.

[4] Diego Orlando Barragan Guerrero (2007), Optical Character Recognition (OCR), MatLab Central, Files Exchange. Available: http://www.mathworks.com/matlabcentral/fileexchange/18169-optical-character-recognition-ocr. Accessed: November 2010.

Chapter 5

# Preprocessing for Images Captured by Cameras

Chih-Chang Yu, Ming-Gang Wen, Kuo-Chin Fan and Hsin-Te Lue

Additional information is available at the end of the chapter

http://dx.doi.org/10.5772/52110

## 1. Introduction

Due to the rapid development of mobile devices equipped with cameras, the realization of what you get is what you see is not a dream anymore. In general, texts in images often draw people's attention due to the following reasons: semantic meanings to objects in the image (e.g., the name of the book), information about the environment (e.g., a traffic sign), or commercial purpose (e.g., an advertisement). The mass development of mobile device with low cost cameras boosts the demand of recognizing characters in nature scenes via mobile devices such as smartphones. Employing text detection algorithms along with character recognition techniques on mobile devices assists users in understanding or gathering useful information around them. A useful mobile application is the translation tool. Using handwriting as the input is widely used in current translation tools on smartphones. However, capturing images and recognizing texts directly is more intuitive and convenient for users. A translation tool with character recognition techniques recognizes texts on the road signs or restaurant menus. Such application greatly helps travelers and blinds.

The mobility advantage inspires users to capture text images using mobile devices rather than scanners, especially in outdoors. Optical character recognition (OCR) is a very mature technique accomplished by many previous researchers. However, camera-based OCR is a more difficult task than traditional OCR using scanners. Scanned images are captured with high resolution, even illumination, simple background, high contrast, and no perspective distortion. These properties ensure that high recognition rates can be achieved when employing OCR. Conversely, images captured by cameras on mobile devices include many external or unwanted environmental effects which deeply affect the performance of OCR. These images are often captured with low resolution and fluctuations such as noises, uneven illuminations or perspective distortions, etc. In that case, low quality images cause the camera-based OCR more challenging than traditional OCR. The reason is that the extracted character blobs are usually broken or stuck together (also called as "ligature") in low quality images. It is a prerequisite to clearly detect foreground texts before proceeding to later recognition task. To facilitate the processing of camera-based OCR, a good preprocessing is highly required.

This chapter discusses how to segment text images into individual single characters to facilitate later OCR kernel processing. Before the character segmentation procedure, several works such as text region detection and text-line construction need to be done in advance. First, regions in images are classified into text and non-text region (e.g. graphics, trademarks, etc.). Second, the text components are grouped to form text-lines via a bottom-up approach. After text-line construction, typographical structure is analyzed to distinguish inverted (upside-down) texts. Finally, a character segmentation method is introduced to segment ligatures, which often appear on text images captured by cameras. In the following sections, these processes will be described in detail.

## 2. Related works

Instead of discussing the character recognition techniques, this chapter focuses on the new challenges imposed by the imperfect capturing conditions mentioned in the first section. More specifically, some methods are proposed to detect foreground texts and segment each character from an image correctly. In the proposed preprocessing system, there are three main procedures: text detection, text-line construction and character segmentation. Before that, a brief review of several works done by previous researchers is described in the following subsections.

### 2.1. Text detection

The current text detection researches are roughly divided into rule-based and classifier-based approaches. Rule-based methods [1-5] formulate rules with prior-knowledge to distinguish text and non-text blocks. Conditional constraints are often adopted in these rules, such as the sizes of connected components, edge information, color information and texture information. Adopting edge information is inspired by the observations that texts often cluster together and have high contrast to backgrounds. Regions with large enough variances and sufficient amount of edge pixels are regarded as the text candidates. Color information is utilized with region growing and clustering methods [6, 7]. The rules formulated by experienced experts filter texts efficiently but may not be robust. Texts themselves can be regarded as textures [8]. In this type of approach, images are transformed to frequency domains by using filters such as DCT [9], FFT [10], Wavelet [11], Gabor filter [12], etc. to reveal distinct textural properties so that text regions can be separated from background regions.

The classifier-based methods [13-16] utilize the extracted features as the input of specific classifiers, such as neural networks or Support Vector Machines (SVM) to classify text and non-text components. The classifiers usually need enough samples to be trained well. Moreover, the parameters of these classifiers often have to be tuned case by case to get the best classification results.

## 2.2. Text-line construction

After finding text components, these components are linked one another to form meaningful text-lines (i.e. words and sentences). Text-lines are constructed based on the distance between two text blocks with the observation that the row spacing is often larger than the character spacing in most documents. In traditional page segmentation, top-down approaches such as X-Y Cut [18, 19] and the run-length smearing algorithm (RLSA) [20] are widely used to find paragraphs, text-lines, and characters, and then segment them by horizontal and vertical projections. However, both methods are infeasible to segment the document when the image is skewed.

From another point of view, when document images are with unknown structures, the bottom-up methods are more practical than the top-down methods to construct text-lines. Hough transform is a well-known algorithm to find potential alignments in images. However, Hough transform is a computationally expensive method. The minimum spanning tree methods [21, 22] are employed according to the properties of text clustering and typesetting. The extracted minimum spanning trees are not considered the text-line structures yet; some criteria are further adopted to delete redundant or add additional edges to form complete text-lines. Basu et al. [23] propose a water flow method to construct text-lines. Hypothetical water flows from both left and right image margins to opposite image margins. Areas are wetted after the flood. In their approach, text regions are obstructions which block water flows so that the un-wetted areas can be linked to form text-lines. The disadvantage of water flow algorithm is that the threshold of the flow filter is empirically determined.

## 2.3. Character segmentation

Traditional character segmentation techniques are categorized into projection methods, minimal segmentation cost path method, recognition-feedback-based methods, and classifier-based methods. Projection methods [3, 24] project the image along the horizontal and vertical directions. The locations with no projection values are believed to be the locations of spacing. The projection methods are efficient but have difficulties in resolving ligatures and broken characters. More specifically, when ligatures occur, the amount of spacing is often less than the number of characters. Conversely, the amount of spacing is often more than the number of characters when one character breaks into several blobs. Hence, confirming segmentation locations using the projection method only is risky in camera-based OCR because ligatures and broken characters are very likely to occur. If characters are stuck together severely, the segmentation results will be wrong. Another situation is the emergence of broken characters. Broken characters result in over-segmentation due to the occurrence of many locations with no projection values. It is infeasible to segment characters by using projection method if images are skewed or contain italic fonts. Hence, the projection methods often collaborate with other methods for correct segmentation result. The minimal segmentation cost method is to find a segmentation path with minimal cost in images. The weights of foregrounds and backgrounds are pre-specified. To reduce the complexity of finding the optimal segmentation path, certain constraints such as path movement range and divided zones are integrated with dynamic programming [25, 26].

The recognition-feedback-based methods, [27, 29] provide a recovery mechanism for wrong segmentations. These methods seek some segmentation points to divide ligatures into several segmented blocks. The segmented blocks are then fed into the recognition kernel. If the recognition rate of the segmented block is above a certain threshold, the segmentation point is considered as legal. Otherwise, the segmented block is illegal and the corresponding segmentation point is abandoned. This method is more reliable than the projection methods, but the computation cost is also more expensive. Classifier-based methods [30, 31] select segmentation points using classifiers trained by correct segmentation samples. The drawback of classifier-based method is that classifiers require enough training samples to obtain better segmentation results.

## 3. Preprocessing

The main challenge for the preprocessing system is that the captured images are often with low resolution. Although cameras on mobile devices are capable of taking higher resolution images, the computation cost is still an issue nowadays. The preprocessing system consists of three modules: text detection, text-line construction, and character segmentation to provide acceptable inputs (i.e. individual character images) for OCR.

### 3.1. System flowchart

The flowchart of the preprocessing system is illustrated in Figure 1. In the text detection module, foreground blobs are separated from backgrounds. These foreground blobs are classified into text connected components (CC) and non-text CCs using the text-noise filter. In the text-line construction module, the text CCs are used to construct rough text-lines first. Then the text-line completeness and reading order confirmation are achieved via the features of employed typographical structure. In the character segmentation module, each text CC is classified as a single character or a ligature. If the text CC is classified as a ligature, it is segmented via the proposed segmentation mechanism.

### 3.2. Text detection

The first work of the preprocessing system is to find the locations of texts. Text images include texts, graphic, backgrounds, and tables. In general, texts are with high contrast to the backgrounds. Based on this observation, foregrounds can be separated from backgrounds by image binarization. The segmented foregrounds are labeled as connected components (CCs) by 8-ways connected component labeling method. However, binarizing all images using a fixed threshold is improper because the external lighting conditions of

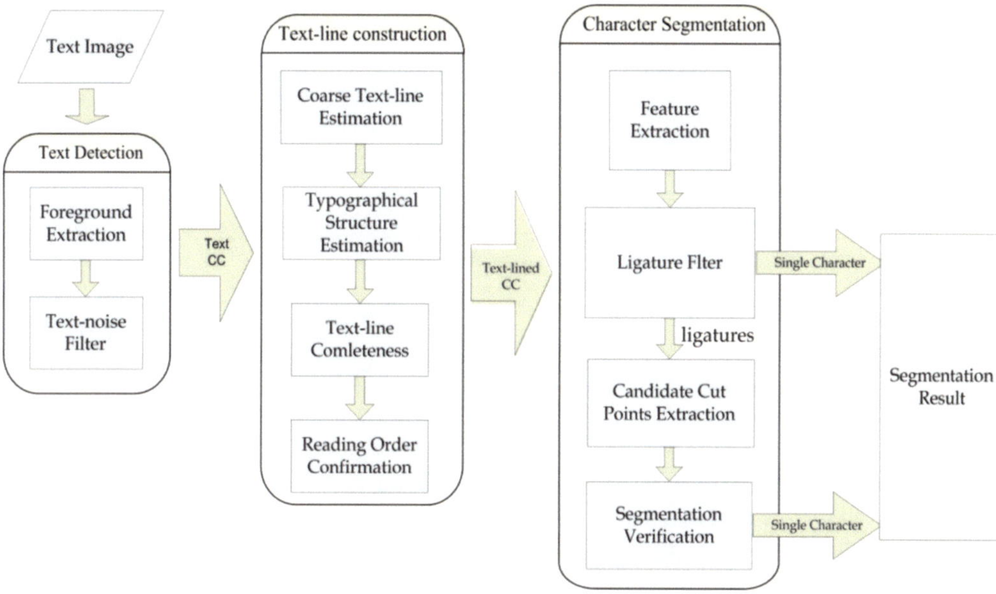


**Figure 1.** Flowchart of the preprocessing system.

text images are usually not the same. A two-stage binarization mechanism which adopts the well-known Otsu's method [32] is proposed. In the first stage, foreground blobs are extracted using a global threshold which is automatically found by the Otsu's method. The found foreground blobs contain noises, pictures, and texts. To reduce the computational cost of the text-line construction module, these blobs are classified into text and non-text CCs using a text-noise filter. Only the text CCs are used to construct a rough text-line in the text-line construction module. Afterwards, Otsu's method is performed again in a small region of each individual text-line area to complete the text CCs. It is helpful for the character segmentation module when the contours of text CCs are clearer after the binarization in the second stage.

A statistical approach is adopted to distinguish text CCs from non-text CCs. The widths and heights of CCs form two histograms. Figure 2 (a) is an example of the width histogram. Every 5 bins of the histogram in Figure 2 (a) are summed up to form the second histogram (see Figure 2 (b)). The majority of the second histogram can be acquired and the average width is calculated by the width values belong to the major bin. As shown in Figure 2 (b), the majority bin is bin #3, which corresponds to the $11^{th}$ -$15^{th}$ bin of the histogram in Figure 2(a). Hence, the average width of CCs is 13 in this case. Same procedure can be applied to the height histogram to obtain the average height of CCs. CCs sizes of which are larger than the ratio of product of average width and average height are labeled as non-text CCs.

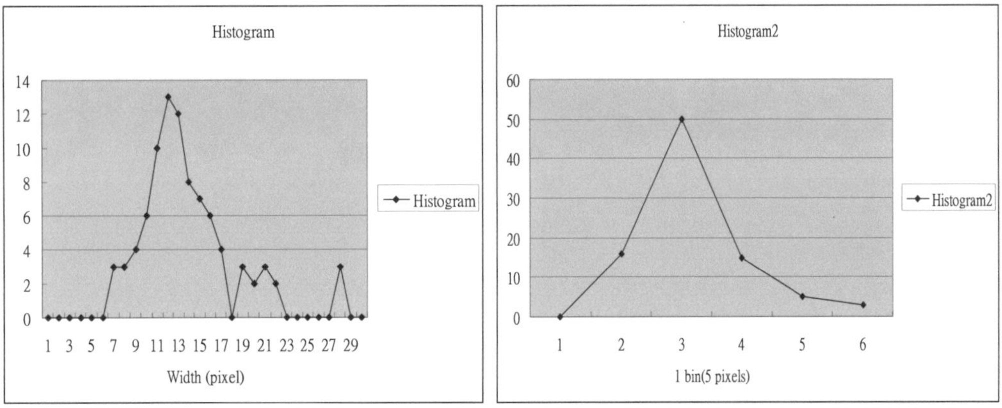


(a) (b)

**Figure 2.** Example of histogram used for finding the average width of text CCs.(a) Histogram of the widths of CCs and (b) histogram which sums up every 5 bins of (a).

The CCs are normalized to a fixed size before passing the text-noise filter. Then, auto-regressive (AR) features [42] are extracted from the CCs as the inputs of neural network for text-noise classification. The misclassified text CCs in this procedure are recovered using the properties of text clusters and text-lines during the text-line construction procedure, which will be described in the following subsection.

### 3.3. Text-line construction

The goal of the text-line construction is to find the reading order of a text and construct a linked-list of characters. A distance-based method is designed herein to construct text-lines according to the following characteristic: the row spacing is often greater than the word spacing in most document layouts. Instead of calculating the distance between the central points of two text CCs, the distance between two CCs is estimated by the "out-length". The out-length is defined as the length of the segment between the bounding boxes of two text CCs (see Figure 3). The advantage of using the out-length measurement is that the out-length values remain small even the widths of text CCs are large (this usually happens on ligatures) as long as they are on the same text-line. Figure 4 illustrate the consideration of neighboring CCs for each CC by using the out-length. If we consider the distances between the central points of CCs, CC1 and CC2 will be considered as close CCs and the text-line will thereby be constructed in a wrong direction. Instead, CC3 is closer to CC2 than CC1 using the out-length measurement. Hence, a correct text-line can be constructed.

A two-stage statistical method is proposed herein to find the reading order of text-lines. In the first stage, for each text CC, a neighboring candidate CC which has the smallest out-length to it is chosen. Then, the angle $\theta$ between the horizontal line and the line linking the central points of these two neighboring CCs is computed (see Figure 4). A histogram is constructed and the angle $\theta_m$ with the majority votes in the histogram is utilized to determine the coarse reading order (that is, the orientation) of the document. The coarse reading order estimated in the first stage is temporally assumed as the correct reading order to construct the initial text-lines. For each CC, only the smallest and second smallest out-length values are considered according to the fact that a character in text-lines has two neighbors at most. The text-line construction algorithm is stated as follows:

**Step 1.** For an unvisited $CC_i$ and its neighboring $CC_j$, angle $\theta_{ij}$ which is the angle between $CC_i$ and $CC_j$ are evaluated by the following equation

$$\theta_m - \varepsilon < \theta_{ij} < \theta_m + \varepsilon \tag{1}$$

where $\theta_m$ is the temporary reading order orientation, and ε is a tolerance threshold. The purpose of Eq. (1) is to link several CCs into a text-line along a straight direction. If $\theta_{ij}$ satisfies the inequality in Eq. (1), go to Step 2. Otherwise, select another neighboring $CC_k$ with the second smallest out-length and check the inequality again using angle $\theta_{ik}$. If $\theta_{ik}$ satisfies the inequality in Eq. (1) is satisfied for $\theta_{ik}$, go to Step 3. If both $\theta_{ij}$ and $\theta_{ik}$ cannot satisfy Eq. (1), go to step 4.

**Step 2.** Link $CC_i$ to $CC_j$. Go to step 1 and check the next text candidate.
**Step 3.** Link $CC_i$ to $CC_k$. Go to step 1 and check the next text candidate.
**Step 4.** $CC_i$ cannot be connected with any $CC$ at this stage. Find another unvisited $CC_p$ and go to step 1. If all CCs have been visited, terminate the algorithm.

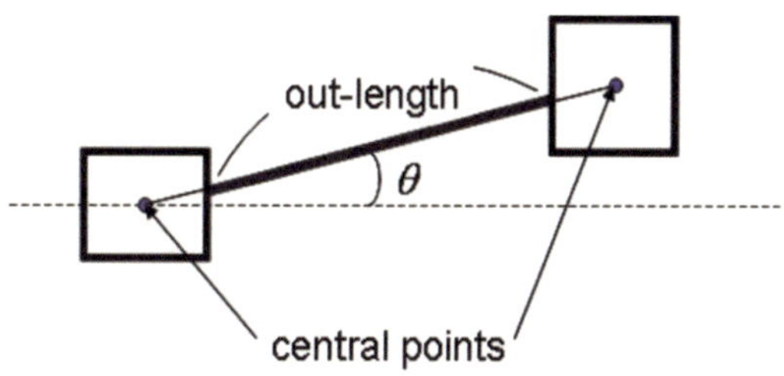


**Figure 3.** Illustration of out-length and slant angle between two CCs.

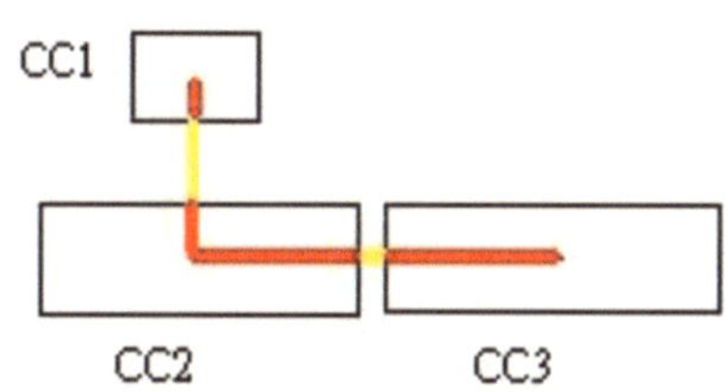


**Figure 4.** Illustration that CC3 is closer to CC2 than CC1 by using out-length, but CC1 is closer than CC3 estimated by using the distance between the central points of the CCs.

Figure 5 (a) depicts the link between all CCs and their corresponding nearest CCs using the out-length measurement. Figure 5 (b) illustrates the link of the second nearest CCs. The coarse orientation $\theta_m$ of text-lines in Figure 5 is horizontal. After performing the algorithm, most CCs are linked to form some text-lines, as shown in Figure 5 (c). Some estimated text-lines in Figure 5 (c) are not accurate enough. These inaccurate text-lines will be refined in the next stage.

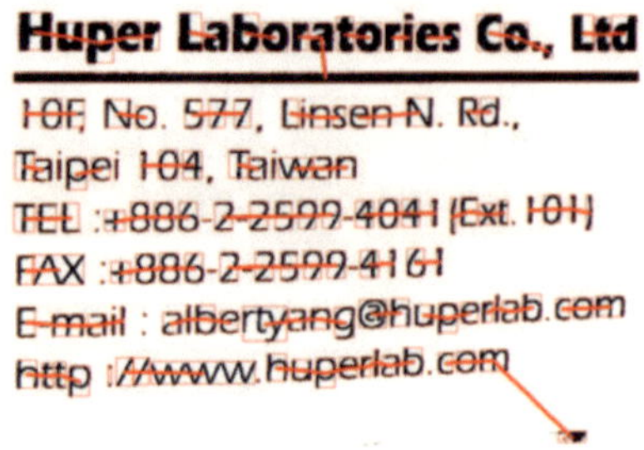


(a)

(b)

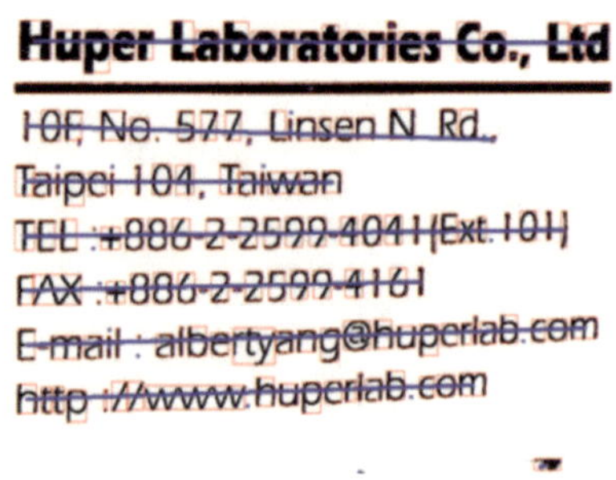


(c)

**Figure 5.** Illustration of the coarse text-line construction in the first stage. (a) Links of the nearest neighbors (b) links of the second nearest neighbor (c) results of performing the text-line construction algorithm.

In the second stage, the extracted text-lines are further refined using typographical structures and the geometry information of CCs in text-lines. Typographical structures [34] have been designed since the era of typewriter and are still preserved in the printed fonts today. Figure 6 illustrates the four lines (called Typo-lines) which bound all printed English characters in three areas. The four lines are named as the *top line*, *upper line*, *baseline*, and *bottom line*. The three areas within the four lines are called the upper, central, and lower zones. The printed alphanumeric characters and punctuation marks locate in particular positions according to the design of typographical structure. For instance, capital letters only appear in the upper zone and central zone. The printed alphanumeric characters and punctuation marks are classified into seven categories, called Typo-classes, according to their locations in the Typo-lines. The seven Typo-classes are listed below:

1. *Full*: the character occupies three zones, such as j, left parenthesis, right parenthesis, and so on.
2. *High*: the character is located in both upper and central zones, such as capital letters, numerals, b, d, and so on.
3. *Short*: the character is only located in the central zone, such as a, c, e, and so on.
4. *Deep*: the character appears in central zone and lower zone. Only the four lowercase letters g, p, q, and y belong to this Typo-class.
5. *Subscript*: the punctuation mark is closer to the baseline, such as comma, period, and so on.
6. *Superscript*: the punctuation is closer to the upper line, such as quotation marks, double quotation marks, and so on.
7. *Unknown*: the class is given when the Typo-class cannot be confirmed due to the lack of certain Typo-lines.

**Figure 6.** Typographical structure

To determine the typographical structure, a Typo-line extraction algorithm which integrates k-means and least mean square error (LMSE) algorithm is proposed. First, the y coordinates of the top edges of all CCs which belong to the same text-line are classified into two clusters using the k-means algorithm. Second, the LMSE algorithm is applied to each cluster to determine the corresponding Typo-lines (top line and upper line). The baseline and bottom line can also be extracted using the same procedure. Figure 7 depicts the extracted text-line in the first stage and the Typo-lines which are obtained in the second stage.

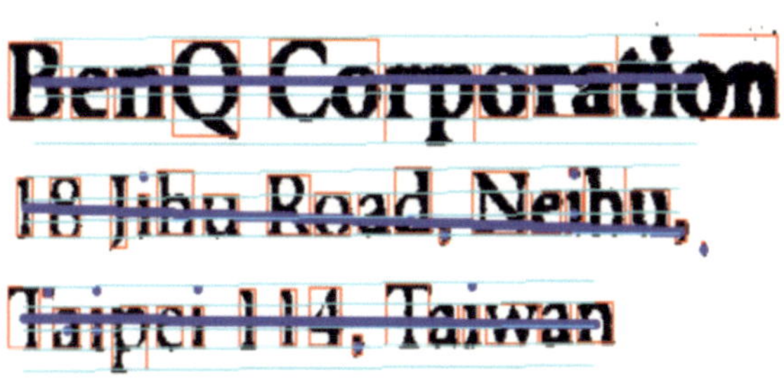


**Figure 7.** Initial text-line and extracted Typo-lines

The LMSE algorithm for finding Typo-lines is described as follows. The line formulation to represent a Typo-line is

$$y = f(x) = a + bx \tag{2}$$

Then the least square error $E$ can be formulated as

$$E = \sum_i \left[ y_i - f(x_i) \right]^2 = \sum_i \left[ y_i - \left( a + bx_i \right) \right]^2 \tag{3}$$

The least square error is minimal when $E$ is zero. The first derivative is applied on $E$:

$$\begin{aligned} \frac{\partial E}{\partial a} &= 2\sum_{i=1}^{n} \left[ y_i - \left( a + bx_i \right) \right] = 0, \\ \frac{\partial E}{\partial b} &= 2\sum_{i=1}^{n} \left[ y_i - \left( a + bx_i \right) \right] x_i = 0 \end{aligned} \tag{4}$$

Equation (4) can be extended as follow:

$$\begin{aligned} \sum_{i=1}^{n} y_i &= \sum_{i=1}^{n} a + \sum_{i=1}^{n} bx_i = a\sum_{i=1}^{n} 1 + b\sum_{i=1}^{n} x_i, \\ \sum_{i=1}^{n} y_i x_i &= \sum_{i=1}^{n} ax_i + \sum_{i=1}^{n} bx_i^2 = a\sum_{i=1}^{n} x_i + b\sum_{i=1}^{n} x_i^2 \end{aligned} \tag{5}$$

Finally, the two unknowns $a$ and $b$ can be solved by

$$\begin{aligned} a &= \frac{\left( \sum_{i=1}^{n} y_i \right)\left( \sum_{i=1}^{n} x_i^2 \right) - \left( \sum_{i=1}^{n} x_i \right)\left( \sum_{i=1}^{n} y_i x_i \right)}{n\left( \sum_{i=1}^{n} x_i^2 \right) - \left( \sum_{i=1}^{n} x_i \right)^2}, \\ b &= \frac{n\left( \sum_{i=1}^{n} y_i x_i \right) - \left( \sum_{i=1}^{n} y_i \right)\left( \sum_{i=1}^{n} x_i \right)}{n\left( \sum_{i=1}^{n} x_i^2 \right) - \left( \sum_{i=1}^{n} x_i \right)^2} \end{aligned} \tag{6}$$

The orientation of texts is refined by taking the mean of the upper line and baseline. However, both the correct text CCs or upside-down text CCs generate a horizontal text-line. To solve this problem, the coarse reading order is also further confirmed in this stage. The confirmation is accomplished by analyzing the Typo-classes of the characters. The characters of *Full* and *Short* types remain the same when the image is rotated 180 degrees, but the *High* and *Deep* types do not. An observation is that all lowercase letters consist of 13 *Short* types, 8 *High* types, 4 *Deep* types and 1 *Full* type. The reading order can be confirmed by a cue that the appearance rates of the *High* and *Deep* type characters are significantly different when the texts are upside-down. Baker and Piper [35] calculated the appearance rates of 100362 lowercase letters in newspapers and novels. The appearance rates of the Typo-classes are listed in Table 1. The reading order is correct if the appearance rate of the *High* type is significantly larger than that of the *Deep* type. Hence, if the documents are captured with a slanted angle, the images can be de-skewed according to the slope of Typo-lines.

| Typo-Class | Appearance rate |
|---|---|
| Full | 0.2 |
| High | 35 |
| Short | 59.1 |
| Deep | 6 |

**Table 1.** Appearance rate of Typo-class

The details of reading order confirmation process is summarized as follows:

1. If the extracted text-line is not horizontal, rotate the image to horizontal according to the orientation of the estimated text-line.
2. Extract Typo-lines and verify whether the number of the High type characters is larger than that of the Deep type characters or not. If the number of the High type characters is greater than that of the Deep type characters, the reading order orientation is correct. Otherwise, rotate the image by 180 degree and inverse the order of text CCs in the text-line.

In the aforementioned text-noise filter, the text CCs may be wrongly classified as noises due to the low quality of images. These mis-classified text CCs are often located around or inside the text-lines (e.g. the dots or commas). Sometimes these missing text CCs result in breaking the text-lines (see Figure 15). To solve this problem, the bounding boxes of all estimated text-lines are slightly extended to seek possible merge. If two text-lines are overlapped after an extension, they are merged into a single text-line. Moreover, if the mis-classified text CCs fall in the bounding box of the text-lines, they are reconsidered as the text CCs and linked to the existed text CCs in the text-lines. The bounding boxes of the text-lines are extended by twice of the average width of characters to recover the mis-classified CCs nearby. By utilizing the characteristics of the typographical structure, the text CCs that are mis-classified as noises by the text-noise filter can be recovered.

### 3.4. Character segmentation

In traditional character segmentation, the ligatures often result from the specific character sequences with the specific font. For example, the character sequences "ti" with the font "Times new roman" are usually considered as the character "d". In terms of the images captured by cameras, the characters are touched severely due to the blurred character boundaries. In this section, a character segmentation mechanism with the ligature filter is introduced. The text CCs are classified as a single character or ligature using the devised filter. The proposed filter consists of two stages. In the first stage, seven intrinsic features of CCs are obtained after using the projection method on text CCs. The vertical/horizontal projection is obtained by calculating the amount of foreground pixels in the vertical/horizontal direction respectively. Denote that the vertical projection and horizontal projection are $P_v$ and $P_h$ respectively. The intrinsic features are described as follows:

- $c_1$: the height-width ratio of the CC.
- $c_2$: the index of the maximum value of $P_v$ with respect to the left boundary of the CC.
- $c_3$: the index of the maximum value of $P_h$ with respect to the upper boundary of the CC.
- $c_4$: maximum value of $P_v$ divided by the height of CC.
- $c_5$: maximum value of $P_h$ divided by the width of CC.
- $c_6$: find the maximum value of $P_v'$ divided by the height of CC where $P_v'$ is the histogram which averages $P_v$ every 5 bins.
- $c_7$: find the maximum value of $P_h'$ divided by the height of CC where $P_h'$ is the histogram which averages $P_h$ every 5 bins.

The feature set C={$c_1$,$c_2$,$c_3$,$c_4$,$c_5$,$c_6$,$c_7$} is trained by two SVMs to classify CCs as a single character or a ligature. The feature set {$c_1$, $c_2$, $c_3$, $c_4$, $c_5$} is used as the input for the first SVM, and {$c_1$, $c_6$, $c_7$} is used for the second one. Some *High* type characters such as "ti" and "fl" are usually misclassified as "d" and "H" respectively. To cope with this problem, if the CC is considered as a single character by the first SVM and the Typo-class of the CC is *High* type as well, the CC is further verified by the second SVM. The positive and negative image samples for SVM training include 7 common types of font (Arial, Arial Narrow, Courier New, Time New Roman, Mingliu, PMingliu, and KaiU) and 4 different font sizes (32, 48, 52, and 72). The positive samples consist of single alphanumerical characters and punctuations. The negative samples are composed of two connected alphanumerical characters. The illustration of negative image samples is shown in Figure 8.

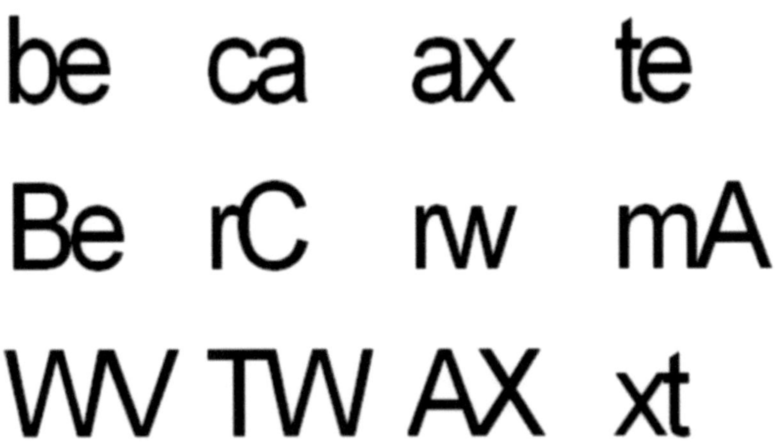


**Figure 8.** Illustration of negative samples of SVM database.

Text CCs which cannot pass both SVM classifiers are considered to be possible ligatures. These CCs will enter the second stage. In the second stage, the periphery features are extracted from the CCs. The periphery features are composed of 32 character contour values $f_i$, where $i$ = 1, 2,..., 32 as shown in Figure 9. In Figure 10, the closer the peripheral feature to the central position, the larger weight it is assigned. $f_i$ is defined as follow:

$$f_i = W_{i \bmod 8} \frac{p_i}{l_i} \tag{7}$$

where the weight $W_{i\bmod 8}$ can be obtained by referring to Figure 10. If $0 < i < 9$ or $16 < i < 25$, $l_i$ is the character width. Otherwise, $l_i$ is the character height. $P_i$ is the distance between the boundary to the contour, i.e. the length of the blue band in Figure 9, where $0 < i < 9$ is the length of the boundary to the left contour, and so on. The 32 periphery features and an additional feature, the height-width ratio of CC, are concatenated to form a feature vector $F$={ $f_1, f_2, \ldots, f_{33}$}.

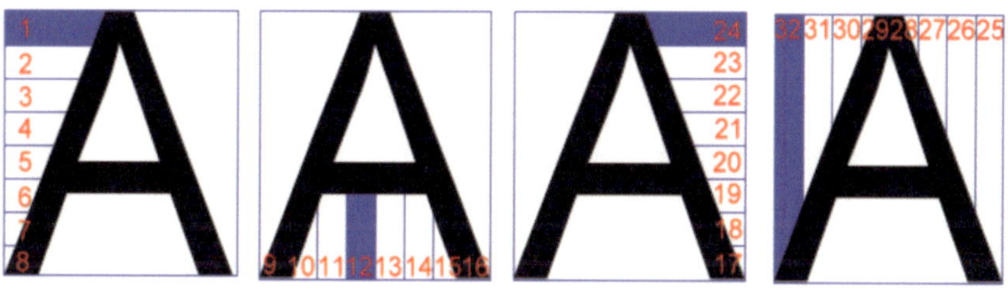

**Figure 9.** Illustration of 32 periphery features

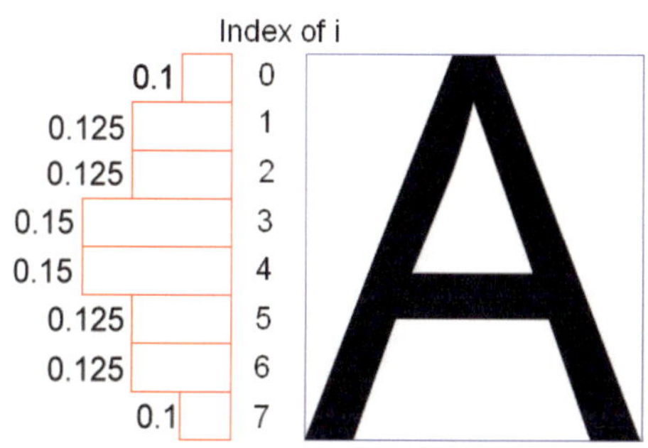


**Figure 10.** Illustration of weights of periphery features

The feature vector $F$ is compared with the feature vector $T$, which is obtained from the templates. Suppose there are $n$ templates need to be compared. For each periphery feature $f_i$, the score $d_{ij}$ is defined as follow:

$$d_{ij} = \begin{cases} 1 \quad if \quad \left|f_i - T_i^j\right| < th_1 \quad \& \quad \left|f_{33} - T_{33}^j\right| < th_3 \\ -1 \quad if \quad \left|f_i - T_i^j\right| > th_2 \quad \& \quad \left|f_{33} - T_{33}^j\right| < th_3, i = 1,\ldots,32 \quad j = 1,\ldots,n \\ 0 \quad otherwise \end{cases} \tag{8}$$

two scores $PV_j$ and $NV_j$ are obtained by

$$PV_j = \sum_{i=1}^{32} d_{ij}, \forall d_{ij} > 0, NV_j = \sum_{i=1}^{32} d_{ij}, \forall d_{ij} < 0, j = 1,\ldots,n \tag{9}$$

Then, the final similarity $PV_{max}$ and $NV_{min}$ are obtained by finding the maximum value of $PV_j$ and the minimum value of $NV_j$ for $j$=1,...,$n$ respectively. If $PV_{max}$ is larger than a threshold and $NV_{min}$ is smaller than another threshold as well, the CC is considered as a single character. Otherwise, the CC is considered as a ligature.

If the CCs are regarded as ligatures by the ligature filter, the CCs will enter to the character segmentation mechanism. The character segmentation mechanism consists of three steps:

1. Search the cut point candidates.
2. Segment ligatures using dynamic programming.
3. Verify the segmentation result.

Three features are utilized in searching possible cut points in a ligature: the vertical projection, the vertical profile, and the gray level vertical projection. Figure 11 (c) shows the vertical projection obtained from the image in Figure 11 (b). The vertical profile, also called the Caliper distance [31], is the distance between the top contour pixel and the bottom contour pixel in each bin. For example, shown in Figure 11 (e) is the vertical profile obtained from the image in Figure 11 (d).

(a) (b) (c) (d) (e)

**Figure 11.** Illustration of vertical projection and vertical profile (a) Original character image, (b) accumulation of pixels in obtaining vertical projection, (c) the vertical projection of (b), (d) accumulation of pixels in vertical profile, and (e) the vertical profile of (d).

Define $G$ as the set of the gray level projection of CC. That is, $G = \{g(0), g(1),...,g(w\text{-}1)\}$ where $w$ is the width of CC. The gray level projection $g(x)$ is formulated as follows:

$$g(x) = \sum_{y=0}^{h} \left| I(x,y) - 255 \right| \tag{10}$$

where $I(x,y)$ is the gray level value at pixel $(x,y)$ and $h$ is the height of the image. Figure 12 illustrates the process in obtaining the gray level projection in a gray level image. Figure 12 (b) depicts the projection result using Eq. (10). Figure 12 (c) is the final result after normalizing the gray level projection $g(x)$.

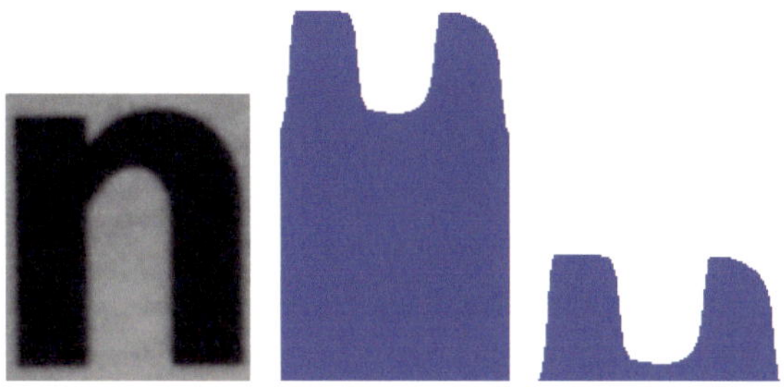

(a) (b) (c)

**Figure 12.** Illustration of gray level projection (a) Original image, (b) the gray level projection, and (c) the normalized gray level projection.

Denote the histograms of the three features mentioned above are *V*. The following equation is used to evaluate the validity of being a cut point at location *x*:

$$p(x) = \frac{V(lp) - 2V(x) + V(rp)}{V(x)+1}, \quad x = 1,\ldots,w \tag{11}$$

where *V(lp)* is the first peak in the left of *x*, *V(rp)* is the first peak in the right of *x*, and *V(x)* is the value of *x*. The larger value of *p(x)*, the higher possibility *x* is a cut point. A selection rule is designed according to the following two criteria. The first criterion is that the number of cut points increases when the width-height ratio of CC increases. Hence, more points with larger values of *p(x)* have a higher tendency to be chosen as cut points. The second criterion is that the cut points near an already selected cut point should be ignored to reduce computation cost due to the restriction of minimum stroke width of a character. Figure 13 depicts the selection of cut point candidates. Given a ligature image shown in Figure 13(a), the cut point between 'n' and 'o' cannot be found by using the vertical projection only (see Figure 13 (f)). However, it can be successfully found by utilizing the vertical profile or Gray level projection as shown in Figure 13 (g) and (f).

If there are *n* cut point candidates, there will be 2^n combinations of selecting cut points, and only one combination of all possibilities segments the ligature image correctly. It is too difficult to find the correct combination without an efficient pruning mechanism. The periphery features of a character image are utilized again as the inputs of SVM to output a confidence value for evaluating the quality of the segmentation result. A combination of the cut points which has the highest confidence value is considered as the final segmentation result. The maximum confidence value can be efficiently computed using Dynamic Programming (DP). Suppose the number of cut point candidates plus the left and right boundary of the ligature image is $n, 0 \le i \le i+k \le j \le n$, where *i, j, k, n, a, b* are integers, and *i, i+k, j* are the indices of cut points. The boundary conditions of DP are described as

$$m(i,j) = \begin{cases} 0, & if \quad i = j \\ Max\{(m(i,i+k) \times a + m(i+k,j) \times b) / (a+b), m(i,j)\}, & if \quad i < j \end{cases} \tag{12}$$

where $m(i, j)$ is the confident value of the image between cut points $i$ and $j$. $a$ and $b$ are the number of segmented characters in the image between $i$ and $i+k$, $i+k$ and $j$, respectively. Figure 14 is an example of explaining the character segmentation procedure. Figure 14 (a) shows the image of a business card. The personal information in the business card is erased to protect personal privacy. Figure 14 (b) is the text-detection result. Each red rectangle in Figure 14 (b) indicates one CC. CCs identified as ligatures are further segmented by the character segmentation process. Take the ligature CC, "Support", as an example (see Figure 14 (c)). In this example, $m(i,j)$ is the confident value ranged from 0 to 4 given by SVM. There are 2 values in each block of the DP table in Figure 14 (d). The upper value is the confident value of the character image between row $i$ and column $j$, whereas the lower value indicates the selected cut point index in the character image between row $i$ and column $j$. If the confident value of the whole image between row $i$ and column $j$ is larger than the average confident value of the image divided into 2 parts between ($i$, $i+k$) and ($i+k$, $j$), then the cut point index will be set to -1. The final segmentation combination of the CC (0, 1) (1, 3) (3, 4) (4, 5) (5, 6) (6, 8) (8, 9) derived by DP is obtained (see the upper left corner of Figure 14 (c)). As shown in Figure 14 (e), the final segmentation result can then be obtained with each blue rectangle indicating one segmented character.

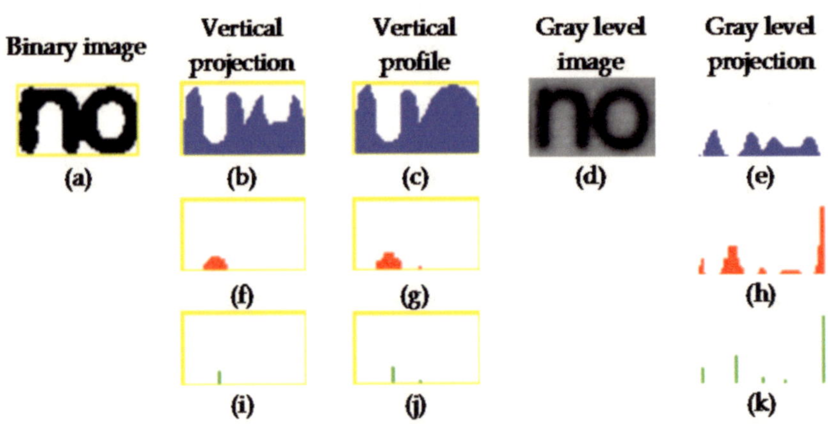


**Figure 13.** Illustration of cut point candidate searching (a) Binary image, (b) vertical projection, (c) vertical profile, (d) gray level image, (e) gray level projection, (f)-(h) results are obtained by performing Eq. (8) on (b)(c)(e), and (i)-(k) results after cut points selection.

In the character segmentation procedure, it is inevitable to encounter the over-segmentation problem. To remedy this, the procedure verifies the segmentation result by merely using the Typo-class information. For example, character 'm' is usually segmented into two parts, recognized as 'r n' or 'n 7', which is unreasonable because the typo class of 'm' is *Short* and the typo classes of 'n 7' are *Short* and *High*. Table 2 tabulates the designed check table for verification with each element representing one unreasonable situation. If a character is segmented into the specific combination as listed in Table 2, the segmentation of the character is ignored to preserve the original character by not performing the segmentation task on it.

**Figure 14.** Example of cut points selection using DP. (a)Origin image, (b)result of text detection and connected component labeling (c)possible cut points in a CC "Support" (d) the corresponding DP table of (c) (e)final character segmentation result.

| Text | Segmentation combination | Type | Text | Segmentation combination | Type |
|---|---|---|---|---|---|
| M | r,n、n,7、n,1 | 3 | C | C,: | 1 |
| N | r,1、r,7 | 3 | c | c,: | 3 |
| W | v,v | 3 | B | I,3 | 1 |
| W | V,V | 1 | D | I,3 | 1 |
| H | I,7、t,1、t,7 | 1 | | | |

**Table 2.** Check table for verifying the segmentation result.

## 4. Experiments

In the experiments, text images captured from fifty business cards by a two- million-pixel webcam with resolution 1600×1200 are collected as testing images. Testing images includes the business cards with simple binary backgrounds and complex color backgrounds. There are 9,550 characters and 419 touched characters (1,050 single characters in the touched characters) for a total of 10,600 characters in the testing images. The experiments demonstrate the visual results of reading order confirmation, ligature filter, and character segmentation.

Figure 15 illustrates the experimental result on the process of correcting the reading order. The image is captured in an incorrect reading order (see Figure 15(a)). Text CCs are extracted using binarization and connected component labeling (see Figure 14(b)). Figure 14(c) shows the result of text-line construction. Texts in the left side of Figure 14(d) show the estimated orientation of text-lines. The major angle is the $\theta_m$ which is described in section 3.3. The right side of Figure 14(d) is the result using the introduced reading order confirmation algorithm.

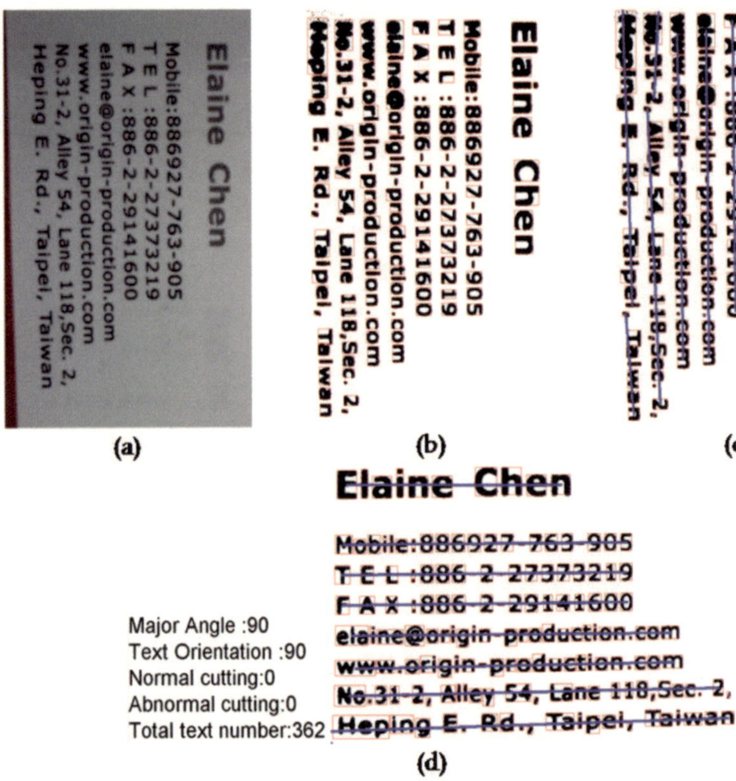


**Figure 15.** Illustration that reading order confirmation. (a) Source image, (b) performing connected component method in binary image (a), (c) connected component linking, (d) reading order estimation, and (e) image rotation result.

In the second experiment, fifty images of business card are considered as testing images for evaluating the accuracy rate of the ligature filter. The accuracy rate is defined as the number of correct filtered CCs divided by number of total CCs. The average accuracy rate of the proposed ligature filter is 92.14%. Figure 16 shows two examples of the results of ligature filter. CCs with numbers above indicate that they are not ligatures.

(a)

(b)

(c)

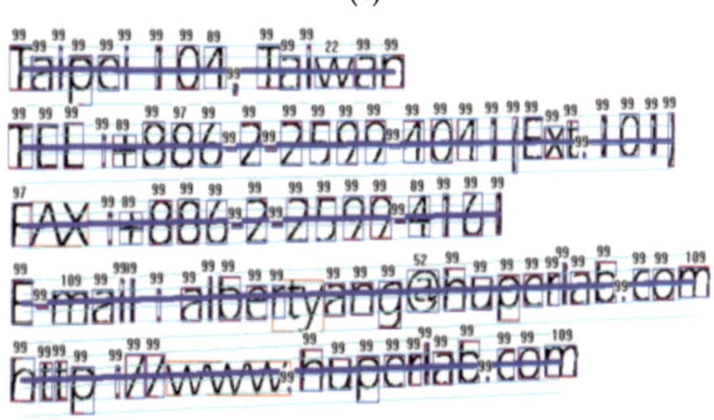

(d)

**Figure 16.** Results of ligature filter (a),(c) cut source image and (b),(d) the corresponding filtering result.

In the third experiment, same 50 images are used for analyzing the performance of the character segmentation procedure. The accuracy rate of character segmentation is defined as the number of correct segmented ligatures divided by the number of all ligatures. In our experiments, the overall accuracy rate of character segmentation is 98.57%. Figure 17 is a worse case of the character segmentation. The uneven illumination and blur result in severe ligatures after text detection module. It is difficult to find good cut points to segment these ligatures precisely.

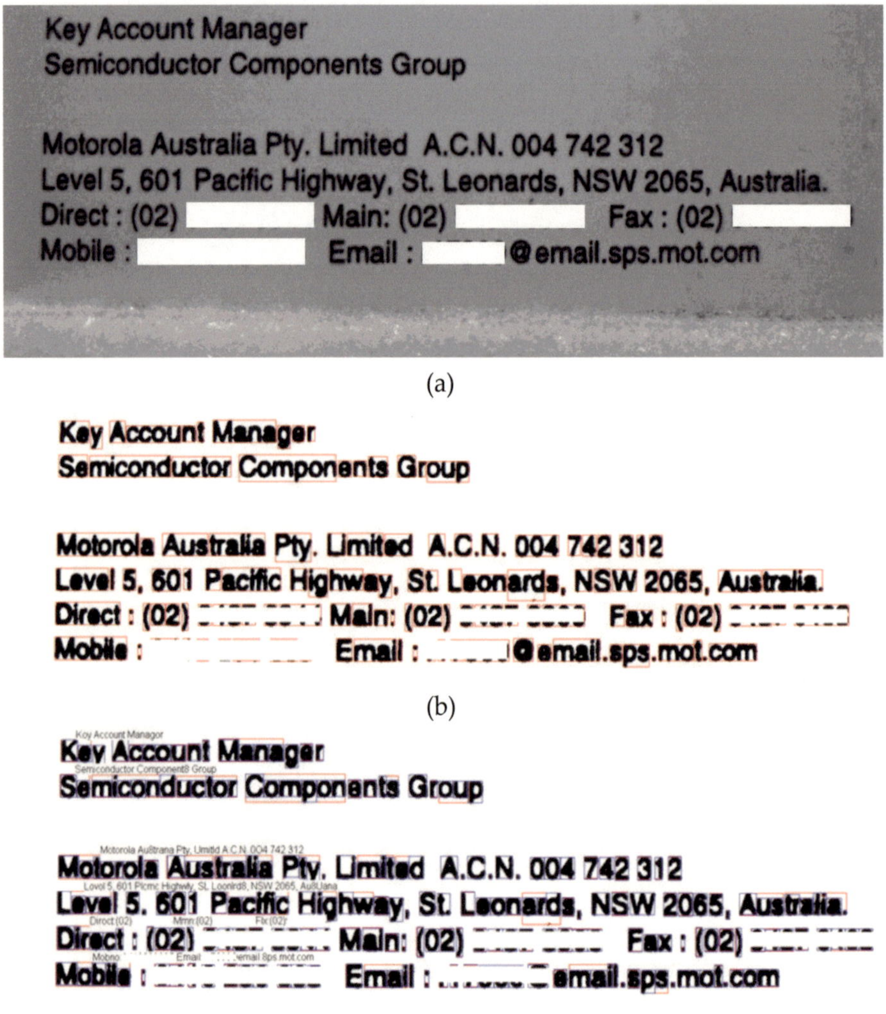


**Figure 17.** Bad result of character segmentation. Uneven illumination and blur appear severely in image. (a) Original image, (b) binarized image, and (c) character segmentation and recognition result.

The character recognition method proposed in [36] is implemented to evaluate the overall performance of the preprocessing system. The recognition rate of characters is 94.90%. Recognizing blurred and ligatures caused by illumination variation and out of focus is challenging. However, the proposed preprocessing system can overcome these difficulties and achieve a high recognition rate.

## 5. Conclusions

A preprocessing system dedicated to text images captured by cameras is introduced in this chapter. The preprocessing plays a crucial role in dominating the success of later character recognition because text images captured by cameras are usually accompanied with severe uneven illuminations. Three modules in the preprocessing system are introduced in detail: A text detection module, a text-line construction module, and a character segmentation module. Experimental results demonstrate the feasibility and validity of each module of the preprocessing system. The characteristics of the preprocessing system are summarized as follows:

1. *A text-noise filter which filters out non-text CCs efficiently.* A two-stage binarization is used for detecting texts in images and sharpening the contour of CCs. Text and non-text CCs are classified by the devised text-noise filter.
2. *Reading order determination by typographical structures.* When text-lines are constructed, the reading order of the text-lines is still unknown because there are two possible reading orientations of a text-line. A reading order confirmation scheme is proposed by analyzing the typographical structures.
3. *A ligature filter with character segmentation mechanism for improving the efficiency of character segmentation.* The intrinsic features and periphery features are used for classifying ligatures and individual characters. The character segmentation mechanism is only used for ligatures so that the efficiency of the character segmentation module can be improved.

Built upon this work, some works can be accomplished in the future:

1. *Detect texts in the complex background.* The proposed text detection method is appropriate for document images but has defects on complex background. To induce color information of text images and clustering method to the text detection module may be a good try because texts in the same text-line usually have similar colors.
2. *Detect and recognize texts on irregular surface.* The introduced modules are effective for recognizing texts on document images. However, texts often locate on non-plane surface such as a cylinder. It will be helpful to recognizing these texts correctly.
3. *Merge broken characters.* Both broken characters and ligatures cannot be recognized well by OCR. The introduced method solves the ligature problem but do not coping with the broken character problem. A preprocessing system is more complete than that of this work by involving some mechanisms to merge broken characters.
4. *Correct Perspective distortion.* Document images without the margin are hard to correct perspective distortion. Other information needs to be considered for performing affine transformation in a distorted document image.

## Author details

Chih-Chang Yu*
*Department of Computer Science and Information Engineering,*
*Vanunug University, Zhongli, Taiwan (R.O.C.)*

* Corresponding Author

Ming-Gang Wen
*Department of Computer Science and Information Engineering,*
*National United University, Miaoli, Taiwan (R.O.C.)*

Kuo-Chin Fan and Hsin-Te Lue
*Department of Computer Science and Information Engineering,*
*National Central University, Zhongli, Taiwan (R.O.C.)*

## Acknowledgement

The authors would like to thank the National Science Council of Taiwan for financially supporting this research under Contract No. 101-2221-E-238-012-.

## 6. References

[1] Chen X, Yang J, Zhang J & Waibel A (2004) Automatic detection and recognition of signs from natural scenes. IEEE Transaction on Image Processing, vol. 13, (January 2004), pp. 87-99, ISSN 1057-7149
[2] Ezaki N, Bulacu M & Schomaker L (2004) Text detection from natural scene images: towards a system for visually impaired persons. Proceedings of the 17th International Conference on Pattern Recognition, vol. 2, pp. 683-686, ISBN 0-7695-2128-2, Cambridge, UK, August, 2004
[3] Lienhart R & Wernicke A (2002) Localizing and segmenting text in images and videos. IEEE Transaction on Circuits System and Video Technology, vol. 12, (April 2002), pp. 256-268, ISSN 1051-8215
[4] Lyu M R; Song J & Cai M. (2005) A comprehensive method for multilingual video text detection, localization, and extraction. IEEE Transaction on Circuits System and Video Technology, vol. 15, (February 2005), pp. 243-255, ISSN 1051-8215
[5] Wu W, Chen X & Yang J (2005) Detection of text on road signs from video. IEEE Transaction on Intelligent Transportation Systems, vol. 6, (Dec. 2005), pp. 378-390, ISSN 1524-9050
[6] Zhong T, Karu K & Jain A K (1995) Locating text in complex color images," Pattern Recognition, vol. 28, (Oct. 1995), pp. 1523-1535 ISSN 0031-3203
[7] Kim K C, Byun H R, Song Y J, Choi Y W, Chi S Y, Kim K K & Chung Y K (2004) Scene text extraction in natural scene images using hierarchical feature combining and verification. Proceedings of the 17th International Conference on Pattern Recognition, vol. 2, pp. 679-682, ISBN 0-7695-2128-2, Cambridge, UK, August, 2004
[8] Kim, K. I.; Jung, K. & H. Kim (2003). Texture-based approach for text detection in images using support vector machines and continuously adaptive mean shift algorithm. IEEE Transaction on Pattern Analysis and Machine Intelligence, vol. 25, (Dec. 2003), pp. 1631-1639, ISSN 0162-8828
[9] Lim, Y. K.; Choi, S. H. & Lee, S. W. (2000). Text extraction in MPEG compressed video for content-based indexing. Proceedings of the 15th International Conference on Pattern Recognition, pp. 409-412, ISBN 0-7695-0750-6, Barcelona, Spain, September 3-7, 2000

[10] Chun, B. T.; Bae, Y. & Kim, T. Y. (1999). Automatic text extraction in digital videos using FFT and neural network. Proceedings of the IEEE International Conference on Fuzzy Systems, vol. 2, pp. 1112-1115, Seoul, South Korea, August 22-25, 1999, ISBN 0-7803-5406-0

[11] Gllavata, J.; Ewerth, R. & Freisleben, B. (2004). Text detection in images based on unsupervised classification of high-frequency wavelet coefficients. Proceedings of the 17th International Conference on Pattern Recognition, vol. 1, pp. 425-428, ISBN 0-7695-2128-2, Cambridge, UK, August, 2004

[12] Thillou, C.; Ferreira, S. & Gosselin B. (2005). An embedded application for degraded text recognition. EURASIP Journal on Advances in Signal Processing, vol. 2005, pp. 2127-2135, August 2005, ISSN 1687-6180

[13] Hu, S. & Chen, M. (2005). Adaptive Fréchet kernel based support vector machine for text detection. Proceedings of IEEE International Conference on Acoustics, Speech and Signal Processing, vol. 5, pp. 365-368, ISBN 0-7803-8874-7, 18-23 March, 2005

[14] Yamguchi T. & Maruyama, M. (2004). Character extraction from natural scene images by hierarchical classifiers. Proceedings of the 17th International Conference on Pattern Recognition, vol. 2, pp. 687-690, ISBN 0-7695-2128-2, Cambridge, UK, August, 2004

[15] Bargeron, D.; Viola, P. & Simard, P. (2005). Boosting-based transductive learning for text detection. Proceedings of the 8th International Conference on Document Analysis and Recognition, vol. 2, pp. 1166-1177, ISBN 0-7695-2420-6, Seoul, Korea, August 29 – September 1, 2005

[16] Jung, K. (2001). Neural network-based text location in color images. Pattern Recognition Letters, vol. 22, Issue 14, (December 2001), pp. 1503-1515, ISSN: 0167-8655

[17] Jung, K.; Kim, K. I. & Jain, A. K. (2004). Text information extraction in images and video: a survey. Pattern Recognition, vol. 37, (May 2004), pp. 977-997, ISSN 0031-3203

[18] Fan, K. C. & Wang, L. S. (1998). Classification of machine-printed and handwritten texts using character block layout variance. Pattern Recognition, vol. 31, (September 1998), pp. 1275-1284, ISSN 0031-3203

[19] Meunier, J. L. (2005). Optimized XY-cut for determining a page reading order. Proceedings of the 8th International Conference on Document Analysis and Recognition, vol. 1, pp. 347- 351., ISBN 0-7695-2420-6, Seoul, Korea, 29 Aug.-1 Sept. 2005

[20] Gatos, B.; Antonacopoulos, A. & Stamatopoulos, N. (2007). Handwriting segmentation contest," Proceedings of the 9th International Conference on Document Analysis and Recognition, pp. 1284-1288, ISBN 978-0-7695-2822-9, Curitiba, Brazil, September 23-26, 2007

[21] Yin, F. & Liu, C. L. (2009). Handwritten Chinese text line segmentation by clustering with distance metric learning. Pattern Recognition, vol. 42, (Dec. 2009), pp. 3146-3157, ISSN 0031-3203

[22] Simon, A.; Pret, J. C. & Johnson, A. P. (1997). A fast algorithm for bottom-up document layout analysis. IEEE Transaction on Pattern Analysis and Machine Intelligence, vol. 19, (March 1997), pp. 273-277, ISSN 0162-8828

[23] Basu, S.; Chaudhuri, C.; Kundu, M.; Nasipuri, M. & Basu, D. K. (2007). Text line extraction from multi-skewed handwritten document. Pattern Recognition, vol. 40, (June 2007), pp. 1825-1839, ISSN 0031-3203

[24] Thillou, C. M.; Ferreira, S.; Demeyer, J.; Minetti, C. & Gosselin, B. (2007). A multifunctional reading assistant for the visually impaired. EURASIP Journal on Image and Video Processing, vol. 3, (November 2007), pp. 1-11, ISSN: 1687-5281

[25] Chen, Y. K. and Wang, J. F. (2000). Segmentation of single- or multiple touching handwritten numeral string using background and foreground analysis. IEEE Transaction on Pattern Analysis and Machine Intelligence, vol. 22, (November 2000), pp. 1304-1317, ISSN 0162-8828
[26] Tse, J.; Curtis, D.; Jones, C. & Yfantis, E. (2007). An OCR-independent character segmentation using shortest-path in grayscale document images. Proceedings of the 6th International Conference on Machine Learning and Applications, pp. 142-147, ISBN 0-7695-3069-9, Cincinnati, USA, December 13-15, 2007.
[27] Liu, C. L.; Sako, H. & Fujisawa, H. (2004). Effects of classifier structures and training regimes on integrated segmentation and recognition of handwritten numeral strings. IEEE Transaction on Pattern Analysis and Machine Intelligence, vol. 26, (November 2004), pp. 1395-1407, ISSN 0162-8828
[28] Casey R. G. & Lecolinet, E. (1996). A survey of methods and strategies in character segmentation. IEEE Transaction on Pattern Analysis and Machine Intelligence, vol. 18, ( July 1996), pp. 690-706, ISSN 0162-8828
[29] Vellasques, E.; Oliveira, L. S.; Britto, A. S.; Koerich, A. L. & Sabourin, R. (2008). Filtering segmentation cuts for digit string recognition. Pattern Recognition, vol. 41, (October 2008), pp. 3044-3053, ISSN 0031-3203
[30] Marinai, S.; Gori, M. & Soda, G. (2005). Artificial neural networks for document analysis and recognition. IEEE Transaction on Pattern Analysis and Machine Intelligence, vol. 27, (January 2005), pp. 23-35, ISSN 0162-8828
[31] Thillou, C. M.; Mancas, M. & Gosselin, B. (2005). Camera-based degraded character segmentation into individual components. Proceedings of the 8th International Conference on Document Analysis and Recognition, vol. 2, pp. 755-759, ISBN 0-7695-2420-6, Seoul, Korea, 29 August-1 September, 2005.
[32] Otsu, N. (1979). A threshold selection method from gray level histograms. IEEE Transactions on Systems, Man, and Cybernetics, vol. 9, (January 1979), pp. 62-66, ISSN 0018-9472
[33] Kim, K. I.; Jung, K.; Park, S. H. & Kim, H. J. (2002). Support vector machines for texture classification. IEEE Transaction on Pattern Analysis and Machine Intelligence, vol. 24, (November 2002), pp. 1542-1550, ISSN 0162-8828
[34] Zramdini, A. & Ingold, R. (1998). Optical font recognition using typographical features. IEEE Transaction on Pattern Analysis and Machine Intelligence, vol. 20, (August 1998), pp. 877-882, ISSN 0162-8828
[35] Beker H. & Piper, F. (1983). Cipher systems: The protection of communication, John Wiley & Sons, ISBN 978-0471891925
[36] Chang, F.; Chou, C. H.; Lin, C. C. & Chen, C. J. (2004). A prototype classification method and its application to handwritten character recognition. Proceedings of IEEE International Conference on Systems, Man and Cybernetics, vol. 5, pp. 4738-4743, ISBN: 0-7803-8566-7, The Hague, Netherlands, October 10-13, 2004.

Chapter 6

# Character Recognition from Virtual Scenes and Vehicle License Plates Using Genetic Algorithms and Neural Networks

Stephen Karungaru, Kenji Terada and Minoru Fukumi

Additional information is available at the end of the chapter

http://dx.doi.org/10.5772/51473

## 1. Introduction

Character recognition remains one of the vital research areas mainly because its application to human-machine and machine-machine communication. One example application that needs this technology is vehicle number plate recognition. With millions of vehicles on the roads today, human resources alone are insufficient in recognizing, tracking or controlling their movements. Another area in character recognition is in virtual scenes. In such scenes, the characters are written in the air by hand and captured using a cheap USB camera placed in front of a subject. Such characters are termed "Air Characters" in this work.

In this chapter, we present a character recognition method for virtual scenes (air characters) and vehicle number plate recognition using neural networks and evolutionary computation. We combine neural networks learning, image processing and template matching to create a novel character recognition system. To speed up the system and deal with size and orientation issues, we employ a genetic algorithm. Furthermore, to control the size of both the neural network inputs and the template, we also apply a genetic algorithm to guide the search.

Fortunately, many useful technologies in automatic detection and recognition have already been proposed to recognize characters. In vehicle license plate detection and recognition research is widely carried out by many researchers in many countries because of the many applications that benefit from it ranging from traffic control, crime prevention, automatic parking authentication systems, etc. Recognition of air characters will open new areas in human-machine interfaces especially in replacing the TV remote control devices and enabling non-verbal communication. Three steps are necessary in such systems. That is, the size and orientation invariant segmentation of the characters, normalization of other factors like brightness, contrast, illumination, etc. and the recognition of the characters themselves.

In [1] we proposed a robust license plate recognition method which recognized characters using a combination of neural networks, template matching and genetic algorithms. In this work, we improve the system by the introduction of the the bilateral filter for noise reduction,the variable threshold method for better image binalization and linear regression to extract more shape features that creates a better feature vector.

Today there are many OCR devices in use based on a plethora of different algorithms [21]. Examples include a wavelet transform based method for extracting license plates from cluttered images achieving a 92.4% accuracy [2] and a morphology-based method for detecting license plates from cluttered images with a detection accuracy of 98% [3] . Hough transform combined with other preprocessing methods is used by [4, 5]. In [6] an efficient object detection method is proposed. More recently, license plate recognition from low-quality videos using morphological and Adaboost algorithm was proposed by [7]. It uses the haar like features proposed by [8] for face detection. Furthermore, in our earlier work [9], we proposed a license plate detection algorithm using genetic algorithms. All of the popular algorithms sport high accuracy and most high speed, but still many suffer from a fairly simple flaw: mis-recognition that is often very unnatural to the human point of view. That is, mistaking a "5" for an "S", or a "B" for a "8",etc.

In this work, we extend and largely improve the work in [1] to also recognize the characters using more features and a hybrid system consisting of neural networks and template matching. The genetic algorithm used in [1] has been re-designed to improve its detection accuracy. We extract bifurcation, end and corner points from candidate characters and used a hybrid system made of neural networks, template matching and genetic algorithms to solve such mis-recognition problems. We also test this method using air characters that prove that the method is effective for different types of characters. However, the results are affected by character segmentation whose results are not perfect yet.

The effectiveness of various types of neural networks to solve a variety of problems has recently been shown in [10] for partially connected neural networks (PCNN), [11] for recurrent neural networks (RNN) and [12] for perceptron neural networks. This adds confidence to the use of neural network in learning problems. Character recognition using neural networks to determine a threshold is proposed by [13]. However, since character shearing is not handled exhaustively, the accuracy is not high enough. As stated, although a lot of work has been done in this area, as far as we can tell, our proposed use of genetic algorithms and artificial templates has not been used anywhere else.

## 2. Database

### 2.1. License plates

This work uses license plates images of vehicles that were taken near a parking lot with the target vehicle coming towards the camera and then turning towards the right or left[1].

The license plates are divided into several categories based on colors and arrangement of the characters on the plates. In private vehicles, the plates have a black background and white characters, for taxis it is the exact opposite, white backgrounds with black characters and a variety of other kinds based on special regions, etc. Moreover, there are single and double row plates. The characters on the plates are all alphanumeric (All upper-case). However, the alphabets $I, O$ and $Z$ are not used in the license plates.

In the database used in our experiments, there are 6444 images of 46 cars each captured in a different number of frames. Each of the images is 320*240 pixels. In some of the images, there are no vehicles and hence no license plates to detect. Although, there are single and double row license plates, the background color of plates is either black or white. Moreover, the number of characters in the plates may also differ. Therefore, the length of the license plates is also different. A sample of these plates is shown in Fig. 1.

The details of the extraction, from the database, of the license plates locations and the character segmentation methods adapted in this work can be found in [1].

**Figure 1.** Example of plates in the Database

## 2.2. Air characters

The database for the air characters is created using images captured in our laboratory. An USB camera is placed on top of a computer display in front of a subject. In this experiment, the subject is asked to use the right hand's pointing finger to write characters in the air in front of the camera. Preprocessing steps required include the detection of the face region to make sure that it does not interfere with the character segmentation because both region are characterised by similar skin color. The tip of the finger is extracted and then tracked to trace the character. The process is as follow:

- An open palm in front of the camera indicates the home position. This is important to disable the unnecessary detections at the beginning.
- Extract the face region to make sure the skin pixels inside it don't interfere with the tracking.
- If only the pointing finger is visible, start tracing the movement.
- To end a character, pause for about 1 second.

The detection of the face can be accomplished using several methods. In this work, we use the method that uses neural networks and genetic algorithms proposed in [20].

The segmentation of the palm region uses colour, based on the HSV colour space and dynamic thresholds. Colour based extraction is chosen because it is fast to process and invariant to rotation. The conversion from the RGB color space to the HSV color space can be performed using the following expressions.

$$H = arcos \frac{\frac{1}{2}((R-G)+(R-B))}{\sqrt{(R-G)^2+(R-B)+(G-B)}} \tag{1}$$

$$S = 1 - 3\frac{min(R,G,B)}{R+B+G} \tag{2}$$

$$V = \frac{1}{3}(R+B+G) \tag{3}$$

An example air character capture scene is shown in Fig. 2.

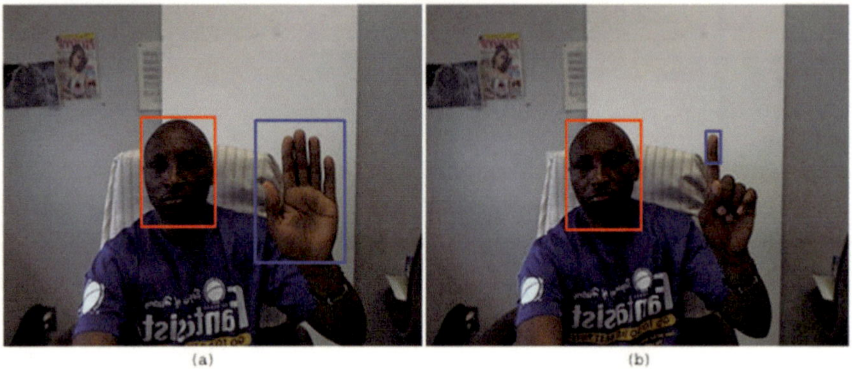

**Figure 2.** Air character capture scene. (a) Home position (b)Start tracing position

## 3. Character region segmentation

Candidate character regions should be extracted from target images to improve the search accuracy and speed up the process. Raster scanning images for a character is both slow and inefficient. Therefore, a character segmentation method is vital.

Character segmentation is a process in which the areas that are likely to contain characters (search candidates) are extracted from the image. Thereafter, character recognition methods are applied only inside the segmented candidate regions, hence, speeding up the search. However, character segmentation is not such a trivial problem. Although it is assumed that only one character will be included in each segmented area, this is not usually the case. Any method assuming one character per region will thus fail because such recognition methods (for example, template matching) rely on the number of characters and the size of the extracted region to set their parameters. Therefore character segmentation must be accurate otherwise the results of recognition will be adversely affected.

### 3.1. Noise reduction

Once the character candidate regions have been determined, noise reduction is carried out before image binalization by smoothing the region using the bilateral filter. Smoothing reduces the noise and average brightness of an image. The bilateral filter is defined by eq.4.

$$f(i,j) = \frac{\sum_{n=-\omega}^{\omega}\sum_{m=-\omega}^{\omega} f(i+m,j+n)\cdot exp(-\frac{m^2+n^2}{2\sigma_1^2})exp(-\frac{(f(i,j)-f(i+m,j+n))^2}{2\sigma_2^2})}{\sum_{n=-\omega}^{\omega}\sum_{m=-\omega}^{\omega} exp(-\frac{m^2+n^2}{2\sigma_1^2})exp(-\frac{(f(i,j)-f(i+m,j+n))^2}{2\sigma_2^2})} \tag{4}$$

where:

$\sigma_1$,$\sigma_2$ are the geometric spreads chosen based on the desired amount of low-pass filtering required.

However, with the bilateral filter, we must decide the optimal window size during smoothing. The best results were obtained with filter window sizes of 5*5 and 7*7. In addition, the value of parameters $\sigma_1$ and $\sigma_2$ is set to 5.

## 3.2. Image binalization

The most basic image binalization technique is the selection of a single threshold value for the whole image. All the grey levels below this value are classified as black, and those above white. However, it is almost impractical to clearly segment an image into objects and background with a single threshold value because of noise and illumination effects.

Therefore, in this work, to binalize the image, the Variable Threshold Method (VTM) is used. It sets a domain in an image and uses the average of the brightness in the domain to set a two level threshold. The processing windows are set in the image beginning at the top left corner of the image. Inside a window, the extraction thresholds are automatically set using average region brightness. However, it is not easy to decide the optimal size of the window for best extraction accuracy and short processing time. Therefore, we experimented using several window sizes between 5 and 20.

To improve the performance of the conventional VTM method, we employ the Discriminant Analysis (DA) method to automatically determine the threshold in the windows. The DA method classifies data into two classes solving for eigenvectors which maximize between-class variance and minimizes the within-class variance. The algorithm proceeds as follows:

For a given image, where $\omega_i$, $M_i$, $\sigma_i^2$ and $M_T$ represents the total number of pixels in class, class average brightness, class variance and overall average brightness respectively, the within-class variance ($\sigma_W^2$) is given by:

$$\sigma_W^2 = \frac{\omega_1\sigma_1^2 + \omega_2\sigma_2^2}{\omega_1 + \omega_2} \tag{5}$$

and the between-class variance ($\sigma_B^2$) can be calculated using:

$$\sigma_B^2 = \frac{\omega_1\omega_2(M_1 - M_2)^2}{(\omega_1 + \omega_2)^2} \tag{6}$$

The total variance is given by:

$$\sigma_T^2 = \sigma_W^2 + \sigma_B^2 \tag{7}$$

The threshold can be determined by maximizing $\sigma_B^2$ in the following equation.

$$\frac{\sigma_B^2}{\sigma_W^2} = \frac{\sigma_B^2}{\sigma_T^2 - \sigma_B^2} \tag{8}$$

After image binalization, labeling is carried out to extract the blobs. We expect one blob per segment. Therefore, we select the largest blob as the candidate and delete the others as noise. The major advantage of noise deletion is the reduction in the number of the blobs. This improves the systems speed by eliminating unnecessary computation. The results of this process are shown in Fig. 3.

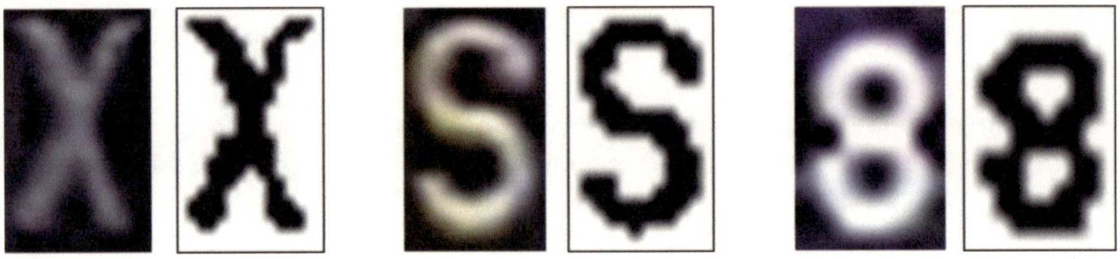

**Figure 3.** Binalization using the VTM and DA methods.

## 4. Feature extraction

Two types of features are used to recognize the characters, brightness and shape. Brightness features can be captured from the image data directly. For shape features, after image thinning, linear regression is used to extract straight lines and circular regions common in several characters and numbers.

### 4.1. Image thinning

A image skeleton is useful because it represents the shape of the object in a relatively small number of pixels [16]. This reduction of information speeds up the other analysis or recognition processes performed after. Thinning is an iterative technique, which extracts the skeleton of an object as a result. In every iteration, the edge pixels having more than one adjacent background pixels are eroded if their removal does not change the topology of the character.

We employ a skeletonization method called the Zhang-Suen Thinning Algorithm [17] because it is fast and easy to process. This skeletonization algorithm is a parallel method that obtains a new value depending only on the previous iteration's value. The algorithm can be implemented using two iterations. In the first iteration, a pixel is deleted (in order) if

- it has at lease two and at most six neighbours
- left, top and bottom neighbours exist
- right, top and bottom neighbours exist

The second iteration phase is similar to the first except the order of the last two processes is reversed. The algorithm terminates if no more pixels can be deleted after the two iterations. Figure 4 shows some example results achieved using the Zhang-Suen Thinning Algorithm.

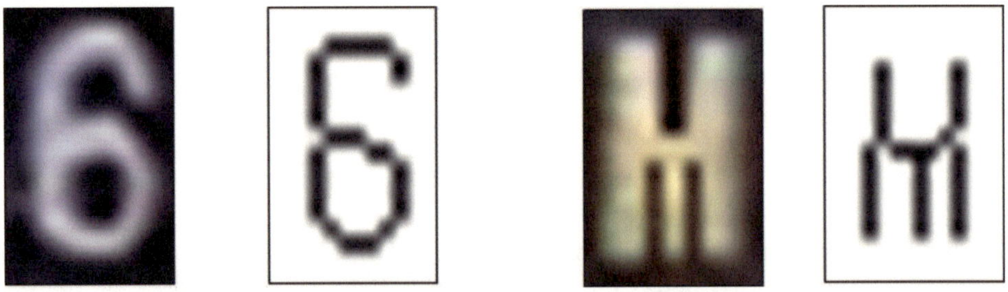

**Figure 4.** Thinning results using the Zhang-Suen Thinning Algorithm.

However, the results were not perfect for all characters. A closer observation of the "M" in Fig. 4 shows that some areas still have more than one pixel width. A pruning algorithm is therefore necessary to remove such noise. The results of pruning are shown in Fig.5.

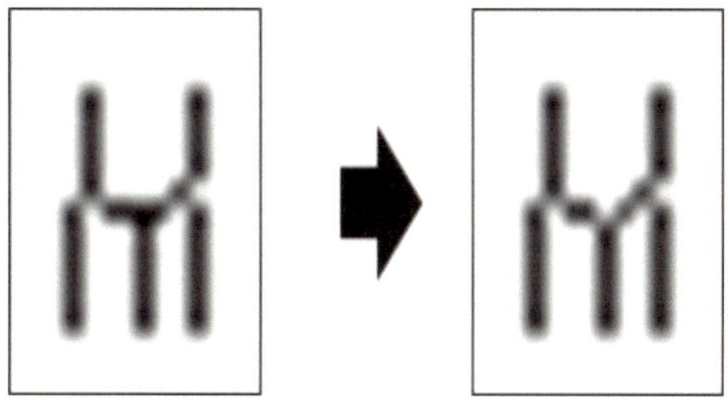

**Figure 5.** Noise pruning results.

### 4.2. Bifurcation and end points extraction

To define the shapes of the characters, it is important to extract the bifurcation and end-points from the results of the thinning operation. We define a bifurcation point as one with three neighbors and an endpoint as one with only one neighbor. In this work, we deal with license plate characters which are printed and hand written virtual characters. Table 1 shows the number of bifurcation and end-points for each character extracted manually by visual observation.

Extraction of the bifurcation and end points from virtual characters produces similar results to those shown in table 1 because they are based on our intuition about how characters should look like.

However, printed characters like the ones on license plates produce different rather surprising results. For such characters, the binalization and thinning results are somewhat different. For example Fig.6 shows the thinning results of the character "V" extracted from a license plate.

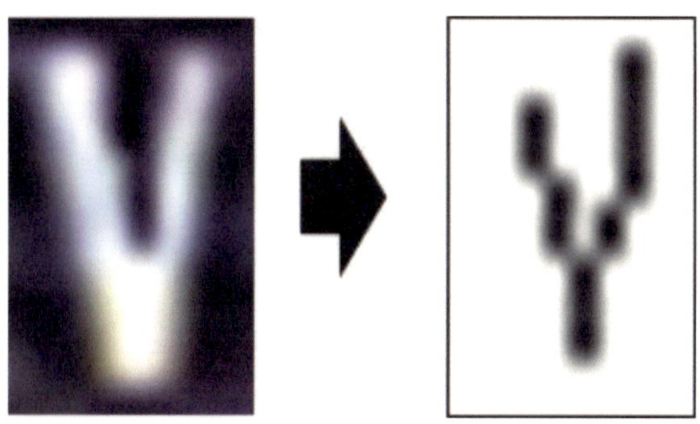

**Figure 6.** Noise pruning results.

Whereas the manual extraction gives no bifurcation points and 2 end points, the results of automatic extraction are 1 bifurcation point and 3 end points. In fact, "V" and "Y" have the same number of bifurcation and end points. Therefore, there are significant differences in the number of bifurcation and end points for the virtual and printed characters. In

| Chara-cter | Bifur points | End pts | Char-cter | Bifur pts | End pts | Char-cter | Bifur pts | End pts |
|---|---|---|---|---|---|---|---|---|
| 0 | 0 | 0 | C | 0 | 2 | O | 0 | 0 |
| 1 | 0 | 2 | D | 0 | 0 | P | 1 | 1 |
| 2 | 0 | 2 | E | 1 | 3 | Q | 1 | 2(1) |
| 3 | 0 | 2 | F | 1 | 3 | R | 1(2) | 2 |
| 4 | 1(2) | 2 | G | 1(0) | 3(2) | S | 0 | 2 |
| 5 | 0 | 2 | H | 2 | 4 | T | 1 | 3 |
| 6 | 1 | 1 | I | 0 | 2 | U | 0 | 2 |
| 7 | 0 | 2 | J | 1(0) | 3(2) | V | 0(1) | 2(3) |
| 8 | 1(2) | 0 | K | 1(3) | 4 | W | 0(3) | 2(5) |
| 9 | 1 | 1 | L | 0 | 2 | X | 1(2) | 4 |
| A | 2 | 2 | M | 0(5) | 2(3) | Y | 1 | 3 |
| B | 1(2) | 0 | N | 0(2) | 2(4) | Z | 0 | 2 |

**Table 1.** Manual bifurcation and end-points extraction.

table 1, the values in the brackets show extracted points for the character when the value was different for the virtual and printed extractions. As shown in the table, characters "4","8","B","G","J","K","M","N","Q","R","V","W" and "Y" are affected.

Figure 7 shows a set of bifurcation and end points extracted from license plate characters.

### 4.3. Corner points extraction

Bifurcation and end points provide information about the general shape of the characters and can help divide the character in segments for further processing. These segments are assumed to contain either straight lines or curves. However, to help differentiate characters like "S" and "5" or "2" and "Z" which have two end points each and no bifurcation points, or "B" and "8" with two bifurcation points and no end points, it is important to extract the corner points. Corner points help further classify segments with both straight and curved sections.

### 4.4. Shape features extraction

To extract the shape features, the bifurcation and end points are used. We check for straight lines and circles between a combination of the points.

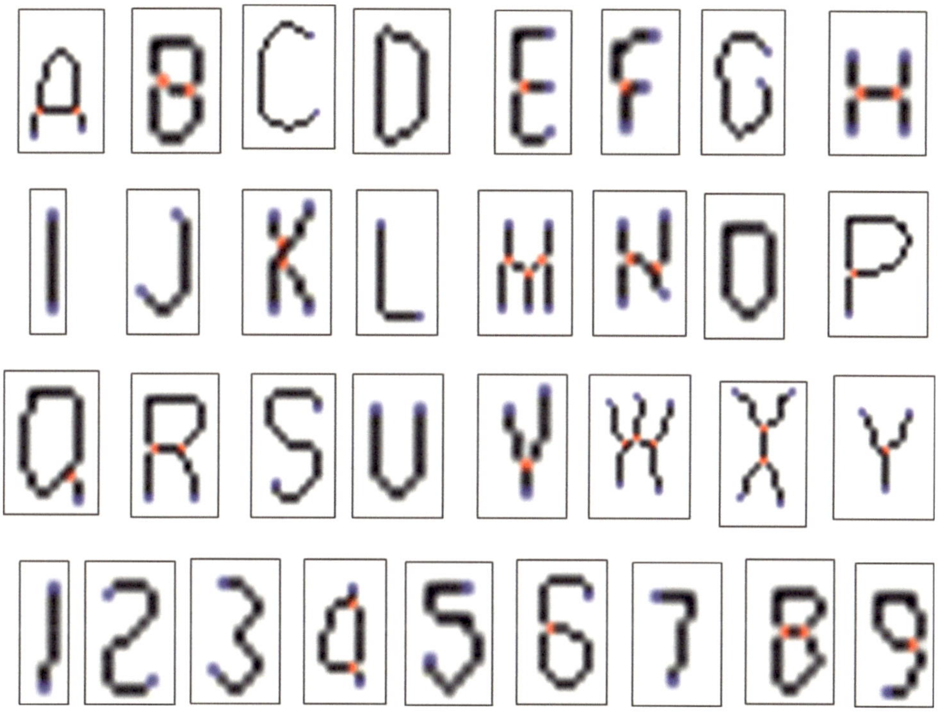

**Figure 7.** Bifurcation (red) and end (blue) points extracted from license plate characters.
3

*4.4.1. Number of segments and length*

Based on the number of bifurcation and end points, we can determine the number of segments making up the character. Each segment is created between bifurcation points, end points or a combination of both types of points. Moreover, each segment length in pixels can then be calculated. This length is then normalized by dividing it by the height of the character. The normalization should offer some size invariance during training and testing.

*4.4.2. Lines: Linear regression*

There is need to determine which of the segments are lines and which are circles. Initially, we should assume that the segment is a line and use a line extractor to find it. Hough transform [18] is a widely used line extractor. However, in this work, we cannot use it because we need to determine how well the extracted line fits the data. Therefore, we use linear regression to fit the line because we can calculate an error that tells us how well the lines fit.

Linear regression [19] is the least squares estimator of a linear regression model with a single explanatory variable. It fits a straight line through the set of points by minimizing the vertical distances between the points of the data set and the fitted line. The fitted line has the slope equal to the correlation between y and x corrected by the ratio of standard deviations of these variables.

After fitting a segment, we set a threshold for the error to decide if the segment is a line or should be passed to the curves(circle) extractor.

*4.4.3. Curves*

Most characters contain some form of circle like curve. Therefore, we can process for circularity as a character feature. This value is calculated between 0 to 1. As circularity approaches 1, a near perfect circle is extracted. It can be calculated using Eq. 9. Area and circumference are used.

$$\frac{4S\pi}{L^2} \tag{9}$$

Where $S$ is the enclosed area and $L$ is the circumference.

The area and circumference can be easily calculated from the segment information.

## 5. Character recognition

In this work, we chose Neural Networks (NN) as the main classifiers because of their proven effectiveness to learn multi-dimensional and non-linear data [10–12]. There are 26 alphabets and 10 numerals that must be recognized.

### 5.1. Neural network

Although neural networks can learn from large non-linear data, the processes requires thousands of training examples and huge computation time. Therefore, to effectively use neural networks in real time, their structure should be simple and the number of classes to be learned should be minimized. In this work, instead of creating one neural network to learn the 36 characters, we use "divide and conquer" method to train highly specialized compact forms.

The subdivisions are based the following features:

- Number of bifurcation points
- Number of end points
- Number of segments
- Number of straight segments
- Straight Line angles
- Number of curved segments
- Circularity (0 to 1 value) of each curved segment
- Length of segment

Table 2 shows a list of all the features extracted from the characters.

Using this information, we can divide the characters into seven neural networks as shown in Table 3.

The neural networks are selected to be 3 layered trained using the back propagation algorithm [14]. The size of the training sample is 15x20pixels. There are also nodes to represent the presence of lines(1), angles(3), circles(1) and their numbers(2). Therefore, the number of units in the input layer is 307.

The system is trained to produce an output of 0.95 for the node representing the character or numeral being learned and 0.05 for all the other output nodes. To further reduce the size of these neural networks, improving the training and test speeds, structural learning with knowledge [15] is used to supplement the error back propagation method.

| Chara-cter | Bifur points | End points | Corner points | Straight Lines | Angles | Curves |
|---|---|---|---|---|---|---|
| 0 | 0 | 0 | 0 | 0 | 0 | 1 |
| D | 0 | 0 | 0 | 2 | 0 | 2 |
| 0 | 0 | 0 | 0 | 0 | 0 | 1 |
| 1 | 0 | 2 | 2 | 1 | 0 | 0 |
| 2 | 0 | 2 | 3 | 3 | 0 | 1 |
| 3 | 0 | 2 | 2 | 0 | 0 | 1 |
| 5 | 0 | 2 | 3 | 3 | 0 | 1 |
| 7 | 0 | 2 | 1 | 2 | 1 | 0 |
| C | 0 | 2 | 0 | 1 | 0 | 2 |
| G | 0 | 2 | 0 | 0 | 0 | 1 |
| I | 0 | 2 | 2 | 1 | 0 | 0 |
| J | 0 | 2 | 0 | 1 | 0 | 1 |
| L | 0 | 2 | 1 | 2 | 0 | 0 |
| S | 0 | 2 | 2 | 4 | 0 | 2 |
| U | 0 | 2 | 0 | 0 | 0 | 1 |
| Z | 0 | 2 | 0 | 3 | 1 | 0 |
| 6 | 1 | 1 | 1 | 2 | 0 | 1 |
| 9 | 1 | 1 | 1 | 2 | 0 | 2 |
| E | 1 | 3 | 2 | 5 | 0 | 0 |
| F | 1 | 3 | 1 | 4 | 0 | 0 |
| P | 1 | 1 | 1 | 3 | 0 | 1 |
| Q | 1 | 1 | 1 | 2 | 0 | 1 |
| T | 1 | 3 | 0 | 2 | 0 | 0 |
| V | 1 | 3 | 0 | 3 | 2 | 0 |
| Y | 1 | 3 | 0 | 3 | 2 | 0 |
| 4 | 2 | 2 | 1 | 4 | 0 | 1 |
| 8 | 2 | 0 | 0 | 0 | 0 | 2 |
| A | 2 | 2 | 0 | 2 | 2 | 1 |
| B | 2 | 0 | 2 | 2 | 0 | 2 |
| H | 2 | 5 | 0 | 5 | 0 | 0 |
| K | 2 | 4 | 0 | 4 | 2 | 0 |
| N | 2 | 4 | 0 | 5 | 2 | 0 |
| R | 2 | 2 | 1 | 5 | 1 | 1 |
| X | 2 | 5 | 0 | 5 | 4 | 0 |
| M | 3 | 5 | 0 | 7 | 2 | 0 |
| W | 3 | 5 | 0 | 7 | 2 | 0 |

**Table 2.** All extracted character features.

# 6. Genetic algorithm

The neural network training and the character template creation data is extracted using a genetic algorithm for better normalization. The genetic algorithms can extract character

| | Features | Characters in Group |
|---|---|---|
| 1 | No Bifurcation or End points | 0, D, O |
| 2 | Angled lines (3 or less) | 7, Z, V, Y, A |
| 3 | Angled lines (3 or more) | 4, K, N, X, M, W |
| 4 | More than 3 straight lines(no angles) | E, F, H, T |
| 5 | Curves and Straight Lines | 2, 5, J, R, Q, P, B |
| 6 | Curves Only | 3, C, U, 6, 9, 8, S |
| 7 | Straight lines only | 1, I, L |

**Table 3.** All extracted character features.

regions invariant to size and orientation. The two characteristics are vital especially in neural network training.

Based on the selected character region size, the largest parameter that must be coded is 20. Therefore, 5 bits are used to code each parameter and the orientation angle. This information is used to determine the length of the genetic algorithm chromosome. The genetic algorithm determines the position, size and shearing angle of each sample. Moreover, the scaling rates and the translation values each require 5 bits. Therefore, the genetic algorithm chromosome length is 36. This genetic algorithm is binary coded to allow for bit manipulation during training.

The GA chromosome is designed as follows;

1. The position of the sample is represented by $l_x$ and $l_y$.
2. Translation in the $x$ and $y$ directions by $t_x$ and $t_y$ respectively.
3. Rotation angle by $ang$. The angle changes are from $-20 \leq ang \leq 20$
4. The scaling rate by $scl$. Scale of 1 is 20 pixels. The maximum allowed expansion is up 32 pixels (This is the maximum number we can represent using binary code).

The character segmentation genetic algorithm's chromosome is shown in Fig.8.

The fitness of the GA is based on the color of the characters. During reproduction, we save the elite solution, and then use the top 40% of the fittest individuals to reproduce 80% of the next population. The remaining 20% of the next population is reproduced by selection of one of the parents from the top 40% group and the other from the remainder of the population. This method improves the search space by ensuring that we not only retain the best individuals for reproduction but also explore the rest of the population for other possible candidates. The matching process is terminated after 50 generation and the elite solution is the character for training the neural network or creation of the template.

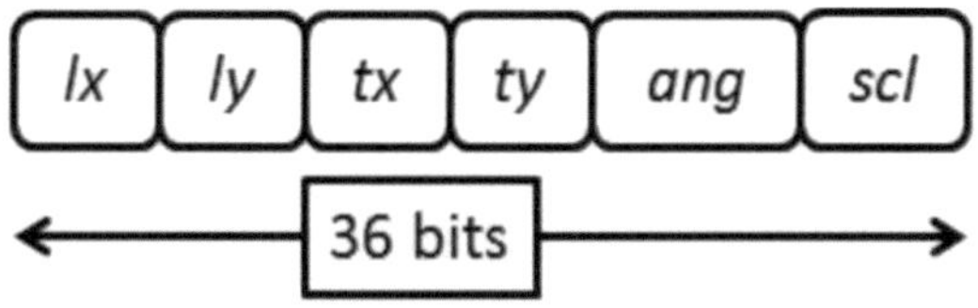


**Figure 8.** Character segmentation GA's structure.

## 7. Template matching

Although template matching is computationally expensive especially for large images, it is used in this work as a preprocessing step to help divide the characters into different higher classes. To reduce the computational cost, we have selected a relatively small character region.

The templates used in this work for each of the characters are constructed from the same data used to train the neural network. Therefore the initial size of the template is 15*20 pixels. Each template is the average of 10 images selected at random from the minimum 20 images extracted for neural network training. Note that the height and the width of the template are fixed.

## 8. Experiments

This work uses license plates images of vehicles that were taken near a parking lot with the target vehicle coming towards the camera and then turning towards the right or left[1] for license plate character recognition and air characters captured in our laboratory as explained in sec. 2.2. We use 3 subjects each writing the characters a total of 4 times.

However, the characters "I", "O","T" and "Z" are missing in the license plate database.

This work is carried out using a computer with the following specifications. The processor is Intel core 7 CPU, operation at 3.47GHz and an installed memory of 4GB.

### 8.1. Procedure

The overall system procedure is as follows.

#### *8.1.1. Training*

1. Train the neural networks separately, for the licence plates and air characters
2. For the license plate, there are about 10 examples per character
3. For the air characters, use 3 characters from each subject, total 9 examples each.

#### *8.1.2. Testing*

1. Extract the character features and use them to decide the neural network to learn.
2. Use template matching to make an initial guess.
3. Run the neural network to confirm the results from step 2.
4. If results of steps 2 and 3 are same, end.
5. Otherwise use the results of the neural network as the final result.

## 9. Results

There are two experiments in this work. License plate and air character recognition. The experiments are still ongoing but we can report that we achieved better results than those in [1], in license plate recognition. The air characters have so far produced an accuracy of over 94%.

For each character region, the neural network and template matching method were initially tested individually. To use the two methods in a hybrid system, this time we make an initial guess using the template matching method and confirm the results using a neural network.

The results of these computer simulations for character recognition are shown in table 4. These are the average results for all the 30 characters learned. The total number of characters used for testing was 4268.

Table 4 shows the results of character recognition for license plates recognition.

| | Percentage Accuracy (%) | | | |
|---|---|---|---|---|
| Method | Letters | Numbers | Average | Average time (Msec) |
| NN only | 96.1 | 97.3 | 95.2 | 5.0 |
| TM only | 89.3 | 91.0 | 90.3 | 5.0 |
| Hybrid | 96.3 | 98.3 | 96.8 | 6.0 |

**Table 4.** Character Recognition Results for license plates

Table 5 shows the results of character recognition for air characters.

| | Percentage Accuracy (%) | | | |
|---|---|---|---|---|
| Method | Letters | Numbers | Average | Average time (Msec) |
| NN only | 92 | 94 | 93 | 12.0 |
| TM only | 90 | 89 | 90 | 13.0 |
| Hybrid | 93 | 95 | 94 | 15.0 |

**Table 5.** Character Recognition Results for air characters

For comparison, the method described in [1] achieved an accuracy of 94% using a neural network and template matching for licence plate detection only. The results of this work show a 3% accuracy improvement because of the different features used.

## 10. Discussion

Initially, we hoped to use the same neural network to recognize all characters weather printed or virtual. However, although human visual observation make it look like they are similar, the results of the thinning process produced completely different rather surprising results. Therefore, two system are required.

Neural network training depends on the number of training samples available. In this work, the samples used per character vary between a minimum of 10 samples for letters $(U, X)$ to a maximum of 200 for letter $W$ and numerals $(7, 9)$. Generally, neural network require a lot of data to train. This phenomenon is also observed here where the accuracy results of characters with more training samples are better.

The air character data collection needs some improvement to reduce the processing time. Although face detection is useful for position extraction etc, it takes valuable time that could be used to improve the character segmentation process.

## 11. Conclusion

In this chapter, we presented a character recognition method for virtual scenes (air characters) and vehicle number plate recognition using neural networks, template matching and evolutionary computation. We combine neural networks learning, image processing and template matching to create a novel character recognition system. To speed up the system and deal with, size and orientation issues, we employ a genetic algorithm. In addition, to control the size of both the neural network inputs and the template, we apply a genetic algorithm to guide the search. Average accuracy of about 97% and 94% were achieved for the license plate and virtual characters respectively.

In future we must find ways to combine the different recognition systems to universally recognize all characters and expand the work to include the recognition of lower case characters as well. Computation time especially for air character recognition must also be improved.

## Author details

Stephen Karungaru, Kenji Terada and Minoru Fukumi
*Department of Information Science and Intelligent Systems, University of Tokushima, Japan*

## 12. References

[1] Stephen Karungaru, Minoru Fukumi, Norio Akamatsu and Takuya Akashi (2009). Detection and Recognition of Vehicle License Plate using Template Matching, Genetic Algorithms and Neural Networks, *Trans. of International Journal of Innovative Computing*, Information and Control, Vol.5, No.7, pp.1975-1985.

[2] Ching-Tang Hsieh, Yu-Shan Juan, Kuo-Ming Hung (2005). Multiple License Plate Detection for Complex Background, *Advanced Information Networking and Applications* , pp.389-392.

[3] Jun-Wei Hsieh, Shih-Hao Yu, Yung-Sheng Chen (2002). Morphology-Based License Plate Detection from Complex Scenes, *Proc. of International Conference on Pattern Recognition* , pp. 176-179.

[4] Yanamura Y., Goto M., Nishiyama D, Soga M, Nakatani H, Saji H (2003). Extraction And Tracking Of The License Plate Using Hough Transform And Voted Block Matching, Proc. of IEEE IV Intelligent Vehicles Symposium , pp.243-6.

[5] Kamat V., Ganesan S (1995). An efficient implementation of the Hough transform for detecting vehicle license plates using DSPĄfS, *Proc. of Real-Time Technology and Applications Symposium*, pp.58-9.

[6] Viola P., Jones M (2001). Rapid Object Detection Using a Boosted Cascade of Simple Features, *Proc. of Computer Vision and Pattern Recognition* , vol.1, pp.511-518.

[7] Chih-Chiang Chen, Jun-Wei Hsieh (2007). License Plate Recognition from Low-Quality Videos. *Proc. of the IAPR Conference on Machine Vision Applications*, pp. 122-125.

[8] P. Viola and M. J. Jones (2004). Robust real-time face detection, *International Journal of Computer Vision*, vol. 57, no. 2, pp. 137-154.

[9] Stephen Karungaru, Minoru Fukumi and Norio Akamatsu (2005). License Plate Localization Using Template Matching, *Proc. of 9th International Conference on Mechtronics Technology*, Vol.1, No.T4-3, pp.1-5, Kuala Lumpur.

[10] Y. Abe, M. Konishi and J. Imai (2007). Neural network based diagnosis system for looper height controller of hot strip mills, *International Journal Innovative Computing, Information and Control* , vol.3, no.4, pp.919-935.

[11] Fekih, A., H. Xu and F. Chowdhury (2007). Neural networks based system identification techniques for model based fault detection of nonlinear systems, *International Journal Innovative Computing , Information and Control*, vol.3, no.5, pp.1073-1085.

[12] L. Mi and F. Takeda (2007). Analysis on the robustness of the pressure-based individual identification system based on neural networks, *International Journal Innovative Computing, Information and Control*, vol.3, no.1, pp.97-110.

[13] M.Fukumi, Y.Takeuchi H.Fukumoto, Y.Mitsukura, and M.Khalid (2005). Neural Network Based Threshold Determination for Malaysia License Plate Character Recognition, *Proc. of 9th International Conference on Mechatronics Technology*, Vol.1, No.T1-4, pp.1-5, Kuala Lumpur.

[14] Kah-Kay Sung (1996). Learning and example selection for object and pattern recognition, PhD Thesis, MIT AI Lab.

[15] M. Ishikawa (1993), Structure learning with forgetting, *Neural networks journal* , Vol. 9, No. 3, pp 509-521.

[16] Parker, J., R. (1994) "Practical Computer Vision using C", Wiley Computer Publishing.

[17] Zhang, T. Y. and Suen, Ching Y. (1984) "A Fast Parallel Algorithms For Thinning Digital Patterns", Communication of the ACM, Vol 27, No. 3, Maret 1984, pp.236-239.

[18] Duda, R. O. and P. E. Hart (1972) "Use of the Hough Transformation to Detect Lines and Curves in Pictures," Comm. ACM, Vol. 15, pp. 11-5.

[19] Kenney, J. F. and Keeping, E. S. (1962) "Linear Regression and Correlation." Ch. 15 in Mathematics of Statistics, Pt. 1, 3rd ed. Princeton, NJ: Van Nostrand, pp. 252-285

[20] Stephen Karungaru, Minoru Fukumi, Norio Akamatsu (2005), "Genetic Algorithms Based On-line Size and Rotation Invariant Face Detection," Journal of Signal Processing, Vol.9, No.6, pp.497-503, November 2005.

[21] Eric W. Brown, 2010, "Character Recognition by Feature Point Extraction", http://www.ccs.neu.edu/home/feneric/charrec.html.

Chapter 7

# A Novel Method for Multifont Arabic Characters Features Extraction

Nadia Ben Amor and Najoua Essoukri Ben Amara

Additional information is available at the end of the chapter

http://dx.doi.org/10.5772/52245

## 1. Introduction

Recently, many researchers around the world focused on Arabic document analysis, promising results have been reported.

However, there are not standard databases in Arabic to be considered as a benchmark. Each of research groups implemented their own system of set of data they gathered and different recognition rates were reported. Therefore, it is very difficult to give comparative and objective results for the proposed methods.

The aim of our work is to test several feature extraction algorithm and classification method using the same data base that we developed and which is composed of some 664 488 Arabic characters in nine different fonts and to conclude as far as the best suitable method for Arabic morphological specificities.

## 2. A review of Arabic characteristics

In this section we present a description of the important aspects of Arabic characters since the characteristics of Arabic writing is different from other alphabets.

Arabic script is cursive in both its handwritten and printed forms and letter shape is context sensitive.

The cursive nature of Arabic script is the main challenge to any Arabic text recognition system. Besides, Arabic script cursiveness obeys well-defined rules: some letters of the alphabet are never connected to their successors while others link to their within-word successors by a horizontal connection line.

In addition to the cursive aspect, we can also note the multitude of directions that can be described by the same Arabic character, especially in the multifont context.

Arabic writing may be classified into three different styles [1, 9]:

- Typewritten: This is a computer generated style. It is the simplest one because the characters are written without ligature or overlaps Figure1.

**Figure 1.** Example of typewritten Arabic style

- Typeset: This style is more difficult than typewritten because it has many ligatures and overlaps. It is used to write books and newspapers.

Nowadays, this style may also be generated using computers Figure2.

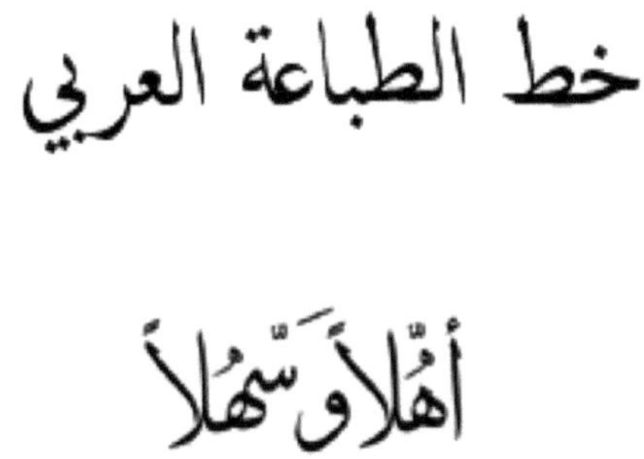


**Figure 2.** Example of typeset Arabic style

- Handwritten: This is the most difficult style because of the variation of writing the Arabic alphabets from one writer to another.

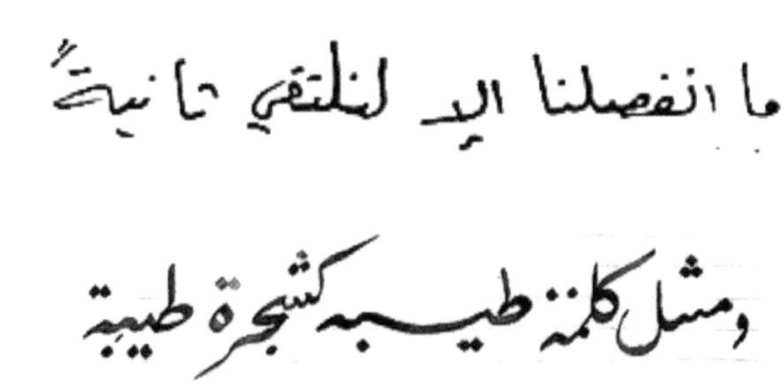


**Figure 3.** Examples of handwritten Arabic

Besides to different style of writing, there are many fonts in Arabic which make the recognition process more and more difficult.

In our work we have been dealing with multifont Arabic isolated characters. In fact, Segmenting Arabic script into characters is very difficult and always generates errors in the segmentation–based system. This work solves the cursiveness problem by presenting a segmentation–free system.

Due to the lack of common Arabic script data base, we had to develop our own one including all the shapes of the Arabic characters, beforehand segmented.

These characters was considered in nine different fonts which are Arabic transparent, Badr, AlHada, Diwani, Kufi, Cordoba, Andalus, Ferisi and Salam (Figure 4, Figure 5).

**Figure 4.** Samples of isolated Arabic characters considered in nine different fonts.

Besides, theses characters were considered in the different shapes they could have depending on their position within a word. Some samples of these different shapes are represented in the figure 5.

In fact, more and more Arabic documents are compound and use the multifont context, such as the newspapers and the magazines or even the official documents. Figure 6, extracted from an official Tunisian Newspaper, includes three different fonts which are Arabic Transparent, Ferisi and Andalus, used in the big title and the subtitles.

| Characters / Fonts | Noun | He | Ta | Sad | Fe | Ain | Kaf | Ke |
|---|---|---|---|---|---|---|---|---|
| Arabic Transparent | ن ننن | ه ههه | ط ططط | ص صصص | ف ففف | ع ععع | ق ققق | ك ككك |
| Badr | ن ننن | ه ههه | ط ططط | ص صصص | ف ففف | ع ععع | ق ققق | ك ككك |
| Diwani | ن ننن | ه ههه | ط ططط | ص صصص | ف ففف | ع ععع | ق ققق | ك ككك |
| Kufi | ن ننن | ه ههه | ط ططط | ص صصص | ف ففف | ع ععع | ق ققق | ك ككك |
| AlHada | ن ننن | ه ههه | ط ططط | ص صصص | ف ففف | ع ععع | ق ققق | ك ككك |
| Andalus | ن ننن | ه ههه | ط ططط | ص صصص | ف ففف | ع ععع | ق ققق | ك ككك |
| Cortoba | ن ننن | ه ههه | ط ططط | ص صصص | ف ففف | ع ععع | ق ققق | ك ككك |
| Ferisi | ن ننن | ه ههه | ط ططط | ص صصص | ف ففف | ع ععع | ق ققق | ك ككك |
| Salam | ن ننن | ه ههه | ط ططط | ص صصص | ف ففف | ع ععع | ق ققق | ك ككك |

**Figure 5.** Samples of different Arabic characters shape according to their font and position in a word.

**Figure 6.** Examples of Arabic multifont documents, extracted from two official newspapers

We have developed so far several processes for mutltifont Arabic characters recognition. All of these methods have proved the importance of the cooperation of different types of information at different levels (feature extraction, classification, post-processing...). This cooperation helps to overcome the variability of Arabic script especially in a multifont context [12, 13, 14, 15].

In this paper we highlight the role of Contourlets in the feature extraction step in an Arabic OCR context. This will allow us to compare the Contourlets performances with those of Wavelets and the Standard Hough Transform (SHT) that we previously used for the same purpose in our multifont Arabic recognition system. This comparison will lead to conclude as far as the precious contribution of the Contourlets in Arabic characters recognition field.

In the following section, we present the first approaches we developed in the features extraction step, then we introduce the Contourlet transform in the 3rd section. In section 4, we detail the system performances and experimental results. And finally, we conclude this paper in Section 5.

## 3. Wavelets and SHT approach for Arabic characters feature extraction

Feature extraction is a preliminary step for characters recognition. However, there is no perfect edge detector or feature extraction algorithm.

Many approaches have been so far developed for many alphabets such as Latin and Japanese. Yet given the specificity of this kind of writing we cannot apply them, as they are, for Arabic characters. Indeed, Arabic writing presents a very specific morphology. Thus the field remains one of the most challenging even though some works have been done [6, 17].

Arabic script is mainly composed of graphemes of cursive and structural nature. That's why we developed first two approaches based on wavelets transform and standard Hough transform-SHT. Wavelet transform is suitable for extracting cursive characteristics, while SHT is well known for extracting directional features.

Even though these methods have allowed us to achieve good recognition rates, it is worth mentioning that they presented some weaknesses regarding the pure directional and cursive aspect of some Arabic characters such as....

In fact, the wavelet transform has been proven to be powerful in many signal and image processing applications such as compression [11], noise removal, image edge enhancement and feature extraction.

However, wavelets are not optimal in capturing the two-dimensional singularities found in images. They are not effective in representing the images with smooth contours in different directions even though they offer multi-scale and time-frequency localization of an image (Figure7, Figure8). Wavelets are known to be quite efficient in representing image textures, but they show up insufficient as far as the smooth contour localization is concerned [16].

Typically, a separable 2-D wavelet transform provides:

- multiresolution, which is the ability to visualize the transform with varying resolution from coarse to fine

- localization, which is the ability of the basis elements to be localized in both the spacial and frequency domains
- critical sampling, which is the ability for the basis elements to have little redundancy.

**Figure 7.** Examples with good recognition results using wavelets as feature extractor (cursive aspect)

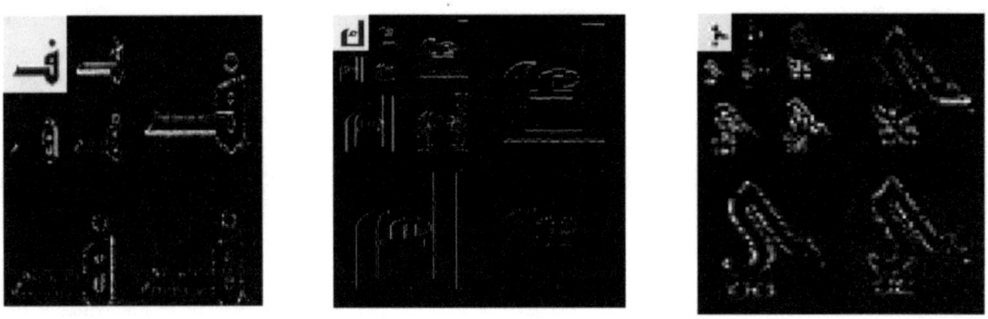

**Figure 8.** Examples with less good recognition results using wavelets as feature extractor (directional aspect)

However, it is not capable of providing:

- directionality, which is having basis elements defined in a variety of directions
- anisotropy, which is having basis elements defined in various aspect ratios and shapes.

In fact, despite its efficiency the wavelet transform can only capture limited directional information. This can affect the performance of the recognition system especially that the cursive nature of Arabic characters leads to a large number of directions to be considered. Thus the introduction of a directional based feature extraction method was a necessity.

The other features extraction method we focused on, was the SHT.

The SHT is known to be the popular and powerful technique for finding multiple lines in a binary image, and has been used in various applications.

It is very useful when dealing with the identification of features of a particular shape within a character image such as straight lines, but it fails as soon as it's a question of curves and circles localization [9]. This fact is shown in Figure9 and Figure10.

**Figure 9.** Examples of characters where the SHT fails in capturing cursive forms

**Figure 10.** Examples of characters where the SHT manages in capturing straight forms

Besides, trying to take advantage of these two previous methods, we have integrated them in a hybrid approach. This hybridization allowed localizing image texture as well as straight lines and directional features. In spite of the improvement of the results, the computation time had considerably increased [14].

## 4. Discrete Contourlet transform and feature extraction

Recently, several transforms have been proposed for image analysis that have incorporated directionality and multi-resolution which could more efficiently capture edges in the processed images. In fact, much more elaborated techniques of signal processing emerged such as Steerable Pyramid [4], Curvelets [3] and Contourlets [7] which are some well known examples. The Contourlet transform is one of the new geometrical image transforms, which seems to be promising since it allows extracting both directional and cursive primitives.

The contourlet transform uses a stage of subband decomposition followed by a directional transform. In the contourlet transform, a Laplacian pyramid is applied in the first stage, while directional filter banks (DFB) are used in the angular decomposition stage [7].

Unlike Wavelets, the contourlet transform is a directional transform capable of capturing contours and fine details in images.

In addition, the contourlet expansion is composed of basis functions oriented at a variety of directions in multiple scales. With this rich set of basis functions, the contourlets can effectively capture smooth contours.

Contourlets not only possess the main features of wavelets (multiscale and time-frequency localization), but also offer a high degree of directionality and anisotropy. Precisely, Contourlets transform involves basis functions that are oriented at any power of two's number of directions with flexible aspect ratios. [8]

The double filter bank structure of the contourlet is shown in Figure 11 for obtaining sparse expansions for typical images having smooth contours.

### 4.1. Laplacian Pyramid decomposition

The first filter bank, known as the Laplacian Pyramid (LP), is utilized to generate a multiscale representation of an image of interest. LP decomposition at each level generates a down-sampled low-pass version of the original image and the difference between the original and the prediction, which results in a band-pass image. The LP decomposition is shown in Figure 12. In LP decomposition process, H and G are one dimensional low pass analysis and synthesis filters respectively. M is the sampling matrix. Here, the band-pass image obtained in LP decomposition is then processed by the directional filter bank stage to reveal the directional details at each specific scale level.

The output values from the second filter bank are called "contourlet coefficients". Any analysis performed with the contourlet coefficients is considered as in the "contourlet domain."

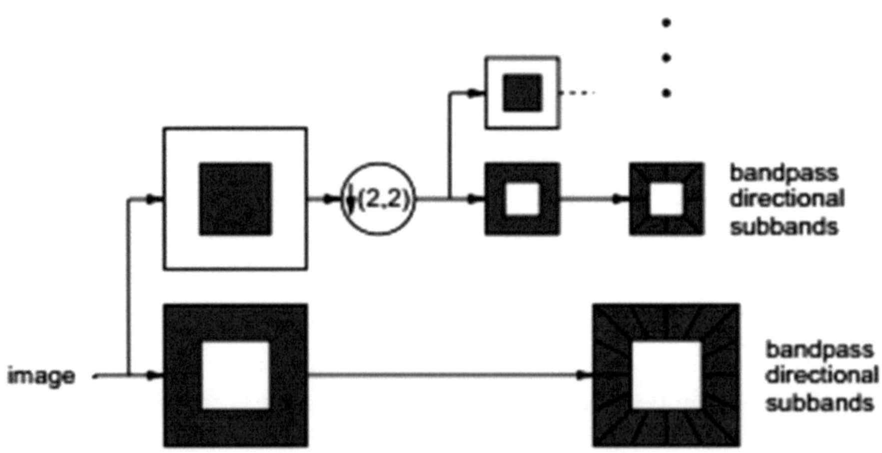


**Figure 11.** Double Filter Bank Decomposition of Contourlets transform.

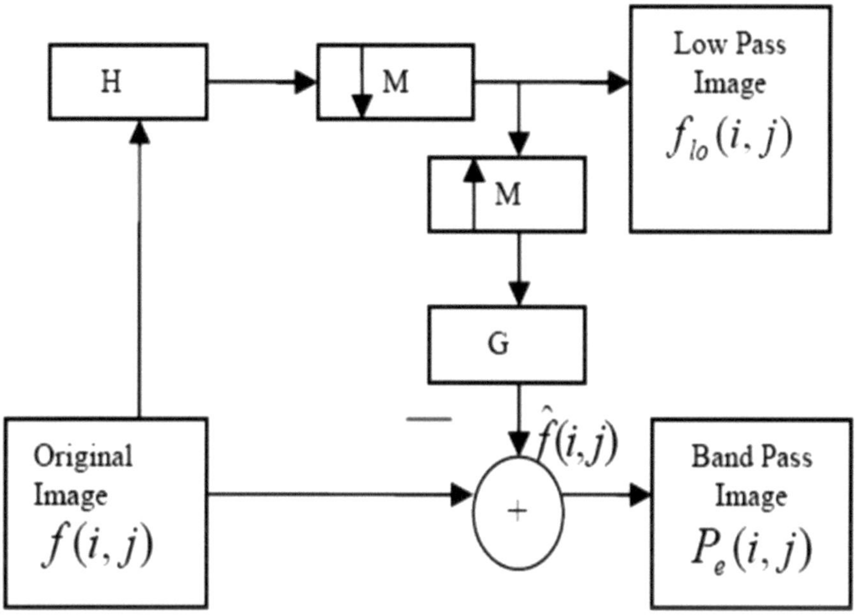


**Figure 12.** The principle of LP

## 4.2. Directional Filter Bank decomposition

Directional Filter Bank (DFB) is designed to capture the high frequency content like smooth contours and directional edges. Several implementations of these DFBs are available in the literature [8]. Combination of a Laplacian Pyramid (LP) and a DFB gives a double filter bank structure known as contourlet filter bank. Band pass images from the LP are fed to DFB so that directional information can be captured.

The scheme can be iterated on the coarse image. This combination of LP and DFB stages results in a double iterated filter bank structure known as contourlet filter bank, which decomposes the given image into directional sub-bands at multiple scales.

Since the purpose of using Contourlets is to focus on the cursive nature of the Arabic characters, we take an example of a cursive area and examine the behaviour of both wavelets and Contourlets on it Figure13.

Figure.13.a shows how wavelets arrange each others along the edge at different resolutions. The small blue squares represent the wavelets at the finest resolution, the green ones represent intermediate resolution and the red squares represent wavelets at the coarsest resolution. Figure.13.b shows the alignment of Contourlets and we can notice that the squares are replaced by rectangles.

Besides, we notice that, at each resolution, the edge can be represented by a far less number of contourlets than wavelets. As Wavelets are isotropic they can not take advantage of the underlying geometry of the edge. They approximate the edge as a collection of dots (small squares) so many points are needed to represent an edge. While contourlets are representing the edge as a collection of small needles hence only a few needle shaped line segments can represent the edge.

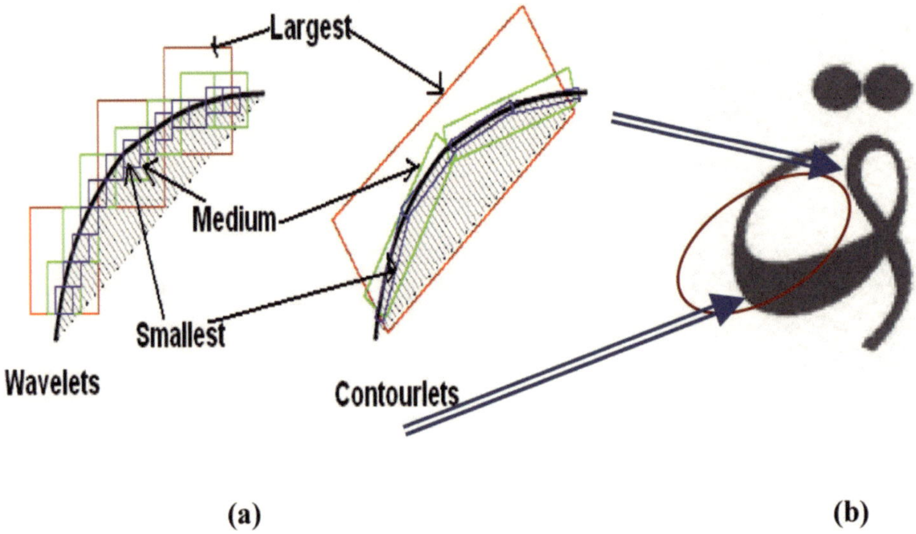


**Figure 13.** Wavelets (a) vs. Contourlets (b)

To sum up, one contourlet may be assumed to be formed by grouping several wavelets at the same resolution.

In the Figure 14, we present some examples of Arabic characters images decomposition, using Contourlets, wavelet and SHT. The better quality comparing with Wavelets and SHT is obvious.

## 5. Experimental results

Due to the lack of a standard database in Arabic to be considered as a benchmark, we developed our own database including all the Arabic characters beforehand segmented and presented in the different shapes they could have in a word.

All images in the database are processed in the grey level in the Tiff format.

Each image is decomposed in the contourlet domain. The resulting coefficients are structured in a special cellular form. Many experiments were conducted and we retained the Standard Deviation (SD) vector as a set of features.

Edge and texture orientations are captured by using contourlet decomposition with 3 level (0, 2 and 3) decomposition. At each level, the numbers of directional subbands are 3, 4 and 8 respectively. 'Pkva' filters are used for LP decomposition and directional subband decomposition.

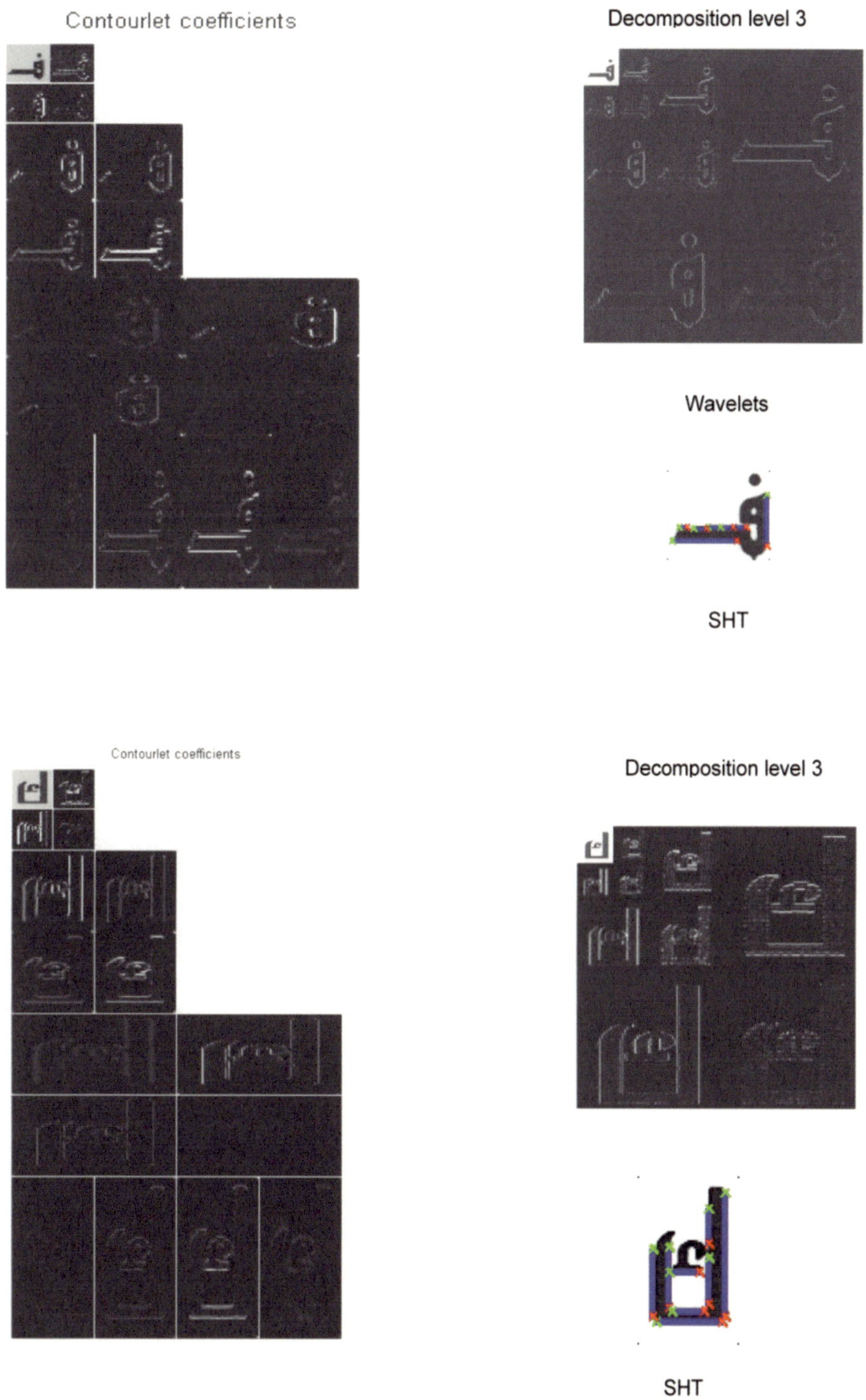


(a) Better straight lines and directions detection than wavelets and SHT.

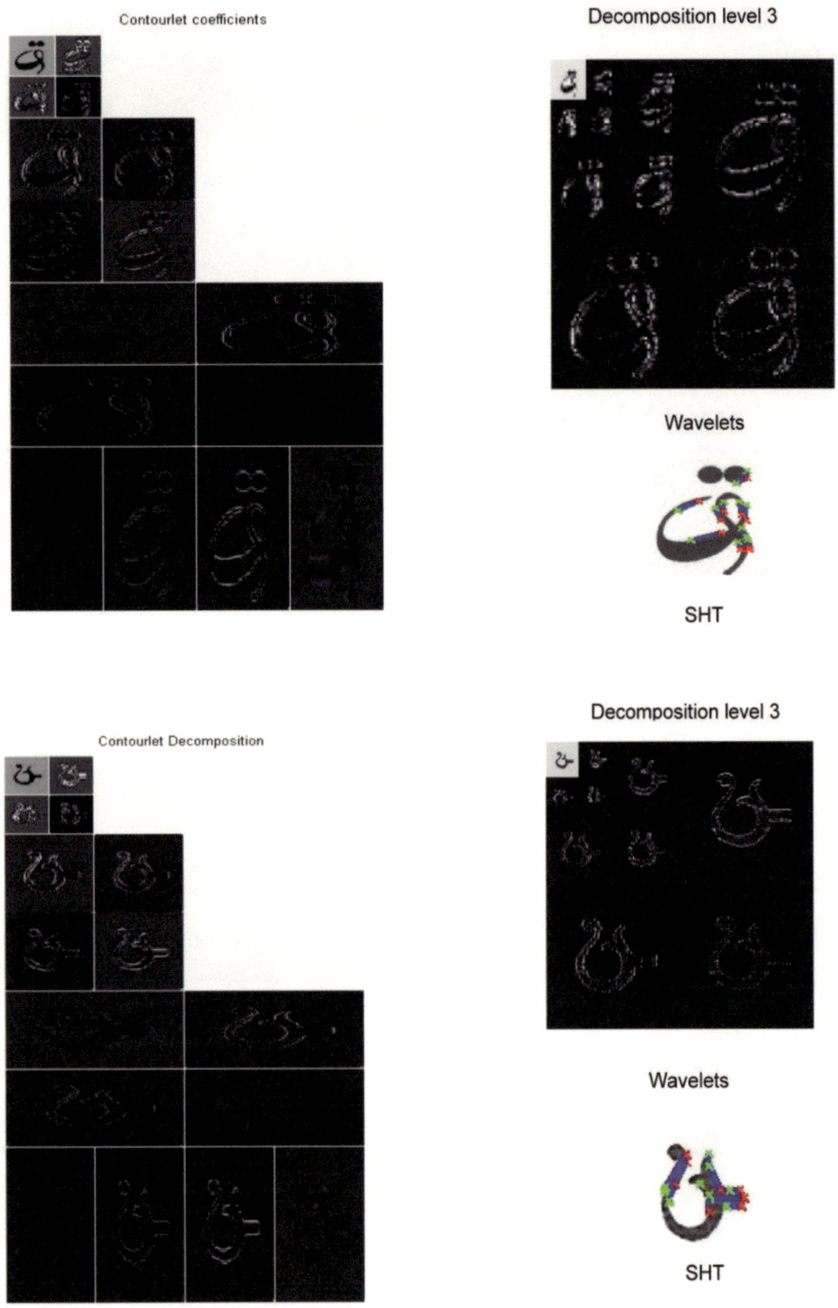


(b) Better curves and directions detection than wavelets and SHT.

**Figure 14.** Examples of images of features extraction using Contourlets, Wavelets and SHT: Better quality and recognition rates than Wavelets at greater level of resolution. Better curves detection than SHT.

As a result of this process, we obtain as output, a cell-vector where except output {1} corresponding to the lowpass subband. Each cell corresponds to one pyramidal level and is a cell-vector that contains band-pass directional subbands from the DFB at that level. These parameters result in a 16-dimentional feature vector (n=16). Standard deviation vector used as image feature is computed on each directional sub-band of the contourlet decomposed image and then normalized. This normalized feature vectors are used to feed the entry of the Artificial Neural Network classification stage.

Two architectures of neural network were implemented: a global Multilayer Perceptron (MLP) and a modular one.

In Table 1, we present the different recognition rates achieved when using Contourlets [13], Wavelets [10] and SHT [11] in features extraction. These results show the efficiency of contourlet transform compared to those obtained previously with the SHT and wavelet transform even though the used directional filter is a predefined one.

| Features extraction / Classification | | Contourlets | | Wavelets | | SHT |
|---|---|---|---|---|---|---|
| Characters | | Modular MLP | Global MLP | Modular MLP | Global MLP | Modular MLP |
| ا | Alif | 99.43 | 99.58 | 99.52 | 97.70 | 99.10 |
| ب | Ba' | 99.41 | 99.85 | 99.43 | 98.85 | 95.13 |
| ت | Ta' | 98.66 | 99.56 | 98.56 | 96.79 | 97.16 |
| ث | Tha' | 99.18 | 99.31 | 99.04 | 98.75 | 98.86 |
| ج | Jim | 99.28 | 100 | 97.99 | 97.50 | 97.02 |
| ح | Ha' | 99.90 | 100 | 99.43 | 98 | 96.80 |
| خ | Kha' | 99.40 | 100 | 98.85 | 97.23 | 96.26 |
| د | Dal | 99.27 | 99.73 | 100 | 98.37 | 95.69 |
| ذ | Dhal | 98.43 | 99.60 | 98.18 | 97.96 | 96.73 |
| ر | Ra' | 98.84 | 99.51 | 97.89 | 96.79 | 96.73 |
| ز | Zay | 98.57 | 99.74 | 95.41 | 95.08 | 96.55 |
| س | Sin | 99.15 | 99.85 | 99.52 | 98.18 | 94.65 |
| ش | Chin | 98.59 | 99.90 | 98.76 | 97.75 | 96.16 |
| ص | <u>S</u>ad | 98.35 | 99.83 | 99.52 | 100 | 96.24 |
| ض | Dhad | 97.96 | 99.71 | 96.47 | 96.55 | 94.62 |

| Features extraction / Classification | | Contourlets | | Wavelets | | SHT |
|---|---|---|---|---|---|---|
| Characters | | Modular MLP | Global MLP | Modular MLP | Global MLP | Modular MLP |
| ط | Ṯa' | 98.83 | 99.76 | 98.37 | 98.23 | 94.64 |
| ظ | D̲h̲a' | 98.87 | 99.22 | 98.66 | 97.85 | 95.24 |
| ع | 'Ayn | 99.23 | 99.82 | 98.47 | 95.61 | 96.76 |
| غ | Ghayn | 99.18 | 99.78 | 98.76 | 98.63 | 96.22 |
| ف | Fa' | 98.29 | 99.20 | 99.23 | 100 | 95.50 |
| ق | Qaf | 99.69 | 99.64 | 98 | 98.97 | 95.34 |
| ك | Kaf | 99.02 | 99.71 | 99.52 | 98.69 | 95.16 |
| ل | Lam | 99.45 | 99.60 | 100 | 98.93 | 98.38 |
| م | Mim | 99.24 | 99.47 | 99.33 | 99.16 | 97.02 |
| ن | Noun | 99.19 | 99.42 | 97.51 | 96.92 | 97.18 |
| ه | Ha' | 98.40 | 99.85 | 98.76 | 98.37 | 98.55 |
| و | Waw | 99.31 | 98.98 | 98.95 | 97.86 | 97.31 |
| ي | Ya' | 99.66 | 99.88 | 98.09 | 98.12 | 97.98 |
| Average rate (%) | | 99.03 | 99.66 | 98.65 | 97.95 | 96.53 |

**Table 1.** Recognition rate per character corresponding to the MLP models

## 6. Conclusion and perspectives

In this paper, we were interested in the challenges of Arabic characters feature extraction especially in a multifont context. We proposed a new approach for Arabic character recognition based on contourlet transform for feature extraction.

The achieved results show the efficiency of this transform compared with the Wavelet transform and the SHT. They proved its superiority in describing the different morphological variations of Arabic isolated characters. In fact, the contourlet transform have the advantage of highlighting both directional and cursive nature of Arabic scripts.

As a major perspective to this work we can consider to optimize the Contourlets Algorithm, by developing an adaptive filter depending on the character's class and form. Such as implementing filters adapting the most recognized directions by the SHT and of course the main directions of the Arabic scrip itself.

## Author details

Nadia Ben Amor
*National Engineering School of Tunis, Country*

Najoua Essoukri Ben Amara
*National Engineering School of Sousse, Country*

## 7. References

[1] B. Al-Badr and S. A. Mahmoud. Survey and bibliography of Arabic optical text recognition. Signal Processing, 41(1):49–77, 1995.
[2] D.Y .Po and Minh N Do. "Directional Multiscale Modelling of Images Using the Contourlet-transform", IEEE Transactions on Image Processing, 2006 Vol. 15, No. 6, pp 1610- 1620.
[3] E. J. Candes and D. L. Donoho, "Curvelets – a suprizingly effective nonadaptive representation for objects with edges," in Curve and Surface Fitting, Saint- Malo, Vanderbuilt Univ. Press, 1999.
[4] E. P. Simoncelli and W. T. Freeman, "The steerable pyramid: A flexible architecture for multi-scale derivative computation" 2nd IEEE International Conference on Image Processing.Washington, October, 1995DC. vol III, pp 444-447.
[5] E. W. Brown, "Character Recognition by Feature Point Extraction", Northeastern University internal paper 1992.
[6] M.Hamdani , H. El Abed, M. Kherallah, and A. M. Alimi, " Combining multiple HMMs using online and offline features for offline Arabic handwriting recognition," In Proceedings of the 10th International Conference on Document Analysis and Recognition (ICDAR), vol. 1, pp. 201–205, July 2009.
[7] M. N. Do and M. Vetterli, "Contourlets", in Beyond Wavelets, Academic Press, New York, 2003.
[8] M. N. Do, "Directional multiresolution image representation", Ph.D. Thesis. Department of Communication Systems, Swiss Federal Institute of Technology Lausanne, November 2001.
[9] M. S. Khorsheed. Off-line arabic character recognition - a review. Pattern Analysis & Applications, 5:31–45, 2002.
[10] N Aggarwal and WC Karl. Line detection in images through regularized Hough transform. IEEE Trans. on Image processing, 15:582–591, 2006.
[11] N.Ben Amor, N. Essoukri Ben Amara "DICOM Image Compression By Wavelet Transform". Proc. IEEE International Conference on Systems, Man and Cybernetics, Vol. 2, 6-9 October 2002 Hammamet, Tunisie.
[12] N.Ben Amor, N. Essoukri Ben Amara "Applying Neural Networks and Wavelet Transform to Multifont Arabic Character Recognition" International Conference on

Computing, Communications and Control Technologies (CCCT 2004), Austin (Texas), USA, on August 14-17, 2004.

[13] N.Ben Amor, N. Essoukri Ben Amara "Multifont Arabic Characters Recognition Using Hough Transform and Neural Networks" the Third International Symposium on Neural Networks (ISNN 2006) Chengdu China,May 28-31, 2006, J. Wang et al. (Eds.): (ISNN 2006), Lecture Notes in Computer Sciences LNCS 3972, 2006.© Springer-Verlag Berlin Heidelberg 2006, , pp. 293 – 298.

[14] [N.Ben Amor, N. Essoukri Ben Amara "A hybrid Approach for Features Selection in multifont Arabic isolated characters Recognition" the International Conference on Computer & Communication (ICCCE06), Malaysia, 9-11 May 2006.

[15] N.Ben Amor, N. Essoukri Ben Amara " Multifont Arabic Isolated Character Recognition Using Contourlets and Artificial Neural Networks" 11th International Conference on Frontiers in Handwriting Recognition 19-21 August 2008 (ICFHR 08]

[16] S.Esakkirajan, T. Veerakumar, V.Senthil Murugan, R. Sudhakar, "Image compression using contourlet transform and multistage vector quantization", *GVIP Journal,* volume 6, Issue 1, pp.19-28, July 2006.

[17] T.J. Klassen, Towards NN Recognition of Handwritten Arabic Letters, Project Report, 2001.

Chapter 8

# Decision Tree as an Accelerator for Support Vector Machines

Fu Chang and Chan-Cheng Liu

Additional information is available at the end of the chapter

http://dx.doi.org/10.5772/52227

## 1. Introduction

Support vector machine (SVM) is known to be a very powerful learning machine for pattern classification, of which optical character recognition (OCR) naturally falls as a branch. There are, however, a few hindrances in making an immediate application of SVM for the OCR purpose. First, to construct a well-performing SVM character recognizer has to deal with a large set of training samples (hundreds of thousands in the Chinese OCR, for example). There are two types of SVMs: linear and non-linear SVMs. Training a linear SVM is relatively inexpensive, while training a non-linear SVM is of the order $n^p$, where $n$ is the number of training samples and $p \geq 2$. Thus, the sheer size of samples has the potential of incurring a high training cost on an OCR application. Second, a normal OCR task also deals with a large number of class types. There are, for example, thousands of character class types being handled in the Chinese OCR. There are also hundreds of them being handled in the English OCR, if touched English letters are considered as separate class types from untouched letters. Since SVM training deals with one pair of class types at a time, we need to train $l(l\text{-}1)/2$ one-against-one (1A1) classifiers (Kerr et al. [1]) or $l$ one-against-others (1AO) classifiers (Bottou et al. [2]), where $l$ is the number of class types. Such a gigantic collection of classifiers not only poses a problem to the training but also to the testing of SVMs. Third, SVM training also involves a number of parameters whose values affect the generalization power of classifiers. This means that searching for optimal parameter values is necessary and it constitutes another heavy load to the SVM training. The above three factors, when put together, will demand months of computing time to complete a whole round of conventional SVM trainings, including linear and non-linear SVM trainings, and also demands an unusual amount of time in conducting a conventional online OCR task.

To cope with the above problems, we propose two methods, both of which involve the use of decision tree (Breiman et al. [3]) to speed up the computation. The first method, called *decision tree support vector machine* (DTSVM) (Chang et al. [4]) is developed by us to expedite SVM training. The second method, called *random forest decomposition* (RFD), generalizes a technique of ours (Liu et al. [5]) to speed up a testing process.

DTSVM decomposes a given data space with a decision tree. It then trains SVMs on each of the decomposed regions. In so doing, DTSVM can enjoy the following advantages. First, training non-linear SVMs on decomposed regions of size $\sigma$ reduces the complexity from $n^p$ to $(n/\sigma) \times \sigma^p = n\sigma^{p-1}$. Second, the decision tree may decompose the data space so that certain decomposed regions become homogeneous (i.e., they contain samples of the same class type), thereby reducing the cost of SVM training that is applied only to the remaining samples. Since DTSVM trains SVMs on regions of size $\sigma$, it leaves $\sigma$ an additional parameter to the parameters $\boldsymbol{\theta}$ associated with SVMs. The third advantage of DTSVM then lies in the fact that DTSVM handles all values of $\boldsymbol{\theta}$ only on the regions of lowest $\sigma$-size, and focus on very few selected values of $\boldsymbol{\theta}$ on the regions of higher $\sigma$-sizes, thereby making further savings in the training cost.

While DTSVM speeds up SVM training, it may not help reduce the time consumed in SVM testing. To achieve the latter goal, we propose to use *multiple* trees to decompose the data space. In this method, each tree employs a subset of randomly drawn features, instead of the set of all features. The collection of these trees is called a *random forest*. The RFD method proposed by us differs from the traditional random forest method (Ho [6], Breiman [7]) in the following way. The traditional method determines the class type for each test sample **x**, while RFD determines a number of class types for **x**. RFD is thus a learning algorithm whose objective is to reduce the number of class types for each test sample. There are a few parameters whose values need to be determined in the RFD's learning process, including the number of trees, the common size of each tree's decomposed regions, and one more parameter to be described in Section 3. The values of these parameters will be determined under the constraint that they lead to a restricted classifier whose generalization power is not inferior to the un-restricted classifier. The generalization power of a classifier can be estimated as the accuracy rate obtained in a validation process. The RFD thus assumes that a classifier is constructed in advance. In our case, it is the DTSVM classifier.

DTSVM is very handy for constructing classifiers and for conducting other tasks, including the selection of linear or non-linear SVMs, the selection of critical features, etc. RFD, on the other hand, is handy for putting a classifier to use in an online process. The results reported in this chapter showed that DTSVM and RFD could substantially speed up SVM training and testing, respectively, and still achieved comparable test accuracy. The reason for the no loss of test accuracy is the following. DTSVM and RFD trainings, similar to SVM training, involve a search for optimal parameters, thus bringing about the best possible classifiers as an outcome.

In this chapter, we apply DTSVM and RFD methods to three data sets of very large scale: ETL8B (comprised of 152,960 samples and 956 class types), ETL9B (comprised of 607,200 samples and 3,036 class types), and ACP (comprised of 548,508 samples and 919 class types). The features to be extracted from ETL8B and ETL9B are those described in Chou et al. [8] and Chang et al. [9]; those extracted from ACP are described in Lin et al. [10].

On the three data sets, we conducted our experiments in the following manner. We first trained linear and non-linear DTSVMs on the experimental data sets with some reasonable parameter values. We then computed DTSVMs' performance scores, including training time, test speed, and test accuracy rates. Although a strict comparison between DTSVMs and global SVMs (gSVMs, i.e., SVMs that are trained on the full training data set) may not be possible, due to the extremely slow training process of gSVMs, it is possible to estimate the speedup factors achieved by DTSVMs. To show the effectiveness of DTSVM, we further compare DTSVM classifiers with the classifiers obtained by *k*-nearest neighbor (kNN) and decision tree (without the addition of SVMs) methods.

The rest of this chapter is organized as follows. Section 2 reviews the DTSVM method. In Section 3, we describe the RFD learning algorithm. In Section 4, we describe our experimental results. Section 5 contains some concluding remarks.

## 2. Decision Tree Support Vector Machine (DTSVM)

In this section, we describe DTSVM as a method to speed up the training of SVMs over large-scale data sets. We divide the section into two sub-sections. In the first sub-section, we describe the decision tree that is used in DTSVM, and in RFD as well, for decomposing the data space. In the second sub-section, we describe the learning algorithm of DTSVM.

An implementation of DTSVM is available at

http://ocrwks11.iis.sinica.edu.tw/~dar/Download/WebPages/DTSVM.htm,

which contains source codes, experimental data sets, and an instruction file to use the codes.

### 2.1 The Decision Tree as a Decomposition Scheme

The decomposition scheme adopted in the DTSVM and RFD methods is basically a CART (Breiman et al., 1984) or a binary C4.5 (Quinlan, 1986) that allows two child nodes to grow from each node that is not a leaf. To grow a binary tree, we follow a recursive process, whereby each training sample flowing to a node is sent to its left-hand or right-hand child node. At a given node $E$, a certain feature $f$ of the training samples flowing to $E$ is compared with a certain value $v$ so that all samples with $f < v$ are sent to the left-hand child node, and the remaining samples are sent to the right-hand child node. The optimal values of $(f, v)$ are determined as follows:

$$(f^*,v^*) = \arg\max_{(f,v)} IR(f,v),$$

where

$$IR(f,v) = I(S) - \frac{|S_{f<v}|}{|S|} I(S_{f<v}) - \frac{|S_{f\geq v}|}{|S|} I(S_{f\geq v}),$$

$S$ is the set of all samples flowing to $E$; $S_{f<v}$ consists of the elements of $S$ with $f < v$; $S_{f \geq v} = S \setminus S_{f<v}$; $|X|$ is the size of any data set $X$; and $I(X)$ is the impurity of $X$. The impurity function used in our experiments is the entropy measure, defined as

$$I(S) = -\sum_y p(S_y) \log p(S_y),$$

where $p(S_y)$ is the proportion of $S$'s samples whose class type is $y$.

For both DTSVM and RFD, we do not grow a decision tree to its full scale. Instead, we stop splitting a node $E$ when one of the following conditions is satisfied: (i) the number of samples that flow to $E$ is smaller than a *ceiling size* $\sigma$; or (ii) when $IR(f, v) = 0$ for all $f$ and $v$ at $E$. The value of $\sigma$ in the first condition is determined in a data-driven fashion, which we describe in Section 2.2. The second condition occurs mainly in the following cases. (a) All the samples that flow to $E$ are homogeneous; or (b) a subset of them is homogeneous and the remaining samples, although differ in class type, are identical to some members of the homogeneous subset.

## 2.2. The DTSVM learning algorithm

After growing a tree, we train an SVM on each of its leaves, using samples that flow to each leaf as training data. A tree and all SVMs associated with its leaves constitute a DTSVM classifier. In the training phase, all the SVMs in a DTSVM classifier are trained with the same parameter values. In the validation or the testing phase, we input a given data point **x** to the tree. If **x** reaches a homogeneous leaf, we classify **x** as the common class type of those samples; otherwise, we classify it with the SVM associated with that leaf.

When a learning data set is given, we divide a given learning data set into a training and validation constituent. We then build a DTSVM classifier on the training constituent and determine its optimal parameter values with the help of the validation constituent. The parameters associated with a DTSVM classifier are: (i) $\sigma$, the ceiling size of the decision tree; and (ii) the SVM parameters. Their optimal values are determined in the following manner.

We begin by training a binary tree with an initial ceiling size $\sigma_0$, and then train SVMs on the leaves with SVM-parameters $\boldsymbol{\theta} \in \Theta$, where $\Theta$ is the set of all possible SVM-parameter values whose effects we want to evaluate. Note that we express $\boldsymbol{\theta}$ in boldface to indicate that it may consist of more than one parameter. Let $var(\sigma_0, \boldsymbol{\theta})$ be the validation accuracy rate achieved by the resultant DTSVM classifier.

Next, we construct DTSVM classifiers with larger ceiling sizes $\sigma_1, \sigma_2, \ldots$, with $\sigma_0 < \sigma_1 < \sigma_2 < \ldots$ On the leaves of these trees, we only train their associated SVMs with $k$ top-ranked $\boldsymbol{\theta}$. To do this, we rank $\boldsymbol{\theta}$ in descending order of $var(\sigma_0, \boldsymbol{\theta})$. Let $\Theta_k$ be the set that consists of $k$ top-ranked $\boldsymbol{\theta}$. We then implement the following sub-process, denoted as *SubProcess*($\boldsymbol{\theta}$), for each $\boldsymbol{\theta} \in \Theta_k$.

1. Set $t = 0$ and get the binary tree with the ceiling size $\sigma_0$.

2. Increase $t$ by 1. Modify the tree with ceiling size $\sigma_{t-1}$ to obtain a tree with ceiling size $\sigma_t$. This is done by moving from the root towards the leaves and retaining each node whose size or whose parent's size is greater than $\sigma_t$. Then, train SVMs on the leaves with SVM-parameters $\theta$. Let $var(\sigma_t, \theta)$ be the validation accuracy of the resultant DTSVM classifier.
3. If $var(\sigma_t, \theta) - var(\sigma_{t-1}, \theta) \geq 0.5\%$ and $\sigma_t$ is less than the size of the training constituent, proceed to step 2.
4. If $var(\sigma_t, \theta) - var(\sigma_{t-1}, \theta) < 0.5\%$, then $\sigma(\theta) = \sigma_{t-1}$; otherwise, $\sigma(\theta) = \sigma_t$.

When we have completed *SubProcess*($\theta$) for all $\theta \in \Theta_{[k]}$, we define

$$\theta_{opt} = \arg\max_{\theta \in \Theta_k} var(\sigma(\theta), \theta) \text{ and } \sigma_{opt} = \sigma(\theta_{opt}).$$

We then output the DTSVM classifier with the SVM-parameter $\theta_{opt}$ and the ceiling size $\sigma_{opt}$.

In our experiments, training linear SVMs involved only one parameter $C$, the cost penalty factor, whose values were taken from $\Phi = \{10^a: a = -1, 0, \ldots, 5\}$. Training non-linear SVMs involved two parameters, $C$ and $\gamma$, where $\gamma$ appears in an RBF kernel function. The values of $C$ were also from $\Phi$, while the values of $\gamma$ were taken from $\Psi = \{10^b: b = -1, -2, \ldots, -9\}$. Furthermore, we fixed the number of top-ranked parameters at $k = 3$ for linear SVMs and at $k = 5$ for non-linear SVMs. For the sequence of ceiling sizes, we had only two such numbers: the initial ceiling size $\sigma_0 = 1{,}500$ and the next ceiling size $\sigma_1 = n+1$, where $n$ is the number of training samples. The reason for these two numbers is as follows. On a tree with the initial ceiling size $\sigma_0$, we needed to train SVMs with all combinations of parameter values. So, we set $\sigma_0$ at a sufficiently low level to save a tremendous amount of training time. At the next stage, we immediately jumped to the root level of a tree, because in the three experimental data sets, the number of training samples per class type was not high, even though the total number of training samples was very large, so we did not want to waste time on any intermediate level between $\sigma_0$ and $\sigma_1$.

## 3. Random Forest Decomposition (RFD)

In this section, we address the acceleration of SVM testing, using RFD as the method to construct a multiple decomposition scheme. The implementation of the RFD method is available at the following website.

http://ocrwks11.iis.sinica.edu.tw/~dar/Download/WebPages/RFD.htm

To speed up SVM testing, we assume that all the required SVM classifiers have been constructed. Suppose that there are $l$ class types and we want to conduct 1A1 classification, then there are $l(l-1)/2$ SVMs in total. To classify a data point **x**, we first apply our multiple decomposition scheme to pull out $m$ candidate class types for **x**, where $m$ depends on **x** and $m < l$. We then apply $m(m-1)/2$ SVMs to **x**, each of which involves a pair of candidate class types. If, on the other hand, we want to conduct 1AO classification, then there are $l$ SVMs and we apply $m$ of them to **x**.

In the above process, we use random forest (RF) as the multiple decomposition scheme. An RF is a collection of trees, each of which is trained on a separate subset of features that is drawn randomly from the set of all features. When the total number of features is $F$, we train all such trees on a subset of $[F/2]$ features, where $[F/2]$ is the integral part of $F/2$. Moreover, we train all these trees with a common ceiling size. At each leaf of an RF, we store the class types of the training samples that flow to this leaf, instead of the training samples themselves.

When an RF is given, let $\tau$ = the number of trees in the RF and $\sigma$ = the common ceiling size of these trees. For a given data point **x**, we first send **x** to all the $\tau$ trees and examine the leaves to which **x** flows. Next, we pull out the class types that are stored in at least $\mu$ leaves. We then classify **x** under the restriction that only these class types are considered as the candidate class types of **x**.

The RFE training process thus involves the construction of an RF of $\tau$ trees with a common ceiling size $\sigma$, which we denote as RF($\tau$, $\sigma$). For each data point **x**, let $M(\mathbf{x}, \tau, \sigma, \mu)$ be the collection of class types such that

$$M(\mathbf{x},\tau,\sigma,\mu) = \{l:\ l \text{ is stored in at least } \mu \text{ leaves of } \mathrm{RF}(\tau,\sigma) \text{ to which } \mathbf{x} \text{ flows}\}.$$

To find the optimal values of $\tau$, $\sigma$, and $\mu$, we divide a given learning data set into a training constituent and a validation constituent. For each possible value of $\tau$ and $\sigma$, we train a random forest RF($\tau$, $\sigma$) on the training constituent. Then, for each possible value of $\mu$, we compute the validation accuracy rate $var(\tau, \sigma, \mu)$ on the validation constituent, where

$$var(\tau,\sigma,\mu) = \frac{|\{\mathbf{x} \in \mathrm{V}:\ \text{the SVMs restricted to } M(\mathbf{x},\tau,\sigma,\mu) \text{ correctly classifies } \mathbf{x}\}|}{|\mathrm{V}|},$$

V is the set of all validation samples, and $|\mathrm{X}|$ is the size of any data set X.

To make an exhaustive search for the highest possible value of $var(\tau, \sigma, \mu)$ proves to be very time consuming. So we propose the following two-stage search strategy. At the first stage, we fix $\mu = 1$ and search for sufficiently low $\tau^*$ and $\sigma^*$ such that $var(\tau^*, \sigma^*, 1) \geq var_{baseline}$, where $var_{baseline}$ is the validation accuracy rate achieved by the unrestricted SVMs. At the second stage, we look for the largest $\mu^*$ such that $var(\tau^*, \sigma^*, \mu^*) \geq var_{baseline}$.

We fix $\mu = 1$ at the first stage based on the following observation. For any value of values of $\mathbf{x}$, $\tau$, and $\sigma$, we have $M(\mathbf{x}, \tau, \sigma, 1) \supseteq M(\mathbf{x}, \tau, \sigma, 2) \supseteq \ldots$, and $var(\tau, \sigma, 1) \geq var(\tau, \sigma, 2) \geq \ldots$ So, if $var(\tau, \sigma, \mu) \geq var_{baseline}$ for some $\mu$, we must have $var(\tau, \sigma, 1) \geq var_{baseline}$.

The first stage of our search strategy is detailed as follows.

1. Set $\tau = 15$ and $\sigma = 500$, namely, grow 15 trees with a common ceiling size 500.
2. If $var(\tau, \sigma, 1) \geq var_{baseline}$, stop the process. Otherwise, change the common ceiling size of the $\tau$ trees from $\sigma$ to $4\times\sigma$.
3. If $var(\tau, \sigma, 1) \geq var_{baseline}$, stop the process. Otherwise, increase $\tau$ by 5; namely, grow 5 more trees with a common ceiling size $\sigma$.

4. Go to step 2.

The procedure must stop at a finite number of iteration. In the worst case, it stops when $\sigma$ reaches the root level and all class types are candidate class types. The resultant $\tau$ and $\sigma$ in this procedure are denoted as $\tau^*$ and $\sigma^*$. At the next stage, we look for

$$\mu^* = \arg\max_{1 \le \mu \le \tau^*} \{\mu : var(\tau^*, \sigma^*, \mu) \ge var_{baseline}\}$$

under the constraint that $\tau = \tau^*$, $\sigma = \sigma^*$, and $var(\tau^*, \sigma^*, \mu^*) \ge var_{baseline}$.

# 4. Experimental results

In this section, we describe the data sets in the experiments and the features extracted out the character images. We then present and discuss the experimental results.

## 4.1. The data sets and features

To demonstrate the effects of the proposed methods, we applied DTSVM and RFD to the data sets: ACP, ETL8B, and ETL9B. The ACP data set derived from a task of classifying textual components on machine-printed documents written in Chinese and English. In the original work described in [10], all textual components were classified into 3 types: alphanumeric (A), Chinese (C), and punctuation (P). Once classified, those components would be sent to a separate recognizer for further classification. In the current task, we expanded the 3 class types into 863 alphanumeric types and 55 punctuation types. So, there would be no separate recognizers for alphanumeric or punctuation types. Moreover, there were a lot more class types in the alphanumeric category than one might expect, because we considered touched characters as separate types from all other types. On the other hand, all Chinese components were considered as one type, since we had to first merge them into characters and send the characters into a Chinese recognizer.

When textual component was segmented from a document image, we extract the following features out of it.

*Density.* A 64×64 bitmap image is divided into 8×8 regions, each comprising 64 pixels. For each region, the counts of black pixels are used as a density feature. The total number of features in the density category is 64.

*Cross Count.* A cross count is the average number of black intervals that lie within eight consecutive scan lines that run through a bitmap in either a horizontal or vertical direction. The total number of features in the cross-count category is 16.

*Aspect Ratio.* For a textual component *TC* that appears in a horizontal textline *H*, we obtain the following features: 1) bit '1' for the slot indicating that *H* is a horizontal textline; 2) '0' for the slot indicating that *H* is a vertical textline; 3) the ratio between *TC*'s height and *H*'s height; 4) the ratio between *TC*'s height and *TC*'s width; 5) the ratio between *TC*'s top gap and *H*'s height; and 6) the ratio between *TC*'s bottom gap and *H*'s height. We follow the same procedure for a textual component that appears in a vertical textline. The total number of features in the aspect-ratio category is 6.

ETL8B and ETL9B are well known data sets comprising 955 and 3,035 Chinese/Hiragana handwritten characters respectively. For all the characters contained in the two data sets, we used a feature extraction method consisting of the following basic techniques: non-linear normalization (Lee and Park [11], Yamada et al. [12]), directional feature extraction (Chou et al. [8]), and feature blurring (Liu et al. [13]). These three techniques were considered as major breakthroughs in handwritten Chinese/Hiragana character recognition (Umeda [14]). The total number of features extracted out of each character is 256.

The feature vectors extracted out of the three data sets can be found at the following website.

http://ocrwks11.iis.sinica.edu.tw/~dar/Download/WebPages/RFD.htm

When conducting both training and testing, we decompose each data set into training, validation, and test constituents at the ratio of 4:1:1. We use samples in the training constituent to train classifiers. We then use samples in the validation constituent for finding optimal parameters. Finally, we apply the classifiers trained with optimal parameters to the test constituent for computing the test accuracy rate. Table 1 contains detailed information for all the data sets and the constituents derived from them.

| | ACP | ETL8B | ETL9B |
|---|---|---|---|
| Number of Class Types | 919 | 955 | 3,035 |
| Number of Features | 86 | 256 | 256 |
| Number of Samples | 545,698 | 152,960 | 607,200 |
| Training Constituent | 363,789 | 102,292 | 406,824 |
| Validation Constituent | 90,944 | 25,812 | 100,188 |
| Test Constituent | 90,965 | 24,856 | 100,188 |

**Table 1.** The three data sets used in our experiments.

## 4.2. Results of DTSVM

Two types of DTSVM were studied in our experiments. They were linear DTSVM (L-DTSVM) and non-linear DTSVM (N-DTSVM). We compared them with linear gSVM (L-gSVM) and non-linear gSVM (N-gSVM). In addition to these four SVM methods, we also included decision tree and kNN for comparison. To train SVMs for L-DTSVM and L-gSVM, we employed LIBLINEAR (Fan et al. [15]). On the other hand, we used LIBSVM (Fan et al. [16]) to train SVMs for N-DTSVM and N-gSVM.

For all the SVM methods, we only conducted 1A1 classification. While 1AO is another option to take, it is too costly compared to 1A1. A 1AO-training involves samples of all class types, while a 1A1-training involves samples of only two class types. In the 1A1 training, we needed to train $l(l-1)/2$ SVMs. In the testing, however, we performed a DAG testing process (Platt et al. [17]) that involved only $l$ SVMs for classifying a test sample. More about DAG will be given in Section 4.3.

We display in Figure 1 the training times of the six compared methods, expressed in *seconds*. The results demonstrated that DTSVM conducted training substantially faster than gSVM. The speedup factor of L-DTSVM relative to L-gSVM was between 1.6 and 2.0, while the speedup factor of N-DTSVM relative to N-gSVM was between 6.7 and 14.4. The results also showed that the non-linear SVM methods were a lot more time-consuming than linear SVM methods. On the other hand, decision tree and kNN are fast in training.

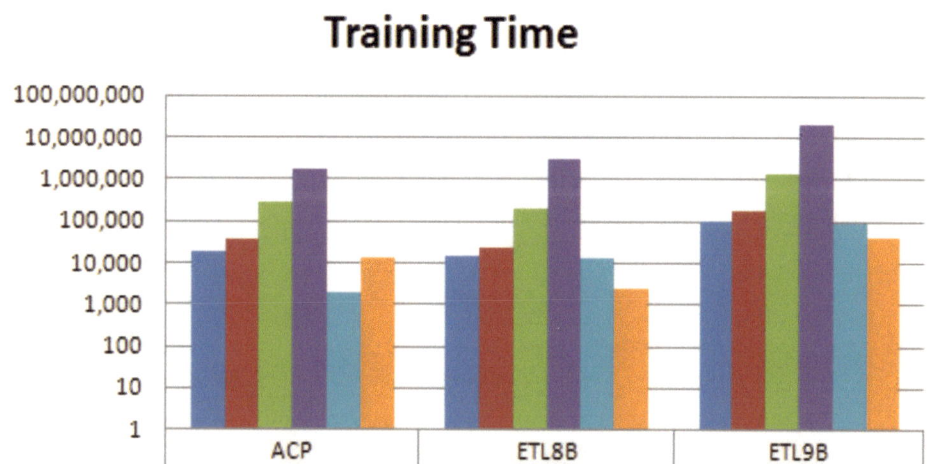


| | ACP | ETL8B | ETL9B |
|---|---|---|---|
| L-DTSVM | 19,306 | 14,287 | 100,009 |
| L-gSVM | 37,779 | 24,038 | 168,266 |
| N-DTSVM | 264,628 | 203,476 | 1,424,332 |
| N-gSVM | 1,777,715 | 2,939,804 | 20,578,628 |
| Decision Tree | 2,007 | 12,668 | 88,676 |
| kNN | 13,595 | 2,430 | 38,991 |

**Figure 1.** Training times of the six compared methods, expressed in seconds. DTSVMs outperformed gSVMs and decision tree outperformed all the six methods.

Figure 2 shows the test accuracy rates achieved by all the compared methods. All the SVM methods achieved about the same rates. Moreover, they outperformed decision tree and kNN on all the data sets. Decision tree, in particular, performed poorly on data sets ETL8B and ETL9B; kNN fell behind the SVM methods by a visible amount on ETL9B.

Figure 3 shows the test speeds of all the compared methods, expressed in *characters per second*. L-DTSVM achieved a staggering high speed on the data set ACP. The two linear SVM methods conducted testing much faster than the two non-linear SVM methods.

Decision tree, again, was faster in testing; kNN was slow, unsurprisingly, because it had to compare a test sample against all training samples.

All the times or speeds reported in this chapter were measured on Quad-Core Intel Xeon E5335 CPU 2.0GHz with a 32GB RAM. In our experiments, we took advantage of parallelism to shorten the wall-clock time. However, all the times reported here are CPU times. Furthermore, we were able to train all gSVMs on ACP and ETL8B, but we did not complete the training of gSVMs on ETL9B. Instead, we estimated the total training time based on the SVM training that we had performed for DTSVMs on the root level.

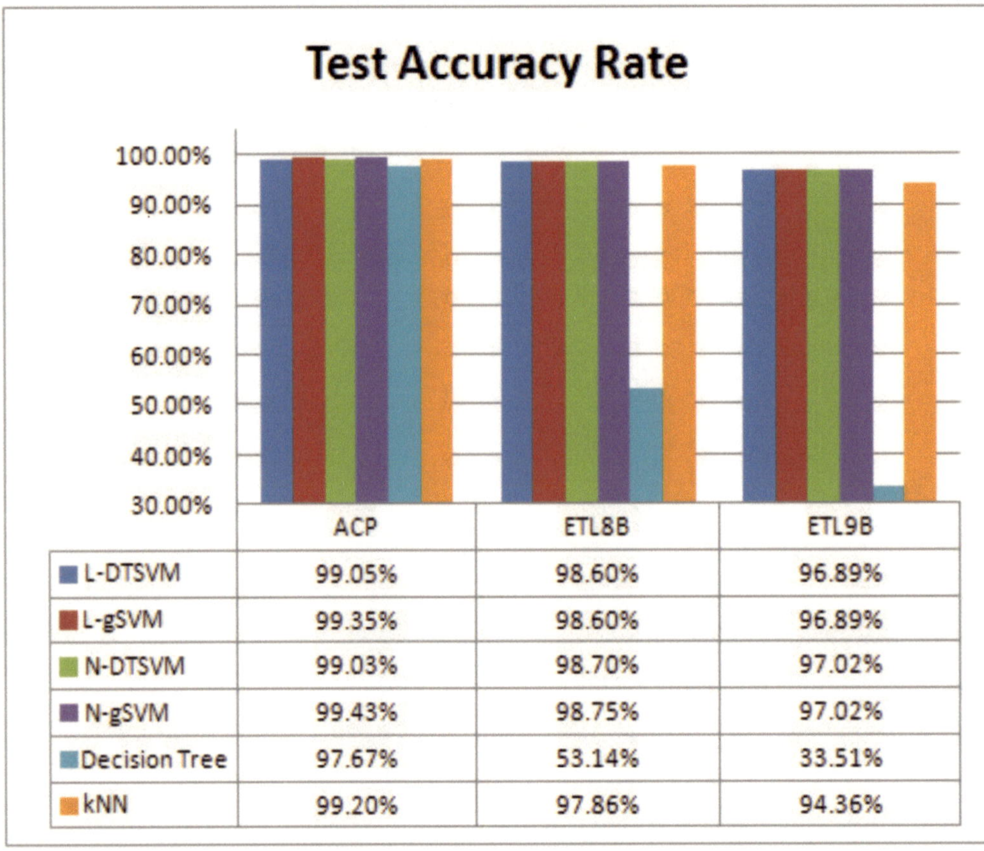


| | ACP | ETL8B | ETL9B |
|---|---|---|---|
| L-DTSVM | 99.05% | 98.60% | 96.89% |
| L-gSVM | 99.35% | 98.60% | 96.89% |
| N-DTSVM | 99.03% | 98.70% | 97.02% |
| N-gSVM | 99.43% | 98.75% | 97.02% |
| Decision Tree | 97.67% | 53.14% | 33.51% |
| kNN | 99.20% | 97.86% | 94.36% |

**Figure 2.** Test accuracy rates of the six compared methods. SVMs achieved comparable accuracy rates to each other; they outperformed decision tree and kNN.

We also show in Table 2 the optimal parameter values for all compared methods, except the decision tree that involves no parameters. On the data set ACP, $\sigma^* = 1{,}500$, explaining why L-DTSVM and N-DTSVM conducted training and testing at such a high speed. On ETL8B and ETL9B, $\sigma^*$ = root, implying that DTSVM classifiers were trained on the root, the same site where gSVM classifiers were trained. This explains why DTSVM and gSVM conducted testing at the same speed. However, DTSVMs consumed less time in training than gSVMs because not all local SVMs of the DTSVM classifiers were trained on the root level.

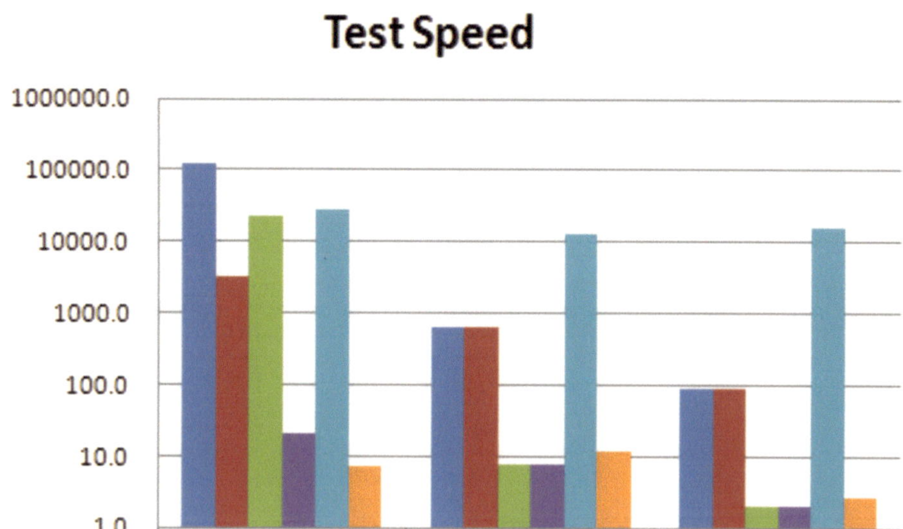


| | ACP | ETL8B | ETL9B |
|---|---|---|---|
| L-DTSVM | 126516.0 | 622.2 | 91.6 |
| L-gSVM | 3317.5 | 622.4 | 91.6 |
| N-DTSVM | 22477.1 | 7.9 | 2.0 |
| N-gSVM | 21.5 | 8.0 | 2.0 |
| Decision Tree | 28813.7 | 13479.4 | 16151.5 |
| kNN | 7.2 | 12.2 | 2.8 |

**Figure 3.** Test speeds of the six compared methods, expressed in characters per second. L-DTSVM outperformed all other SVM methods; decision tree outperformed all other methods, except L-DTSVM on the data set ACP.

Finally, we remark that, on the ACP data set, DTSVM training not only settled at a low ceiling size (1,500) but also resulted in a tree with some homogeneous leaves. In fact, 63.2% of the ACP training samples flowed to leaves with a single class type, the Chinese type. So in the testing phase, a large proportion of ACP test samples also flowed to homogeneous leaves, leaving no further effort for classifying them. The ETL8B and ETL9B data sets, on the other hand, comprised a large number of small-sized class types and no large-sized class type. So the DTSVM training settled at the root level on the two data sets.

### 4.3. Results of RFD

The RFD method is associated with an SVM training method. When applying RFD, we must have all the associated SVM classifiers constructed.

If, for example, gSVM is the training method, RFD will work with all the 1A1 classifiers ($l$, $l'$), where $l$ and $l'$ are any two class types. We first describe how we use these classifiers in the DAG testing process. When a test sample **x** is given, we first tag all class types as *likely* types. We next apply a classifier ($l_1$, $l_2$) to **x**. If **x** is classified as $l_1$, we re-tag $l_2$ as unlikely and replace it by a likely type $l_3$. We then apply the classifier ($l_1$, $l_3$) to **x**. This process goes on until only one likely type is left, which we take as **x**'s class type.

| Data Set | Method | $\sigma^*$ | $C^*$ | $\gamma^*$ | $k^*$ |
|---|---|---|---|---|---|
| ACP | L-DTSVM | 1,500 | 1 | | |
| | L-gSVM | | 1 | | |
| | N-DTSVM | 1,500 | $10^2$ | $10^{-1}$ | |
| | N-gSVM | | 10 | $10^{-1}$ | |
| | kNN | | | | 3 |
| ETL8B | L-DTSVM | root | $10^5$ | | |
| | L-gSVM | | $10^5$ | | |
| | N-DTSVM | root | $10^4$ | $10^{-8}$ | |
| | N-gSVM | | $10^5$ | $10^{-9}$ | |
| | kNN | | | | 10 |
| ETL9B | L-DTSVM | root | 10 | | |
| | L-gSVM | | 10 | | |
| | N-DTSVM | root | $10^3$ | $10^{-7}$ | |
| | N-gSVM | | $10^3$ | $10^{-7}$ | |
| | kNN | | | | 12 |

**Table 2.** Optimal parameter values for all the methods except decision tree. Empty cells imply that the corresponding categories are not applicable.

When the RFD method is employed, we first send **x** to the corresponding RF and find the *m* candidate class types for **x**. We tag these class types as likely types and the remaining class types as unlikely types. We then proceed as in the DAG process until only one likely type is left.

If, on the other hand, RFD works with a DTSVM classifier, **x**'s candidate class types must fall into two subsets: one is associated with the decision tree of the DTSVM classifier and the other is with the RF derived by the RFD method. So we extract the class types from the intersection of these two subsets and tag them as the likely types. We then proceed as in the DAG process.

We show in Tables 3 and 4 the results of applying the RFD method to L-DTSVM, L-gSVM, N-DTSVM and N-gSVM classifiers. Table 3 displays the times to train the corresponding RFs and the optimal parameters associated with them. It is shown that all the RFs comprise

15 decision trees and almost all of them settled at the ceiling size 500, except the RFs for accelerating DTSVMs on the ACP data set settling at the ceiling size 2,000.

| Data Set | Method | Training Time | $\tau^*$ | $\sigma^*$ | $\mu^*$ |
|---|---|---|---|---|---|
| ACP | L-DTSVM | 381,645 | 15 | 2,000 | 3 |
| | L-gSVM | 380,617 | 15 | 500 | 4 |
| | N-DTSVM | 381,676 | 15 | 2,000 | 4 |
| | N-gSVM | 381,450 | 15 | 500 | 9 |
| ETL8B | L-DTSVM | 190,232 | 15 | 500 | 3 |
| | L-gSVM | 190,232 | 15 | 500 | 3 |
| | N-DTSVM | 202,241 | 15 | 500 | 2 |
| | N-gSVM | 202,241 | 15 | 500 | 2 |
| ETL9B | L-DTSVM | 3,263,999 | 15 | 500 | 1 |
| | L-gSVM | 3,263,999 | 15 | 500 | 1 |
| | N-DTSVM | 3,490,394 | 15 | 500 | 1 |
| | N-gSVM | 3,490,394 | 15 | 500 | 1 |

**Table 3.** Training times and optimal parameters for the RFs associated with all the SVM methods.

Table 4 displays the testing times achieved by all the SVM methods with or without the RFD to speed up. The effects of RFD were manifest on all SVM classifiers and all data sets, except for the DTSVM classifier on the ACP data set. The reason for the exceptional case is easy to understand. DTSVM classifiers ran very fast on the ACP data set; to speed it up by another device (i.e., an RF) would not be economical, due to the fact that this device would incur its own computing cost to the process.

### 4.4. Summary

We summarize the results in Sections 4.2 and 4.3 as follows.

1. Among all the competing methods, we judge L-DTSVM to be the champion, since it achieved comparable test accuracy rates to all other SVM methods, required the least times to train and to test among all SVM methods, and outperformed decision tree the kNN by large. This is a rather welcomed result, since L-DTSVM conducted much faster training and testing than other SVM methods.
2. The decision tree and kNN, although were fast in training, achieved worse test accuracy rates than the SVM methods. Moreover, the kNN method was slow for testing. We thus found these two methods unsuitable for our purpose.
3. The DTSVM method proved to be very effective for speeding up SVM training and achieved comparable test accuracy rates to gSVM. This was even true when linear SVM was adopted as the learning machine.

| Data Set | Classifier | With RFD | Without RFD |
|---|---|---|---|
| ACP | L-DTSVM | 29249.2 | 126516.0 |
| | L-gSVM | 21565.9 | 3317.5 |
| | N-DTSVM | 16354.7 | 22477.1 |
| | N-gSVM | 819.5 | 21.5 |
| ETL8B | L-DTSVM | 2766.7 | 622.2 |
| | L-gSVM | 2766.7 | 622.4 |
| | N-DTSVM | 30.7 | 7.9 |
| | N-gSVM | 30.7 | 8.0 |
| ETL9B | L-DTSVM | 519.1 | 91.6 |
| | L-gSVM | 519.1 | 91.6 |
| | N-DTSVM | 6.6 | 2.0 |
| | N-gSVM | 6.6 | 2.0 |

**Table 4.** Testing times achieved by all the SVM methods with or without RFD to speed up.

4. The RFD method proved to be very effective to speed up SVM testing. This claim was found to be true for all but one case, in which the DTSVM method was already very fast to require any further acceleration.

## 5. Conclusion

Having applied the DTSVM and RFD methods to three data sets comprising machine-printed and handwritten characters, we showed that we were able to substantially reduce the time in training and testing SVMs, and still achieved comparable test accuracy. One pleasant result obtained in the experiments was that linear DTSVM classifiers performed the best among all SVM methods, in the sense that they attained better or comparable test accuracy rates and consumed the least amount of time in training and testing.

## Author details

Fu Chang* and Chan-Cheng Liu
*Institute of Information Science, Academia Sinica, Taipei, Taiwan*

## 6. References

[1] Knerr S, Personnaz L, Dreyfus G (1990) Single-layer Learning Revisited: A Stepwise Procedure for Building and Training A Neural Network. In J. Fogelman,

* Corresponding Author

editor, Neurocomputing: Algorithms, Architectures and Applications. Springer-Verlag.

[2] Bottou L, Cortes C, Denker J, Drucker H, Guyon I, Jackel L, LeCun Y, Müller U, Sackinger E, Simard P, Vapnik V (1994) Comparison of Classifier Methods: A Case Study in Handwriting Digit Recognition. Int. Conf. on Pattern Recognition; pp. 77–87.

[3] Breiman L, Friedman JH, Olshen RA, Stone CJ (1984) Classification and Regression Trees. Chapman and Hall.

[4] Chang F, Guo CY, Lin XR, Lu CJ (2010) Tree Decomposition for Large-Scale SVM Problems. Journal of Machine Learning Research; 11: 2935–2972.

[5] Liu YH, Lin CC, Lin WH, Chang F (2007) Accelerating Feature-Vector Matching Using Multiple-Tree and Sub-Vector Methods. Pattern Recognition; 40(9): 2392-2399.

[6] Ho TK (1998) The Random Subspace Method for Constructing Decision Forests. IEEE Transactions on Pattern Analysis and Machine Intelligence; 20(8): 832–844.

[7] Breiman L (2006) Random Forests. Machine Learning. 45(1): 5-32.

[8] Chou CH, Lin CC, Liu YH, Chang F (2006) A Prototype Classification Method and Its Use in A Hybrid Solution for Multiclass Pattern Recognition. Pattern Recognition; 39(4): 624-634.

[9] Chang F (2008) Techniques for Solving The Large-Scale Classification Problem in Chinese Handwriting Recognition. Arabic and Chinese Handwriting Recognition, Lecture Notes in Computer Science; 4768: 161-169.

[10] Lin XR, Guo CY, Chang F (2011) Classifying Textual Components of Bilingual Documents with Decision-Tree Support Vector Machines. Int. Conf. on Document Analysis and Recognition; PP. 498-502.

[11] Lee SW, Park JS (1994) Nonlinear Shape Normalization Methods for The Recognition of Large-Set Handwritten Characters. Pattern Recognition; 27(7): 895-902.

[12] Yamada H, Yamamoto K, Saito T (1990) A Nonlinear Normalization Method for Handprinted Kanji Character Recognition – Line Density Equalization. Pattern Recognition 23(9): 1023-1029.

[13] Liu CL, Kim IJ, Kim JH (1997) High Accuracy Handwritten Chinese Character Recognition by Improved Feature Matching Method. Int. Conf. Document Analysis and Recognition; pp. 1033-1037.

[14] Umeda M (1996) Advances in Recognition Methods for Handwritten Kanji Characters. IEICE Trans. Information and Systems; E79-D(5): 401-410.

[15] Fan RE, Chang KW, Hsieh CJ, Wang XR, Lin CJ (2008) LIBLINEAR: A Library for Large Linear Classification. Journal of Machine Learning Research; 9: 1871-1874.

[16] Fan RE, Chen PH, Lin CJ (2005) Working Set Selection Using Second Order Information for Training SVM. Journal of Machine Learning Research; 6: 1889-1918.

[17] Platt JC, Cristianini N, Shawe-Taylor J. (2000) Large Margin DAGs for Multiclass Classification. In S. A. Solla, T. K. Leen and K.-R. Müller, editors, Advances in Neural Information Processing Systems. MIT Press.

Chapter 9

# Generating Training Sets for the Automatic Recognition of Handwritten Documents

Gabriel Pereira e Silva and Rafael Dueire Lins

Additional information is available at the end of the chapter

http://dx.doi.org/10.5772//52074

## 1. Introduction

Handwritten character recognition is a task of high complexity even for humans, sometimes. People have different writing "style", which may vary according to psychological state, the kind of document written, and even physical elements such as the texture of the paper and kind of pencil or pen used. Despite such wide range of variation possibilities, some elements tend to remain unchanged in a way that other people, in general, can recognize one´s writing and even identify the authorship of a document. Very seldom one is unable to identify one's own writing. Very seldom someone is unable to identify his own writing.

The basis for pattern recognition rests on two corner stones. The first one is to find the minimal set of features that presents all maximum diversity within the universe of study. The second one is to find a suitable training set that also covers all possible data to be classified. Due to the variation of writing styles between people, one should not expect that a general classifier yields good recognition performance in a general context. Thus, one tends to either have general classifiers for very specific restricted vocabularies (such as digits), or to have personalized recognizers for general contexts. The scope of the present work is the latter. In such context it is a burden and very difficult to generate a good training set to allow the classifier to reach a reasonable recognition rate.

This paper proposes a new approach for the automatic generation of the training set for the handwritten recognizer of a given person. The first step for that is to select a set of documents representative of the author's style. In the Internet one may find several public domain sites with font sets. In particular the site Fontspace [21] offers 282 different cursive font sets for download (e.g Brannboll Small, Jenna Sue, Signerica Fat, The Only Exception, Homemade Apple, Santos Dumont, etc). Figure 1 presents an example of some of them. The key idea presented here is "approximating" the author writing by a cursive typographical font, which is skeletonized and a "standard" training set is generated. Such strategy, detailed as follows, was adopted with success with documents of the Nabuco bequest [12] and of the Thanatos Project [1].

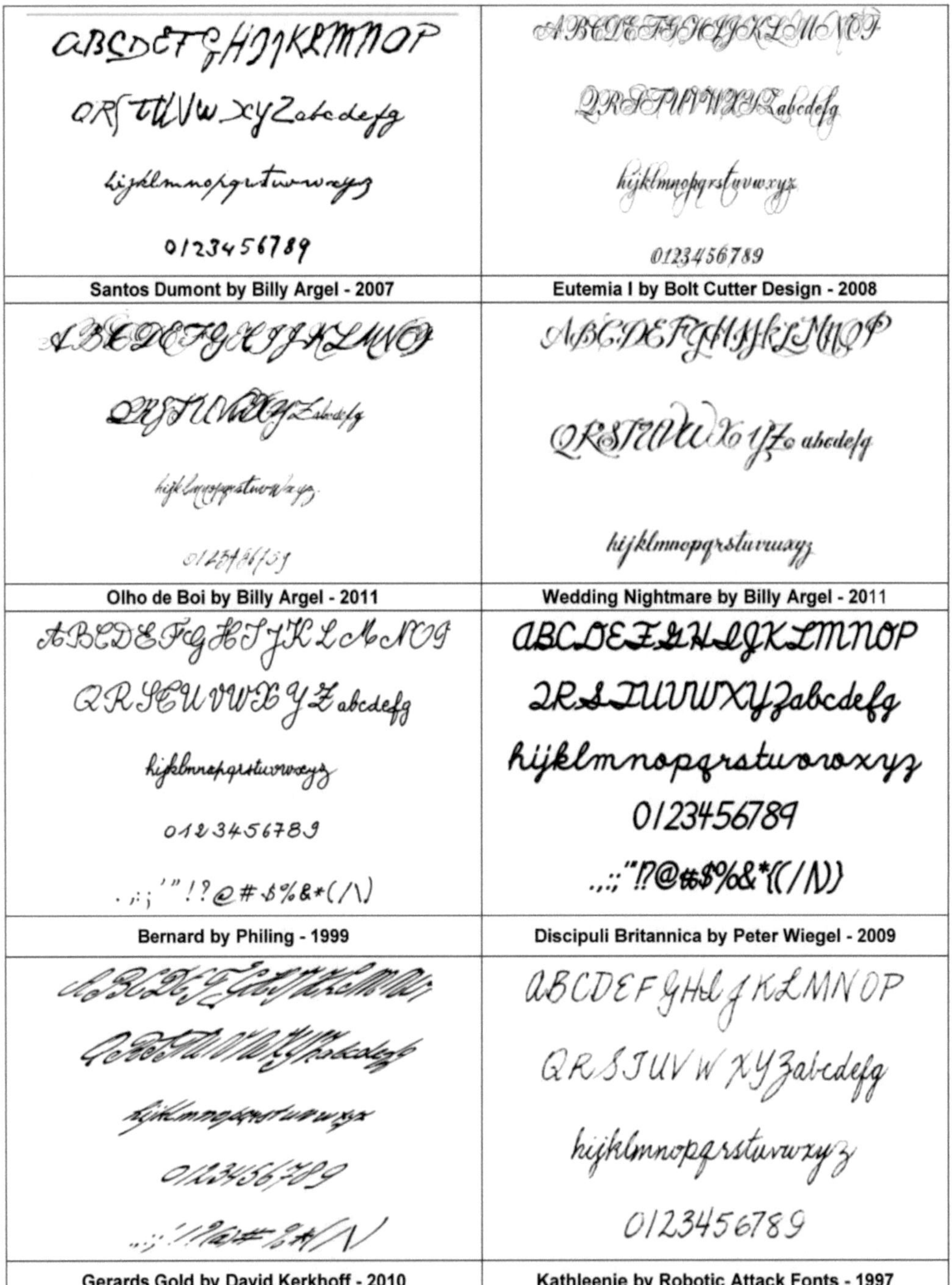


**Figure 1.** Examples of cursive font sets extracted from Fontspace [1]

## 2. The proposed method

The choice of a representative training set together with a good set of features is fundamental for the success of automatic pattern recognition. These two factors are tightly linked to each other and in such a way as to grant good recognition results. To obtain a good training set for handwriting recognition of a given author during a period of time in which the writing features are stable (they changes with age, psychological and health factors, etc.) one has to group together the documents that have similar properties. A subset of them that is representative of the set of documents (in general the size of the training set is about 10% of the size of the whole data "universe") is chosen in such a way as to cover the whole diversity of the documents to be transcribed.

The development of the proposed method starts by using a set of cursive fonts. In the Internet one may find several public domain sites with font sets. In particular the site Fontspace [21] offers 282 different cursive font sets for download.

The central difficulty in generating the training set for handwritten documents is to have a "font set" of a specific author to extract the convenient features for patter matching.

The strategy adopted here is:

1. Select a number of documents that is representative of the author.
2. Process the documents to:
    a. remove digitalization borders that may frame the image,
    b. correct skew,
    c. filter-out back-to-front interference (bleeding),
    d. binarize the document.
3. Transcribe the document into text by a human reader.
4. The user should select a number of a cursive font set that bears "some resemblance" to the original author handwriting.
5. The text version of the document is typeset in each of the cursive font sets chosen in step 4 (above).
6. All the typeset versions of the document are converted into image.
7. The image of the original document is skeletonised and then dilated.
8. Segment the image in boxes around each letter (font cases) of the skeletonised and dilated version of the original image and the synthetically generated images.
9. Apply a deformation transform to make each font case in the synthetic images coincide with the font case of the skeletonised-dilated version of the original document.
10. Extract the features from each document and place in a vector.
11. Take the Hamming distance between the feature vectors of the synthetic and original images.
12. The font set used to generate the synthetic document which provides the smallest Hamming distance is the one to be used as the training set.

The structural features used for pattern recognition, mentioned in step 10 above, are:

- Geometric Moments [15] [9];

- Concavity Measurements [16];
- Shape Representation of Profile [14];
- Distance between barycentre points between two consecutive characters;
- Maximum and minimum heights of two consecutive characters.
- Maximum and minimum distance between concavities of two consecutive characters.

The image filtering operations listed in step 2 were performed using HistDoc v.2.0 environment [13] which offers a wide number of tools for historic document image processing including the several algorithms for the removal of back-to-front interference and binarizarion. The skeletonization and dilation processes in this work were performed using the filters available in ImageJ [20].

Step 9, performing image vectorization, is important to increase the likelihood between the synthetic and the original documents. Such operation is applied to each character in each synthetically generated image by deforming the bounding-box and the strokes until there is a perfect match between the synthetic and the original one. In this "deformation" process some statistical analysis is performed to infer data about inter character and inter word spacing, line and character skew, inter line separation, etc.

The feature vector of a document brings an account of the basic features of the author calligraphy. The Hamming distance between the feature vectors of the synthetic and original images, which is part of step 11, brings an account of their similarity, and is calculated using the formula:

$$H_w = \sum_{n=1}^{N\ features} \left| f_{on} - f_{sn} \right|$$

where $f_{on}$ and $f_{sn}$ are the components of the feature vectors of the original and synthetic images, respectively. The choice of a vector of features such that one could extract "information" about the calligraphic pattern of the author shares some ideas with the work in reference [5]. The font set that provides the smallest Hamming distance to the original set is chosen to synthetically generate the whole training dictionary to the classifier.

In what follows the steps described above are detailed in two files of historical documents: the handwritten letters of Joaquim Nabuco that are about one century old and the hand filled information on the books of pre-printed forms of civil certificates from the state of Pernambuco-Brazil, from mid 20$^{th}$ century.

## 3. Results

The strategy presented above for developing the training set was tested in two sets of documents: letters from Nabuco bequest and death certificates from the Thanatos project [1].

### 3.1. Transcribing Nabuco´s letters

The Nabuco Project [12] was an initiative of the second author of this paper. It started in 1991 with the aim to preserve the file of letters of Joaquim Nabuco, a Brazilian statesman, writer, and diplomat, one of the key figures in the campaign for freeing black slaves in Brazil (b.1861-d.1910). The Nabuco file encompasses over 6,500 documents and about 30,000 pages of active and passive correspondence (including postcards, typed and handwritten letters), a bequest of historical documents of paramount importance to understand the formation of the political and social structure of the countries in the Americas and their relationship with other countries. The letters of Nabuco were catalogued and some of them summarized [2] [4], but the bequest was never fully transcribed. The Nabuco Project is acknowledged as being the pioneering initiative in Latin America to attempt to generate a digital library of historic documents. Figure 2 presents an example of letter in Nabuco bequest, written in a blank sheet of paper without lines, which presents a textured background due to paper aging, a horizontal folding mark in its central part, a light back-to-front interference (bleeding) as the letter was written on both sides of the sheet of paper. The image was acquired with an operator driven flatbed scanner, using 200 dpi resolution, in true color. There is no marginal noise (borders) framing the image and its skew is negligible.

To automatically generate the training set for recognizing the handwritten letters from Nabuco file a visual inspection was made to find letters that could represent the whole universe of letters. From the Nabuco file 50 letters were chosen and transcribed by historians, yielding 50 text files, totaling 3,584 words. Twenty-five letters (1,469 words) were used to develop the feature set used for training the classifier, and the remaining ones for ground-truth testing. All the selected documents were processed performing the steps listed in step 2 above, which encompasses marginal border removal, image de-skew, removal of back-to-front interference and binarization. An example of resulting document after filtering and binarization using the HistDoc v.2.0 environment [13] may be found in Figure 3. The image in Figure 2 is skeletonized and then dilated using the filters in ImageJ [20]; the resulting image is presented in Figure 4.

The synthetic image generation is performed by choosing a subset of the cursive fontsets available that resemble the writing of the original document. In the case of Nabuco, the subset selected encompassed 15 of the 282 cursive font sets available in Fontspace [21] (e.g Brannboll Small, Jenna Sue, Signerica Fat, The Only Exception, Homemade Apple, Santos Dumont, etc) that were closer to the author's writing style during the period of interest. The text of the original document was (human) transcribed into a text file, which was typeset using the choosen cursive fontsets. The text of document in Figure 2 typeset using the fonts in "Signerica Fat" type font is shown in Figure 5. The image shown in Figure 5 is now vectorized and "approximated" to the original skeletonized and dilated image by "deforming" each "letter case" and strokes until matching, as much as possible. The resulting image is presented in Figure 6.

The feature vector of each of the synthetic images "deformed" in such a way to the character case to match the original font case was extracted and the Hamming distance of each of them to the skelotonized-dilated original image was calculated. The image that exhibited the minimum distance was the "Signerica Fat" font set presented in Figure 6.

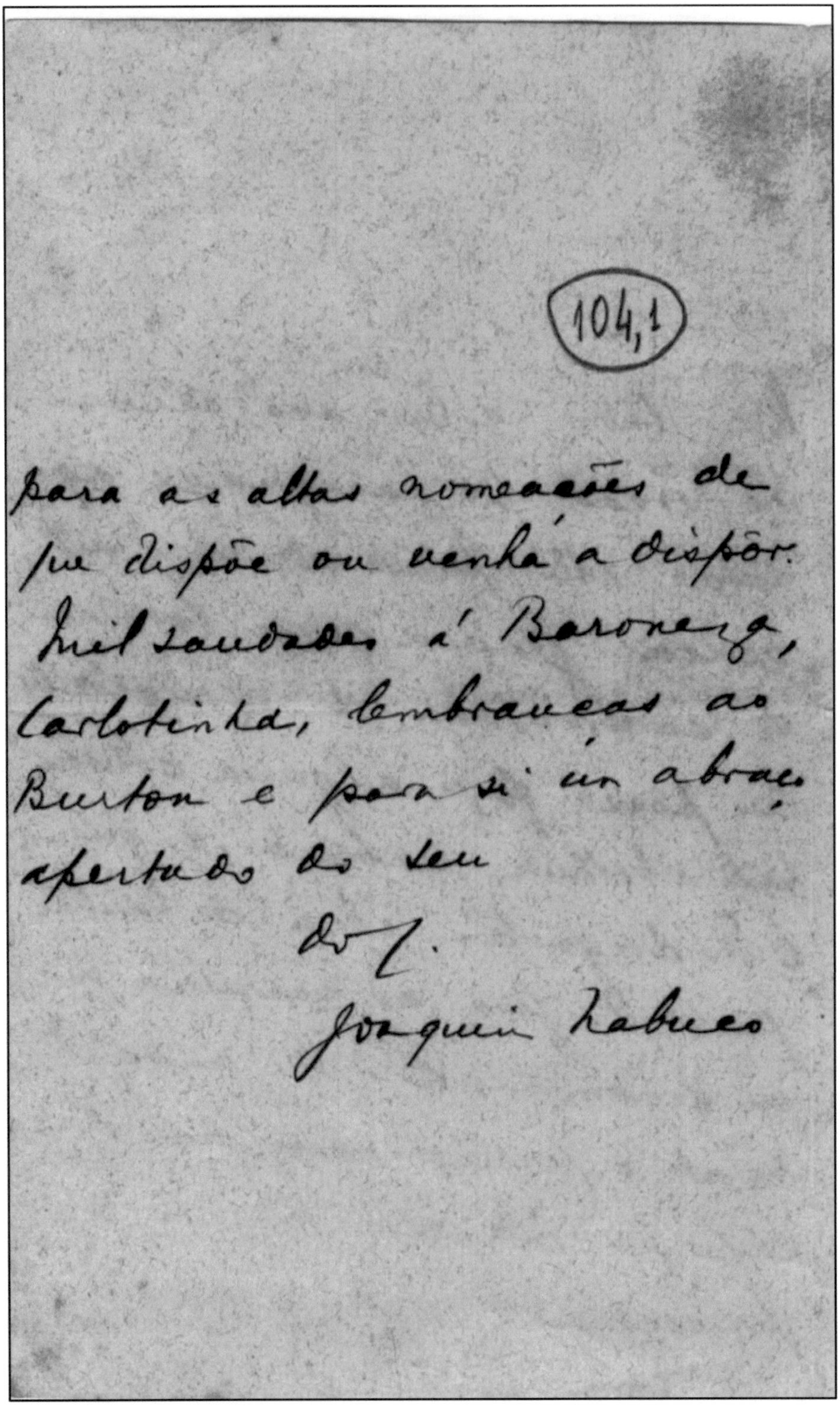

para as altas nomeações de
que dispõe ou venha a dispôr.
Mil saudades á Baroneza,
Carlotinha, lembranças ao
Burton e para si um abraço
apertado do seu
[illegible]
Joaquim Nabuco

**Figure 2.** Letter from Nabuco bequest.

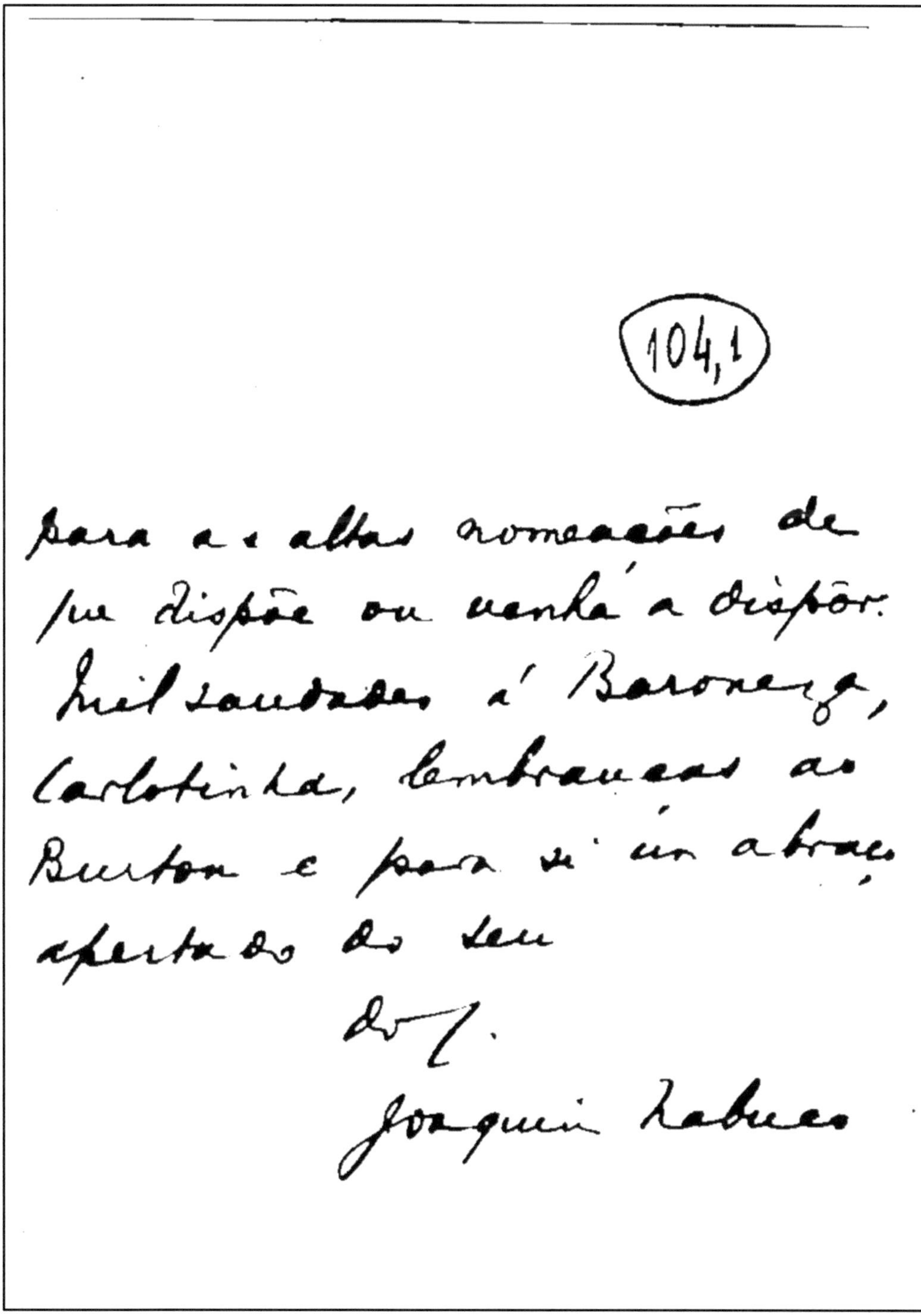
104,1

para as altas nomeações de
que dispõe ou venha á dispôr.
Mil saudades á Baroneza,
Carlotinha, lembranças ao
Burton e para si um abraço
apertado do seu
Am.º
Joaquim Nabuco

**Figure 3.** Document shown if Figure 2 after filtering and binarization.

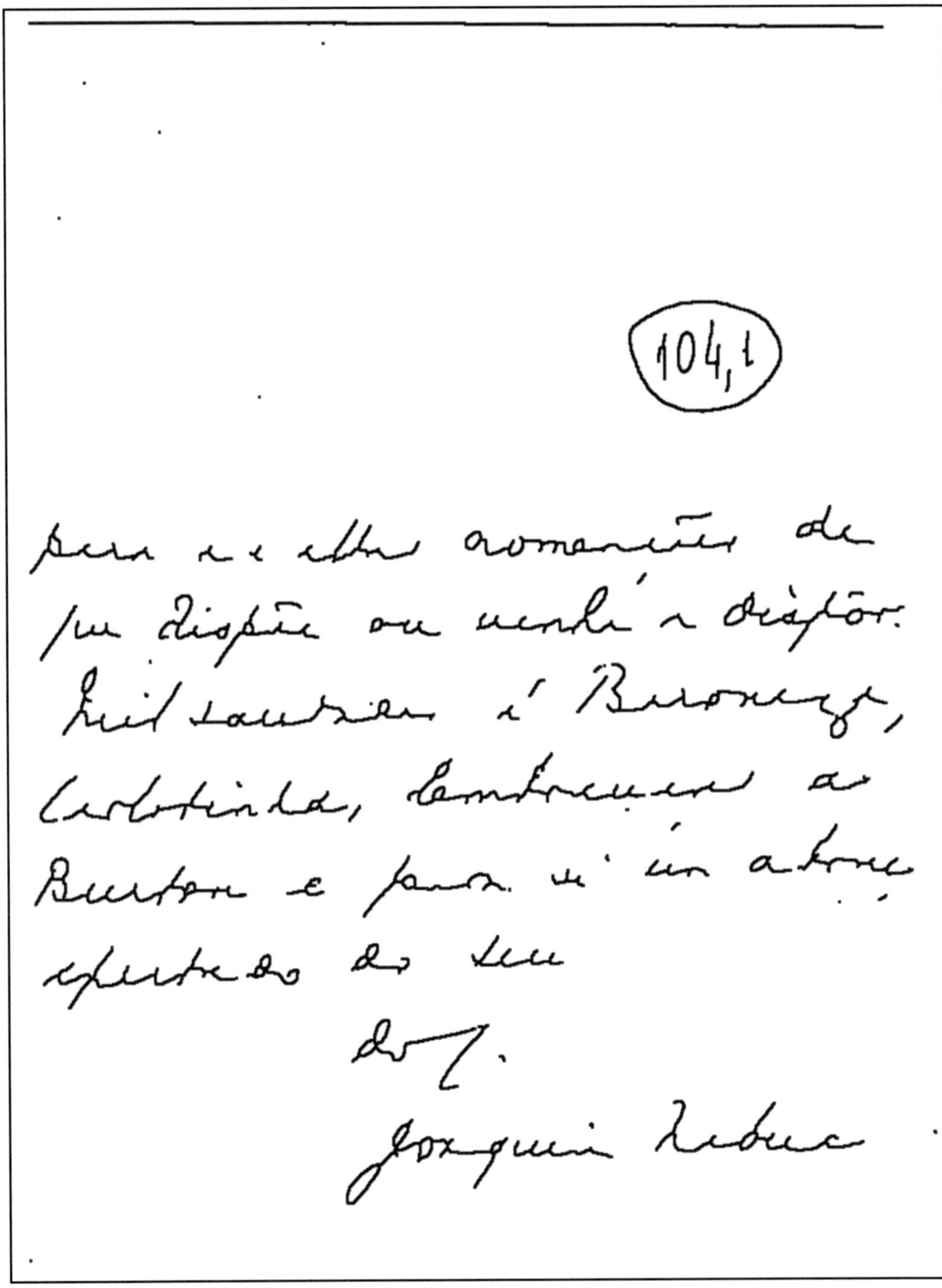


**Figure 4.** Skeletonized and dilated version of letter shown if Figure 3

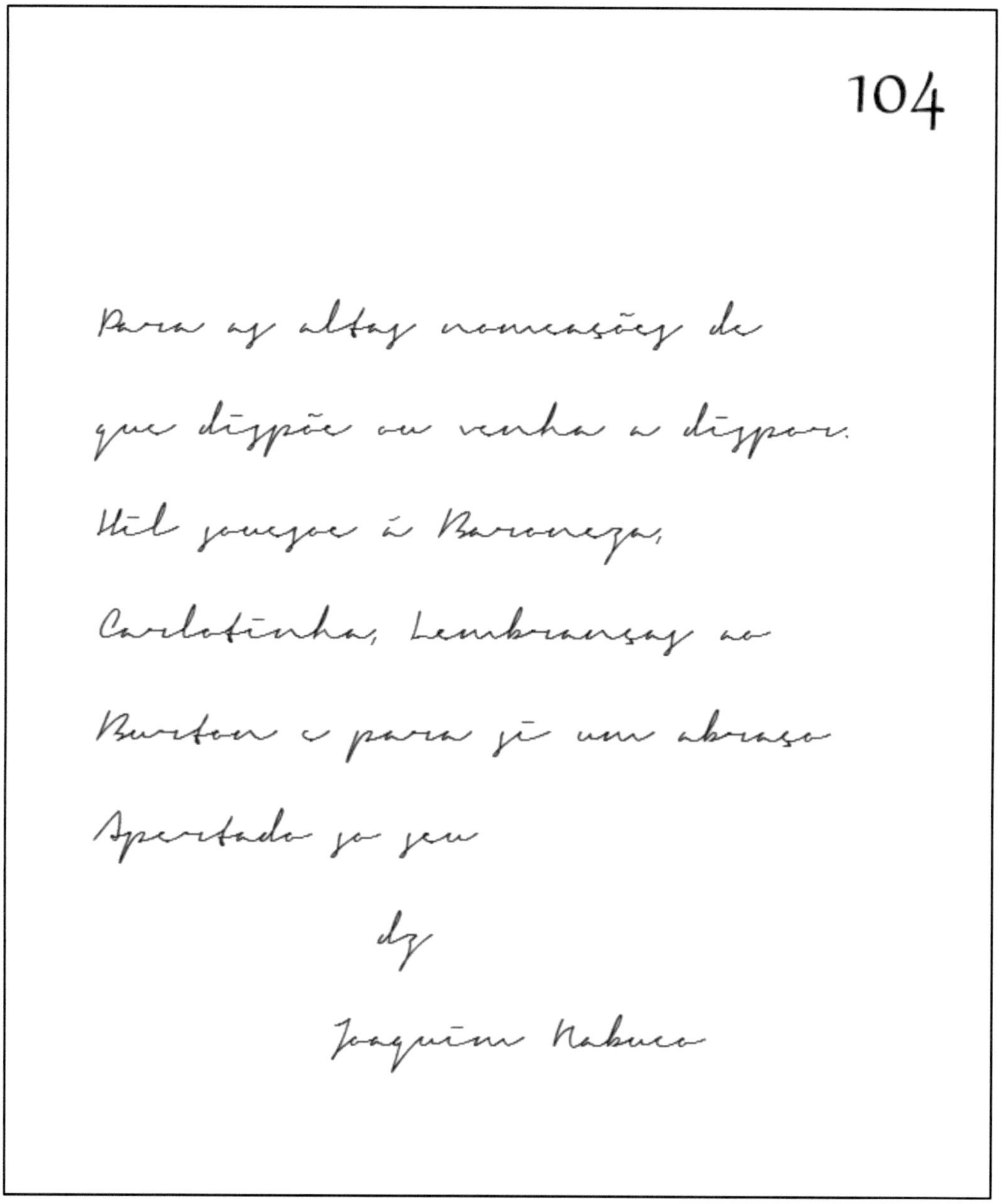


**Figure 5.** Synthetic skeletonized image generated from typesetting the text of the original document with the "Signerica Fat" font set.

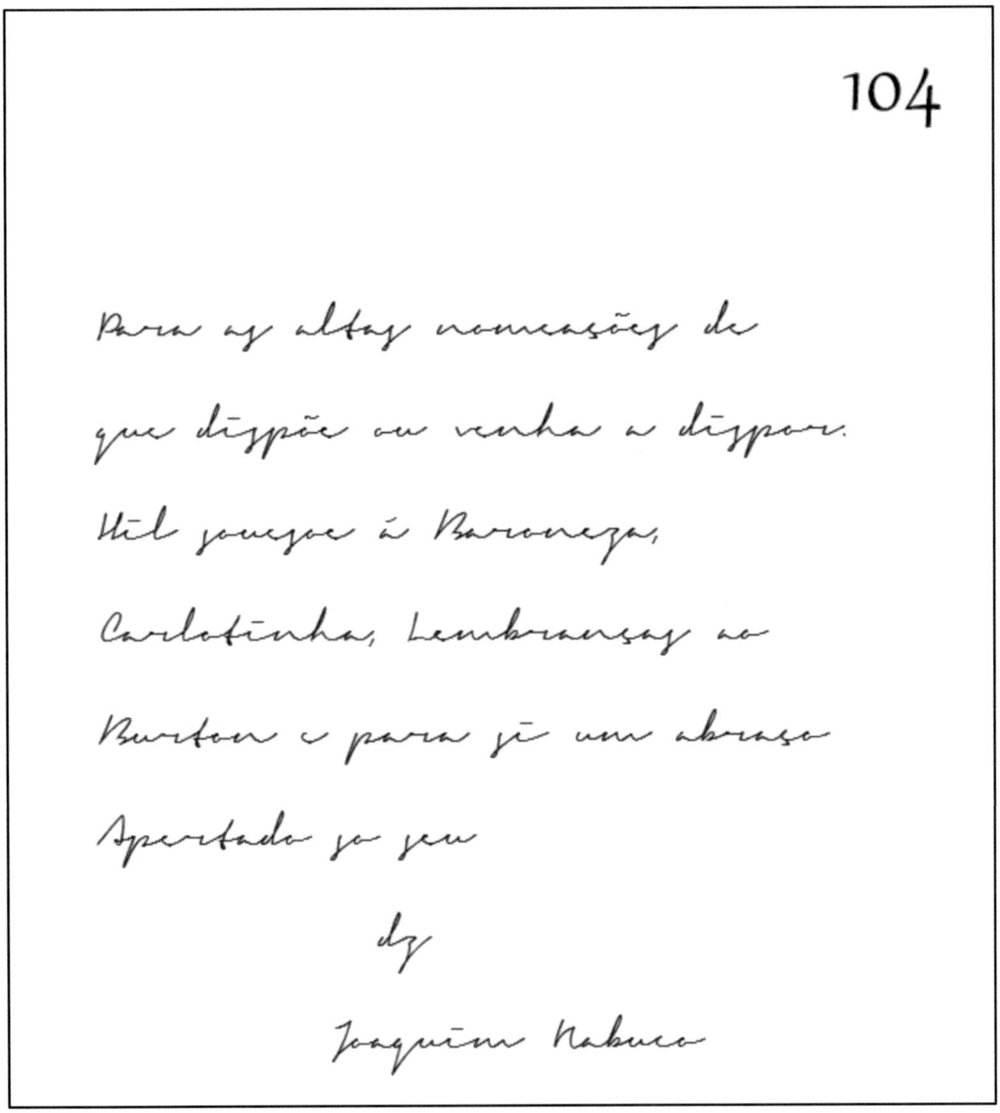


**Figure 6.** Image of Figure 5 after vectorization and deformation to make a font case matching to the original document after skeletonization and dilatation (Figure 4).

The comparison of the images of Figure 2 and Figure 5 shows several small differences, but there is a mapping path between each letter in the original text (ASCII character) and a "font" that resembles the author calligraphic pattern, which allows the automatic generation of a dictionary of patterns to be used as a training set for the recognizer.

The comparison of the images of Figure 2 and Figure 5 shows several small differences, but there is a mapping path between each letter in the original text (ASCII character) and a "font" that resembles the author calligraphic pattern, which allows the automatic generation of a dictionary of patterns to be used as a training set for the recognizer.

A MLP [8] and two SOM [10] fuzzy classifiers were used in parallel and the majority vote is taken for the transcription of the 25 letters in the document test set, totaling 2,115 words (with at least three letters), both trained with the same dictionary of synthesized words. The result obtained was of 61% (1,294 words) correctly transcribed and 17% (364 words) mismatched into (incorrect) valid words. Testing the whole set of fifty letters (3,584 words), that include the 25 letters used to develop the training set the results were of 67% words correctly transcribed and 15% of "false-positive" words . The result of the classifier applied to the remaining 25 letters yielded a precision and recall of 72%. Table 1 shows the significance of the recognition rate reached may be seen if one attempts to automatically recognize the document in Figure 2 with the classifier trained using the approach presented here and three of the best OCR softwares available today in the market: the Abby FineReader version 12 [19], Omnipage [23] and OCRopus 0.3.1 (alpha3) [22] that calls Tesseract.

Table 1 witnesses the suitability of the melhod proposed here. It is interesting to notice that even the human reader does not know what Joaquim Nabuco meant with the symbol (?) just before his signature. The transcription automatically made using the methodology proposed here may be considered very successful, overall if compared with the transcriptions obtained by the commercial OCRs tested (Tesseract produced no output at all). One interesting fact to observe is that although the grammatically correct accent in the third line of the text is "à", Nabuco´s writing was very calligraphically "imprecise" and looks as "á", as automatically transcribed. One may not consider that an error or even that he mispelled the lexeme "à", because the "á" in isolation does not exist in Portuguese. The addition of a dictionary may solve such a problem as well as some other as for instance the transcribed word "Hil" does not exist in Portuguese and the only possible valid candidate is the correct word "Mil" (one thousand).

## 3.2. Word recognition in death certificates

Death certificates provide important data such as *causa mortis*, age of death, birth and death places, parental information, etc. Such information may be used to analyze not only what caused the death of the person, but also a large number of demographic information such as internal migration, the relation of death cause with marital status, sex, profession, etc.

Images were acquired by The Family Search International Institute using a camera-based platform.

| | | |
|---|---|---|
| | | |
| 104<br><br>Para as altas nomeações de que dispõe ou venha a dispor.<br>Mil saudades à Baroneza, Carlotinha, Lembranças ao Burton e para si um abraço Apertado do seu<br><br>???<br><br>Joaquim Nabuco | | 104<br><br>Para as altas nomeações de que dispõe ou venha a dispor.<br>Hil souesoe á Baroneza, Carlotinha, Lembranças ao Burton e para si um abraço Apertado do seu<br><br>dz<br><br>Joaquim Nabuco |
| **Human transcribed text** | | **Proposed Method** |
| 1*^ | -* * ‘ ^ ^^“f* ^CjL-íU As<br>À-«-$tjt_Jt-C<br><br>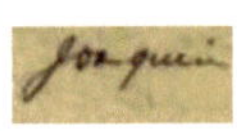 | |
| **Omnipage** | **Abby FineReader Professional Edition 12** | **OCRopus/Tesseract** |

**Table 1.** Human transcribed text of the document in Figure 2 and the automatic transcriptions by the Proposed Method, Omnipage, Abby FineReader and Tesseract.

Thanatos [1] is a platform designed to extract information from the Death Certificate Records in Pernambuco (Brazil), a collection of "books" kept by the local authorities from the 16th century onwards. The current phase of the Thanatos project focuses on the books from the 19th century. During such period, registration books were pre-printed with blank spaces to be filled in by the notary, as shown in Figure 7. Pre-processing is performed to remove noisy borders using the algorithm described in reference [6] incorporated in the

HistDoc Plarform as this step influences all the result of the other subsequent algorithms, the result of which is shown in Figure 8. Image processing continues on the border-removed image (Figure 8) to make image-size (resolution) uniform, binarize, correct skew (using the algorithm Ávila and Lins [3], 2005 also implemented in HistDoc [13]), remove salt-and-pepper and clutter noises, and finally splitting an image in two images each of them corresponding to one death certificate as shown in Figure 9.

Notaries in Brazil are a concession of the State. They are a permanent position many people exercise throughout their lives. Thus, most record books are written by a single person, allowing one to use the strategy proposed here to train the classifier to recognize the content of the different fields. Masks are then applied to extract the content of each of the fields filled in by notaries to extract the content.

They are:

- Nº (Register number) – placed at the top of the left margin of the register. It conveys numerical information only. Example: Nº 19.945.
- Data (Date) – the date is written in words and the information is filled in three fields for day, month, and year in this sequence. Example: Aos vinte e três dias do mês de janeiro de mil novecentos e sessenta e seis (At the twenty three days of the month of January of one thousand nine hundred and sixty six).
- Nome do cartório (Notary name) – this field holds the name of the place where the notary office was found. Example: neste cartório da Encruzilhada (at this notary office at Encruzilhada).
- Município do Cartório (City of the notary office) – Example: município de Recife (at the city of Recife).
- Estado do Cartório (State of the notary office) - Example: Estado de Pernambuco (State of Pernambuco).
- Nome do Declarante (Name of declarer) – Name of who attended the office to inform the death. Example: compareceu Guilherme dos Santos (attended Guilherme dos Santos).
- Nome do Médico (Name of the Medical Doctor) – Name of the M.D. who checked the death. Example: exibindo um atestado de óbito firmado pelo doutor José Ricardo (showing a death declaration signed by doctor José Ricardo).
- Causa mortis – Specifies the reason of the death in the declaration from the M.D. Example: dando como causa da morte edema pulmonar, o qual fica arquivado (that states as cause of death lung edema, which is filed).

The first strategy reported in reference [1] for information recognition in the Thanatos platform was to transcribe the fields using the commercial OCR tool ABBYY FineReader 12 Professional Editor [19]. The results obtained were zero correct recognition for all fields, including even the numerical ones. Such disappointing results forced the development of a recognition tool for the Thanatos platform based in the approach in reference [17] that makes use of a set of geometrical and perceptual features extracted from "zoning" the image.

"Zoning" may be seen as splitting a complex pattern in several simpler ones [18] [11] [7]. The original Thanatos strategy used dictionaries to analyze the possible "answers" to the blank fields. The original results of tests performed with 300 death certificates extracted from the same book of death records [1] were already considered reasonable and are shown in the first column of Table 2.

The adoption of the strategy presented here to generate the features of the writer through the modification of a cursive type font text was adopted. The list of all cities and places (villages, neighborhoods, etc) in the state of Pernambuco was collected from IBGE (the Brazilian Geographic and Statistical Institute) a social science research institute responsible for demographic and economic statistics and data collection in Brazil. Another list of family names was also generated having as basis the local phone directory. Those lists were "typeset" using the synthetic set of features extracted and then used to train the classifiers. The results obtained adopting this strategy is presented in the New column in Table 2. It is important to stress that the same parallel architecture (MLP + 2 SOM) fuzzy classifiers with majority vote was used in both cases, only with different training sets.

| Field | Thanatos | New |
|---|---|---|
| Name of Notary | 98.0% | 98.5% |
| City of the Notary | 71.0% | 94.0% |
| State of the Notary | 98.0% | 100.0% |
| Place of death | 31.0% | 73.0% |
| Numbers in writing - Time of obit | 69.0% | 91.0% |
| Numbers in writing - Date of death | 69.0% | 91.0% |
| Numbers in writing - Date of birth | 69.0% | 91.0% |
| Color of skin | 100.0% | 100.0% |
| Marital status | 100.0% | 100.0% |

**Table 2.** Recognition rate for non-numerical fields in 300 certificates.

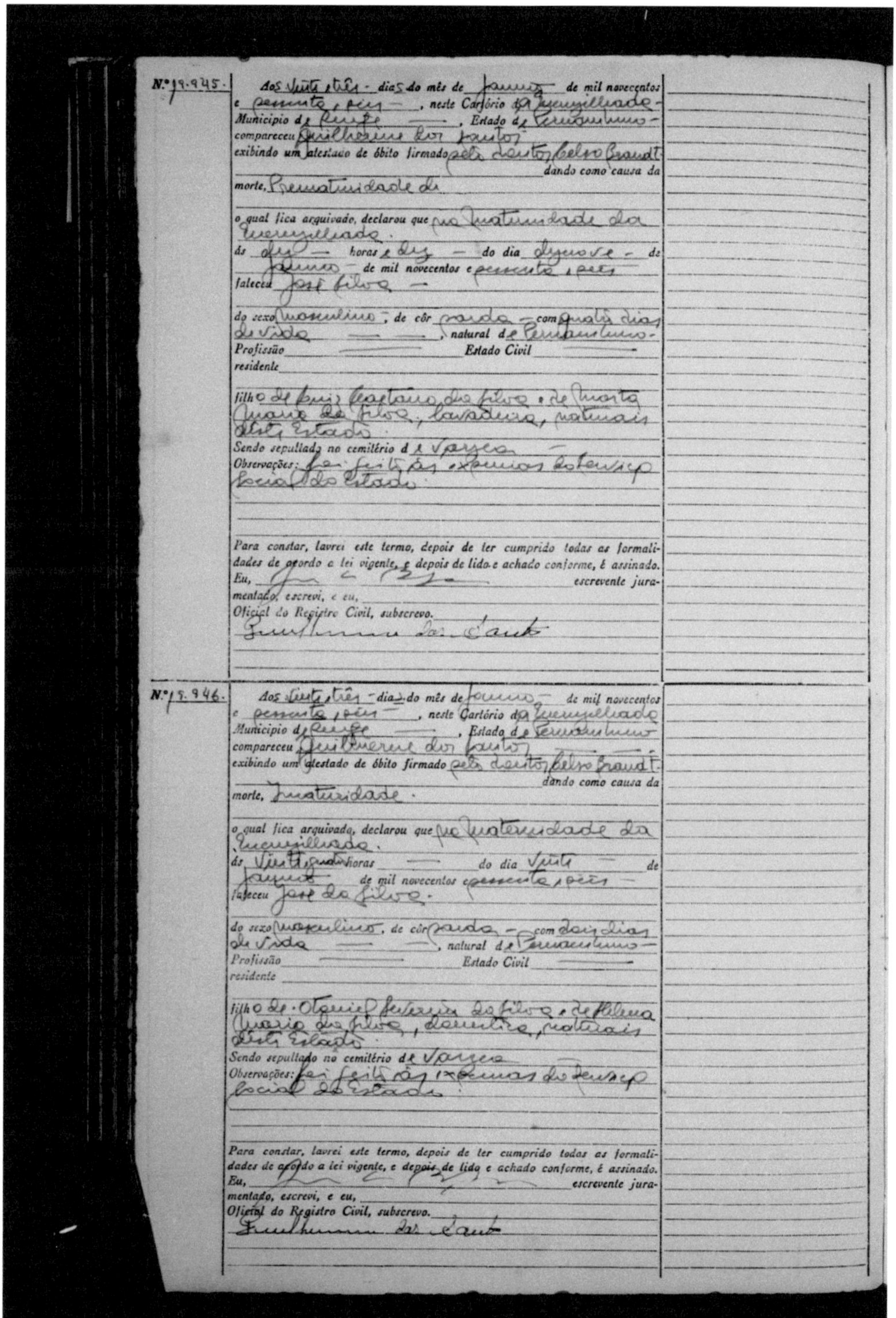

N.º 19.945.

Aos vinte e três dias do mês de janeiro de mil novecentos e sessenta e seis, neste Cartório da Encruzilhada, Município do Recife, Estado de Pernambuco, compareceu Guilherme dos Santos exibindo um atestado de óbito firmado pelo doutor Celso Brandt dando como causa da morte, Prematuridade de ...

o qual fica arquivado, declarou que na Maternidade da Encruzilhada. às dez horas e dez do dia dezenove de janeiro de mil novecentos e sessenta e seis faleceu José Silva

do sexo masculino, de côr parda com quatro dias de vida, natural de Pernambuco.
Profissão ______ Estado Civil ______
residente ______

filho de Luiz Caetano da Silva e de Marta Maria da Silva, lavadeira, naturais deste Estado.
Sendo sepultado no cemitério de Várzea
Observações: Foi feito os exames ...

Para constar, lavrei este termo, depois de ter cumprido todas as formalidades de acordo a lei vigente, e depois de lido e achado conforme, é assinado. Eu, ______ escrevente juramentado, escrevi, e eu, Oficial do Registro Civil, subscrevo.

N.º 19.946.

Aos vinte e três dias do mês de janeiro de mil novecentos e sessenta e seis, neste Cartório da Encruzilhada, Município do Recife, Estado de Pernambuco, compareceu Guilherme dos Santos exibindo um atestado de óbito firmado pelo doutor Celso Brandt dando como causa da morte, Prematuridade.

o qual fica arquivado, declarou que na Maternidade da Encruzilhada. às vinte e ... horas do dia vinte de janeiro de mil novecentos e sessenta e seis faleceu José da Silva.

do sexo masculino, de côr parda com dois dias de vida, natural de Pernambuco.
Profissão ______ Estado Civil ______
residente ______

filho de Otaniel Ferreira da Silva e de Helena Maria da Silva, doméstica, naturais deste Estado.
Sendo sepultado no cemitério de Várzea
Observações: Foi feito os exames ...

Para constar, lavrei este termo, depois de ter cumprido todas as formalidades de acordo a lei vigente, e depois de lido e achado conforme, é assinado. Eu, ______ escrevente juramentado, escrevi, e eu, Oficial do Registro Civil, subscrevo.

**Figure 7.** Original image from a book of printed forms of death certificates in Pernambuco (Brazil) – 1966.

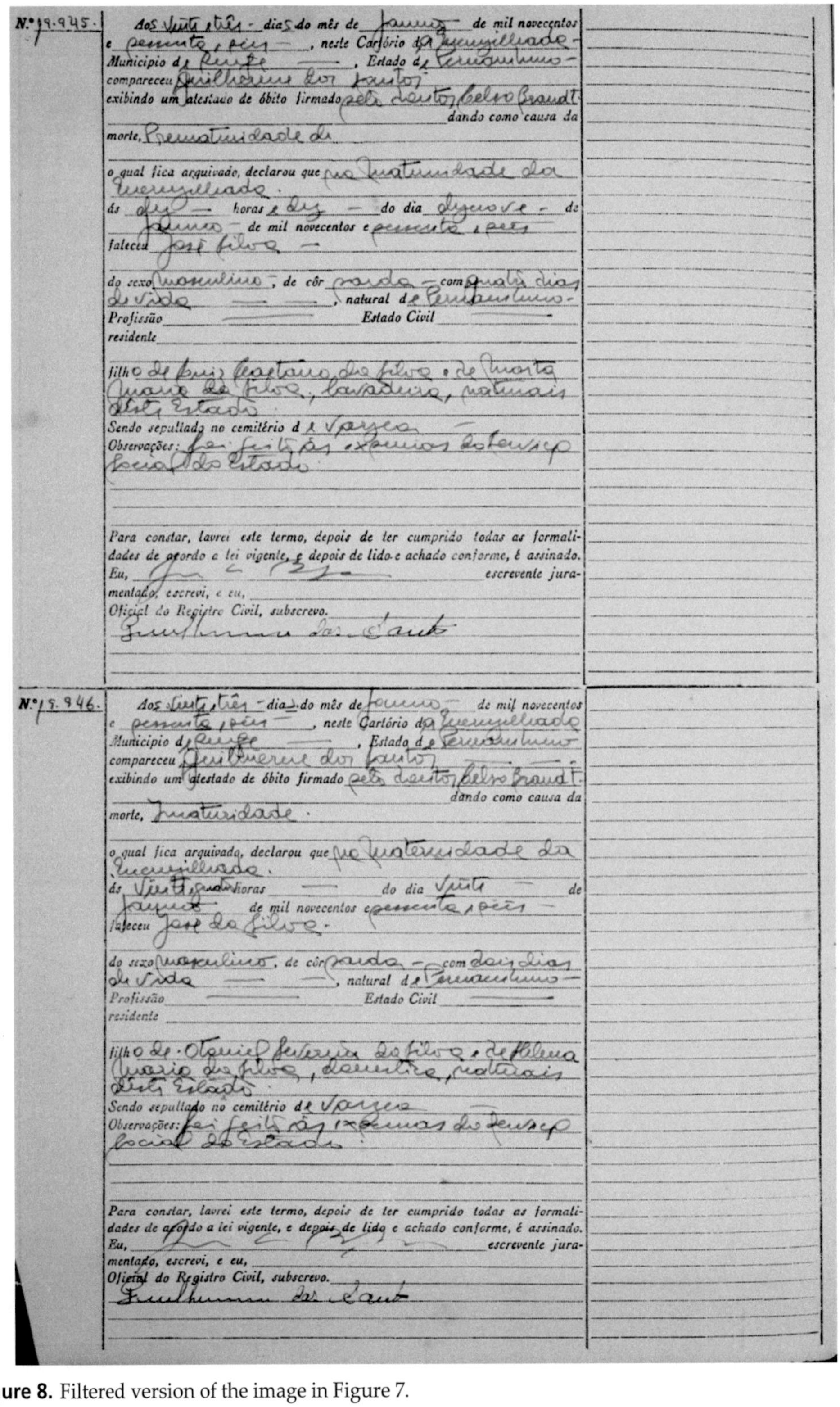

**Figure 8.** Filtered version of the image in Figure 7.

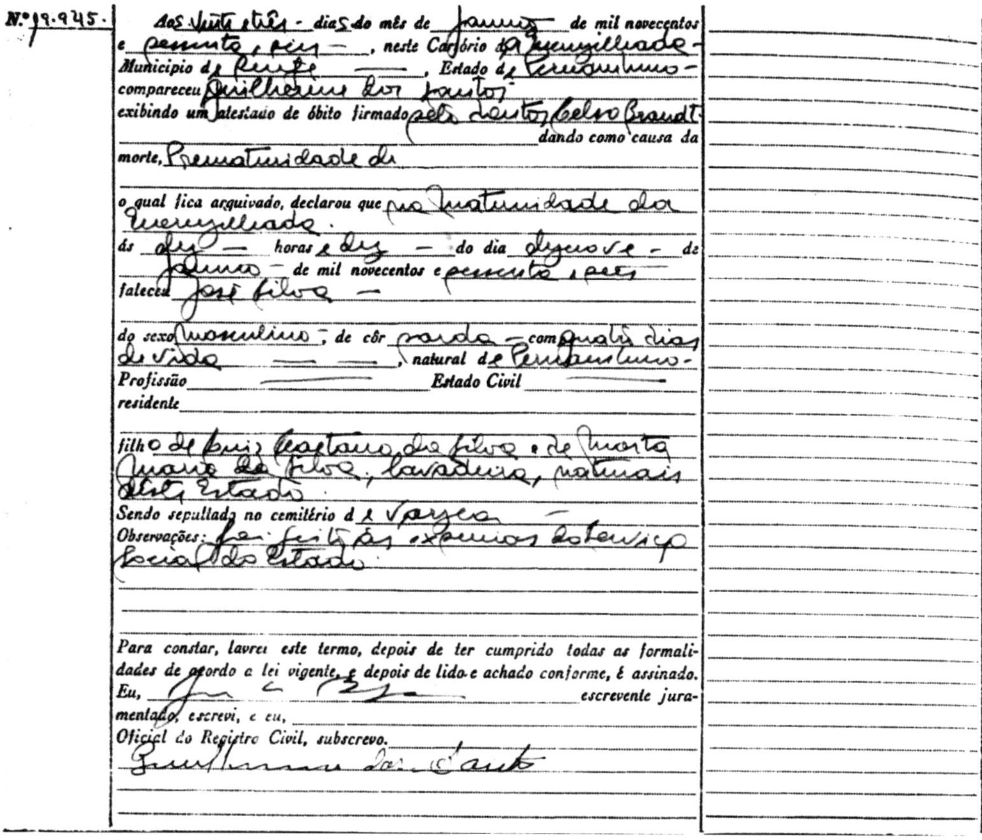

N.° 19.945.

Aos vinte e três dias do mês de janeiro de mil novecentos e cinquenta e seis, neste Cartório da Encruzilhada Município do Recife, Estado de Pernambuco compareceu Guilherme dos Santos exibindo um atestado de óbito firmado pelo doutor Celso Brandt dando como causa da morte, Prematuridade de

o qual fica arquivado, declarou que na Maternidade da Encruzilhada.
às dez horas e dez do dia dezenove de janeiro de mil novecentos e cinquenta e seis
faleceu José Silva
do sexo masculino, de côr parda com quatro dias de vida, natural de Pernambuco.
Profissão Estado Civil
residente

filho de Luiz Caetano da Silva e de Maria Joana da Silva, lavadeira, naturais deste Estado
Sendo sepultado no cemitério de Várzea
Observações: Foi feito às expensas do Serviço Social do Estado

Para constar, lavrei este termo, depois de ter cumprido todas as formalidades de acordo a lei vigente, e depois de lido e achado conforme, é assinado. Eu, escrevente juramentado, escrevi, e eu, Oficial do Registro Civil, subscrevo.
Guilherme dos Santos

**Figure 9.** Monochromatic version of Death Certificate after filtering and splitting the image in Figure 8.

The column Thanatos refers to the results obtained in reference [1], while **New** presents the results of the strategy presented in this paper. Table 2 shows that the new strategy presented here presented either no loss or gains in the recognition rate of all fields recognized in relation to the results presented in reference [1]. In the case of the field "Place of death" the increase in recognition rate reached 42%.

## 4. Conclusions and lines for further work

Handwritten recognition to gain any degree of success either chooses a limited dictionary and allows a large number of writers or widens the vocabulary and largely restricts the numbers of writers. In both cases, the choice of the training set is of central importance for the success of any classification strategy and must be representative of the whole "universe" one wants to correctly recognize. This paper presents a new way of automatically generating the training set for the recognition of a large set of words written by a single user. It has as starting point different sets cursive type fonts, which are modified and compared to the original writing to "match their features". Once the "matching path" is found it is applied to a large dictionary in that encompasses the vocabulary of the document, generating the training set to be used for the whole batch of documents to be transcribed.

The strategy presented here was used with success in two sets of documents. In the case of the transcription of the handwritten letters in the bequest of Joaquim Nabuco it reached the correct rate of 67% transcribed words (of more than three letters), a result that may be considered successful at least for keyword indexing of such historical documents. In the case of death certificates of the Thanatos project, whose vocabulary is far more restricted the results presented either no loss or gains in the recognition rate of all fields recognized in relation to the previous results, reaching an average of 93.79% correct field recognition.

The statistical data collected inter character and inter word spacing, line and character skew, inter line separation were not used to enrich the generation of entries in the dictionary of the training set. Its use is left as a possibility for further work.

## Author details

Gabriel Pereira e Silva and Rafael Dueire Lins
*Universidade Federal de Pernambuco, Brazil*

## Acknowledgement

The authors are grateful to the organizers of the Fontspace site for setting such a useful site, fundamental for the development of this work. The authors also thank the Family Search International Institute for the initiative of digitizing the death certificate records of Pernambuco (Brazil) and to Tribunal de Justiça de Pernambuco (TJPE) to allow the use of such data for research purposes.

Research presented here is partly sponsored by CNPq-Conselho Nacional de Pesquisas e Desenvolvimento Tecnológico, Brazilian Government.

## 5. References

[1] A. Almeida, R.D.Lins, and G.F. Pereira e Silva. Thanatos. Automatically Retrieving Information from Death Certificates in Brazil. Proceedings of the 2011 Workshop on Historical Document Imaging and Processing, pp. 146-153, ACM Press, 2011.

[2] A. I. de S. L. Andrade, C. L. de S. L. Rêgo, T. C. de S. Dantas, Catálogo da Correspondência de Joaquim Nabuco 1903-1906, volume I 1865-1884, volume II 1885-1889, volume III 1890-1910, Editora Massangana, ISBN 857019126X, 1980. (Available at: www.fundaj.gov.br/geral/2010anojn/catalogo_nabuco_v2.pdf)

[3] B. T. Ávila and R. D. Lins. A Fast Orientation and Skew Detection Algorithm for Monochromatic Document Images. 2005 ACM International Conference on Document Engineering, p.118 - 126. ACM Press, 2005.

[4] L. Bethell, J. M. De Carvalho. Joaquim Nabuco, British Abolitionists, and the End of Slavery in Brazil: Correspondence 1880-1905, Institute for the Studies of the Americas, 2009. ISBN-13: 978-1900039956.

[5] M. Bulacu and L. Schomaker. Text-independent writer identification and verfication using textural and allographic features. IEEE Trans. on PAMI, 29(4):701.717, April 2007.

[6] A. de A. Formiga and R. D. Lins. Efficient Removal of Noisy Borders of Monochromatic Documents. International Conference on Image Analysis and Recognition, 2009, LNCS v.5627. p.158 – 167, Springer Verlag, 2009.

[7] C. O. A. Freitas, L.S. Oliveira, S.B.K. Aires, F. Bortolozzi, Zoning and metaclasses for character recognition. ACM–SAC 2007. P. 632-636, 2007.

[8] S. Haykin, Neural Networks: A Comprehensive Foundation. Hardcover (2nd Edition), 1998.

[9] M. Hu, "Visual pattern recognition by moment invariants", IEEE Transactions on Information Theory, 8(2):179-187, 1962.

[10] T. Kohonen, Self-Organizing Maps, Springer Series in Information Sciences,Springer, second edition, vol. 30, 1997.

[11] Z.C. Li, C.Y. Suen, J. Guo, A Regional Decomposition Method for Recognizing Handprinted Characters, IEEE Transactions on Systems, Man, and Cybernetics, N. 25, p. 998-1010, 1995.

[12] R.D.Lins. Nabuco - Two Decades of Document Processing in Latin America, Journal of Universal Computer Science, v. 17(1), pp. 151-161, 2011.

[13] R.D.Lins, G.F. Pereira e Silva, A.de A. Formiga. HistDoc v. 2.0: enhancing a platform to process historical documents. Proceedings of the 2011 Workshop on Historical Document Imaging and Processing, pp. 169-176, ACM Press, 2011.

[14] C. Liu, Y. Liu, and R. Dai, "Preprocessing and statistical/structural feature extraction for handwritten numeral recognition", Progress of Handwriting Recognition, A.C. Downton and S. Impedovo eds., World Scientific, 1997.

[15] C. Liu, K. Nakashima, H. Sako, and H. Fujisawa, "Handwritten digit recognition: benchmarking of state-of-the-art techniques", Pattern Recognition, 36(10):2271-2285, 2003.

[16] L. Oliveira, R. Sabourin, F. Bortolozzi, and C. Suen, "Automatic recognition of handwritten numerical strings: A recognition and verification strategy", IEEE Trans. on Pattern Analysis and Machine Intelligence, 24(11):1438-1454, 2002.

[17] G. F. Pereira e Silva and R. D. Lins. An Automatic Method for Enhancing Character Recognition in Degraded Historical Documents. ICDAR 2011, Beijing, September, IEEE Press, 2011.

[18] C.Y. Suen, J. Guo, Z.C Li, Analysis and Recognition of Alphanumeric Handprints by parts, IEEE Transactions on Systems,Man, and Cybernetics, N. 24, p. 614-631, 1994.

[19] ABBYY FineReader 12 Professional Editor, http://finereader.abbyy.com/ , last visited on 13.04.2012.

[20] IMAGEJ. http://rsbweb.nih.gov/ij/ , last visited on 13.04.2012.

[21] http://www.fontspace.com/category/cursive?p=19 , last visited on 13.04.2012.

[22] OCRopus 0.3.1 (alpha3): http://code.google.com/p/ocropus/
[23] Nuance OminiPage Professional 16: http://www.nuance.com/for-individuals/by-product/omnipage/index.htm

Chapter 10

# Stroke-Based Cursive Character Recognition

K.C. Santosh and Eizaburo Iwata

Additional information is available at the end of the chapter

http://dx.doi.org/10.5772/51471

## 1. Introduction

Human eye can see and read what is written or displayed either in natural handwriting or in printed format. The same work in case the machine does is called handwriting recognition. Handwriting recognition can be broken down into two categories: off-line and on-line.

**Off-line character recognition** – Off-line character recognition takes a raster image from a scanner (scanned images of the paper documents), digital camera or other digital input sources. The image is binarised based on for instance, color pattern (color or gray scale) so that the image pixels are either 1 or 0.

**On-line character recognition** – In on-line, the current information is presented to the system and recognition (of character or word) is carried out at the same time. Basically, it accepts a string of $(x, y)$ coordinate pairs from an electronic pen touching a pressure sensitive digital tablet.

In this chapter, we keep focusing on on-line writer independent cursive character recognition engine. In what follows, we explain the importance of on-line handwriting recognition over off-line, the necessity of writer independent system and the importance as well as scope of cursive scripts like Devanagari. Devanagari is considered as one of the known cursive scripts [20, 29]. However, we aim to include other scripts related to the current study.

### 1.1. Why on-line?

With the advent of handwriting recognition technology since a few decades [3, 31], applications are challenging. For example, OCR is becoming an integral part of document scanners, and is used in many applications such as postal processing, script recognition, banking, security (signature verification, for instance) and language identification. In handwriting recognition, feature selection has been an important issue [43]. Both structural and statistical features as well as their combination have been widely used [15, 18]. These features tend to vary since characters' shapes vary widely. As a consequence, local structural properties like intersection of lines, number of holes, concave arcs, end points and junctions change time to time. These are mainly due to

- *deformations* can be from any range of shape variations including geometric transformation such as translation, rotation, scaling and even stretching; and
- *defects* yield imperfections due to printing, optics, scanning, binarisation as well as poor segmentation.

In the state-of-the-art of handwritten character recognition, several different studies have shown that off-line handwriting recognition offers less classification rate compared to on-line [31, 42]. Furthermore, on-line data offers significant reduction in memory and therefore space complexity. Another advantage is that the digital pen or a digital form on a tablet device immediately transforms your handwriting into a digital representation that can be reused later without having any risk of degradation usually associated with ancient handwriting. Based on all these reasons, one can cite a few examples [7, 13, 32, 45] where they mainly focus on temporal information as well as writing order recovery from static handwriting image. On-line handwriting recognition systems provide interesting results.

On-line character recognition involves the automatic conversion of stroke as it is written on a special digitiser or PDA, where a sensor picks up the pen-tip movements as well as pen-up/pen-down switching. Such data is known as digital ink and can be regarded as a dynamic representation of handwriting. The obtained signal is converted into letter codes which are usable within computer and character-processing applications.

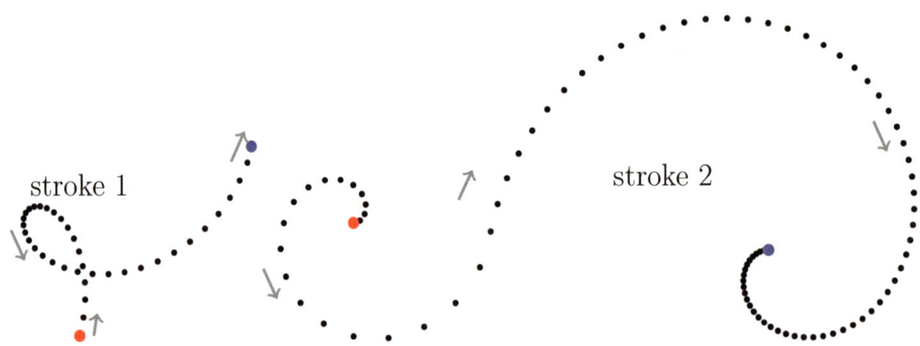


**Figure 1.** On-line stroke sequences in the form of 2D $(x, y)$ coordinates. In this illustration, initial pen-tip position is coloured with red and pen-up (final point) is coloured with blue.

The elements of an on-line handwriting recognition interface typically include:

1. a pen or stylus for the user to write with, and a touch sensitive surface, which may be integrated with, or adjacent to, an output display.
2. a software application i.e., a recogniser which interprets the movements of the stylus across the writing surface, translating the resulting strokes into digital character.

Globally, it resembles one of the applications of pen computing i.e., computer user-interface using a pen (or stylus) and tablet, rather than devices such as a keyboard, joysticks or a mouse. Pen computing can be extended to the usage of mobile devices such as wireless tablet personal computers, PDAs and GPS receivers.

Historically, pen computing (defined as a computer system employing a user-interface using a pointing device plus handwriting recognition as the primary means for interactive user input) predates the use of a mouse and graphical display by at least two decades, starting with the Stylator [12] and RAND tablet [16] systems of the 1950s and early 1960s.

### 1.2. Why writer independent?

As mentioned before, on-line handwriting recognition systems provide interesting results almost over all types scripts. The recognition systems vary widely which can be due to nature of the scripts employed along with the associated particular difficulties including the intended applications. The performance of the application-based (commercial) recogniser is used to determine by its speed in addition to accuracy.

Among many, more specifically, template based approaches have a long standing record [4, 11, 19, 36, 41]. In many of the cases, writer independent recogniser has been made since every new user does not require training – which is widely acceptable. In such a context, the expected recognition system should automatically update or adapt the new users once they provide input or previously trained recogniser should be able to discriminate new users.

### 1.3. Why Devanagari?

In a few points, interesting scope will be summarised.

1. Pencil and paper can be preferable for anyone during a first draft preparation instead of using keyboard and other computer input interfaces, especially when writing in languages and scripts for which keyboards are cumbersome. Devanagari keyboards for instance, are quite difficult to use. Devanagari characters follow a complex structure and may count up to more than 500 symbols [20, 29].
2. Devanagari is a script used to write several Indian languages, including Nepali, Sanskrit, Hindi, Marathi, Pali, Kashmiri, Sindhi, and sometimes Punjabi. According to the 2001 Indian census, 258 million people in India used Devanagari.
3. Writing one's own style brings unevenness in writing units, which is the most difficult part to recognise. Variation in basic writing units such as number of strokes, their order, shapes and sizes, tilting angles and similarities among classes of characters are considered as the important issues. In contrast to Roman script, it happens more in cursive scripts like Devanagari.

   Devanagari is written from left to right with a horizontal line on the *top* which is the *shirorekha*. Every character requires one *shirorekha* from which text(s) is(are) suspended. The way of writing Devanagari has its own particularities. In what follows, in particular, we shortly explain a few major points associated difficulties.

   - Many of the characters are similar to each other in structure. Visually very similar *symbols* – even from the same writer – may represent different *characters*. While it might seem quite obvious in the following examples to distinguish the first from the second, it can easily be seen that confusion is likely to occur for their handwritten *symbol* counterparts (क, फ), (य, प), (ढ, द), etc.). Fig. 2 shows a few examples of it.
   - The number of strokes, their order, shapes and sizes, directions, skew angle etc. are writing units that are important for symbol recognition and classification. However, these writing units most often vary from one user to another and there is even no guarantee that a same user always writes in a same way. Proposed methods should take this into account.

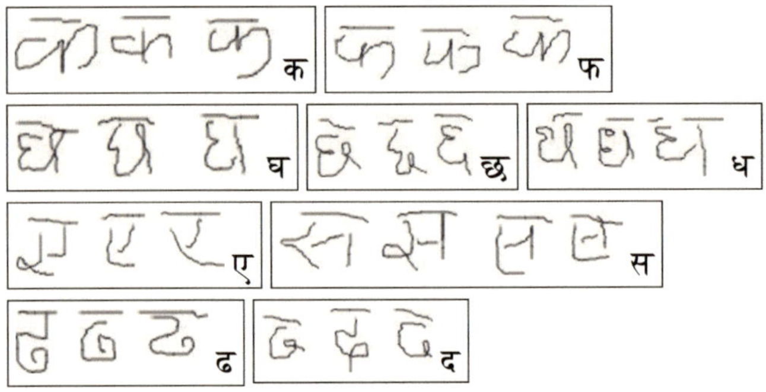


**Figure 2.** A few samples of several different similar classes from Devanagari script.

Based on those major aforementioned reasons, there exists clear motivation to pursue research on Devanagari handwritten character recognition.

### 1.4. Structure of the chapter

The remaining of the paper is organised as follows. In Section 2, we start with detailing the basic concept of character recognition framework in addition to the major highlights on important issues: feature selection, matching and recognition. Section 3 gives a complete outline of how we can efficiently handle optimal recognition performance over cursive scripts like Devangari. In this section, we first provide the complete and then validate the whole process step by step with genuine reasoning and a series of experimental tests over our own dataset but, publicly available. We conclude the chapter in Section 4.

## 2. Character recognition framework

Basically, we can categorise character recognition system into two modules: learning and testing. In learning or training module, following Fig. 3, handwritten strokes are learnt or stored. Testing module follows the former one. The performance of the recognition system is depends on how well handwritten strokes are learnt. It eventually refers to the techniques we employ.

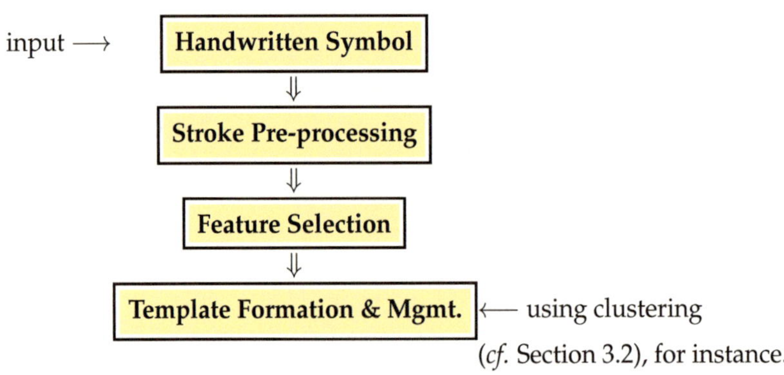


**Figure 3.** Learning strokes from the handwritten symbols. In this illustration, we present a basic concept to form template via clustering of features of the strokes immediately after they are pre-processed.

Basically, learning module employs stroke pre-processing, feature selection and clustering to form template to be stored. Pre-processing and feature selection techniques can be varied from one application to another. For example, noisy stroke elimination or deletion in Roman cannot be directly extended to the cursive scripts like Urdu and Devanagari. In other words, these techniques are found to be application dependent due to their different writing styles. However, they are basically adapted to each other and mostly ad-hoc techniques are built so that optimal recognition performance is possible. In the framework of stroke-based feature extraction and recognition, one can refer to [9, 47], for example. It is important to notice that feature selection usually drives the way we match them. As an example, fixed size feature vectors can be straightforwardly matched while for non-linear feature vector sequences, dynamic programming (elastic matching) has been basically used [22, 23, 26, 33]. The concept was first introduced in the 60's [5]. Once we have an idea to find the similarity between the strokes' features, we follow clustering technique based on their similarity values. The clustering technique will generate templates as the representative of the similar strokes provided. These stored templates will be used for testing in the testing module. Fig. 4 provides a comprehensive idea of it (testing module). More specifically, in this module, every test stroke will be matched with the templates (learnt in training module) so that we can find the most similar one. This procedure will be repeated for all available test strokes. At the end, aggregating all matching scores provides an idea of the test character closer to which one in the template.

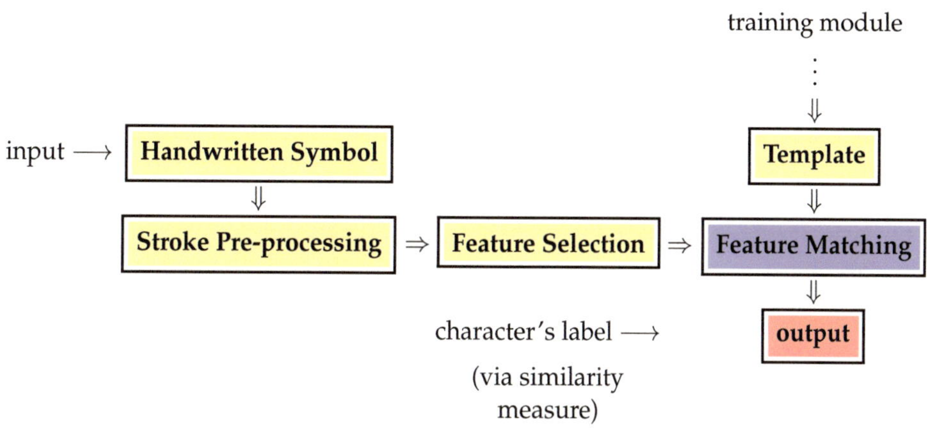


**Figure 4.** An illustration of testing module. As in learning module, test characters are pre-processed and we present a basic concept to form template via clustering of features of the strokes immediately after they are pre-processed.

## 2.1. Preprocessing

Strokes directly collected from users are often incomplete and noisy. Different systems use a variety of different pre-processing techniques before feature extraction [1, 6, 44]. The techniques used in one system may not exactly fit into the other because of different writing styles and nature of the scripts. Very common issues are repeated coordinates deletion [4], noise elimination and normalisation [10, 17].

Besides pre-processing, in this chapter, we mainly focus on feature selection and matching techniques.

## 2.2. Feature selection

If you have complete address of your friend then you can easily find him/her without an additional help from other people on the way. The similar case is happened in character recognition. Here, an address refers to a feature selection. Therefore, the complete or sufficient feature selection from the provided input is the crucial point. In other words, appropriate feature selection can greatly decrease the workload and simplify the subsequent design process of the classifier.

In what follows, we discuss a few but major issues associated with feature selection.

- Pen-flow i.e., speed while writing determines how well the coordinates along the pen trajectory are captured. Speed writing and writing with shivering hands, do not provide complete shape information of the strokes.
- Ratios of the relative height, width and size of letters are not always consistent - which is obvious in natural handwriting.
- Pen-down and pen-up events provide stroke segmentation. But, we do not know which and where the strokes are rewritten or overwritten.
- Slant writing style or writing with some angles to the left or right makes feature selection difficult. For example, in those cases, zoning information using orthogonal projection does not carry consistent information. This means that the zoning features will vary widely as soon as we have different writing styles.

We repeat, features should contain sufficient information to distinguish between classes, be insensitive to irrelevant variability of the input, allow efficient computation of discriminant functions and be able to limit the amount of training data required [24]. However, they vary from one script to another [6, 27, 28, 44].

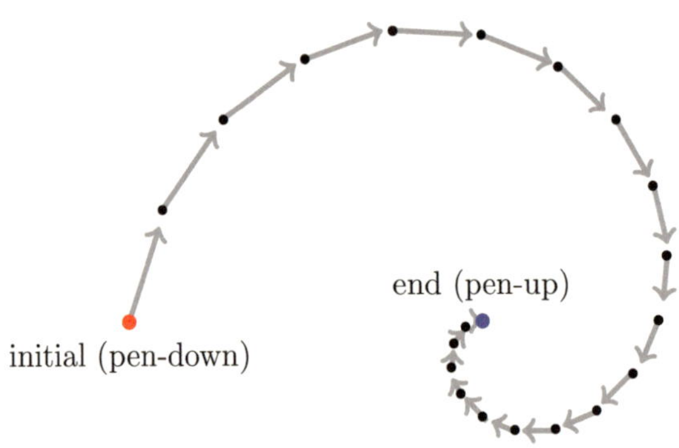


**Figure 5.** An illustration of feature selection: pen-tip position and tangent at every pen-tip position along the pen trajectory.

Feature selection is always application dependent i.e., it relies on what type of scripts (their characteristics and difficulties) used. In our case, we use a feature vector sequence of any stroke is expressed as in [28, 36, 40]:

$$\mathbf{F} = \left[(\mathbf{p}_1, \alpha_{\mathbf{p}_1,\mathbf{p}_2}), (\mathbf{p}_2, \alpha_{\mathbf{p}_2,\mathbf{p}_3}), \ldots, (\mathbf{p}_{l-1}, \alpha_{\mathbf{p}_{l-1},\mathbf{p}_l})\right] \tag{1}$$

where, $\alpha_{\mathbf{p}_{l-1},\mathbf{p}_l} = \arctan\left(\frac{y_l - y_{l-1}}{x_l - x_{l-1}}\right)$. Fig. 5 shows a complete illustration.

Our feature includes a sequence of both pen-tip position and tangent angles sampled from the trajectory of the pen-tip, preserving the directional property of the trajectory path. It is important to remind that stroke direction (either left – right or right – left) leads to very different features although they are geometrically similar. To efficiently handle it, we need both kinds of strokes or samples for training and testing. This does not mean that same writer must be used.

The idea is somehow similar to the directional arrows that are composed of eight types, coded from $0-7$. This can be expressed as, $\begin{matrix} \nwarrow & \uparrow & \nearrow \\ \leftarrow & \circ & \rightarrow \\ \swarrow & \downarrow & \searrow \end{matrix}$.

However, these directional arrows provide only the directional feature of the strokes or line segments. Therefore, more information can be integrated if the relative length of the standard strokes is taken into account [8].

## 2.3. Feature matching

Besides, discussing on classifiers, we explain how features can be matched to obtain similarity or dissimilarity values between them.

Matching techniques are often induced by how features are taken or strokes are represented. For instance, normalising the feature vector sequence into a fixed size vector provides an immediate matching. On the other hand, features having different lengths or non-linear features need dynamic programming for approximate matching, for instance. Considering the latter situation, we explain how dynamic programming is employed.

Dynamic time warping (DTW) allows us to find the dissimilarity between two non-linear sequences potentially having different lengths [22, 23, 26, 33]. It is an algorithm particularly suited to matching sequences with missing information, provided there are long enough segments for matching to occur.

Let us consider two feature sequences

$$\mathbf{X} = \{\mathbf{x}_k\}_{k=1,\ldots,K} \text{ and}$$
$$\mathbf{Y} = \{\mathbf{y}_l\}_{l=1,\ldots,L}$$

of size $K$ and $L$, respectively. The aim of the algorithm is to provide the optimal alignment between both sequences. At first, a matrix $M$ of size $K \times L$ is constructed. Then for each element in matrix $M$, local distance metric $\delta(k,l)$ between the events $e_k$ and $e_l$ is computed i.e., $\delta(k,l) = (e_k - e_l)^2$. Let $D(k,l)$ be the global distance up to $(k,l)$,

$$D(k,l) = \min \begin{bmatrix} D(k-1,l-1), \\ D(k-1,l), \\ D(k,l-1) \end{bmatrix} + \delta(k,l)$$

with an initial condition $D(1,1) = \delta(1,1)$ such that it allows warping path going diagonally from starting node $(1,1)$ to end $(K,L)$. The main aim is to find the path for which the least cost is associated. The warping path therefore provides the difference cost between the compared signatures. Formally, the warping path is,

$$\mathcal{W} = \{w_t\}_{t=1\ldots T},$$

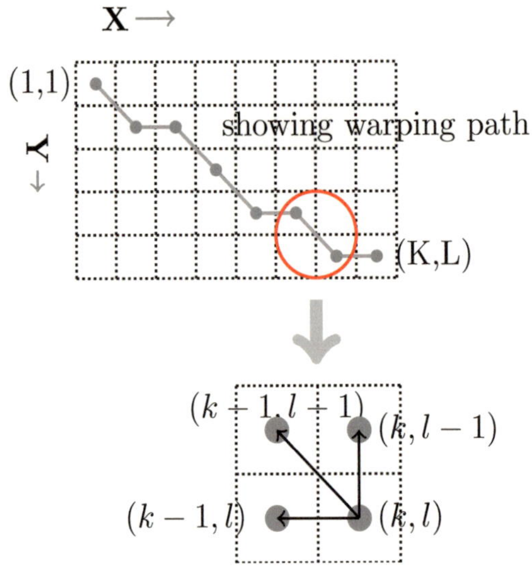


**Figure 6.** Classical DTW algorithm – an alignment illustration between two non-linear sequences **X** and **Y**. In this illustration, diagonal DTW-matrix is shown including how back-tracking has been employed.

where $\max(k,l) \leq T < k+l-1$ and $t^{th}$ element of $\mathcal{W}$ is $w(k,l)_t \in [1:K] \times [1:L]$ for $t \in [1:T]$. The optimised warping path $\mathcal{W}$ satisfies the following three conditions.

**c1.** boundary condition:

$$w_1 = (1,1) \text{ and } w_T = (K,L).$$

**c2.** monotonicity condition:

$$k_1 \leq k_2 \leq \cdots \leq k_K \text{ and } l_1 \leq l_2 \leq \cdots \leq l_L.$$

**c3.** continuity condition:

$$w_{t+1} - w_t \in \{(1,1)(0,1),(1,0)\} \text{ for } t \in [1:T-1].$$

**c1** conveys that the path starts from $(1,1)$ to $(K,L)$, aligning all elements to each other. **c2** forces the path advances one step at a time. **c3** restricts allowable steps in the warping path to adjacent cells, never be back. Note that **c3** implies **c2**.

We then define the global distance between **X** and **Y** as,

$$\Delta(\mathbf{X},\mathbf{Y}) = \frac{D(K,L)}{T}.$$

The last element of the $K \times L$ matrix gives the DTW-distance between **X** and **Y**, which is normalised by $T$ i.e., the number of discrete warping steps along the diagonal DTW-matrix. The overall process is illustrated in Fig. 6.

Until now, we provide a global concept of using DTW distance for non-linear sequences alignment. In order to provide faster matching, we have used local constraint on time warping proposed in [21]. We have $w(k,l)_t$ such that $l - r \leq k \leq l + r$ where $r$ is a term defining a reach i.e., allowed range of warping for a given event in a sequence. With $r$, upper and lower bounding measures can be expressed as,

$$\text{Upper bound } U_k = \max(\mathbf{x}_{k-r} : \mathbf{x}_{k+r})$$
$$\text{Lower bound } L_k = \min(\mathbf{x}_{k-r} : \mathbf{x}_{k+r}).$$

Therefore, for all $i$, an obvious property of $U$ and $L$ is $U_k \geq \mathbf{x}_k \geq L_k$. With this, we can define a lower bounding measure for DTW:

$$\text{LB\_Keogh}(\mathbf{X}, \mathbf{Y}) = \sqrt{\sum_{k=1}^{K} \begin{cases} (\mathbf{y}_k - U_k)^2 & \text{if } \mathbf{y}_k > U_k \\ (\mathbf{y}_k - L_k)^2 & \text{if } \mathbf{y}_k < L_k \\ 0 & \text{otherwise.} \end{cases}}$$

Since this provides a quick introduction of local constraint for lower bounding measure, we refer to [21] for more clarification.

## 2.4. Recognition

From a purely combinatorial point of view, measuring the similarity or dissimilarity between two symbols

$$\mathbf{S}_1 = \left\{\mathbf{s}_1^i\right\}_{i=1...n} \text{ and } \mathbf{S}_2 = \left\{\mathbf{s}_2^j\right\}_{j=1...m}$$

composed, respectively, of $n$ and $m$ strokes, requires a one by one matching score computation of all strokes $\mathbf{s}_1^i$ with all $\mathbf{s}_2^j$. This means that we align individual test strokes of an unknown symbols with the learnt strokes. As soon as we determine the test strokes associated with the known class, the complete symbol can be compared by the fusion of matching information from all test strokes. Such a concept is fundamental under the purview of stroke-based character recognition.

Overall, the concept may not always be sufficient, and these approaches generally need a final, global coherence check to avoid matching of strokes that shows visual similarity but do not respect overall geometric coherence within the complete handwritten character. In other words, matching strategy that happens between test stroke and templates of course, should be intelligent rather than straightforward one-to-many matching concepts. However, it in fact, depends on how template management has been made. In this chapter, this is one of the primary concerns. We highlight the use of relative positioning of the strokes within the handwritten symbol and its direct impact to the performance [40].

# 3. Recognition engine

To make the chapter coherence as well as consistent (to Devanagari character recognition), it refers to the recognition engine which is entirely based on previous studies or works [36–40]. Especially because of the structure of Devanagari, it is necessary to pay attention to the appropriate structuring of the strokes to ease and speed up comparison between the symbols, rather than just relying on global recognition techniques that would be based on a collection of strokes [36]. Therefore, [39, 40] develop a method for analysing handwritten characters based on both the number of strokes and the their spatial information. It consists in four main phases.

**step 1.** Organise the symbols representing the same character into different groups based on the number of strokes.

**step 2.** Find the spatial relation between strokes.

**step 3.** Agglomerate similar strokes from a specific location in a group.

**step 4.** Stroke-wise matching for recognition.

For more clear understanding, we explain the aforementioned steps as follows. For a specific class of character, it is interesting to notice that writing symbols with the equal number of strokes, generally produce visually similar structure and is easier to compare.

In every group within a particular class of character, a representative symbol is synthetically generated from pairwise similar strokes merging, which are positioned identically with respect to the *shirorekha*. It uses DTW algorithm. The learnt strokes are then stored accordingly. It is mainly focused on stroke clustering and management of the learnt strokes.

We align individual test strokes of an unknown symbols with the learnt strokes having both same number of strokes and spatial properties. Overall, symbols can be compared by the fusion of matching information from all test strokes. This eventually build a complete recognition process.

### 3.1. Stroke spatial description and its need

The importance of the location of the strokes is best observed by taking a few pairs of characters that often lead to confusion:

(भ ↔ म), (ध ↔ घ), (थ ↔ य) etc.

The first character in every pair has visually two distinguishing features: its particular location of the *shirorekha* (more to the right) and a small curve in the text. There is no doubt that one of the two features is sufficient to automatically distinguish both characters. However, small curves are usually not robust feature in natural handwriting, finding the location of the *shirorekha* only can avoid possible confusion. Our stroke based spatial relation technique is explained further in the following.

To handle relative positioning of strokes, we use six spatial predicates i.e., $2 \times 3$ relational regions:

$$\mathcal{R} = \begin{bmatrix} \textit{top-left}\ (\text{T–L}) & \textit{top}\ (\text{T}) & \textit{top-right}\ (\text{T–R}) \\ \textit{bottom-left}\ (\text{B–L}) & \textit{bottom}\ (\text{B}) & \textit{bottom-right}\ (\text{B–L}) \end{bmatrix}.$$

For easier understanding, iconic representation of the aforementioned relational matrix $\mathcal{R}$ can be expressed as,

$$\begin{bmatrix} \circ & \circ & \circ \\ \circ & \circ & \bullet \end{bmatrix}$$

where black-dot represents the presence i.e., stroke is found to be in the provided *bottom-right* region.

To confirm the location of the stroke, we use the projection theory: minimum boundary rectangle (MBR) [30] model combined with the stroke's centroid.

Based on [14], we start with checking fundamental topological relations such as *disconnected* (DC), *externally connected* (EC) and *overlap/intersect* (O/I) by considering two strokes $\mathbf{s^j}$ and $\mathbf{s^{j'}}$:

$$\mathbf{s^j} = \left\{\mathbf{p}_k^j\right\}_{k=1...l} \text{ and } \mathbf{s^{j'}} = \left\{\mathbf{p}_{k'}^{j'}\right\}_{k'=1...l'}$$

as follows,

$$\mathbf{s^j} \cap \mathbf{s^{j'}} = \begin{cases} 1 \text{ if } (\mathbf{p}_k^j \cap \mathbf{p}_{k'}^{j'} \neq \emptyset) \Rightarrow \text{EC, O/I} \\ 0 \text{ otherwise} \Rightarrow \text{DC.} \end{cases}$$

We then use the border condition from the geometry of the MBR. It is straightforward for *disconnected* strokes while, is not for *externally connected* and *overlap/intersect* configurations. In the latter case, we check the level of the centroid with respect to the boundary of the MBR. For example, if a boundary of the *shirorekha* is above the centroid level of the *text* stroke, then it is confirmed that the *shirorekha* is on the *top*. This procedure is applied to all of the six previously mentioned spatial predicates. Note that use of angle-based model like bi-centre [25] and angle histogram [46] are not the appropriate choice due to the cursive nature of writing.

On the whole, assuming that the *shirorekha* is on the *top*, the locations of the *text* strokes are estimated. This eventually allows to cross-validate the location of the *shirorekha* along with its size, once *texts'* locations are determined. Fig. 7 shows a real example demonstrating relative positioning between the strokes for a two-stroke symbol क. Besides, symbols with two *shirorekhas* are also possible to treat. In such a situation, the first *shirorekha* according to the order of strokes is taken as reference.

## 3.2. Spatial similarity based clustering

Basically, clustering is a technique for collecting items which are similar in some way. Items of one group are dissimilar with other items belonging to other groups. Consequently, it makes the recognition system compact. To handle this, we present spatial similarity based stroke clustering.

As mentioned in previous work [39, 40], the clustering scheme is a two-step process.

- The first step is to organise symbols representing a same character into different groups, based on the number of strokes used to complete the symbol. Fig. 8 shows an example of it for a class of character अ.
- In the second step, strokes from the specific location are agglomerated hierarchically within the particular group. Once relative position for every stroke is determined as shown in Fig. 8, single-linkage agglomerative hierarchical clustering is used (*cf.* Fig. 10). This means that only strokes which are at a specific location are taken for clustering. As an example, we illustrate it in Fig. 9. This applies to all groups within a class.

In agglomerative hierarchical clustering (*cf.* Fig. 10), we merge two similar strokes and find a new cluster. The distance computation between two strokes follows Section 2.3. The new cluster is computed by averaging both strokes via the use of the discrete warping path along the diagonal DTW-matrix. This process is repeated until it reaches the cluster threshold. The threshold value yields the number of cluster representatives i.e., learnt templates.

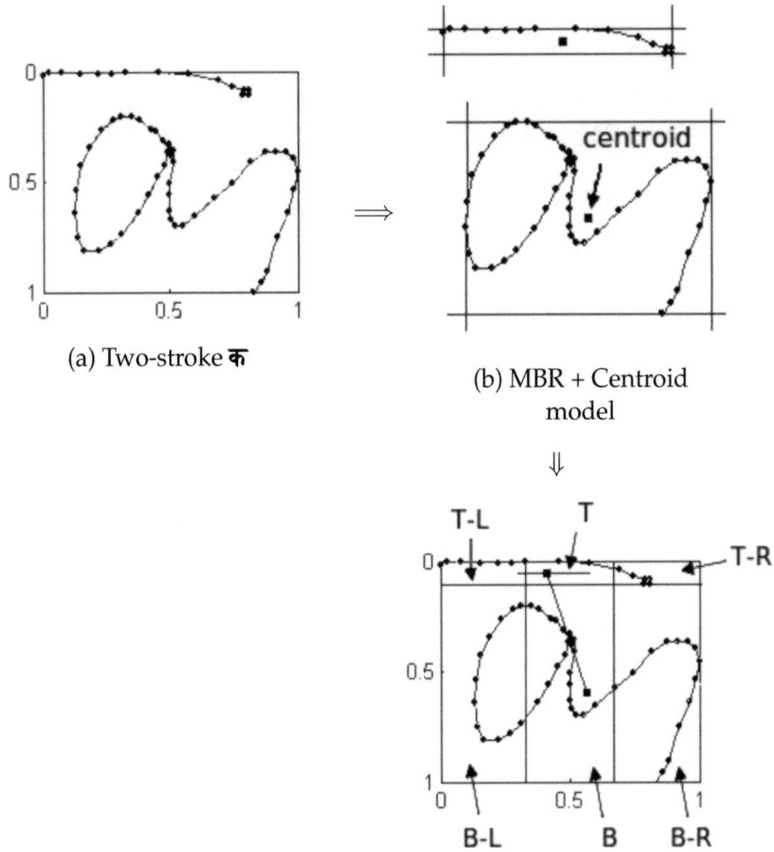


(a) Two-stroke क

(b) MBR + Centroid model

(c) Model realisation

**Figure 7.** Pairwise spatial relation for a two-stroke क [40].

### 3.3. Stroke number and order free recognition

In natural handwriting, number of strokes as well as their order vary widely. This happens from one writing to another, even from the same user – which of course exits from different users. Fig. 11 shows the large variation of stroke numbers as well as the orders.

Once we have organised the symbols (from the particular class) into groups based on the number of strokes used, our stroke clustering has been made according to the relative positioning. As a consequence, while doing recognition, one can write symbol with any numbers and orders because stroke matching is based on relative positioning of the strokes in which group while it does not need to care about the strokes order.

### 3.4. Dataset

In this work, as before, publicly available dataset has been employed (*cf.* Table 1) where a Graphite tablet (WCACOM Co. Ltd.), model ET0405A-U, was used to capture the pen-tip position in the form of 2*D* coordinates at the sampling rate of 20 Hz. The data set is composed of 1800 symbols representing 36 characters, coming from 25 native speakers. Each writer

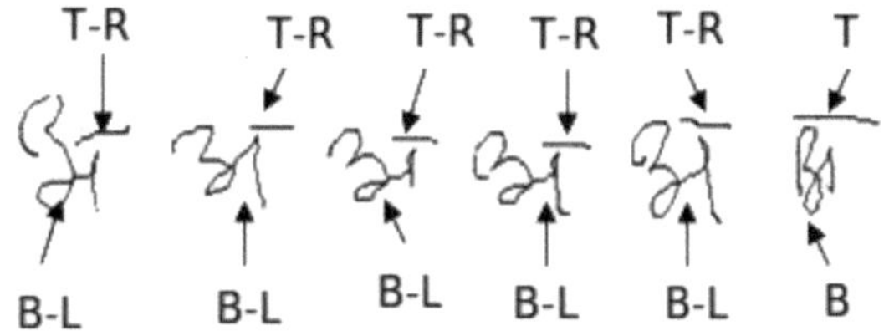


(a) Two-stroke अ

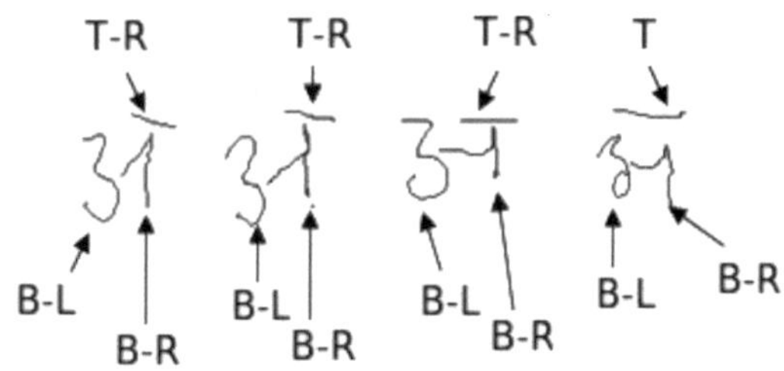


(b) Three-stroke अ

**Figure 8.** Relative positions of strokes for a class अ in two different groups i.e., two-stroke and three-stroke symbols.

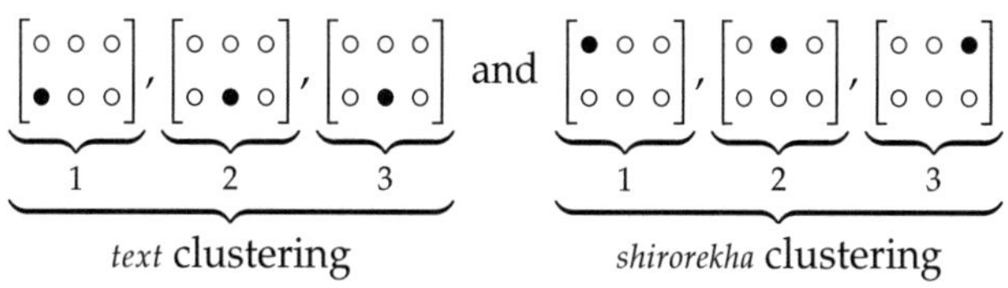


**Figure 9.** Clustering technique for each class. Stroke clustering is based on the relative positioning. As a consequence, we have three clustering blocks for *text* strokes and remaining three for *shirorekha*.

was given the opportunity to write each character twice. No other directions, constraints, or instructions were given to the users.

| Item | Description |
|---|---|
| Classes of character | 36 |
| Users | 25 |
| Dataset size | 1800 |
| Visibility | IAPR tc–11 `http://www.iapr-tc11.org` |

**Table 1.** Dataset formation and its availability.

## 3.5. Recognition performance evaluation

While experimenting, every test sample is matched with training candidates and the closest one is reported. The closest candidate corresponds to the labelled class, which we call 'character recognition'. Formally, recognition rate can be defined as the number of correctly recognised candidates to the total number of test candidates.

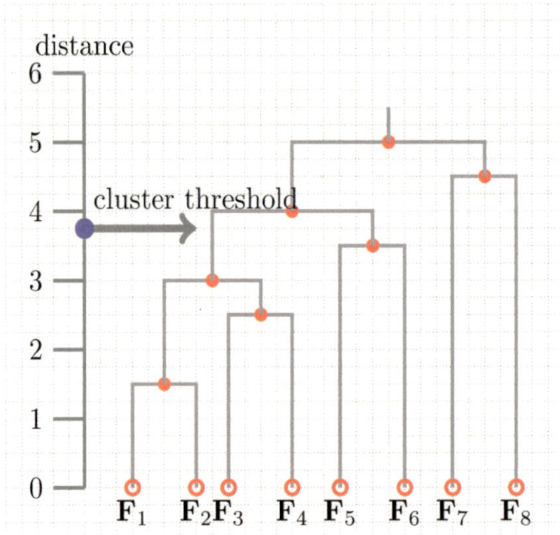


**Figure 10.** Hierarchical stroke clustering concept. At every step, features are merged according to their similarity up to the provided threshold level.

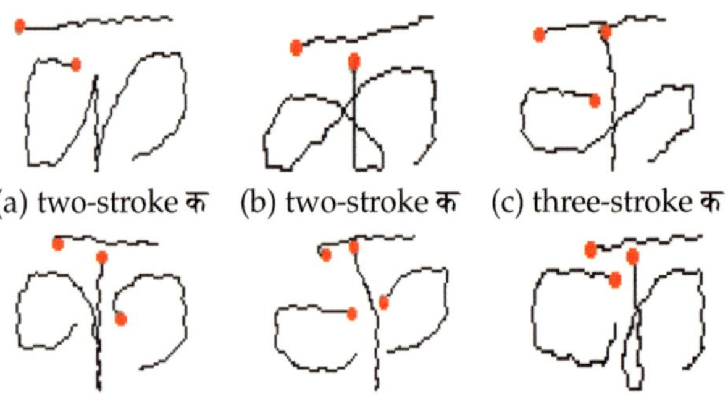

(a) two-stroke क (b) two-stroke क (c) three-stroke क

(d) three-stroke क (e) four-stroke क (f) three-stroke क

**Figure 11.** Different number of strokes and order for a class क. In this illustration, red-dot refers to the initial pen-tip position so that it makes easy to realise how many number of strokes to make a complete symbol. In addition, stroke ordering is different from one to another.

To evaluate the recognition performance, two different protocols can be employed:

1. dichotomous classification and
2. $\mathbb{K}$-fold cross-validation (CV).

In case of dichotomous classification, 15 writers are used for training and the remaining 10 are for testing. On the other hand, $\mathbb{K}$-fold CV has been implemented. Since we have 25 users for data collection, we employ $\mathbb{K} = 5$ in order to make recognition engine writer independent.

In $\mathbb{K}$-fold CV, the original sample for every class is randomly partitioned into $\mathbb{K}$ sub-samples. Of the $\mathbb{K}$ sub-samples, a single sub-sample is used for validation, and the remaining $\mathbb{K} - 1$ sub-samples are used for training. This process is then repeated for $\mathbb{K}$ folds, with each of the $\mathbb{K}$ sub-samples used exactly once. Finally, a single value results from averaging all. The aim of the use of such a series of rigorous tests is to avoid the biasing of the samples that can be

| Method | # of Mis-recognition | # of Rejection | Avg. Error % | Time sec. |
|---|---|---|---|---|
| M1. | 33 | 08 | 05.0 | 04 |
| M2. | 24 | 08 | 03.5 | 02 |

Index:
M1. [40].
M2. [40] + [21] and 5-fold CV.

**Table 2.** Error rates (in %) and running time (in sec. per character). The methods can be differentiated by the additional use of L_B Keogh tool [21] and the evaluation protocol employed.

possible in conventional dichotomous classification. In contrast to the previous studies [40], this will be an interesting evaluation protocol.

### 3.6. Results and discussions

Following evaluation protocols we have mentioned before, Table 2 provides average recognition error rates. In the tests, we have found that the recognition performance has been advanced by approximately more than 2%.

Based on results (*cf.* Table 2), we investigate the recognition performance based on the observed errors. We categorise the origin of the errors that are occurred in our experiments. As said in Section 1.3, these are mainly due to

1. structure similarity,
2. reduced and/or very long ascender and/or descender stroke, and
3. others such as re-writing strokes and mis-writing.

Compared to previous work [40], number of rejection does not change while confusions due to structure similarity has been reduced. This is mainly because of the 5-fold CV evaluation protocol. Besides, running time has been reduced by more than a factor of two i.e., 2 seconds per character, thanks to LB_Keogh tool [21].

## 4. Conclusions

In this chapter, an established as well as validated approach (based on previous studies [36–40]) has been presented for on-line natural handwritten Devanagari character recognition. It uses the number of strokes used to complete a symbol and their spatial relations[1]. Besides, we have provided the dataset publicly available for research purpose. Considering such a dataset, the success rate is approximately 97% in less than 2 seconds per character on average. In this chapter, note that the new evaluation protocol reduces the errors (mainly due to multi-class similarity) and the optimised DTW reduces the delay in processing – which has been new attestation in comparison to the previous studies.

The proposed approach is able to handle handwritten symbols of any stroke and order. Moreover, the stroke-matching technique is interesting and completely controllable. It is primarily due to our symbol categorisation and the use of stroke spatial information in template management. To handle spatial relation efficiently (rather than not just based on orthogonal projection i.e., MBR), more elaborative spatial relation model can be used [35], for

[1] Full credit goes to the work presented in [40] where it has comprehensive study on relative positioning of the handwritten strokes. Once again, to avoid contradictions, this chapter aims to provide coherence as well as consistent studies on Devanagari character recognition.

instance. In addition, use of machine learning techniques like inductive logic programming (ILP) [2, 34] to exploit the complete structural properties in terms of first order logic (FOL) description.

## Acknowledgements

Since the chapter is based on the previous studies, thanks to researchers Cholwich Nattee, School of ICT, SIIT, Thammasat University, Thailand and Bart Lamiroy, Université de Lorraine – Loria Campus Scientifique, France for their efforts. Besides, the dataset is partially based on master thesis: TC-MS-2006-01, conducted in Knowledge Information & Data Management Laboratory, School of ICT, SIIT, Thammasat University under Asian Development Bank – Japan Scholarship Program (ADB-JSP).

## Author details

K.C. Santosh
*INRIA Nancy Grand Est Research Centre, France*

Eizaburo Iwata
*Universal Robot Co. Ltd., Japan*

## 5. References

[1] Alginahi, Y. [2010]. *Preprocessing Techniques in Character Recognition*, intech.
[2] Amin, A. [2000]. Prototyping structural description using an inductive learning program, *International Journal of Intelligent Systems* 15(12): 1103–1123.
[3] Arica, N. & Yarman-Vural, F. [2001]. An overview of character recognition focused on off-line handwriting, *IEEE Transactions on Systems, Man, and Cybernetics, Part C: Applications and Reviews* 31(2): 216 –233.
[4] Bahlmann, C. & Burkhardt, H. [2004]. The writer independent online handwriting recognition system frog on hand and cluster generative statistical dynamic time warping, *IEEE Transactions on Pattern Analysis and Machine Intelligence* 26(3): 299–310.
[5] Bellman, R. & Kalaba, R. [1959]. On adaptive control processes, *Automatic Control* 4(2): 1–9.
[6] Blumenstein, M., Verma, B. & Basli, H. [2003]. A novel feature extraction technique for the recognition of segmented handwritten characters, *Proceedings of International Conference on Document Analysis and Recognition*, p. 137.
[7] Boccignone, G., Chianese, A., Cordella, L. & Marcelli, A. [1993]. Recovering dynamic information from static handwriting, *Pattern Recognition* 26(3): 409 – 418.
[8] Cha, S.-H., Shin, Y.-C. & Srihari, S. N. [1999]. Approximate stroke sequence string matching algorithm for character recognition and analysis, *Proceedings of International Conference on Document Analysis and Recognition*, pp. 53–56.
[9] Chiu, H.-P. & Tseng, D.-C. [1999]. A novel stroke-based feature extraction for handwritten chinese character recognition, *Pattern Recognition* 32(12): 1947–1959.
[10] Chun, L. H., Zhang, P., Dong, X. J., Suen, C. Y. & Bui, T. D. [2005]. The role of size normalization on the recognition rate of handwritten numerals, *IAPR TC3 Workshop of Neural Networks and Learning in Document Analysis and Recognition*, pp. 8–12.
[11] Connell, S. D. & Jain, A. K. [1999]. Template-based online character recognition, *Pattern Recognition* 34: 1–14.

[12] Dimond, T. [1957]. Devices for reading handwritten characters, *Proceedings of the Eastern Joint Computer Conference*, pp. 232–237.

[13] Doermann, D. S. & Rosenfeld, A. [1995]. Recovery of temporal information from static images of handwriting, *International Journal of Computer Vision* 15(1-2): 143–164.

[14] Egenhofer, M. & Herring, J. R. [1991]. Categorizing Binary Topological Relations Between Regions, Lines, and Points in Geographic Databases, *Univ. of Maine, Research Report*.

[15] Foggia, P., Sansone, C., Tortorella, F. & Vento, M. [1999]. Combining statistical and structural approaches for handwritten character description, *Image and Vision Computing* 17(9): 701–711.

[16] Groner, G. [1966]. Real-time recognition of handprinted text, Memorandum RM-5016-ARPA, The Rand Corporation.

[17] Guerfali, W. & Plamondon, R. [1993]. Normalizing and restoring on-line handwriting, *Pattern Recognition* 26(3): 419–431.

[18] Heutte, L., Paquet, T., Moreau, J.-V., Lecourtier, Y. & Olivier, C. [1998]. A structural/statistical feature based vector for handwritten character recognition, *Pattern Recognition Letters* 19(7): 629–641.

[19] Hu, J., Brown, M. K. & Turin, W. [1996]. Hmm based on-line handwriting recognition, *IEEE Transactions on Pattern Analysis and Machine Intelligence* 18: 1039–1045.

[20] Jayadevan, R., Kolhe, S. R., Patil, P. M. & Pal, U. [2011]. Offline recognition of devanagari script: A survey, *IEEE Transactions on Systems, Man, and Cybernetics, Part C* 41(6): 782–796.

[21] Keogh, E. J. [2002]. Exact indexing of dynamic time warping, *Proceedings of 28th International Conference on Very Large Data Bases*, Morgan Kaufmann, pp. 406–417.

[22] Keogh, E. J. & Pazzani, M. J. [1999]. Scaling up dynamic time warping to massive dataset, *European PKDD*, pp. 1–11.

[23] Kruskall, J. B. & Liberman, M. [1983]. The symmetric time warping algorithm: From continuous to discrete, *Time Warps, String Edits and Macromolecules: The Theory and Practice of String Comparison*, Addison-Wesley, pp. 125–161.

[24] Lippmann, R. P. [1989]. Pattern classification using neural networks, *IEEE Comm. Magazine* 27(11): 47–50.

[25] Miyajima, K. & Ralescu, A. [1994]. Spatial organization in 2D segmented images: representation and recognition of primitive spatial relations, *Fuzzy Sets Systems* 65(2-3): 225–236.

[26] Myers, C. S. & Rabiner., L. R. [1981]. A comparative study of several dynamic time-warping algorithms for connected word recognition, *The Bell System Technical Journal* 60(7): 1389–1409.

[27] Namboodiri, A. M. & Jain, A. K. [2004]. Online handwritten script recognition, *IEEE Transactions on Pattern Analysis and Machine Intelligence* 26(1): 124–130.

[28] Okumura, D., Uchida, S. & Sakoe, H. [2005]. An hmm implementation for on-line handwriting recognition - based on pen-coordinate feature and pen-direction feature, *Proceedings of International Conference on Document Analysis and Recognition*, pp. 26–30.

[29] Pal, U. & Chaudhuri, B. B. [2004]. Indian script character recognition: a survey, *Pattern Recognition* 37(9): 1887–1899.

[30] Papadias, D. & Sellis, T. [1994]. *Relation Based Representations for Spatial Knowledge*, PhD Thesis, National Technical Univ. of Athens.

[31] Plamondon, R. & Srihari, S. [2000]. Online and off-line handwriting recognition: a comprehensive survey, *IEEE Transactions on Pattern Analysis and Machine Intelligence* 22(1): 63 –84.

[32] Qiao, Y., Nishiara, M. & Yasuhara, M. [2006]. A framework toward restoration of writing order from single-stroked handwriting image, *IEEE Transactions on Pattern Analysis and Machine Intelligence* 28(11): 1724–1737.
[33] Sakoe, H. [1978]. Dynamic programming algorithm optimization for spoken word recognition, *IEEE Transactions on Acoustics, Speech, and Signal Processing* 26: 43–49.
[34] Santosh, K. C., Lamiroy, B. & Ropers, J.-P. [2009]. Inductive logic programming for symbol recognition, *Proceedings of International Conference on Document Analysis and Recognition*, pp. 1330–1334.
[35] Santosh, K. C., Lamiroy, B. & Wendling, L. [2012]. Symbol recognition using spatial relations, *Pattern Recognition Letters* 33(3): 331–341.
[36] Santosh, K. C. & Nattee, C. [2006a]. Stroke number and order free handwriting recognition for nepali, *in* Q. Yang & G. I. Webb (eds), *Proceedings of the Pacific Rim International Conferences on Artificial Intelligence*, Vol. 4099 of *Lecture Notes in Computer Science*, Springer-Verlag, pp. 990–994.
[37] Santosh, K. C. & Nattee, C. [2006b]. Structural approach on writer independent nepalese natural handwriting recognition, *Proceedings of the International Conference on Cybernetics and Intelligent Systems*, pp. 1–6.
[38] Santosh, K. C. & Nattee, C. [2007]. Template-based nepali natural handwritten alphanumeric character recognition, *Thammasat International Journal of Science and Technology* 12(1): 20–30.
[39] Santosh, K. C., Nattee, C. & Lamiroy, B. [2010]. Spatial similarity based stroke number and order free clustering, *Proceedings of IEEE International Conference on Frontiers in Handwriting Recognition*, pp. 652–657.
[40] Santosh, K. C., Nattee, C. & Lamiroy, B. [2012]. Relative positioning of stroke based clustering: A new approach to on-line handwritten devanagari character recognition, *International Journal of Image and Graphics* 12(2): 1250016-1–25.
[41] Schenkel, M., Guyon, I. & Henderson, D. [1995]. On-line cursive script recognition using time delay neural networks and hidden markov models, *Machine Vision and Applications* 8(4): 215–223.
[42] Tappert, C. C., Suen, C. Y. & Wakahara, T. [1990]. The state of the art in online handwriting recognition, *IEEE Transactions on Pattern Analysis and Machine Intelligence* 12(8): 787–808.
[43] Øivind Due Trier, Jain, A. K. & Taxt, T. [1996]. Feature extraction methods for character recognition – a survey, *Pattern Recognition* 29(4): 641 – 662.
[44] Verma, B., Lu, J., Ghosh, M. & R., G. [2004]. A feature extraction technique for on-line handwriting recognition, *Proceedings of IEEE International Joint Conference on Neural Networks*, pp. 1337–1341.
[45] Viard-Gaudin, C., Lallican, P. M. & Knerr, S. [2005]. Recognition-directed recovering of temporal information from handwriting images, *Pattern Recognition Letters* 26(16): 2537–2548.
[46] Wang, X. & Keller, J. M. [1999]. Human-based spatial relationship generalization through neural/fuzzy approaches, *Fuzzy Sets Systems* 101(1): 5–20.
[47] Zhou, X.-D., Liu, C.-L., Quiniou, S. & Anquetil, E. [2007]. Text/non-text ink stroke classification in japanese handwriting based on markov random fields, *Proceedings of International Conference on Document Analysis and Recognition*, pp. 377–381.

Chapter 11

# Finger Braille Recognition System

Yasuhiro Matsuda and Tsuneshi Isomura

Additional information is available at the end of the chapter

http://dx.doi.org/10.5772/51472

## 1. Introduction

The Ministry of Health, Labour and Welfare of Japan estimates that there are nearly 22,000 deafblind people in Japan (2006). Communication is one of their largest barriers to independent living and participation. Deafblind people use many different communication media, depending on the age of onset of deafness and blindness and the available resources. "*Yubi-Tenji*" (Finger Braille) is one of the tactual communication media utilized by deafblind individuals (see Fig. 1). In two-handed Finger Braille, the sender's index finger, middle finger and ring finger of both hands function like the keys of a Braille typewriter. The sender dots Braille code on the fingers of the receiver. The receiver is assumed to recognize the Braille code. In one-handed Finger Braille, the sender dots the left part of Braille code on the distal interphalangeal (DIP) joints of the three fingers of the receiver, and then the sender dots the right part of Braille code on the proximal interphalangeal (PIP) joints. Deafblind people who are skilled in Finger Braille can communicate words and express various emotions because of the prosody (intonation) of Finger Braille (Fukushima, 1997). Because there is such a small number of non-disabled people who are skilled in Finger Braille, deafblind people communicate only through an interpreter. Thus, the participation of deafblind people is greatly restricted.

Various Finger Braille input devices, including a wearable input device, have been developed. (Uehara et al., 2000) developed a Finger Braille glove system with accelerometers mounted on the fingertips. (Fukumoto et al., 1997) developed a wearable input device with accelerometers mounted on the top of rings. (Hoshino et al., 2002) developed a Finger Braille input system that mounted accelerometers on the middle phalanges. In addition, (Ochi et al., 2003) developed a bracelet-type Finger Braille input device with eighteen mounted accelerometers. These devices require deafblind people to wear gloves, rings or bracelets to input Finger Braille. With these support devices, deafblind people are not only burdened with wearing the sensors, but also they must master a new communication system using such support devices.

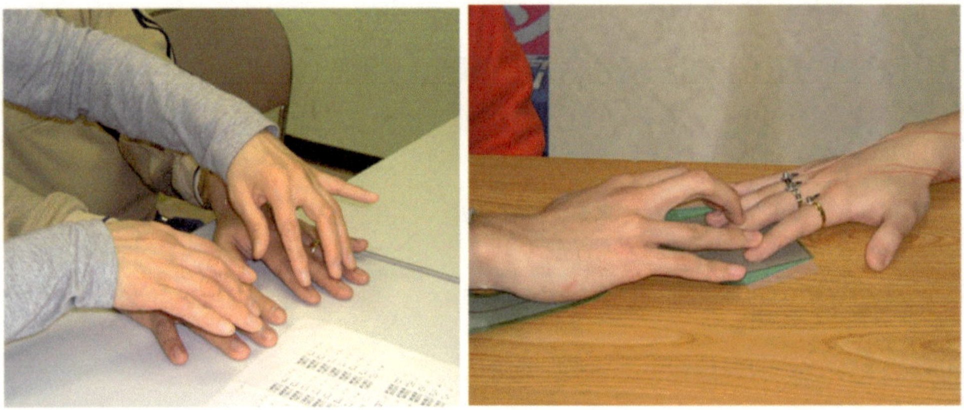

**Figure 1.** Two-handed Finger Braille (left) and one-handed Finger Braille (right)

The objective of this study is the development of a Finger Braille support device which employs communication through skin contact, because skin contact is the only non-verbal communication possible for deafblind people. The concept of the proposed Finger Braille support device is shown in Fig. 2. The advantages of this support device are as follows: both deafblind people and non-disabled people who are not skilled in Finger Braille can communicate using conventional Finger Braille, and all sensors are worn by the non-disabled people. This support device consists of a Finger Braille teaching system and a Finger Braille recognition system. The teaching system recognizes the speech of non-disabled people and displays the associated dot pattern of Finger Braille. Non-disabled people can then dot Finger Braille on the fingers of deafblind people by observing the displayed dot pattern (Matsuda et al., 2010a). The recognition system recognizes the dotting of Finger Braille by the deafblind people and synthesizes the speech for non-disabled people. Thus, deaf-blind people can communicate without being encumbered by the support device.

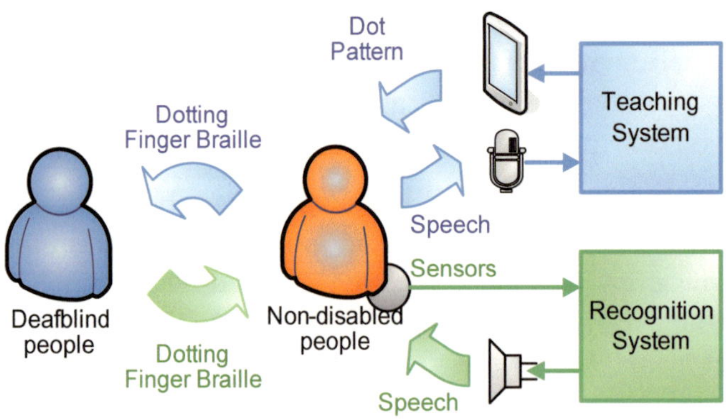


**Figure 2.** Concept of Finger Braille support device

[1] Based on "Development of Finger Braille Recognition System", by Yasuhiro Matsuda, Ischiro Sakuma, Etsuko Kobayashi, Yasuhiko Jimbo, Tatsuhiko Arafune and Tsuneshi Isomura, which appeared in Journal of Biomechanical Science and Engineering, Vol.5, No.1. © 2010 JSME.

To develop the recognition system, some requirements must be fulfilled.

In Finger Braille, the sender dots Braille codes directly on the fingers of the receiver. A rule of Finger Braille is that the sender constantly touches the fingers of the receiver even when not dotting, because the receivers feel uncomfortable in the absence of touching or tactile cues. Therefore, sensors must not hinder the skin contact between deafblind people and non-disabled people. Because of the lack of visual and audio information, deafblind people experience difficulty in mastering a new communication system. Thus, the sensors must be worn by the receiver (non-disabled people). In this study, we adopted small accelerometers mounted on the top of finger rings.

In our concept of assistance, deafblind people are equipped with the recognition system, which non-disabled people can also use. The non-disabled people are unspecified. Thus, the recognition system must be independent of the receiver.

For prosody of Finger Braille, the sender dots long and strong at the end of clauses and sentences. The sender can dot strongly with anger, or weakly with sadness (Matsuda et al., 2010b). Thus, the recognition system must be independent of dotted strength.

To develop the recognition system, we adopted one-handed Finger Braille. Here, the recognition system requires independence of the dotted position and recognition of the dotted positions.

In this chapter we describe the Finger Braille recognition system and present experimental results. We first describe the algorithms for the recognition of dotted fingers and positions. Then, an evaluation experiment was carried out.

## 2. Development of the recognition system

### 2.1. Configuration of the recognition system

Fig. 3 shows the configuration of the Finger Braille recognition system. The non-disabled people wore rings with small piezoelectric accelerometers (yamco 10SW, Yamaichi Electronics) on the index finger, middle finger and ring finger. Each accelerometer was mounted on the top of the ring. The accelerometers were connected to a tablet PC (TC1100, HP) through charge amplifiers (yamco 4101, Yamaichi Electronics) and an A/D converter (USB-9215A-BNC, National Instruments). The sampling frequency was 10 kHz, the measurement range was ±250 m/s$^2$, and the sensibility was 0.2 m/s$^2$. The input voltage of the A/D converter 1V is equal to the acceleration 100 m/s$^2$.

First, the accelerometers detected the accelerations of the dotting, and acceleration data were acquired. Second, the recognition system recognized the dotted fingers and positions. Third, by parsing the recognized Braille codes, the recognition system converted the Braille codes to Japanese text. Finally, the recognition system synthesized the speech of the Japanese text.

The operating system (OS) was Microsoft Windows XP. The programs of recognition of the dotted fingers and positions were programmed in LabVIEW 8.0 (National Instruments). The

Braille code parser was programmed in Win-Prolog 4.500 (Logic Programming Associates). The integrated program was programmed in Microsoft Visual Basic 6. The speech synthesizer was VoiceText (Pentax). Fig. 4 shows an appearance of communication supported by the recognition system.

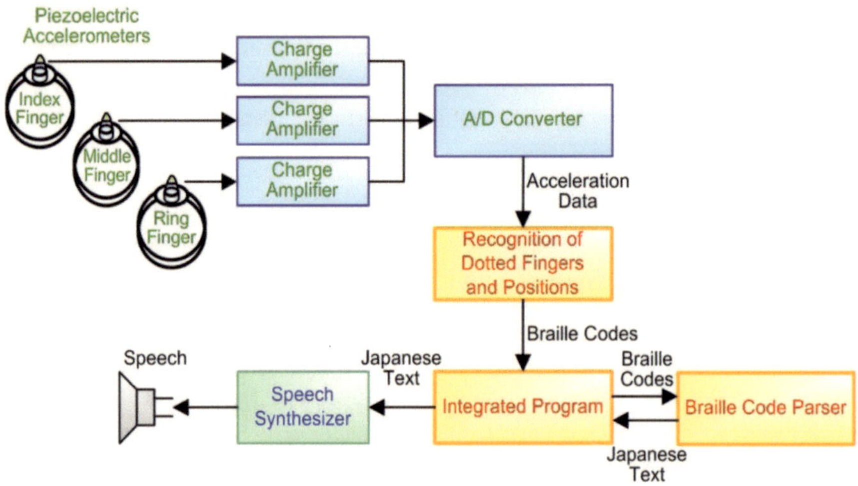


**Figure 3.** Configuration of the recognition system

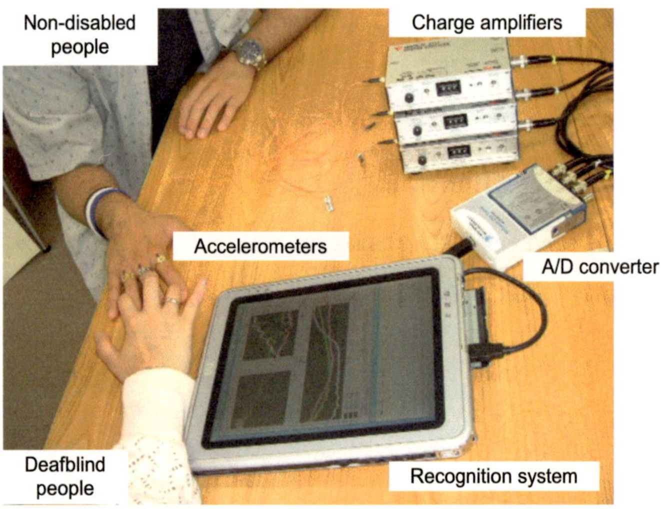


**Figure 4.** Communication supported by the recognition system

## 2.2. Detection of the shock accelerations by dotting

The acceleration data of three fingers were measured continuously and the differential of the sum of the accelerations of three fingers were calculated. If the differential was greater than or equal to 10V/s, the differential data for 100 ms (pre-trigger 20 ms and post-trigger 80 ms) were acquired. If the differential data stayed in between the upper and lower limits (see Fig. 5), these accelerations were recognized as the shock accelerations by dotting.

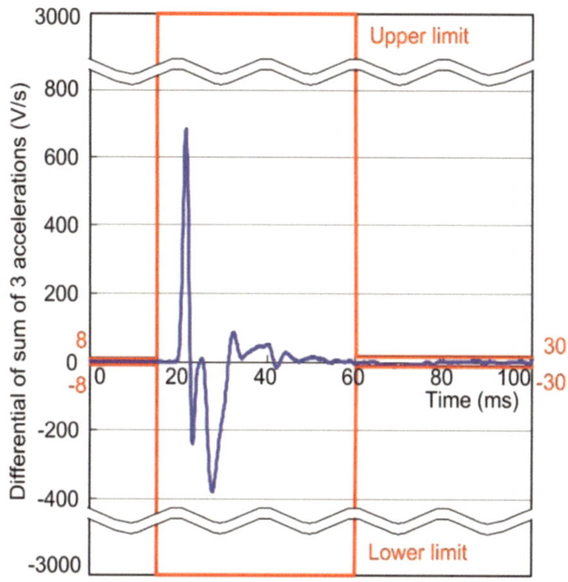


**Figure 5.** Upper and lower limits of the differential of the sum of the accelerations of three fingers to detect the shock acceleration by dotting.

## 2.3. Recognition of dotted fingers

### *2.3.1. Features of shock acceleration by dotting*

Fig. 6 shows features of the accelerations by dotting. When the sender dotted Finger Braille on the fingers of the receiver, the accelerometers detected shock accelerations by the dotting of the mounted finger (self dotting) and shock accelerations by the dotting of the other fingers (cross talk). Fig. 7 shows the shock accelerations by self dotting and cross talk. The accelerations by cross talk were less than the accelerations by self dotting. *AI1, AM1* and *AR1* indicate the amplitudes of accelerations of the index, middle and ring fingers, respectively. The range of the amplitude of acceleration by self dotting and the range of the amplitude of acceleration by cross talk overlap each other. Thus, it is difficult to recognize the acceleration by self dotting by using a constant threshold for the amplitude (Uehara et al., 2000; Matsuda et al., 2010c).

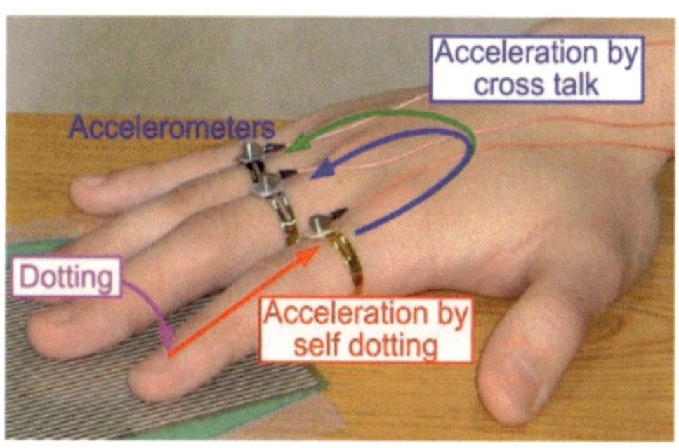


**Figure 6.** Features of the accelerations by dotting

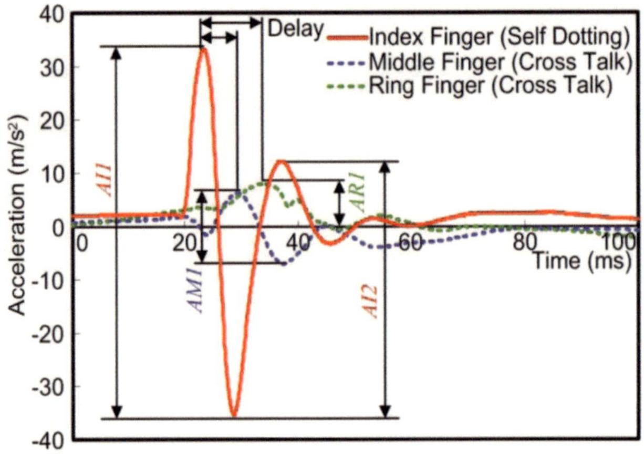


**Figure 7.** Shock accelerations by self dotting and cross talk (dotting on DIP joints: hard impact)

Fig. 8 shows the frequency spectrums of the accelerations by self dotting and cross talk. The acceleration data for 100 ms (pre-trigger 20 ms and post-trigger 80 ms) were recorded. The window function was the Hanning window. The difference of power between self dotting and cross talk was greater at approximately 100 Hz (Fukumoto et al., 1997; Hoshino et al., 2002). *PI*, *PM* and *PR* indicate the powers at 100 Hz of the index, middle and ring fingers, respectively. The range of the power at 100 Hz by self dotting and the range of the power at 100 Hz by cross talk overlap each other. Thus, it is also difficult to recognize the acceleration by self dotting using a constant threshold of power at 100 Hz (Matsuda et al., 2010c).

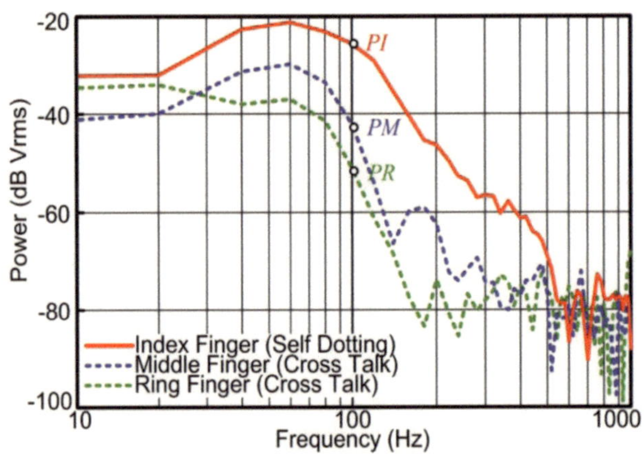


**Figure 8.** Frequency spectrums of accelerations by self dotting and cross talk

Because the accelerations by cross talk must have a delay (adjacent fingers: 5.0 ms, index finger and ring finger: 8.9 ms), the first detected acceleration must be the acceleration by self dotting. In the case of Fig. 6, the acceleration of the index finger is the first detected acceleration. Then by setting the acceleration of the index finger as the dynamic threshold, the recognition system can recognize the acceleration of the middle finger and ring finger. We noted two parameters related to the index finger, the amplitude of acceleration (*AI1*) and the power at 100 Hz (*PI*).

### 2.3.2. *Algorithm for the recognition of the dotted fingers*

We derived an algorithm for the recognition of dotted fingers. For example, the variables and equations in the case of Figs. 7 and 8 are identified.

**Step 1.** Acquire the acceleration data for 100 ms (pre-trigger 20 ms and post-trigger 80 ms) when the shock accelerations by dotting are detected.
**Step 2.** Set the amplitude and power at 100 Hz of the first detected acceleration as the dynamic thresholds (index finger: *AI1*, *PI*).
**Step 3.** If the amplitude of the second detected acceleration is greater than half of the amplitude of the first detected acceleration (middle finger: $AM1>AI1/2$) or the power at 100 Hz of the second detected acceleration is greater than the power at 100 Hz of the first detected acceleration minus 10 dB Vrms (middle finger: $PM>PI-10$), the second detected acceleration is recognized as the acceleration by self dotting.
**Step 4.** If the amplitude of the second detected acceleration is less than or equal to half of the amplitude of the first detected acceleration (middle finger: $AM1\leqq AI1/2$) and the power at 100 Hz of the second detected acceleration is less than or equal to the power at 100 Hz of the first detected acceleration minus 10 dB Vrms (middle finger: $PM\leqq PI-10$), the second detected acceleration is recognized as the acceleration by cross talk.
**Step 5.** If the power at 100 Hz of the second detected acceleration is less than -58 dB Vrms (middle finger: $PM<-58$), the second detected acceleration is recognized as the acceleration by cross talk.
**Step 6.** Steps 3~5 apply to the third detected acceleration (ring finger: *AR1*, *PR*).

## 2.4. Recognition of dotted positions

### 2.4.1. *Features of shock acceleration by dotted positions*

Fig. 9 shows the features of the accelerations by the dotted positions. When the receiver's hand forms a natural longitudinal arch on the desk, the DIP joints are close to the desk, and space exists under the PIP joints. Dotting on the DIP joints causes a hard impact, and dotting on the PIP joints causes a soft impact. Fig. 7 shows the shock accelerations by dotting on the DIP joints. Fig. 10 shows the shock accelerations by dotting on the PIP joints. *AI1* indicates the amplitude of acceleration of the index finger. *AI2* indicates the damping amplitude of the index finger. The difference of each impact is indicated by its damping amplitude. The damping amplitude ratio of accelerations by dotting on the DIP joints (*AI2*/*AI1*) is greater than the damping amplitude ratio of accelerations by dotting on the PIP joints.

### 2.4.2. *Algorithm for the recognition of the dotted positions*

We derived the following algorithm for the recognition of the dotted positions. For this example, the variables and equations for the cases of Figs. 7 and 10 were calculated.

**Step 1.** Calculate the damping amplitude ratio (*AI2*/*AI1*) of the acceleration by self dotting.

**Step 2.** If the damping amplitude ratio is greater than 0.5 (*AI2*/*AI1*>0.5), the acceleration is recognized as the accelerations by dotting on the DIP joints.

**Step 3.** If the damping amplitude ratio is less than or equal to 0.5 (*AI2*/*AI1*≦0.5), the acceleration is recognized as the accelerations by dotting on the PIP joints.

**Step 4.** If the amplitude of the acceleration is greater than 150 m/s$^2$ (*AI1*>150), the acceleration is recognized as the accelerations by dotting on the PIP joints.

**Step 5.** If two or three fingers are dotted at the same time (self dotting), the mean of the damping amplitude ratios is calculated and Steps 2~4 are applied.

After the recognition, the dotted fingers and positions are represented by Braille code. Table 1 lists the Braille code of dotted fingers and positions.

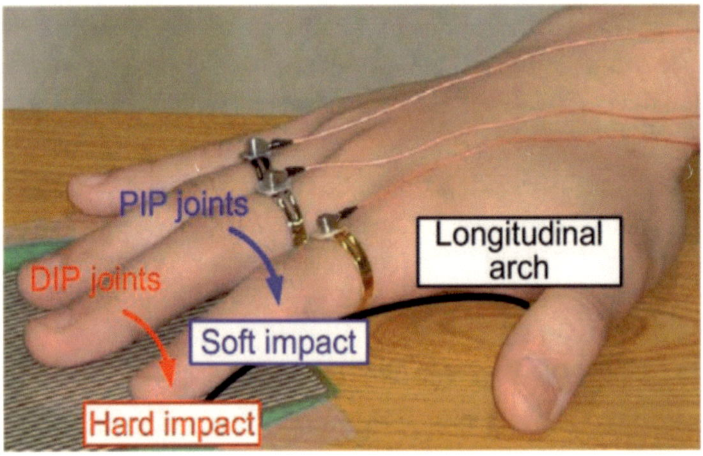


**Figure 9.** Features of the accelerations by dotted positions

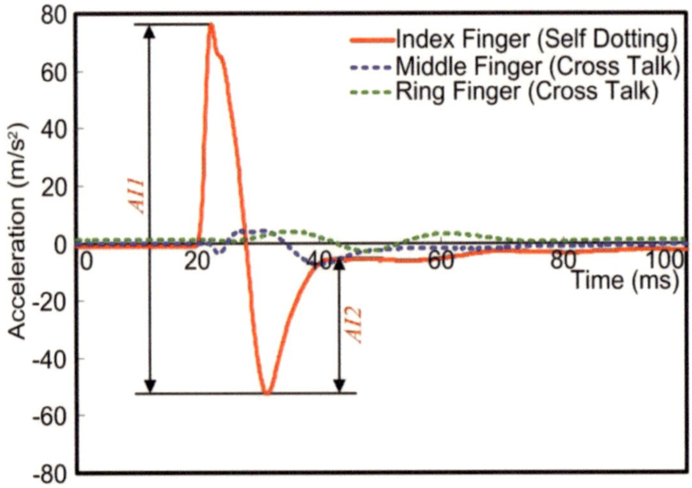


**Figure 10.** Shock accelerations by self dotting and cross talk (dotting on PIP joints: soft impact)

| Dotted fingers | Dotting on DIP joints | Dotting on PIP joints |
|---|---|---|
| Index finger | 11 | 12 |
| Middle finger | 21 | 22 |
| Index + middle fingers | 31 | 32 |
| Ring finger | 41 | 42 |
| Index + ring fingers | 51 | 52 |
| Middle + ring fingers | 61 | 62 |
| Index + middle + ring fingers | 71 | 72 |

**Table 1.** Braille code of dotted fingers and positions

### 2.5. Braille code parser and integrated program

We developed a Braille code parser by applying the technology of natural language processing (BUP system) (Matsumoto et al., 1983). The Braille code parser parsed the Braille code and converted it into Japanese text. The Braille code parser consisted of a dictionary, grammar, BUP translator and control program. The dictionary and the grammar were described in definite clause grammar (DCG). The BUP translator translated the dictionary and grammar into a Prolog program. The control program controlled the execution of parsing.

When the programs for the recognition of dotted fingers and positions recognize a dotting, the integrated program sends a list of recognized Braille code to the Braille code parser. Then the Braille code parser parses the list of Braille code. If the list of Braille code is grammatically correct, the Braille code parser sends the converted Japanese text to the integrated program. If the list of Braille code is grammatically incorrect, the Braille code parser sends a "no" to the integrated program.

Finally, when the integrated program receives the Japanese text from the Braille code parser, the integrated program allows the speech synthesizer to synthesize the Japanese text. Fig. 11 shows a screenshot of the recognition system.

## 3. Evaluation experiment

### 3.1. Method

To evaluate the recognition of sentences dotted by the Finger Braille interpreter, an evaluation experiment of sentence recognition was carried out.

The subject (sender) was a non-disabled Finger Braille interpreter (experiment: 22 years). The subject gave informed consent after hearing a description of the study.

The dialogues (total: 51 sentences, 143 clauses, 288 words, 686 characters) comprised four daily conversations in a Japanese textbook for foreign beginners (3A Corporation, 1998). The numbers of the dottings of the dialogues are listed in Table 2. In Finger Braille, some characters are dotted on both the DIP joints and PIP joints and some characters are dotted only on the DIP joints or the PIP joints. The average of dotted times per character was 1.75.

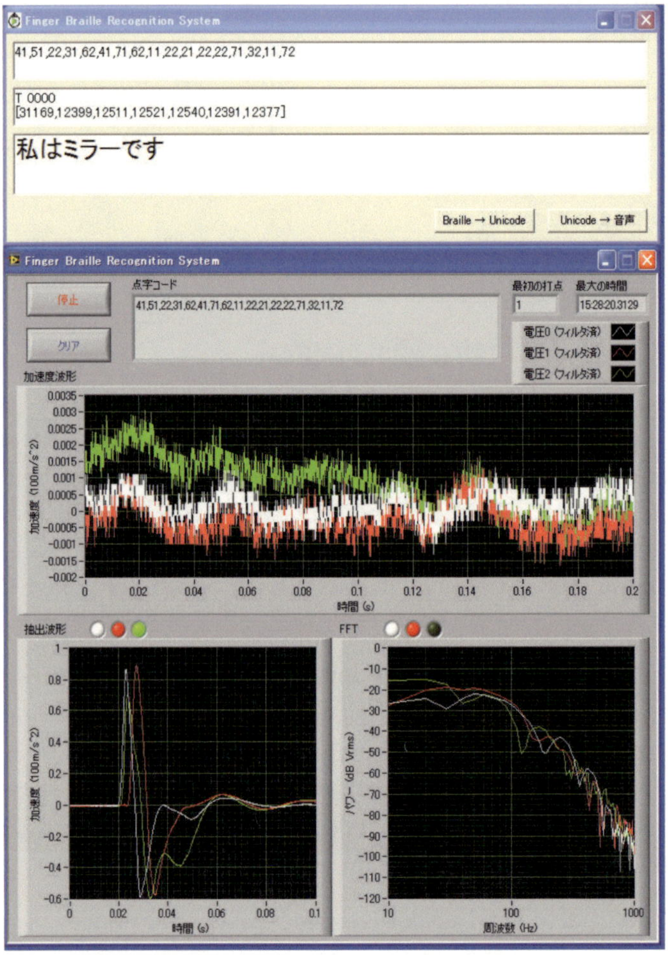


**Figure 11.** Screenshot of the recognition system. Upper window is the integrated program and lower window is the programs of the recognition of dotted fingers and positions.

| Dotted fingers | Dotting on DIP joints | Dotting on PIP joints |
|---|---|---|
| Index finger | 152 | 71 |
| Middle finger | 77 | 161 |
| Ring finger | 70 | 66 |
| Index + middle fingers | 110 | 84 |
| Middle + ring fingers | 54 | 126 |
| Index + ring fingers | 72 | 39 |
| Index + middle + ring fingers | 70 | 72 |

**Table 2.** Numbers of the dottings of the dialogues

The experimental flow is shown in Fig. 12. The experiment included one practice session and four experimental sessions (conversations 1 to 4). In the experiment, a tester and the subject sat face to face. The tester wore the accelerometers. The subject spoke one sentence of the dialogues and then dotted the sentence on the tester's fingers clearly. The tester's hand set on the desk in each conversation and formed the natural longitudinal arch. If the recognition system synthesized the misrecognized speech, the subject would stop dotting or re-dot the dialogues. To prevent unnecessary pause or re-dotting by the subject, the speech synthesizer was turned off during the experiment. The lists of the recognized Braille code were recorded in the hard disk drive of the recognition system.

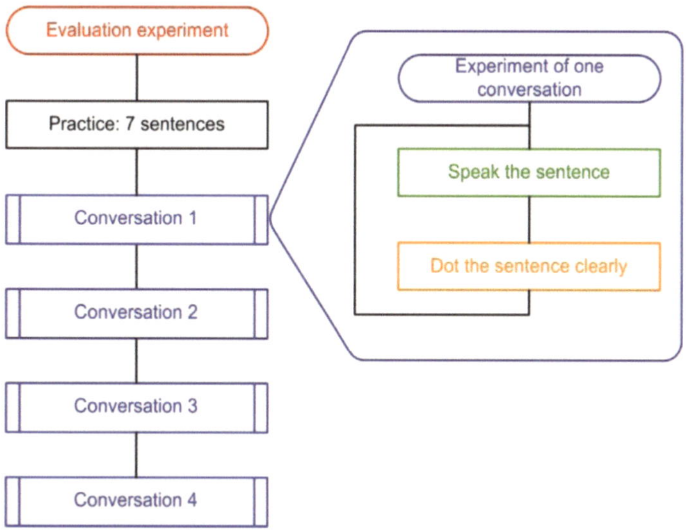


**Figure 12.** Experimental flow

## 3.2. Results

### *3.2.1. Accuracies of recognition of dotted fingers*

The mean of the dotting speed was 37.0 characters/min. This was almost 1/3 of the normal dotting speed.

To evaluate the accuracy of recognition, we checked the lists of the recognized Braille code and calculated the accuracies of the recognition by dotting (each dotting on DIP joints or PIP joints) and by character (one or two dottings). Fig. 13 shows the accuracies of the recognition of dotted fingers as a function of conversation and as a function of the calculation unit. Fig. 14 shows the accuracies of the recognition of dotted fingers by dotting as a function of the dotted fingers and as a function of the dotted positions.

The overall accuracy of the recognition of dotted fingers by dotting was 89.7%. In the experiment of conversation 3, the power at 100 Hz of the middle finger was less 5 dB Vrms. The accuracy of conversation 3 was 77.2%. The accuracy without conversation 3 was 94.3%. The accuracies of the middle finger and middle + ring fingers of the dotting on the PIP joints were less than the other accuracies; the accuracies of the index + middle fingers and middle + ring fingers of the dotting on the PIP joints were also less than the other accuracies.

The overall accuracy of the recognition of dotted fingers by character was 82.6%. The accuracy without conversation 3 was 90.0%.

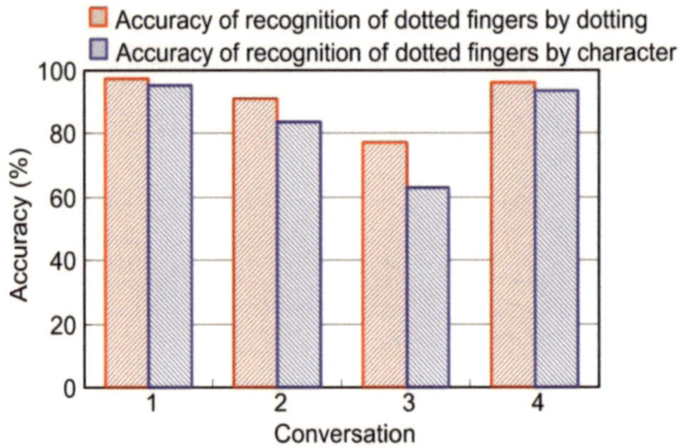


**Figure 13.** Accuracies of the recognition of dotted fingers as a function of conversation and as a function of the calculation unit

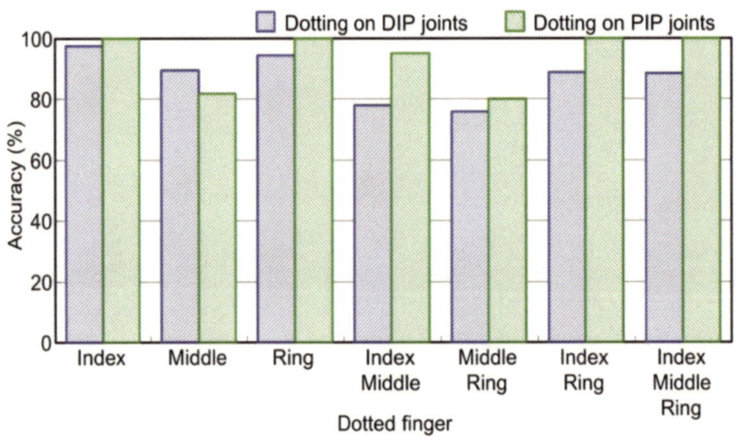


**Figure 14.** Accuracies of the recognition of dotted fingers by dotting as a function of the dotted fingers and as a function of the dotted positions

### *3.2.2. Accuracies of dotting and recognition*

Fig. 15 shows the accuracies of the recognition of dotted positions as a function of conversation and as a function of the calculation unit. Fig. 16 shows the accuracies of the recognition of dotted positions by dotting as a function of the dotted fingers and as a function of the dotted positions.

The overall accuracy of the recognition of dotted positions by dotting was 92.3%. The accuracy of conversation 3 was 88.8%. The accuracy without conversation 3 was 94.9%.The accuracies of the dotting on the PIP joints of the index finger and middle finger were less than the other accuracies.

The overall accuracy of the recognition of dotted positions by character was 88.3%. The accuracy without conversation 3 was 91.2%.

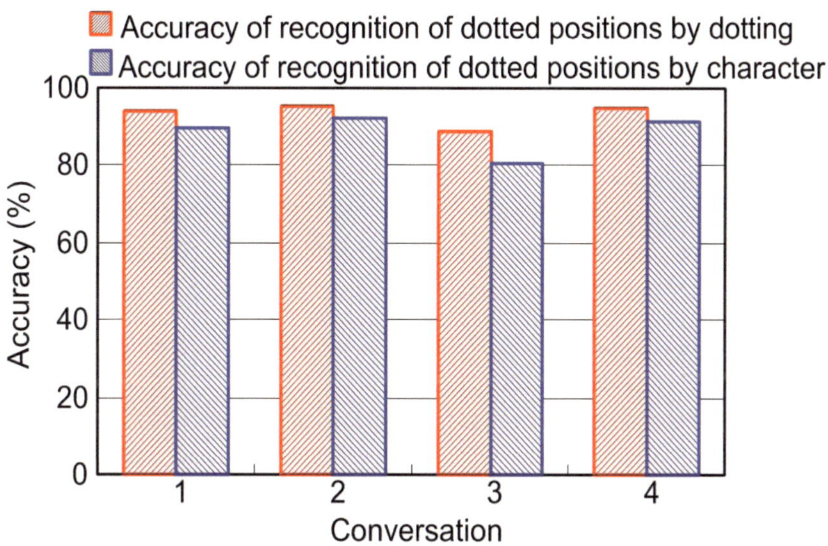


**Figure 15.** Accuracies of the recognition of dotted positions as a function of conversation and as a function of the calculation unit

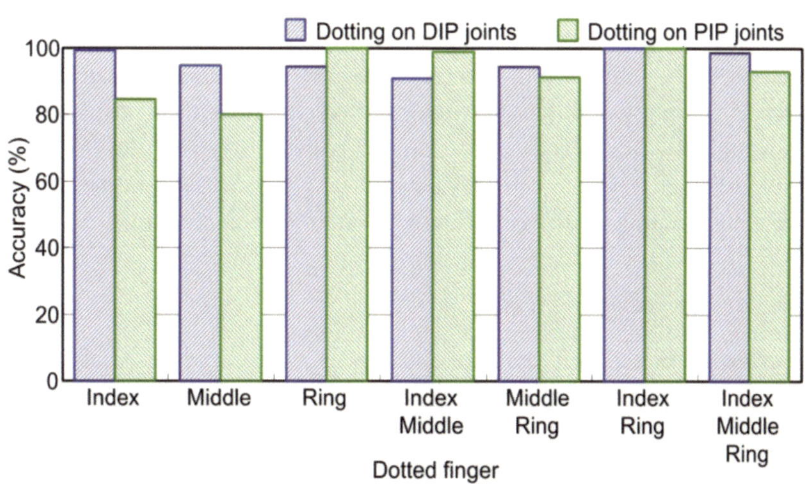


**Figure 16.** Accuracies of the recognition of dotted positions by dotting as a function of the dotted fingers and as a function of the dotted positions

## 3.3. Discussion

### *3.3.1. Accuracies of recognition*

The accuracy of the recognition of dotted fingers by dotting without conversation 3 was 94.3%, and the accuracy of the recognition of dotted positions by dotting without conversation 3 was 94.9%. The accuracy of the recognition of dotted fingers by character without conversation 3 was 90.0%, and the accuracy of the recognition of dotted positions by character without conversation 3 was 91.2%.

In the experiment of conversation 3, the power at 100 Hz of the middle finger was less than 5 dB Vrms, although the power improved in the experiment of conversation 4. This phenomenon was the same as the phenomenon that occurred in the previous experiment (Matsuda et al., 2010c). As real communication using the recognition system, non-disabled people (receiver) can re-set their hand on the desk when they notice a decreased accuracy of recognition. The re-setting of the receiver's hand should be allowed in the communication.

As previously mentioned, (Uehara et al., 2000) developed a Finger Braille glove system with accelerometers mounted on the fingertips. Three Finger Braille interpreters wore the glove system and dotted Finger Braille. The accuracy of recognition was 73.0%. The dialogues that they used were the number of characters; the dotting speed and range of amplitude of acceleration were not clear. But the accuracy of recognition by our recognition system was greater than or equal to the accuracy of recognition by the glove system.

(Hoshino et al., 2002) developed the Finger Braille input system that mounted accelerometers on the middle phalanges. Three visually impaired people and two non-disabled people who were skilled in Finger Braille wore the input system and dotted 100 randomized characters. They reported that the accuracy of recognition was 99.3%. Because the characters did not form sentences, the subjects might not express the prosody of Finger Braille.

To compare our study with these previous studies, our recognition system could recognize the sentences accurately when the interpreter dotted clearly. Although the accuracy of the recognition is high, the Braille code parser can not convert the list of the Braille code which was grammatically incorrect into the Japanese text. Then the recognition system can not synthesize the misrecognized clauses. We have been improving the Braille code parser.

### *3.3.2. Feedback to the deafblind people*

In this experiment, the subject pointed out the importance of feedback from the non-disabled person (receiver) to the deafblind person (sender) as to whether the non-disabled person recognized the Finger Braille correctly. Because of their deafness and blindness, deafblind people cannot confirm the synthesized speech and displayed text of the recognition system. Therefore, deafblind people are uneasy without feedback, and they will find it difficult to keep up with the conversation. Therefore, we have been developing the combination of a recognition system and teaching system to display the dot pattern of the recognized sentence, so that receivers can offer feedback to senders.

# 4. Future plans

## 4.1. Improvement of the mounts of accelerometers

In the previous study, the accuracies of the recognition of the dotted fingers and positions of some subjects are low, when the bottoms of the rings have contacted the desk by dotting, especially the ring finger. Fig. 17 shows the shock accelerations by contact between the bottom of ring and desk. The contact causes different shock accelerations and influences the accuracy of recognition of dotted fingers and positions.

To avoid the shock acceleration by the contact between the bottom of ring and desk, we have been improving the mounts of the accelerometers by two methods (Matsuda et al., 2012). We adopt a cloth band and half-cut ring covered by cloth instead of the previous ring (see Fig. 18). Both the cloth band and half cut ring will not cause the shock acceleration by the contact between the bottom of the mounts and desk.

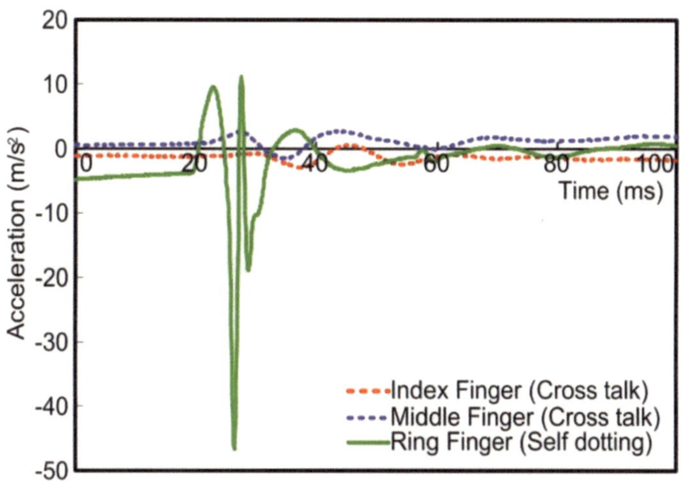


**Figure 17.** Shock accelerations by contact between the bottom of ring and desk

**Figure 18.** Previous ring (left), cloth band (middle) and half-cut ring covered by cloth (right)

### 4.2. Emotion recognition of Finger Braille

In Finger Braille, the sender can express various emotions by changing the duration and strength of dotting (Fukushima, 1997; Matsuda et al, 2010b). The intent of our support device is to assist not only verbal communication but also non-verbal (emotional) communication. To assist in emotional communication, we have been developing an emotion teaching system (Matsuda et al., 2010d) and an emotion recognition system (Matsuda et al, 2010e).

The emotion recognition system is based on the Finger Braille recognition system and recognizes four emotions (joy, sadness, anger and neutral) expressed by the deafblind person. The algorithm of emotion recognition is as follows. First, the emotion recognition system recognizes the dotting by the deafblind person and calculates the duration of dotting and amplitude of acceleration by dotting. Second, the probabilities of four emotions about each dotting are calculated. Third, the means probabilities about a sentence are calculated. The sentence is recognized as the emotion which the mean probability is highest. Regardless of the accuracy of emotion recognition of dotting is not very high, the emotion recognition system can recognize the emotions of sentence accurately.

## 5. Conclusion

In this chapter, we developed a Finger Braille recognition system and derived the algorithms for the recognition of dotted fingers and positions. Next, an evaluation experiment was carried out. The results of the evaluation experiment showed that the accuracy of the recognition of dotted fingers by dotting was 89.7% (94.3% without conversation 3), and the accuracy of the recognition of dotted positions by dotting was 92.3% (94.9% without conversation 3). Therefore, the recognition system could recognize sentences accurately when the interpreter dotted clearly. We confirmed that non-disabled people (receiver) should re-set their hand on the desk when they notice a decrease of the accuracy of recognition.

## Author details

Yasuhiro Matsuda and Tsuneshi Isomura
*Kanagawa Institute of Technology, Japan*

## Acknowledgement

We greatly thank Ms. Satoko Mishina (Finger Braille interpreter) for her support in the evaluation experiment.

This study was supported by the Japan Society for the Promotion of Science under a Grant-in-Aid for Scientific Research (No. 21500522) and the Ministry of Education, Culture, Sports,

Science and Technology of Japan under a Grant-in-Aid for Scientific Research (No. 16700430).

## 6. References

Fukumoto, M. & Tonomura, Y. (1997). Body Coupled FingeRing: Wireless Wearable Keyboard, *Proceedings of the ACM Conference on Human Factors in Computing Systems*, pp.147-154, ISBN 0-201-32229-3, Atlanta, U.S.A., March 1997

Fukushima, S. (1997). *Person with Deafblind and Normalization*, Akashi Shoten, ISBN 4-7503-0982-6, Tokyo, Japan

Hoshino, T., Otake, T. & Yonezawa, Y. (2002). A Study on a Finger-Braille Input System Based on Acceleration of Finger Movements, *IEICE Transactions on Fundamentals of Electronics, Communications and Computer Sciences*, Vol.J85-A, No.3, (March 2002), pp.380-388, ISSN 0913-5707

Matsuda, Y. & Isomura, T. (2010a). Finger Braille Teaching System, In: *Character recognition*, M. Mori, (Ed.), pp.173-188, Sciyo, ISBN 978-953-307-105-3, Rijeka, Croatia

Matsuda, Y.; Sakuma, I.; Jimbo, Y.; Kobayashi, E.; Arafune, T. & Isomura, T. (2010b). Emotional Communication in Finger Braille, *Advances in Human-Computer Interaction*, Vol. 2010, (April 2010), 23 pages, ISSN 1687-5893

Matsuda, Y.; Sakuma, I.; Jimbo, Y.; Kobayashi, E. & Arafune, T. (2010c). Study on Dotted Fingers and Position Recognition System of Finger Braille, In: *Biomechanics 20 Physical Function: Assistance and Improvement Research*, The Society of Biomechanisms Japan, (Ed.), pp.171-182, Keio University Press, ISBN 978-4-7664-1760-9, Tokyo, Japan

Matsuda, Y. & Isomura, T. (2010d). Teaching of Emotional Expression using Finger Braille, *Proceedings of the 2010 IEEE Sixth International Conference on Intelligent Information Hiding and Multimedia Signal Processing*, pp.368-371, ISBN 978-0-7695-4222-5, Darmstadt, Germany, October 15-17, 2010

Matsuda, Y.; Sakuma, I.; Jimbo, Y.; Kobayashi, E.; Arafune, T. & Isomura, T. (2010e). Emotion Recognition of Finger Braille, *International Journal of Innovative Computing, Information and Control*, Vol.6, No.3(B), (March 2010), pp.1363-1377, ISSN 1349-4198

Matsuda, Y. & Isomura, T. (2012). Improvement of Mounts of Accelerometers of Finger Braille Recognition System, *Lecture Notes in Engineering and Computer Science: Proceedings of The International MultiConference of Engineers and Computer Scientists 2012*, Volume I, pp.311-316, ISBN 978-988-19251-1-4, Hong Kong, China, March 14-16, 2012

Matsumoto, Y.; Tanaka, H.; Hirakawa, H.; Miyoshi, H. & Yasukawa, H. (1983). BUP: A Bottom-Up Parser Embedded in Prolog, *New Generation Computing*, Vol.1, No.2, pp.145-158, ISSN 0288-3635

Ochi, T., Kozuki, T. & Suga, H. (2003). Bracelet type braille interface, *Correspondence on Human Interface*, Vol.5, No.1, pp25-27, ISSN 1344-7270

Uehara, N., Aoki, M., Nagashima, Y. & Miyoshi, K. (2000). Bidirectional Telecommunication using Wearable I/O Terminal for Finger Braille, *Proceedings of the Human Interface Symposium 2000*, pp.37-40, ISSN 1345-0794, Tsukuba, Japan, September 2000

3A Corporation (1998). *Minna no Nihongo I Honsatsu (Main Textbook)*, 3A Corporation, ISBN 4-88319-102-8, Tokyo, Japan

Chapter 12

# Usefulness of Only One User's Handwritten Character on Offline Personal Character Recognition

Shinji Tsuruoka, Masahiro Hattori, Yasuji Miyake,
Haruhiko Takase and Hiroharu Kawanaka

Additional information is available at the end of the chapter

http://dx.doi.org/10.5772/53272

## 1. Introduction

The variety of individual person should be respected in present-day life, and in character recognition the usage of characters written by the individual person is one of important problems. Handwritten character recognition is strongly required as a means of input to personal terminal machines such as smartphone, tablet PC and so on. One of problems on handwritten character recognition is low accuracy and the correct rate of the character recognition is not enough for user's request. To improve the accuracy, the characters written by one writer, who is called *"a specific writer"*, are effective for simple characters such as alphabet, numerals and symbols in online system [1-5]. The specific writer's characters employed for on-line character recognition system. However, specific writer's characters are not employed on most offline commercial system.

We are considering the usage of character forms written by a specific writer to improve the recognition rate. The variety of character forms by five writers is shown in Fig. 1. The problem of the grouping the variety of character forms is that the distribution of characters for one category is wide, and that the boundary of the category would be not appropriate for character recognition. We think that the one specific writer would write the similar character forms, and that the distribution of the character by the specific writer is narrower than many writers.

We proposed some personal recognition dictionaries (a pure personal dictionary and three adaptive dictionaries) generated from many characters written by one specific writer [6, 7]. The problem of personal recognition dictionary is the writing cost of the characters written by one specific writer, and personal dictionary has not used on offline OCR system up to the present. In this chapter, we discuss two approaches for generating personal adaptive dictionary in offline character recognition.

**Figure 1.** Variety of character forms written by different writers in Japanese HIRAGANA 'a'.

The first approach employs many characters written by a specific writer and many writers to generate a personal adaptive dictionary. In first approach, we proposed three types, that is, "Renewal type dictionary", "Modification type dictionary", "Mixture type dictionary" [6, 7] made by the compound of many characters by the specific writer and many writers. We evaluated the usefulness such as recognition accuracy, storage size of the three types for Japanese "Hiragana" character at offline. The experimental result shows that the personal dictionary is effective for recognition accuracy in comparison with the general dictionary generated by the characters written by many writers, and that the accuracy improved from 97% to 99%. However, the problem of personal dictionary is a large writing cost for each specific writer.

The second approach employs only one character written by the specific writer for all categories, and the only one character written by the specific writer selects one similar writer registered in recognition system. Some writers would write the similar character forms such as Fig. 2. The personal adaptive dictionary is generates using the characters written by the similar writer and many writers. We proposed two types, that is, "Similar mean dictionary", "Similar feature space dictionary" [9]. We compared two proposed types for Japanese character "Hiragana" at offline. The experimental results show that only one character for all categories is very effective for the improvement of recognition accuracy, and the character recognition rate is improved from 82% for the general dictionary to 91% by the proposed adaptive dictionary.

**Figure 2.** Character forms in the same category Japanese HIRAGANA 'a' by five writers.

Section 2 gives the properties for personal offline character recognition system and the outline of our character recognition system "Weighted Direction Index Histogram Method (WDIHM)" [10,11] which include the feature extraction for histogram of the direction and the modified quadratic discriminant function (MQDF)"[10,11]. Section 3 describes the generating methods of personal adaptive dictionary combined by the characters of specific writer and many writers. Section 4 presents the usage of the characters written by the similar writer of a specific writer, which is low writing cost and that the accuracy of recognition is higher than the general dictionary. We think that the usage of the similar writer is useful for generating the adaptive dictionary.

# 2. Personal offline character recognition system

## 2.1. Usage of characters by a specific writer

The character forms written by individual writers have the variety shown in Fig. 1. Most writers do not write the standard character form, and they have some writing habits. Many researches and developers are interesting in the usage of the characters written by a specific writer. In on-line character recognition, the usage of the characters written by a specific writer is researched widely [1-5]. In offline character recognition, however, the personal recognition dictionary is not used generally at the present, as the writing cost of the characters is large for a specified writer.

We investigated the character forms written by some same writers. The specific writer has a writing habit, and the character forms written by the specific writer are similar each other. We guessed that the personal common feature such as writing habit for each writer is stable shown in Fig.3, and that the personal common feature for each individual writer is useful for personal character recognition. We are considering the extraction method and the usage of the personal common feature for character recognition system. We appear two generating methods of personal dictionary as follows.

1. The usage of many characters written by a specific writer (adaptive dictionary)
2. The usage of only one character written by a specific writer (similar dictionary)

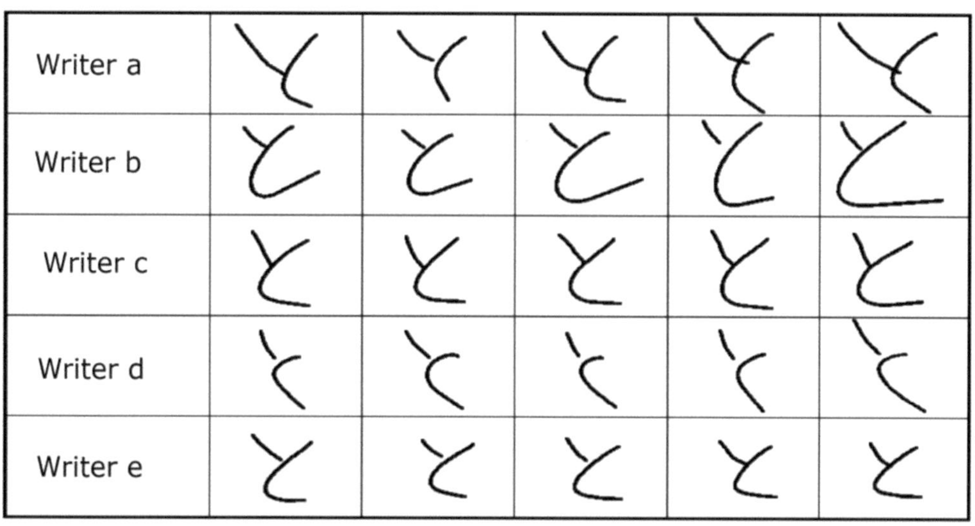


**Figure 3.** Variety of character forms by four writers in Japanese Hiragana 'to'.

## 2.2. Properties for personal offline character recognition system

Personal offline character recognition system should adapt to a specific writer using the characters written by the specific writer. In the initial stage, as the number of the characters written by the specific writer is small, the dictionary of the recognition system should be the general dictionary, which is made from the characters written by many writers. Because the average of the accuracy for every writer should be high, and most of the writers desires the high recognition accuracy in the initial condition.

### 2.2.1. *Calculation cost of a specific writer*

The personal dictionary should be updated to the character form of a specific writer. The calculation cost of the updating the dictionary should be low for each input character. The recognition system with large cost such as neural networks, Dynamic Programming (DP) and Hidden Markov Model (HMM) is not suitable for personal offline character recognition.

### 2.2.2. *Storage size for generating personal dictionary*

The storage size for generating personal dictionary depends on the usage of the learning character, and the less storage of the size is desired. We think that the feature vectors to generate the personal dictionary should be in the mobile terminal machine of the user or cloud, and the writer can use the character forms by many writers.

## 2.3. Outline of character recognition system "Weighted Direction Index Histogram Method (WDIHM)"

We employ "Weighted direction index histogram method (WDIHM) [10, 11]" as the personal character recognition algorithm. The procedure of WDIHM consists of (1) binarization for extracting character area, (2) normalization of position and size (Figure 4(a)), (3) border following and 4-direction index coding (Figure 4(b)), (4) generation of 4-direction index histogram for 7x7 sub-regions (Figure 4(c)), (5) compress of 4x4 (sub-regions) x4 (directions) (= 64 dimension) histograms using Gaussian weighted filter (Figure 4(d),(e)).

This algorithm is popular in off line character recognition for Japanese handwritten characters, and we are developing this algorithm to personal character recognition. The feature vector in the recognition method employs the four direction index histogram, and the dimension of the feature vector is 64 (= 7x7x4).

The mean vector and covariance matrix of feature vector $x = (x_1, x_2, \ldots, x_{64})^T$ for a category $l$ are given in Equation (1), (2)

$$ {}_l\mu = \frac{1}{N}\sum_{i=1}^{N} {}_l x_i \tag{1} $$

$$ {}_l\Sigma = \frac{1}{N}\sum_{i=1}^{N} ({}_l x_i - {}_l\mu)({}_l x_i - {}_l\mu)^T \tag{2} $$

Where, $i = 1, 2, \ldots, N$ and $N$ is the number of learning characters.

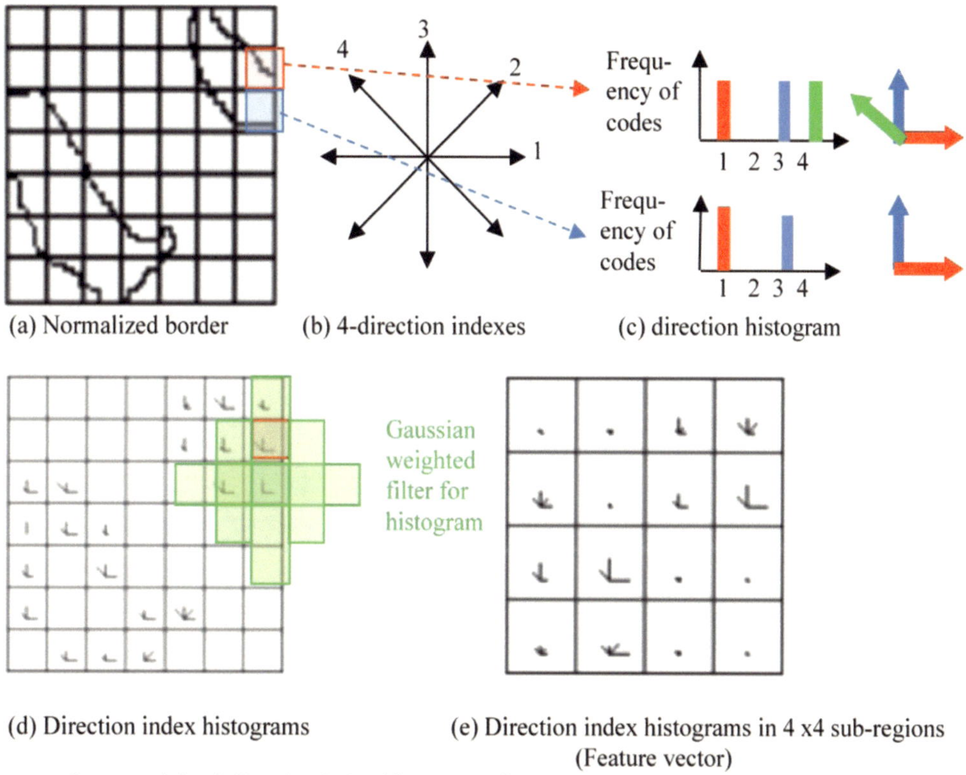


**Figure 4.** Weighted direction index histograms feature (WDIH).

Quadratic discriminate function (QDF) of an n-dimensional feature vector $\boldsymbol{x}$ is given Equation (3) for a category $l$. $P(l)$ is the *a priori* probability for the category $l$.

$$ {}_{1}f(x) = (x - {}_{1}\mu)^{T} \{{}_{1}\Sigma\}^{-1} (x - {}_{1}\mu) + \ln|{}_{1}\Sigma| - 2\log P(l) \tag{3} $$

The QDF becomes optimal in the Bayesian sense for normal distributions with known parameters [11]. On the limited samples, the performance of QDF is degraded because of estimation error, as the parameters become non-optimal. QDF has some problems such as the recognition accuracy, computation time, storage and so on.

We proposed the modified quadratic discriminate function (MQDF) [10, 11] (equation (4)). In our personal character recognition, we employ the modified quadratic discriminate function (MQDF). MQDF for each category is based on the principal component analysis (PCA), and it employs a mean vector, a set of eigenvectors and eigenvalues of a covariance matrix on feature vector for each character category (Fig. 5).

In recognition phase, from the input character the feature vector is extracted, and the MQDF value is calculated for each category. The recognition result, that is the recognized category, is determined by the minimum of the MQDF value for each category.

$$_{l}g(x)=\sum_{i=1}^{k-1}\frac{\{_{l}\varphi_{i}^{T}(x-{}_{l}\mu)\}^{2}}{_{l}\lambda_{i}}+\sum_{i=k}^{n}\frac{\{_{l}\kappa_{i}^{T}(x-{}_{l}\mu)\}^{2}}{_{l}\lambda_{k}}+\ln\left(\prod_{i=1}^{k-1}{}_{l}\lambda_{i}\bullet\prod_{i=k}^{n}{}_{l}\lambda_{k}\right) \tag{4}$$

where, $x$: a feature vector of a character sample

$_{l}\mu$ : mean vector of character in category $l$

$k$ : the number of used eigenvalues ($k < n$) determined by the designer

$n$ : the dimension of feature vectors

$_{l}\varphi_{i}$ : $i$-th eigenvector in category $l$ of covariance matrix

$_{l}\lambda_{i}$ : $i$-th eigenvalue in category $l$ of covariance matrix

$T$ : transpose of a vector

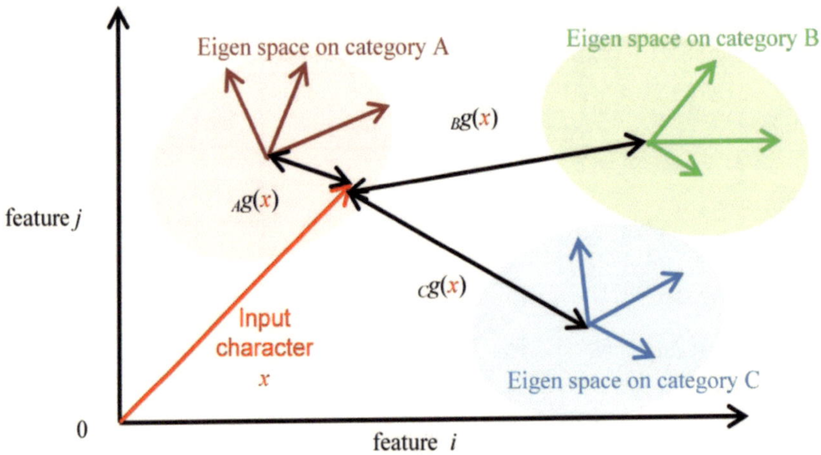


**Figure 5.** Distance using discriminant function MQDF in feature space

The most conventional handwritten OCRs employ a general dictionary, which is generated by many characters written by many general writers to grasp the variety of character forms. The general dictionary consists of the mean vectors, eigenvalues and eigenvectors for each category. The mean vector is made from the feature vectors of learning characters, and the eigenvalues and eigenvectors are calculated by the covariance matrix on the feature vectors. The general dictionary is generated at software developer usually.

## 3. Generating methods of adaptive personal dictionary

### 3.1. Pure personal dictionary and adaptive dictionary

A pure personal dictionary is generated by many characters written by a specific writer, and the dictionary reflects the writing habit of a specific writer. The personal dictionary consists of the personal mean vector and personal covariance matrix for each category (Equation (5), (6)). The recognition accuracy could be the better than the general dictionary by many writers as the distribution of characters written by one specific writer is narrower than the distribution of characters in general dictionary (Fig. 6).

$$ {}_1\mu_p = \frac{1}{N_p}\sum_{i=1}^{Np} {}_1x_{pi} \tag{5} $$

$$ {}_1\Sigma_p = \frac{1}{N_p}\sum_{i=1}^{N} ({}_1x_i - {}_1\mu_p)({}_1x_i - {}_1\mu_p)^T \tag{6} $$

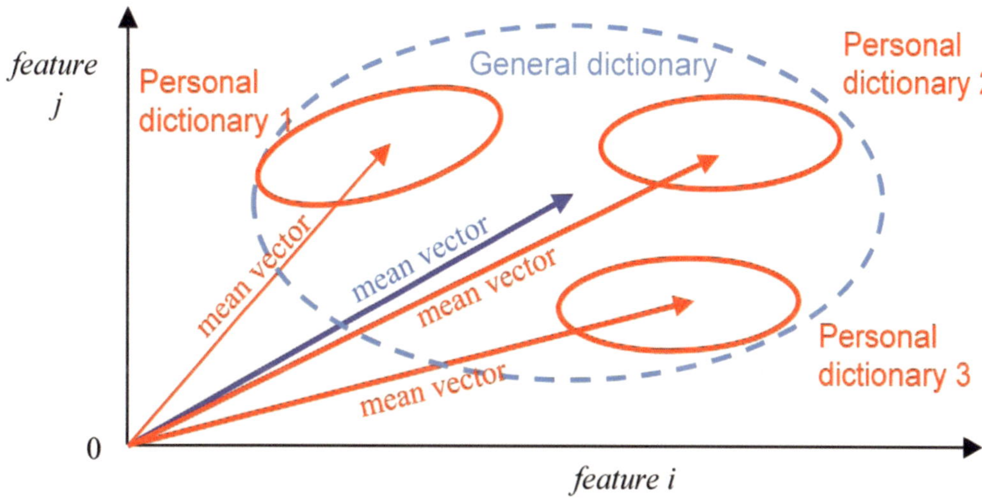


**Figure 6.** Distribution of personal dictionary and general dictionary

We prepared the set of characters written by five writers using mechanical pencil and one character is written for each frame. The set consists of 10 characters per category and the character sets are 46 categories without a voiced consonant mark '゛' and a P-sound mark '゜' in Japanese "Hiragana" characters shown in Table 1. We employed it to generate personal dictionary.

We examined the comparison between the personal and general dictionary for Japanese Hiragana characters (46 categories), and the recognition rates are shown in Fig. 7 when the number of learning characters is ten characters / category [6]. The mean recognition rate of personal dictionary (99.0%) is 2.2 better than the general dictionary (96.8%). The incorrect category of the recognition result is limited at some categories, and the character form of the category is different from the general form. The recognition rates depend on the number of learning characters, and the lack of learning character is one of the important problems. The problem of personal dictionary is the writing cost of a specific writer.

We proposed new three types of adaptive personal dictionary to reduce the writing cost [6, 7]. The adaptive dictionary is made from the characters written by a specific writer and many general writers. The recognition rates of the following three adaptive dictionaries are higher than the pure personal dictionary.

| | | | | | | | | | | | | | | |
|---|---|---|---|---|---|---|---|---|---|---|---|---|---|---|
| あ | か | が | さ | ざ | た | だ | な | は | ば | ぱ | ま | や | ら | わ |
| い | き | ぎ | し | じ | ち | ぢ | に | ひ | び | ぴ | み | | り | ん |
| う | く | ぐ | す | ず | つ | づ | ぬ | ふ | ぶ | ぷ | む | ゆ | る | |
| え | け | げ | せ | ぜ | て | で | ね | へ | べ | ぺ | め | | れ | |
| お | こ | ご | そ | ぞ | と | ど | の | ほ | ぼ | ぽ | も | よ | ろ | を |

**Table 1.** 46 pure sound categories and 25 categories with the voiced consonant mark and the P-sound mark in Japanese HIRAGANA

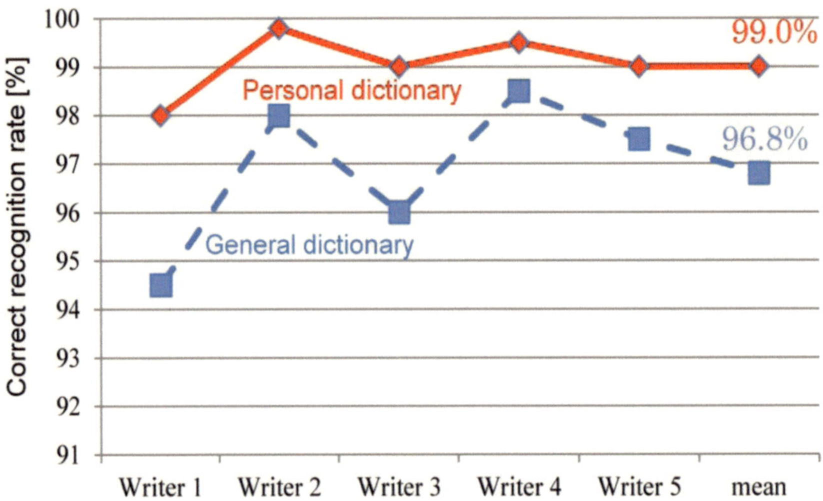


**Figure 7.** Recognition rates of personal dictionary and general dictionary for 46 categories

### 3.2. Renewal type dictionary

The mean vector, eigenvalues and eigenvectors in the renewal type are generated by many characters written by the specific writer and many general writers, when the number of written characters by a specific writer increased (Equation (7) and (8)). The weights of the specific writer and general writer are equal to generate the dictionary. Yoshimura et al presented useful for Japanese character recognition using pattern matching method [8]. The recognition rate of the personal dictionary is better than the general dictionary using WDIHM. The problem is the writing cost by a specific writer, and the number of writing characters is more than 5 characters per category initially to become the recognition rate which is better than the general dictionary.

$$ {}_1\mu_{pr} = \frac{1}{N_p + N}\left(\sum_{i=1}^{Np} {}_1x_{pi} + \sum_{i=1}^{N} {}_1x_i\right) \tag{7} $$

$$ {}_1\Sigma_{pr} = \frac{1}{N_p + N}\left\{\sum_{i=1}^{Np} ({}_1x_i - {}_1\mu_{pr})({}_1x_i - {}_1\mu_{pr})^T + \sum_{i=1}^{N} ({}_1x_i - {}_1\mu)({}_1x_i - {}_1\mu)^T\right\} \tag{8} $$

### 3.3. Modification type dictionary

In modification type dictionary, mean vectors only is updated when the number of written characters by the specific writer increased, and it is the same to pure personal dictionary by Equation (5). The eigenvalues and eigenvectors are the same as the general dictionary from Equation (2), and they are not updated as the stability of eigenvalues and eigenvectors is low when the number of character written by a specific writer is little. The problem of the recognition rate is unstable for some writers when the number of leaning characters is less than 5 characters per categories.

### 3.4. Mixture type dictionary

In mixture type dictionary, the mean vector employs the combination of the general mean vectors and the specific writer's mean vector given by the following equation, where the number of characters by a specific writer $p$ is $N_p$. The eigenvalues and eigenvectors are the same as the general dictionary (Equation (2)).

$$ {}_1\mu_{pm} = \frac{1}{1+N_p}\left({}_1\mu + \sum_{i=1}^{Np} {}_1x_{pi}\right) \tag{9} $$

where, : ${}_1\mu$ mean vector of category $l$ in general dictionary

*Np*: the number of characters written by specific writer $p$

To understand the distributions of three adaptive dictionaries Fig. 8 shows the mean vectors and the existence space of most samples on general dictionary and three type personal dictionaries in feature space, where the mean vector and the existence space are illustrated as an arrow and an ellipse, respectively. The existence space on mixture type and modification type are the same as the general dictionary, and the existence space of the renewal dictionary is narrower than the other dictionaries.

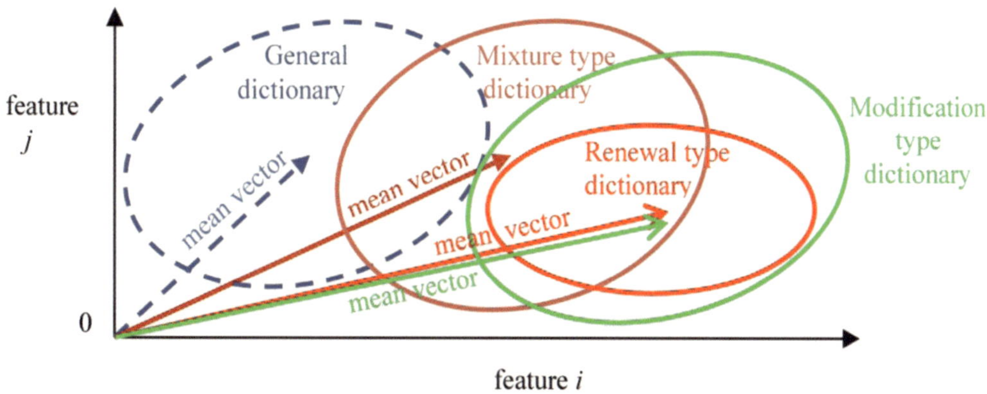


**Figure 8.** Comparison of general dictionary and personal dictionary in feature space.

### 3.5. Comparison of four personal dictionaries

Fig. 9 shows the correct recognition rates on the number of characters written by a specific writer on personal dictionary and three adaptive dictionary types (renewal, modification, mixture) for 46 categories without the voiced consonant mark and the P-sound mark. The general dictionary is made from the characters written by 200 writers per category in the character data base ETL9B by the Electro-Technical Laboratory (ETL) of Japan [at present, the National Institute of Advanced Industrial Science and Technology (AIST) of Japan].

The recognition rate of the modification type at the end of left (the number of characters 0) is the recognition rate of the general dictionary. The recognition rates of modification type and mixture type are better than the general dictionary. The recognition rate of mixture type is better than the other types from 2 learning characters to 8 learning characters. The recognition rates of three adaptive dictionaries are the better than the personal dictionary and the best recognition rate is mixture type dictionary. Table 2 shows the properties of personal dictionary and the adaptive dictionaries, and the recalculation costs of modification and mixture dictionary are less than the personal dictionary and the renewal type as the modification and mixture type dictionary recalculate only the mean vector.

The mixture type dictionary would be the best solution as the personal dictionary from above mentioned experiments. However, the problem of the mixture type dictionary needs at least one character per category, and the specific writer must write the characters for the number of categories. The writing cost of a specific writer is very large when the number of categories is large. For example, the number of Japanese Kanji characters is more than 6000 categories.

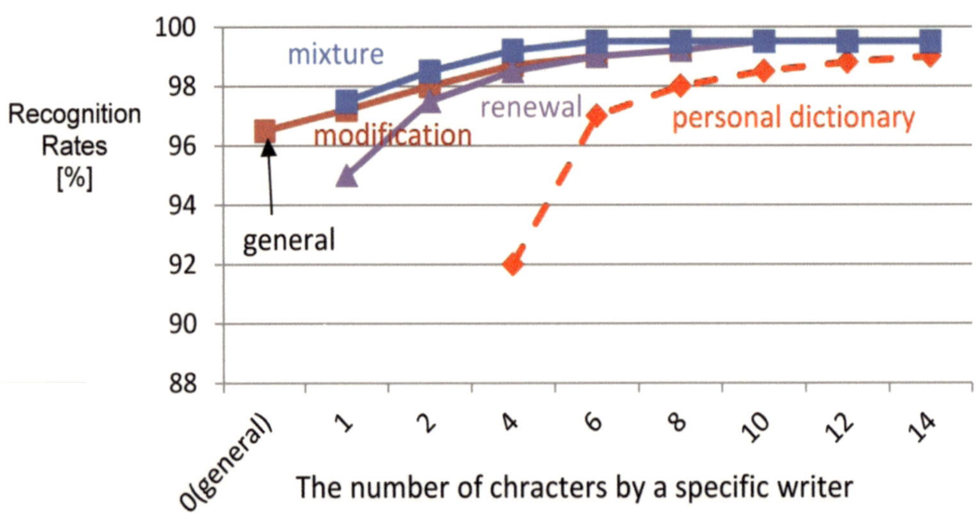


**Figure 9.** The correct recognition rates on the number of learning characters by five writers for 46 categories

| Dictionary type | | | Personal | Renewal | Modification | Mixture |
|---|---|---|---|---|---|---|
| Components | Mean | | personal | personal + general | personal | personal + general |
| | Eigenvalues and Eigenvectors | | personal | personal + general | general | general |
| Recognition rates | The number of characters by a specific writer | less than 6 character | < general | < general in 1, > general in more than 2 | mixture > modification ≧ renewal > personal | |
| | | more than 6 characters | mixture ≧ modification ≧ renewal > personal > general | | | |
| | Recognition rate [%] (10 character / category) | | 99.0 | 99.3 | 99.5 | 99.5 |
| Re-calculation cost | | | 1400 | 1400 | 1 | |
| Storage size | | | 65 | 65 | 1 | |

**Table 2.** Properties of personal dictionary and three adaptive type dictionaries.

## 3.6. Effect of one character per category

We prepared 20 character images per category for ten writers by pen tablet for 71 "HIRAGANA" character categories, and the character categories include 46 pure sound categories, 20 sound categories with a voiced consonant mark ‘゛ ’ and 5 sound categories with a P-sound mark ‘ ゜ ’ shown in Table 1. The resolution of the character is 100 x 100 pixels. We didn't use the time information of tablet and used the image information only. As the feature vector we used the histograms of 4x4 sub-regions, 4 directions, that is, 64 dimensional feature vector.

Fig. 10 shows the correct recognition rates on the number of characters written by a specific writer for all Hiragana 71 categories in mixture type dictionary. The recognition rates of mixture dictionary (93.7% in mixture (10) and 90.8% in mixture (1)) are better than the general dictionary (82.4%). Only one character such as mixture (1) in Fig. 10 is very effective to improve the recognition rate, and the ten characters such as mixture (10) in Fig. 10 can saturate the recognition rates.

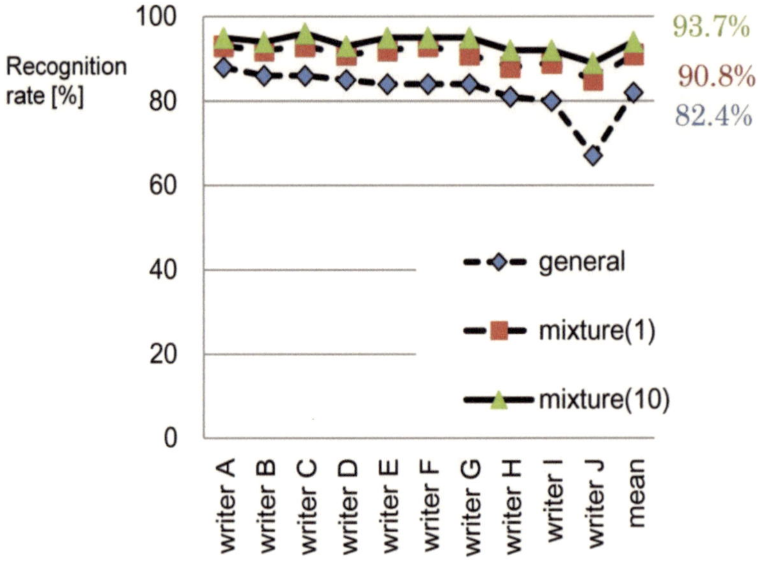


**Figure 10.** Effect of writer's characters in mixture type dictionary for 71 categories

Fig. 11 shows the relation of four mean vectors of personal, mixture (10), mixture (1) and general dictionaries. The mixture (1) approaches personal mean using only one character per category, and it is effective for the improvement of recognition rate.

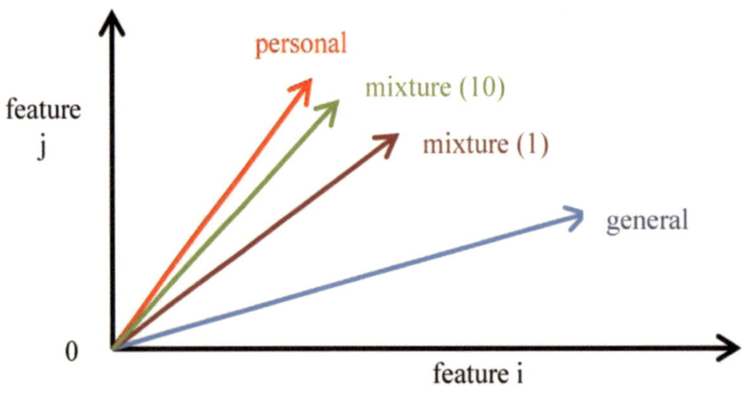


**Figure 11.** Mean vectors of personal, mixture (10), mixture (1) and general dictionaries in feature space

# 4. Usage of one character by a specific writer and similar writers

## 4.1. Outline of usage of one character by a specific writer and similar writers

To resolve the writing cost of a specific writer in the above mentioned discussion, we proposed two new generating methods of adaptive dictionary, especially mixture type dictionary, using only one character for all categories [9]. The key idea is the usage of characters written by the similar writer registered in advance. We assume that the writer's writing feature of one category is much alike to the writer's writing feature of the other category shown in Fig. 12, and that character form of the similar writer selected by one category and one character is similar to the character form by a specific writer in every category, as some writer verification researches appear that the writing feature of one category is similar to every category [12, 13]. Fig. 12 shows that the curvature of arc and the direction of character lines are similar for each writer.

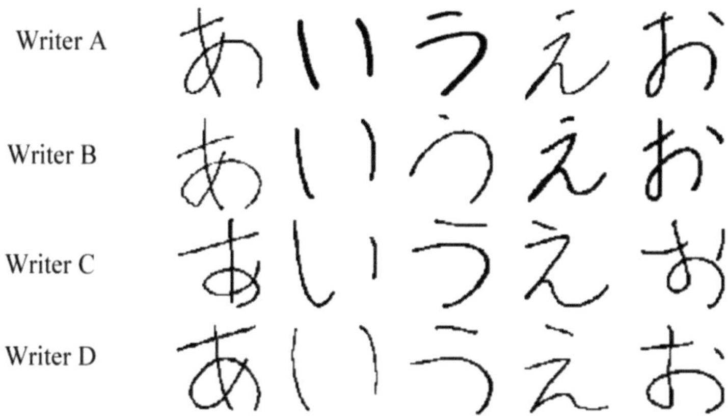


**Figure 12.** Variation of characters written by four writers.

The outline of our proposed method can be explained as the following procedure.

1. In preparing process, some writers write the set of handwritten characters for all categories to generate an adaptive dictionary for each writer such as "Writer A" and "Writer B" in Fig. 12. The feature vector of the character is extracted by WDIHM mentioned in 2.3.
2. An adaptive dictionary, which consists of the mean vector, the eigenvalues and the eigenvectors of the feature vector for each category, is generated from the set of handwritten characters by only one writer. We prepare the adaptive dictionary for each writer, and call the writer "similar writer" in this chapter. The number of similar writers is limited at the initial operation phase of the character recognition system.
3. In learning process, one character written by one specific writer selects the most similar writer by the minimum value of MQDF among the registered similar writers in Fig. 13. The specific writer would be the specific user of a personal terminal machine. In recognition process, the recognition system employs the recognition dictionary of the similar writer for every category. Fig. 14 shows that the similarity on writing habit for two categories, and that the relative position of writers is similar between category A and B. The recognition process using adaptive dictionaries for each similar writer is shown in Fig. 15.
4. The selected adaptive dictionary is updated by the character written by the specific writer to adapt the character form written by the specific writer. Two new adaptive methods are proposed in the following two sections.

When the user employs mobile terminal machines such as smartphone and tablet personal computer (tablet PC), a new user uses the adaptive dictionary of the similar writers in file saver on the Internet shown in Fig. 16. As the adaptive dictionary of the new writer would be updated and be stored in the Internet file saver, the number increases according to the number of users of the proposed system.

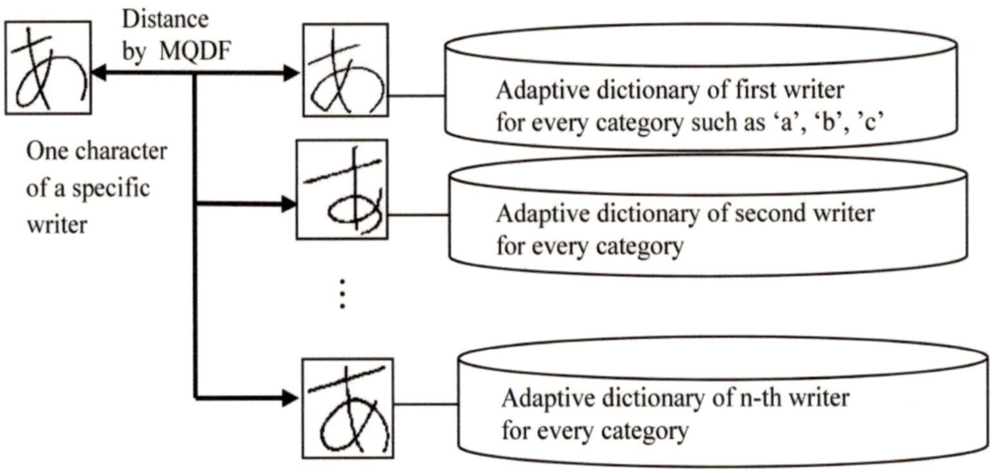


**Figure 13.** Selection of the most similar writer by one character of the specific writer in learning process

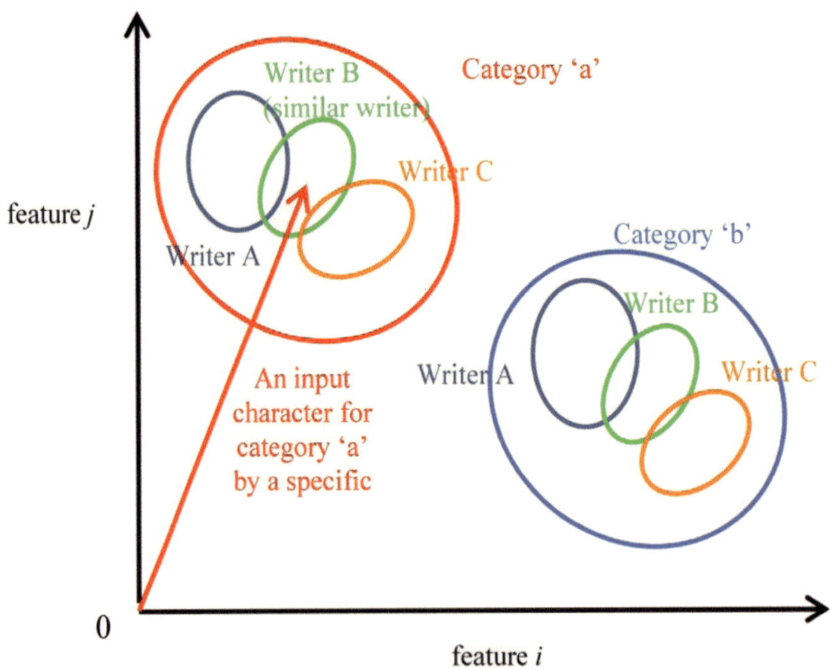


**Figure 14.** Similarity on writing habit for two categories

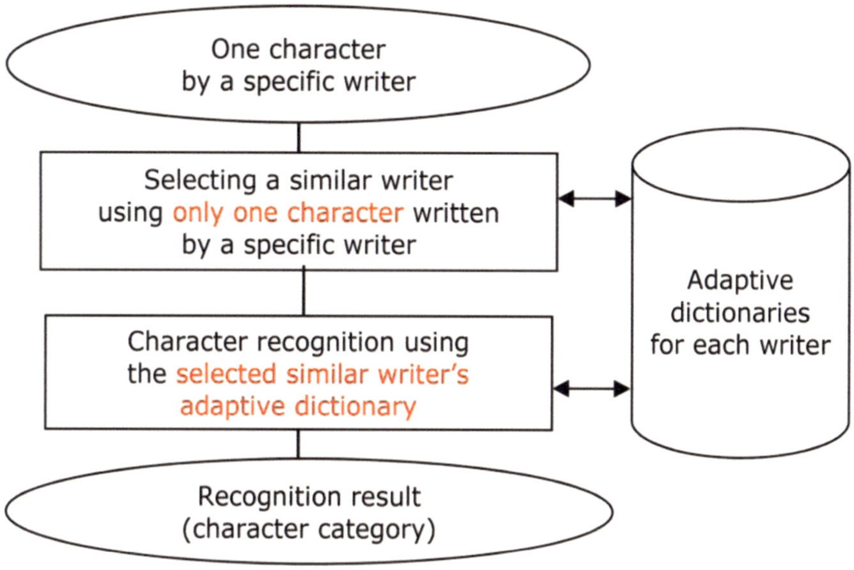


**Figure 15.** Recognition process using adaptive dictionaries for each similar writer

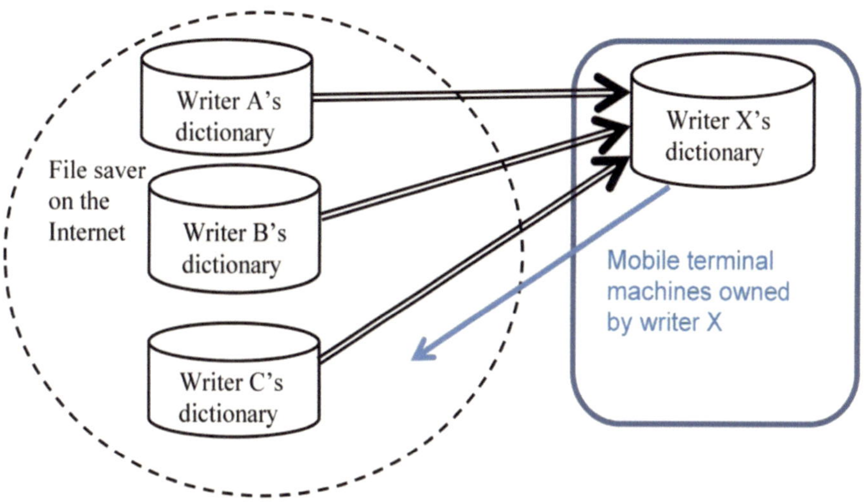


**Figure 16.** Dictionary generating process using character recognition dictionary on the Internet

## 4.2. Similar mean dictionary

The similar mean dictionary consists of the mean vector and the set of the eigenvalues and the eigenvectors for each category. In learning phase, the mean vector only is updated in the learning phase, and the set of the eigenvalues and the eigenvectors is the same as the general dictionary.

In the initial phase, the mean vector is the combination of the general mean and the mean vector of the similar writer for each category by equation (10).

$$ {}_1\mu_s = \frac{1}{1+Ns}({}_1\mu + \sum_{i=1}^{Ns} {}_1x_{s,i}) \tag{10} $$

where, *Ns* : the number of characters written by a similar writer.

In the leaning phase, the mean vector is updated by the character written by the specific writer (user of personal machines) using the following equations.

$$ {}_1\mu_p = \frac{1}{Np}\sum_{i=1}^{Np} {}_1x_{p,i} \tag{11} $$

$$ {}_1\mu_{psm} = \frac{Np}{Ns+Np+1}{}_1\mu_p + \frac{Ns+1}{Ns+Np+1}{}_1\mu_s \tag{12} $$

where, *Np:* the number of characters written by the specific writer.

In the well learned phase, the number of learning characters written by the specific writer becomes large, and the mean vector closes to the mean vector of the specific writer. The set of the eigenvalues and the eigenvectors is the same as the general dictionary.

### 4.3. Similar feature space dictionary

The similar feature space dictionary consists of the mean vector and the set of the eigenvalues and the eigenvectors.

In the initial phase, the mean vector and the set of the eigenvalues and the eigenvectors are generated by the combination of similar writer and general writer. The mean vector in the similar feature space dictionary is the same as the similar mean dictionary mentioned in 4.2. The set of eigenvalues and eigenvectors is not the same with the similar mean dictionary, and it is calculated by the covariance matrix on the feature vectors of characters written by the similar writer and the general writers shown in equation (13).

$$ {}_1\Sigma_{psf} = \frac{1}{Ns+1}{}_1\Sigma g + \frac{Ns}{Ns+1}{}_1\Sigma s \tag{13} $$

In the learning phase, the mean vector only is updated by the character written by the specific writer (user of personal machines) using equation (11) and (12). The set of the eigenvalues and the eigenvectors are not updated.

### 4.4. Comparison of four dictionaries

Two new proposed methods in this paper employ one character written by a specific writer (a new user), and the effort of the user is the minimum to reflect the handwritten feature of a specific writer. The comparison of four dictionaries in initial phase is showed in Table 3.

The similar mean dictionary employs the combined mean vector of characters written by the similar writer and the general writers, and it employs the set of eigenvalues and eigenvectors of the characters written by the general writers. The similar feature space dictionary employs the mean vector and the set of eigenvalues and eigenvectors of characters written by the similar writer and the general writers. The difference of these four dictionaries illustrates in Fig. 17.

| Type of recognition dictionary | The number of characters by a specific writer for 71 categories | The writers of mean vector | The writers of Eigenvalues and Eigenvectors |
|---|---|---|---|
| General | 0 | general | general |
| Mixture type | 71 (minimum) | general+ specific | general |
| Similar mean | 1 | general+ similar | general |
| Similar feature space | 1 | general+ similar | general+ similar |

**Table 3.** Comparison of writing costs for 71 categories and the components of dictionary (mean vector, eigenvalues and eigenvectors) in initial phase

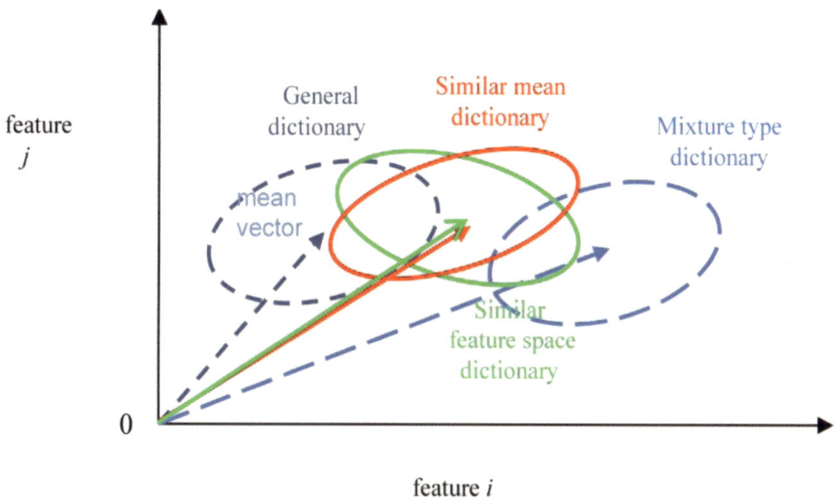


**Figure 17.** Difference of four dictionaries in feature space

## 4.5. Experimental results

### *4.5.1. Similar writer selection by one character in one category*

We examined the recognition rates of HIRAGANA categories to select the category written by the specific writer. The average recognition rate for ten writers is obtained in 20 learning characters per category, and the every combination of 71 categories and ten writers is calculated. The category of the maximum recognition rate among 71 categories is HIRAGANA category 'po', and we select the 'po' category that should be written by the specific writer.

The images in Table 4 and Table 5 show the character forms of HIRAGAN category "e" and category "pa", respectively. The character images in tables show a typical example for each writer. The character forms show the large variety of the writing habit. In Table 4, the MQDF value for one character in category 'po' written by "Writer D" is calculated for nine registered writers using the mixture type dictionary, and "Writer C" is selected by the minimum of MQDF value as the similar writer. MQDF values in category 'e' are shown in Table 4. The MQDF value of the similar writer is the minimum value among the registered nine writers without the specific writer (Writer D), and the character form of the similar writer (Writer C) is similar to the character form of the specific writer (Writer D). The selection procedure of similar writer would be appropriate in this category.

| | Specific writer (Writer D) | Similar Writer (Writer C) | Writer J | Writer A | Writer F |
|---|---|---|---|---|---|
| MQDF value | 149 | 158 | 165 | 167 | 169 |
| Character form |  |  | 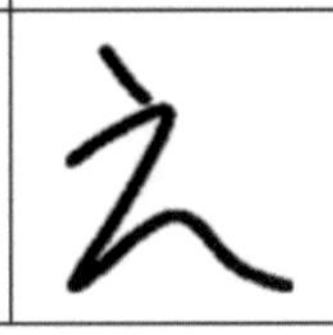 |  | 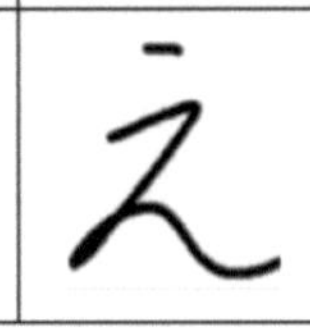 |

**Table 4.** Correct result of character 'e' using similar mean dictionary and similar space dictionary of the similar writer selected by one character 'po' written by a specific writer

Table 5 shows the case of the critical MQDF value of the similar writer. Writer J is selected by the character in category 'po' written by "Writer B". The MQDF value of the similar writer "Writer J" is different from the character form by the specific writer (Writer B), and it is close to the MQDF values of the other writer. The similar writer depends on the written category, and the future problem is the selection of the category for the selection of the similar writer.

| | Specific writer (Writer B) | Similar Writer (Writer J) | Writer E | Writer F | Writer H |
|---|---|---|---|---|---|
| MQDF value | 138 | 147 | 149 | 154 | 155 |
| Character form | 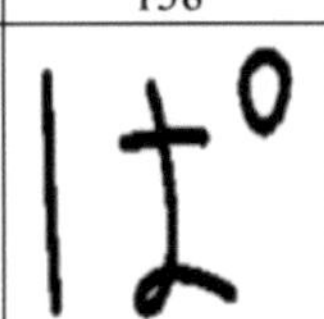 | 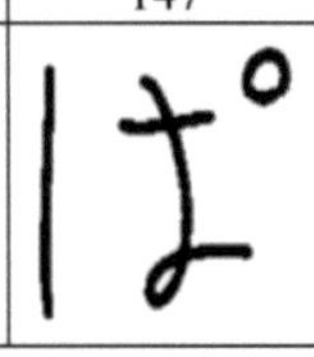 | 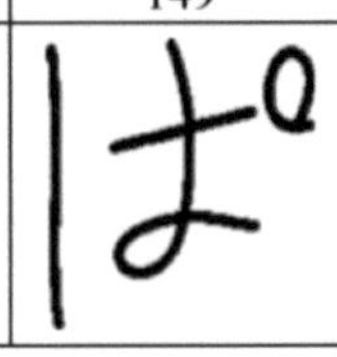 | 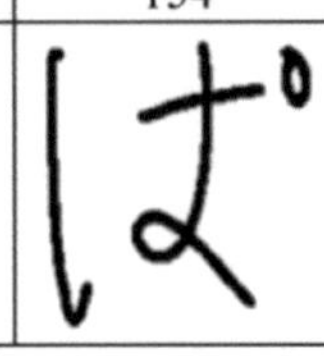 | 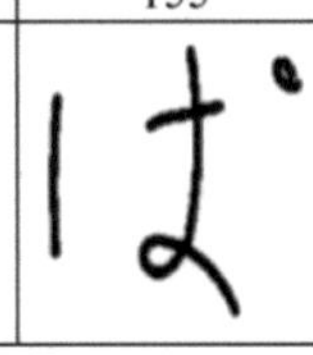 |

**Table 5.** Correct result of character 'pa' using only similar space dictionary

### *4.5.2. The comparison of four dictionaries*

We compared three personal dictionaries (mixture type dictionary, similar mean dictionary and similar feature space dictionary) and the general dictionary. Fig. 18 shows the comparison of the four dictionaries in the correct recognition rates for ten writers, and the order of writers is sorted by the recognition rates using general dictionary. The rates of mixture type dictionary (90.8% in mean) and the similar feature space dictionary (91.0% in mean) are nearly equal, and these rates are better clearly than the rates of the general dictionary (82.4% in mean) and the similar mean dictionary (84.7% in mean) for all writers. The rates of the similar mean dictionary for 7 writers are better than the general dictionary, and the mean rate for ten writers is better than general dictionary. It is more effective for writer with strong writing habit such as Writer J, and the effect of these dictionaries would increase when the number of similar writes would become large. The recognition rate of similar mean dictionary becomes near the general dictionary as the problem of similar mean dictionary would be the mismatch between the mean vector and the set of eigenvalues and eigenvectors. The number of learning character per category to generate similar mean dictionary and similar feature space dictionary is 10 for every category.

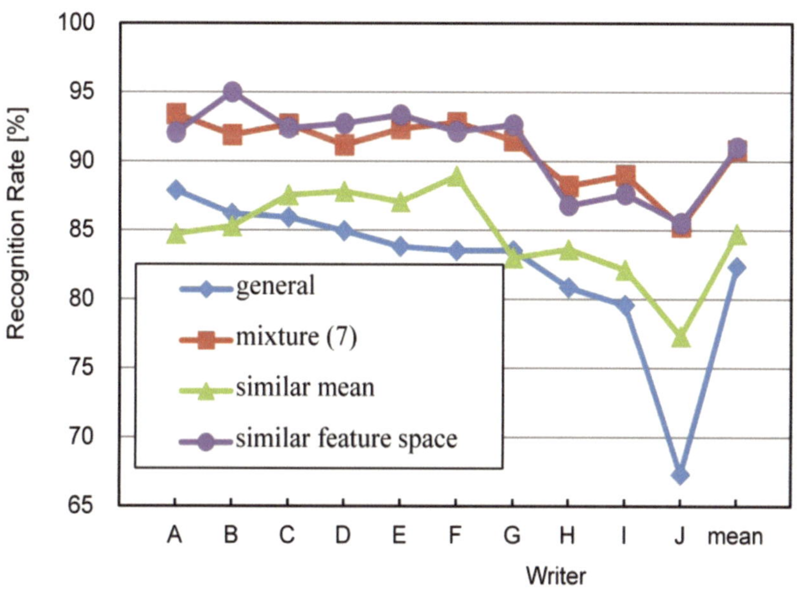


**Figure 18.** The recognition rates by four dictionaries

One character is the least cost to extract the writing habit of writer in similar mean dictionary and similar feature space dictionary. The writing cost of these dictionaries is 1/{(the number of categorty)*(learning characters per category)} of mixture type dictionary. The writing cost of the specific writer is reduced vastly.

Table 6 shows the comparison of correct recognition rates and the writing cost for general dictionary, mixture type dictionary, similar mean dictionary and similar feature space dictionary. It is confirmed that only one character by a specific writer (user) is very effective for handwritten character recognition.

The character image written by the specific writer in Table 4 is the example of the correct recognition result of character 'e' using similar mean dictionary and similar space dictionary of the similar writer selected by one character 'po' written by a specific writer. MQDF value (158) by the similar writer in Table 4 is the minimum value for all categories. However, the character image written by the specific writer in Table 5 is the example of the correct result of character 'pa' using only similar space dictionary, and usig similar mean dictionary arises an incorrect result as MQDF value for category 'pa' is not the minimum MQDF value for the other categories.

| Type of recognition dictionary | Correct recognition rate [%] | The number of characters by a specific writer for 71 categories |
|---|---|---|
| General | 82.4 | 0 |
| Mixture type (7) | 90.8 | 71 x 7 = 497 |
| Similar mean | 84.7 | 1 |
| Similar feature space | 91.0 | 1 |

**Table 6.** Comparison of correct recognition rates

Table 7 shows the incorrect recognition result of character 'wo' using similar mean and similar feature space dictionaries. The MQDF value (159) of the similar writer for category 'wo' is larger than the category 'chi', and the recognition result becomes the category 'chi'. If the similar writer would be 'Writer D', the input character is recognized correctly. We are considering a new selection method of the similar writer to improve the correct recognition rate.

| | Specific writer (Writer F) | Similar Writer (Writer I) | Writer D | Writer A | Writer G |
|---|---|---|---|---|---|
| MQDF value | 133 | 159 | 139 | 147 | 166 |
| Character form |  |  | 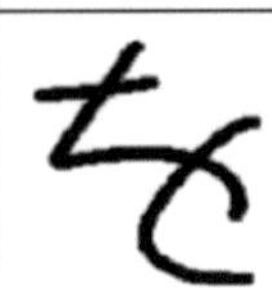 | 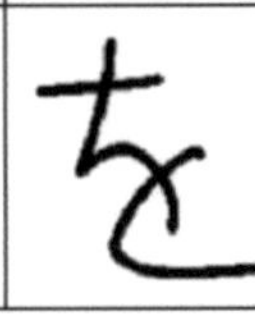 |  |

**Table 7.** Incorrect result of character 'wo' using similar mean and similar feature space dictionaries

The similar mean dictionary and the similar feature dictionary use effectively one character written by the specific writer, and we confirm that the usage of one character will enlarge for personal terminal machines.

## 5. Conclusions

We explained the usefulness of personal dictionary on offline character recognition using our proposed adaptive dictionary. Three adaptive dictionaries (the renewal type, modification type and mixture type) are introduced by our research group, and the recognition rates of the renewal type, modification type and mixture type are 99.3%, 99.5%, 99.5% for 46 categories, respectively. The recognition rate of mixture type is better than the other types from 2 learning characters to 8 learning characters. We think that the mixture type dictionary is most useful for personal terminal machines such as smartphone and tablet personal computer (tablet PC). However the problem of the adaptive dictionary is the writing cost, and to resolve this problem we proposed two dictionary generation methods (similar mean dictionary and similar feature space dictionary) using only one character methods by a specific writer.

We examined the recognition rate using handwritten characters of 71 Japanese "HIRAGANA" categories and we obtained the character recognition rate of 91.0 % (the general dictionary made from ETL9B: 82.4 %). The usage of character forms written by a specific user is very effective even if the number of characters by the user is only one, and the character by the user improves the recognition rate of character recognition system vastly.

The future problems are as follows.

5. The selection of the category for the selection of the similar writer
6. The usage of multiple similar writers and multiple categories
7. The application to Chinese characters

## Author details

Shinji Tsuruoka*
*Graduate School of Regional Innovation Studies, Mie University, Tsu, Mie, Japan*

Masahiro Hattori
*Previously at Graduate School of Engineering, Mie University, Tsu, Japan*

Takuya Kimura
*Previously at Graduate School of Regional Innovation Studies, Mie, University, Tsu, Mie, Japan*

Yasuji Miyake
*Professor Emeritus, Mie University, Tsu, Mie, Japan*

Haruhiko Takase and Hiroharu Kawanaka
*Graduate School of Engineering, Mie University, Tsu, Mie, Japan*

## Acknowledgement

We would like to sincerely thank to Prof. Fumitaka Kimura and Associate Prof. Tetsushi Wakabayashi in Mie University, Japan.

## 6. References

[1] Tappert C.C (1984) Adaptive on-line handwriting recognition, Seventh International Conference on Pattern Recognition (7th ICPR): 1004-1007

* Corresponding Author

[2] Connell S.D, Jain A.K (2001) Template-based online character recognition, Pattern Recognition 34: 1-14
[3] Connell S.D, Jain A.K (2002) Writer Adaptation of Online Handwriting Models, IEEE Trans. PAMI: 329-346
[4] LaViola J J, Zeleznik R C (2007) A Practical Approach for Writer-Dependent Symbol Recognition Using a Writer-Independent Symbol Recognizer, IEEE Trans. PAMI, 29(11):1917-1926
[5] Huang Z, Ding K, Jin L (2009) Writer Adaptive Online Handwriting Recognition Using Incremental Linear Discriminant Analysis, Proc. of International Conference on Document Analysis and Recognition (ICDAR2009):91-95.
[6] Tsuruoka S, Morita H, Kimura F, Miyake Y (1987) Handwritten Character Recognition Adaptable to the Writer. IEICE Trans. on Information and Systems, J70-D (10):1953-1960 [in Japanese]
[7] Tsuruoka S, Morita H, Kimura F, Miyake Y (1988) Handwritten Character Recognition Adaptable to the Writer. Proc. of IAPR Workshop on Computer Vision: 179-182
[8] Yoshimura M, Kimura F, Yoshimura I (1983) On the Effectiveness of Personal Templates in the Character Recognition, IEICE Trans. on Information and Systems, J66-D (4):454-455 [in Japanese]
[9] Tsuruoka S, Hattori M, Kadir M F A, Takano T, Kawanaka H, Takase H, Miyake Y (2010) Personal Dictionaries for Handwritten Character Recognition Using Character Written by a Similar Writer. Proc. of 12th International Conference on Frontiers in Handwriting Recognition (ICFHR2010): 599-604.
[10] Tsuruoka S, Kurita K, Harada T, Kimura F, Miyake Y (1987) Handwritten "KANJI" and "HIRAGANA" Character Recognition Using Weighted Direction Index Histogram Method. IEICE Trans. on Information and Systems, J70-D (7): 1390-1397 [in Japanese]
[11] Kimura F, Takashina K, Tsuruoka S, Miyake Y (1987) Modified Quadratic Discriminant Functions and the Application to Chinese Character Recognition. IEEE Trans. Pattern Anal. Mach. Intell. PAMI-9(1): 149-153
[12] Yoshimura I, Yoshimura M (1991) Off-Line Writer Verification Using Ordinary Characters as the Object, Pattern Recognition, 24(9):909-915
[13] Yoshimura M, Yoshimura I, Kim H. B (1993) A Text-Independent Off-Line Writer Identification Method for Japanese and Korean Sentences, IEICE Trans. on Information and Systems, E76-D (4): 454-461
[14] Cheriet M, Kharma N, Liu C, Suen C Y (2007) Character recognition systems. Wiley & Sons Inc.: 293- 301
[15] Ding K, Jin L (2010) Incremental MQDF Learning for Writer Adaptive Handwriting Recognition, 12th International Conference on Frontiers in Handwriting Recognition (ICFHR 2010): 559-564
[16] Kawazoe Y, Ohyama W, Wakabayashi T, Kimura F (2010) Incremental MQDF Learning for Writer Adaptive Handwriting Recognition, 12th International Conference on Frontiers in Handwriting Recognition (ICFHR 2010): 410-414